My Asian Summer

Laura Pauley

New Generation Publishing

For Summer...

Because life doesn't come with a 'how-to' guide, we simply make it up as we go along (we then make a story out of the adventure!)
Thank you for being the inspiration behind this book, I really do love you around the world and back again...

Testimonials

"What an adventure. A fascinating journey and read.
Inspiration to the brave and bold that travelling with a child can be empowering and enlightening!" Alice B Grist, author of Dirty & Divine http://www.alicegrist.co.uk

"A travelogue like no other…Laura manages to immerse her readers in a story of infinite adventure. A compelling page-turner, you will be swept across numerous Asian countries laughing at the pit of your soul and collecting a body of historical knowledge. You will be encapsulated in a tale of heart-warming love; be exposed to unapologetic honesty and an array of raw-emotion. Consequently, at the end of the book, you will be questioning human nature and what it means to have a rich life." Siân Smith, Editor

Foreword and acknowledgments

Thank you so much for buying this book. After four years of working on it daily, I cannot believe that it is finally finished. I never thought I'd see the day! I have been through so many milestones over the four years; this book has certainly been on a journey.

My hope is that 'My Asian Summer' will inspire people to think about travel outside of the box of tourism. Travelling can offer you an insight into a darker side of the world that you couldn't have imagined before, but I have used humour and creative writing to alleviate some of that darker content that would otherwise be difficult for the reader to digest. On the flip side, travelling can also open your eyes to just how incredible some human beings are! We certainly met some inspirational people along the way...

The unique thing about this book is just how different each chapter is, with some comical, others informative and some displaying unexpected twists and turns. It really is one of those books where you have to read to the end to truly judge it for what it is. The use of italics throughout the chapters has been used to demonstrate my inner thoughts, which is something that I thought would be unique to capture my personality.

I have absolutely no doubts that this book would be nowhere near the caliber that it is without the dedication, support and creative spirit of my editor, Sian Smith. For all the hours that she dedicated to the manuscript: editing for 10-hours straight with me, giving constructive feedback, travelling across the country together to attend a publishing conference; sending me endless editing notes at 3am! Crazy person that she is... not to mention taking my manuscript on every adventure that she did herself! For all of that, I cannot thank her enough.

I would also like to thank my illustrator and childhood friend, Hayley Parish. As a talented artist, I tasked Hayley with drawing some of our travel snaps. I never imagined that her art would be so lifelike. Some of her drawings brought a tear to my eye; the detail in them is so unique and convincing –

just looking at them brings back such fond memories -.what a talent she has. So enjoy these pictures as much as the text, as they really are incredible.

Thank you to my graphic designer and gifted cousin, Jamie. As a book designer by trade, I of course asked him to design the cover. With an idea of what I wanted, Jamie strongly disagreed with my vision (an illustration of Summer and I standing on a bustling city street in Bangkok,) instead he designed the cover to how he knew best. Of course he was absolutely right with his design as the cover is everything that Asia represents – colourful, fun, vibrant, and more than I could ever have asked for.

To my Mum, Nan and Rosie - thank you for babysitting so I could work on this mammoth book! *What would I do without you all*? A special thank you to my Nan for dedicating countless hours babysitting, enabling me to do 'just one more chapter!'

And to my wider family of siblings, cousins, in-laws and friends, for all your encouraging 'how's the book coming along?' dreaded chats when I was pulling my hair out, thinking that I would never see the day that the book was finished.

To my superman: Chris. For all those times you came home at lunchtime and complained that I hadn't made your lunch because I was too busy 'doing my hobby' (cough cough!) For all your unsupportive 'Chris' comments, I love you to pieces. Thank you for being my rock through some incredibly challenging times and making me smile throughout the last few years. Meeting you literally turned my life upside down... what an adventure we have been on, ay?

Cooper and Casey – I am so excited about the adventure and next chapter that is to come with you two. Thank you for giving me yet more reasons to laugh and smile every day.

Lastly: to my forever-inspiring daughter, Summer-Ruby. This book was born out of the idea of showing you a world outside of what you knew. Thank you for forever being my inspiration to do better in life. If you hadn't have come along, who knows where I would be now? Your life has encouraged me to write two books, have a change of career and direction, and most importantly to be a better person. You have made me the person that I am today. If you are to take anything away from both books, it's that you can achieve anything that you want. Life is an adventure – both the good and the bad experiences…so please treat it that way. If you fall down, us Pauley girls simply wipe the dirt from our knees and stand back up. We learn from every experience, with our glass half-full each time.

Between Sian and I, this book was written and edited in: Venice, New York, Malta, Borneo (at an Orangutan Sanctuary,) Singapore, Poland; South Africa (at a wildlife rehabilitation centre,) Gran Canaria, Antalya, Istanbul, Wexford, on a ferry in the middle of the Irish sea; Morocco, Barcelona, Balearic Islands, North and South Wales, Cornwall, West Sussex; Hampshire, London, Bristol - even in hospital whilst in early labour! Here's to the next adventure…

Are you on Instagram? To view the 'My Asian Summer' writing journey, images of the trip and pictures of where my life is now - follow me on: @laurapauley:

#myasiansummer

#myasiansummeredits

#myasiansummerillustrations

***

Chapters:

Introduction:
The last eight years

After releasing my first book, 'My Summer Bump' I spent time writing lifestyle features for magazines such as Mother and Baby and Pregnancy and Birth; I completed restaurant reviews for local newspapers, and even had a weekly column, 'Diary of a slightly mad, single mummy' in a newspaper and magazine.

I quickly returned to work full-time but instead of writing the headlines as a journalist, I became a senior officer in the media department of a fire and rescue service, followed by the NHS.

When Summer was two years old I decided that I wanted to take her travelling. Exactly three years later and that vision finally happened - welcome, *'My Asian Summer.'*

Where am I with my life since returning from Asia? I guess you will have to read to the end of the book to find out…

One:

Why travel?

I was an energetic 18-year-old when I first decided to travel; whilst friends were at college studying for their A Levels, I was backpacking around Australia. It was a turbulent year with many obstacles but it was a great start to adulthood.

Within months of returning to the UK, I took a spontaneous trip to Mexico with a friend, and later that year I went to Seattle to work as a residential nanny. That was all 10 years before I completed this trip around Asia. The only holidays I'd otherwise embarked on were a few beach holidays, a trip to Paris, Barcelona and Dublin. It wasn't that I'd lost my travel bug; it was simply that life had got in the way. Being a single mother, the wheelie bin seemed to go out more often than I did!

I bought my first property when I was 18, so from a young age I had a huge financial commitment. This responsibility led to some poor financial decisions, so the odds were stacked against me for the adventurous and expensive backpacking trip that I was craving. However, I was determined to not let my financial commitments and the fact that I had a young child clip my wings.

I told my family that I was going to save and take Summer travelling on my own. I have always been the type of woman that marches to the beat of her own drum, so they were not surprised.

When Summer was two I started teaching her Spanish and the map of the world. By the time she was three she could name several: continents, countries and landmarks!

The three years of saving for the trip were emotionally-draining. I felt as though my life was on hold because of my newfound weekly restricted budget, which sometimes proved impossible.

With a mound of hard-earned cash and after months of comparing airline tickets, I finally settled on an affordable and truly incredible itinerary that would give us everything that we wanted:

UK - Hong Kong – Thailand (*visiting north, central and south*) – Cambodia (*north to south*) - overland to Vietnam – and finally back to the normality of home...

Why visit Asia?

Asia is the ideal destination for an extended trip as everyday items such as food, accommodation and travel are incredibly cheap. Distances between destinations are also fairly short, which is a huge bonus if you're travelling with a child.

Whilst carrying out my research, I found the continent to be both mesmerising and intriguing. I felt as though the countries I selected would offer us a different perspective on life and how other cultures and communities live.

Each region in Asia is completely different, with its own culture, food, people and beliefs. With a five-year-old's imagination to fire, I figured the history of each country would be brought to life through the numerous temples, palaces, monuments and architecture on offer.

Asia is also very welcoming to families and has some of the friendliest people in the world – *so what better place to take a child?*

If my next explanation is so sugary it sets your teeth on edge - I offer no apology…here were my reasons for taking Summer backpacking around Asia:

Key reasons:

- **Adventure:** Asia has numerous jungle treks that would give us a unique insight into the lives of local people, whilst also appreciating the landscape and learning about nature and wildlife.
- **Accommodation:** Breaking away from western hotels where possible and staying with local families would give us a great appreciation of how others live.

- **Transport:** Using local transport including trains, buses, Longtail boats, bamboo rafts, ferries, overnight trains and Tuk-tuks would not only be adventurous but would allow us to integrate with locals and fellow travellers.
- **Architecture:** The continent is home to some of the earliest architecture and ancient empires of the world. Notably, it has impressive palaces, temples and world heritage sights.
- **Nature**: Asia has breath-taking beaches, national parks, wildlife sanctuaries and vast jungles, not to mention many undiscovered islands.
- **Spirituality:** A chance to visit the orange-robed monks at the temples and monuments would offer a great opportunity to learn about Buddhism.
- **Food and cooking:** Asia would give us the opportunity to step out of western restaurants and take in street food, trying a variety of local herbs and spices and discovering local specialties.
- **Money:** Learning different currencies, bartering for items at the sprawling night and street markets, living on a daily budget and comparing the prices of tours and accommodation would help Summer develop various life skills.
- **Poverty:** Asia has many orphanages and schools that have been set up to help children living in poverty. It would be fantastic to visit such establishments and take the children much-needed gifts.
- **History:** Visiting the endless temples, palaces and monuments across the regions would provide us with a wealth of knowledge. Visiting the 'Killing Fields' in Cambodia in particular would give us the opportunity to learn about modern Cambodia.

For those who are unaware of the 'Killing Fields,' there are a number of fields across the country where people were brutally murdered and buried by the communist, Khmer Rouge, during 1975. The country is still very much re-building itself from this infamous period of history that actually wasn't that long ago.

14

A visit to Vietnam and the 'Cu Chi' underground tunnels that were used as hiding spots by the Viet Cong soldiers in 1968 during the Vietnam War would also be a fascinating sight to see. This would be an unbelievable practical experience to educate Summer about the Vietnam War prior to her learning about it at school.

My diary

Two:

The night before the trip...

It was 10pm. My mum and seventeen-year-old sister, Ellie, hadn't long left after dropping in a handmade goodbye-necklace for Summer. The necklace was full of laminated pictures of family and friends and something that I knew she would cherish when nothing else looked familiar anymore.

Before I went to bed, I wanted one last glimpse of Summer's perfect sleeping face in the comfort of her own bedroom; I knew it would be the last time for a long while.

I pushed open her familiar bedroom door. Unsurprisingly it was covered in art and craft pictures that she'd produced over the years. Overcome with a plethora of emotions, I stepped inside the dark room that was illuminated by twinkling fairy lights.

As expected - Summer was sound asleep, snuggled in a blanket that featured several personalised photographs of her magical five years on this planet; courtesy of the great Nanny June. As always, she was cuddled up to her favourite teddy bear, Duffy.

Her breathing was as rhythmic as usual. Pausing to reflect, I listened and watched her chest rise and fall. Taking in her tiny porcelain-like face, thoughts of the adventure that we were about to embark on raced through my mind like lightening.

Looking around her room, I took in the treasures that we had picked up over the years.

Glancing above, a full-scale beam grew across my face as I stared at the hand-carved Pinocchio that proudly swung before me. A unique memory of trawling through Paris to reach the 'must-see' market (that transpired to merely be no more than an everyday flower market) filled my memory.

Let-down, I span like the Tasmanian-devil in a desperate attempt to escape the hippy-land of flowers, until…swinging proudly from a flower hook was the meticulous-looking Pinocchio.

As my mind drifted further, I felt a bubble of excitement in the pit of my stomach at the prospect of what treasures we would pick up on this trip.

Continuing to stand in silence, I looked around her girly pink bedroom. It seemed unfathomable that after three hard years of saving, we were finally leaving for Asia. In that very moment it felt as though the trip had happened almost overnight.

Glancing at Summer's delicate sleeping face once more, I imagined her future and thought of all the possibilities the world had to offer her and all the things that she would offer the world.

I soundlessly left the mottled light of her treasure-trove of space and whispered, "Night night baby…10 hours to go…"

***

Three:

Meowing through Hong Kong

Walking into the airport hotel at Heathrow, there was only one word to describe how I felt: proud. I had single-handedly tackled London's overground and underground stations, whilst sporting an enormous backpack that was so full I couldn't do it up.

With Summer's backpack strapped to my front, I was sure that I resembled two-turtles stuck together. I also had a carrier bag full of items that I couldn't fit in either of the backpacks, a certain 'Disney Duffy' bear that madam insisted on taking everywhere with her; a takeaway coffee and a bag full of food for the journey to the airport hotel. Most importantly, I had my forever-cheeky five-year-old, Summer-Ruby.

We arrived at the hotel three hours after leaving the house and I was feeling smug. *Who needed to backpack Asia?* Navigating through some of London's biggest stations was a big enough challenge! After enduring the never-ending sequence of stairs I had to climb, and scrambling for that precious standing spot on the tube, I was left feeling the breath of London's quick-tempered commuters and eager-eyed tourists when the driver announced (seconds into the journey) that an incident had disrupted the tube line; meaning that I had to make some drastic alterations to our route. Consequently, I was left tackling the problem of opening a map (a slight issue when you can't even stretch your arm out without touching several people) while also holding onto a bouncing child and countless belongings – all within the confined space of a tube carriage, nonetheless.

Entering the airport hotel, my friend (Carl Baines) was waiting in the reception for us.

Carl coming to Asia was a very rushed and last minute decision. He was a NHS fraud investigator who I'd met through work. If I was honest, I didn't know Carl too well - only really in a work environment. As soon as I told him about the trip, he mentioned how he'd always wanted to see Asia but never had the guts to travel. A single man for several years, the prospect of travelling alone was rather daunting.

In a jokey-way, I found myself casually blurting out, "Well you should come with us?" Before I knew it, he was asking what dates we were going and had booked himself onto the same outward flight. Although a bit shocked at first, I didn't mind all that much - I thought it would be nice to have some adult company on the road.

At 38, Carl was much older than my 29-year-old self. He was divorced and had two children. His ex-wife relocated north shortly after their marriage failed, so sadly contact with the children doesn't happen very often.

Carl openly told me that he hadn't met anyone since his wife, but there certainly wasn't going to be any romance on this trip as Carl was far from my type.

Standing at over 6ft, he was a tall, peculiar-looking, gangly man.

One thing that did intrigue me about him was his wild imagination. At work he would often over-analyse the tiniest of details, and would deliberate constantly over wacky conspiracy theories.

I'd observed a few annoying habits, for example, he always corrected people (particularly if you mispronounced certain words, or didn't tell a story precisely how he remembered it.) Worst of all, he had a bad habit for interrupting people. However, I found myself warming to him because he seemed harmless enough. His peculiar traits certainly made him an interesting character that was for sure.

I suggested to Carl that we both put spending money into an account and that we used that to live on for ease whilst we were away. It was easier than paying for everything separately all the time.

"Hello young Summer," Carl patted Summer's head.

"Are you coming to Asia with us?" Summer casually asked, seemingly without a care in the world.

"I sure am! What an adventure we are going to have, huh?" My new travel companion roared in a cartoon-like, animated voice.

"I know how to say hello in Hong Kong!" Summer proudly announced.

"Meow!"

"Well, I'm not entirely sure where you learnt that, but I don't think it's quite right. My guide book states that it's in fact: 'Neo-Hao.'"

Talk about condescending – just because she's a child. Clearly, he was under-estimating Summer. He would soon learn this fact...

***

Just over 30 hours later, I had found myself wedged between Summer, Carl and a distinct odour. Quickly, I turned my thoughts to what was our first flight to Abu Dhabi.

Whilst the hostess prepared the cabin for take-off, the breeze of her movements guided an unpleasant whiff of sweat towards me. Glancing for the perpetrator, Carl caught my eye with his repeated tapping of his foot into the floor – not to mention the noticeable drips of sweat that were glistering across his face.

"Are you ok?" I asked, slightly puzzled.

"I'm just nervous – I don't like flying." He wiped his brow with his sleeve.

"There are just so many things that could go wrong! We are literally putting our lives in other people's hands for them to do as they please with." He stared towards me with a straight-face.

"Aren't you doing that every day when you board a bus or train? There's no difference really. You stand more chance of dying on one of those than an aeroplane."

"There are so many cover ups that could take place with a plane, though. What you see is what you get with a car crash."

"What do you mean?" I asked, totally confused.

"Let's say a plane goes missing because something has gone wrong – let's just say during a government 'exercise'" he air quoted.

"The government would never want to admit that something went wrong during an exercise, so they would cover it up by saying it was a 'crash!'" he air quoted once again.

"Or let's say that Aliens abducted a plane; again, no government would want to scare the world by saying that's what has happened - even if they can prove it - so they would cover it up. Alternatively, what about a terrorist act – again, no government would want to show defeat so they would cover..."

"Just stop!" I hissed through gritted teeth; aware that people within the cabin were embarrassingly staring our way.

Whispering close to his ear completely irritated, I added: "This isn't a conversation that we should have on a plane - so for now, I think you should keep your conspiracy theories to yourself."

***

Rodrigo (a crew member) approached and asked Carl if I was ok.

Aghast, I glared at Rodrigo confused. Of course I was ok - *why was he singling me out? Were we making too much noise?* In all honesty, Summer had just shouted. I was leaning into her to look out of the window when we were flying over Bagdad. The view (with its brown wrinkled mountains and jagged peaks) was just incredible, making me feel more energised then a thousand vitamin pills!

Rodrigo leant into Carl once again and asked if 'his wife' was ok. *What was it with condescending men on this trip?*

Carl glared my way, prompting me to stare at both men rather puzzled.

"I'm fine," I snapped.

"Is your wife expecting?" Rodrigo asked, ignoring me again and only addressing Carl.

Stunned, I pulled a shell-shocked expression. I felt as though I had time-travelled back to 1927 when Emily Pankhurst was tirelessly campaigning for equal rights for women.

Carl told Rodrigo that we were not married and that I was not 'with child.' I then for some unknown reason found myself explaining to Rodrigo (and consequently those around me) why I was overweight.

"No, I'm not pregnant! However, I'm two stone heavier despite being on a diet for an entire year before this trip. We haven't even landed yet, and (thanks to you) I already feel like a beached-whale! So thank you..." I distinctively made the effort to look at his name badge. "Rodrigo - for pointing out my weight at the start of my big adventure!"

Unsurprisingly, Rodrigo looked instantly embarrassed. Even people in the neighbouring seats were gazing in my direction. Babbling through an apology, Rodrigo stumbled head-first into a lengthy justification.

"I'm sorry madam. I was told that a lady on the left-side of the plane was pregnant and needed assistance." His words echoed through the cabin mirroring a sound effect to a horror movie.

This certainly wasn't a great start to my 'incredible' journey.

***

We had been in Hong Kong for several days and were in love with our hotel. It had a free mini bar in the room that was stocked daily, a kitchen just off the reception where you could help yourself to an array of food and drink, and free washing machines and soap powder – it really was a home from home! At £50 a night, we had never stayed in a hotel quite like it before.

Summer was getting to grips with the language. Despite repeatedly telling her that hello in Hong Kong was 'ni hao,' she thought the similarity between 'ni hao' and 'meow' was hilarious; it was for this reason that she spent the early days 'meowing' at pretty much anyone we passed.

Our first few days in the city were eventful. We battered our way through an overzealous itinerary of places to visit each day and night. We found ourselves leaving the hotel by 9am most mornings (returning at 6pm to quickly freshen up) then going back out until late. Strangely, Summer hadn't moaned that her legs ached once - much to my confusion as my legs felt as though I had run a 26-mile marathon!

I had planned that Hong Kong would be the 'holiday' part of the trip, and Thailand onwards would be the more rustic backpacking element. And the first few days in the city were exactly that. With theme parks visited, lots of tacky market souvenirs bought, and much like any holiday - too much money being spent!

On day three, we decided to visit Victoria Peak, the highest summit in the city with an altitude of over 1,818 feet.

Journeying to the summit was enjoyable as we ascended the mountain on an antique tram that was built in 1888. Well it was for Summer and I... Unbeknown to me, Carl had a terrible fear of heights. Venturing up an extremely high peak on an antique tram was his idea of hell. He spent the entire journey breathing heavily and looking rather wide-eyed.

"Mummy, what's wrong with Carl?" Summer curiously asked; as Carl panted and sweated rather profusely.

"Oh, Carl just doesn't…ummm…"

If I was honest - I didn't know what to say… *Ideally, I didn't want her to be aware of the feeling of fear and then over-think the height herself.*

"I detest heights young Summer, that's what's wrong!" Carl uninvitingly answered, finishing my sentence and totally ruining my mindset about the fear and my general approach to parenting around the topic.

"Why not?" she asked, confused.

"I don't like to not be in control, and on this tram we are sadly not in control!" Carl ranted as he held onto the pole so tight, I could see the veins in his hands protruding through his skin.

"What do you mean?" Summer pressed, clearly not understanding.

"Oh, it doesn't matter." I interrupted, desperately trying to change the subject.

"Oh wow - look at the view Summer!" I attempted to distract her once again.

Failing miserably, Carl completely took over the conversation. *Any normal person would have picked up on this fact...clearly, not Carl.*

"I have a theory that the government 'accidentally'..." he began to spout, using his fingers dramatically to air quote the word, 'accidentally' before continuing... "Kill off holiday makers to get people talking about their country and boost the economy."

I desperately struggled to stop my mouth from turning up at the sides and showcasing a drum-roll of laughter.

"Carl, first it was alien's abducting planes and the government 'covering it up!'" I air quoted him in mockery.

"Now you're saying that the government 'kill'" (I air quoted again) "people on holiday to boost the tourism trade. You don't like governments very much do you, Carl?" I laughed, before continuing: "Anyway, I really don't think that a tourist dying in a certain place would make people want to suddenly holiday there themselves - in fact, it would most likely have the total opposite effect!"

"Not necessarily – you must think about longevity. A tragedy brings the country (that the incident took place in) to the forefront of your mind. It gets people talking and discovering details about it. A year or two down the line, you've heard so much about the place that you suddenly want to visit it yourself...Don't even get me started on when the government promotes its 'developments' for the safety of 'future holiday makers.' This naively makes people believe that they simply *have* to holiday there as it's now the safest place to visit because of all these new measures...I'm telling you I have a point! I'm not a fraud investigator for nothing Laura! This is why I'm good at my job and have won numerous awards – I can work people out!" he sat back smugly, wallowing in self-gratification.

I stared at him astonished. He looked incredibly happy with himself.

"You're mad!" was all I could think to respond, before laughing off his ridiculous theory and admiring the view. *I hope that those around us couldn't understand our conversation.*

"People can be devious Laura – don't forget what I do for a living!" Carl interrupted my thoughts.

How could I forget? It was all he'd rattled on about since we'd landed in Hong Kong...

"Carl, what is your job?" Summer asked, clearly ear-wigging and suddenly intrigued.

"I protect the National Health Service's money, young Summer!" He replied with a gloating expression plastered across his face.

I do hope this sudden onslaught of arrogance wasn't catching...

"What does that mean?"

"When you have a job in our country, you pay money that goes towards the running of hospitals and doctors' surgeries; so that when you hurt yourself you don't have to pay for the treatment. Unfortunately (to put it bluntly) some people steal that money."

"Hu! It's naughty to steal!" Summer looked alarmed.

"Tackling fraud committed against the NHS is the main part of my role - as you know Laura," Carl attempted to engage my interest.

"But I also deal with other crimes that are not fraud but still involve the NHS. This could be: assaults on staff, damage to NHS property or thefts."

"What's 'thefts' mean?" Summer glared at our 'travel buddy' as though he was an alien species. *I was starting to wonder if he was myself? Maybe that brown wrinkled mountain that we'd seen out of the window in Baghdad was in fact a space ship to collect Carl?*

"It's when people are being dishonest and take what isn't rightfully theirs. The money that is funded by the taxpayer is intended for patient care, Summer, but unfortunately on occasions it ends up in the pockets of those who did not legitimately earn it!"

Absorbing Carl's serious expression, I was sure that he'd forgotten he was talking to a five-year-old…

"Laura, do you remember the case of the practice manager who was responsible for administering the payroll? He paid himself overtime amounts of up to £1,000 a month and awarded himself a pay rise every year. His activity resulted in a total criminal benefit of over £200,000! That's the equivalent of buying an entire factory of Barbie dolls!"

"Didn't Mummy tell you? I don't play with Barbie dolls anymore…" I looked fondly at my daughter; she had no idea how much comedy she was bringing to the conversation.

"What happened to the man?" Summer stared up at Carl, prompting me to snigger at their bizarre conversation.

"I investigated him and he was jailed for three years and six months."

"Ok…I think that's enough stories for one day." I said before distracting Summer with something out of the window.

Thankfully, we soon reached the top of the summit where the view was extraordinary.

With Aberdeen Harbour, the surrounding islands and the numerous skyscrapers, my breath was immediately taken away and I could see why the Peak was a tourist magnet. It was incredibly exciting to think that below the 1,818ft drop sat an active, bustling, noisy city as taxi drivers hollered, sped and honked past the traffic, fighting for their next fare.

Not wanting to be near the edge, Carl insisted on standing firmly in the middle of the outlook whilst Summer and I happily peered over the verge; taking in the view of the implausible descent.

"Be careful over there!" Carl shouted from a safe distance.

I had no idea that Carl was so safety conscience. If he thought taking a tram to the peak was a challenge - he hadn't seen anything yet!

Looking down at the city from the famous lookout, I felt excited that I was seeing one of the finest harbours on Earth. Glancing up, I battered the sun's rays away like pesky flies and absorbed the faultless skyline that looked postcard perfect.

Gazing beyond the mountains to the north of the city, the rest of China expressed the story of a hive of activity unravelling at that very moment.

My thoughts fell to the fish market opposite our hotel that I was looking at from the comfort of my high-rise room, early that morning. Despite it being just before seven, their appeared to be a hive of activity as rows-upon-rows of old-fashioned junk boats set about catching their fish of the day.

Sipping on my Nespresso coffee (courtesy of the hotel) I watched as the hard-working, elderly ladies sat on the side of the pavement and prepared their fish for sale.

I felt genuine empathy... that was somebody's grandma grafting away at what looked to be 80 years old!

Everything I'd read about Hong Kong's relentless energy was dramatically confirmed by the Peak's view. Admiring the striking outlook, I felt proud that after the slog of saving I'd finally made it. There I was with my small child looking at the other side of the world!

My thoughts were soon interrupted when a photographer (obviously spotting a photo opportunity of mother and daughter together) grabbed us for a happy snap.

"Carl!" I yelled, waving from across the platform for him to join us.

"Why is Carl shaking his head to say no, Mummy? Does he not want his picture taken?"

"Carl!" I shouted again, this time running towards the bench that he was sat on.

"Come and have your photo taken!" I yelled breathlessly.

"Oh - no thanks. As you know I don't like heights, so the idea of standing by that edge terrifies me. Not to mention how uncomfortable it makes me feel that a stranger would then have a photo of me on his camera. So, I'll pass, thanks..." he paused.

"What do you think he's going to do with a picture of you?" I sniggered.

"What couldn't he do with it? Don't be too trusting Laura!" he said with a cautious look, raising his eyebrows in sync.

"Seriously, you will regret it if you don't join in!" I pulled at his arm regardless, somehow managing to beckon his reluctant body to the edge.

The photographer took some of Carl's fear away by making us erupt into laughter when he produced a box of props, giving both Carl and Summer a pair of sunglasses to match mine.

As the photographer clicked away, he cooed and shouted as though we were professional models pouting for the camera.

"Yes – AMAZING! Wow we nearly have it! Yes, yes – click, click, BOOM!" he dramatically shouted whilst flashing a mouthful of cartoon-white teeth.

Just when I thought it was over: "Man – hug your wife!" he instructed before snapping away and cooing into his huge DSLR.

"Yes – click, click, BOOM!" he screamed as a grin as wide as the African continent stretched across his animated, childlike face.

***

Summer's task of the day was to direct us to the bus stop and attempt to read the timetable to see how long we had to wait. To my delight she successfully navigated us, but unsurprisingly failed to master reading the timetable.

It was 9am (overcast but hot) and like most city bus stops, the queue was longer than a popcorn stand at a cinema, five minutes before the blockbuster of the year is about to start.

I watched inquisitively as a skinny 20-something man who carried a man-bag and looked rather arty, entered a corner shop and bought noodles before joining us in the queue.

Obviously, I was not the only one to notice. Summer instantly turned and asked why he was eating noodles for breakfast. *It was good that she learned this Asian fact early,* especially as there would be times throughout the trip where she would have no choice but to eat noodles for breakfast...*she was yet to learn that!* I squirmed.

After a short while, a double-decker bus approached and we climbed the stairs enthusiastically to sit at the top. I sat next to a young, eccentric girl who had orange hair that was tied into two buns sitting above each of her ears; just like Princess Leia.

She wore a black leather jacket that covered an olive-coloured tassel dress, and had cartoon key rings dangling from the fabric. With frilly black socks that were pulled to her knees, she smiled as I sat down next to her.

"Hey!" I took my seat.

"Hello," she nodded her head in sync to her words.

"You speak English?" I was taken-aback.

"Of course!" she squealed.

"We were taught the language in school."

"You're so lucky; your education is incredible here - much better than in England!" I giggled, prompting her to giggle too.

"Are you here on holiday?"

"Travelling - we're off to Thailand after here!"

"That's wonderful! The riots didn't make you skip Hong Kong then?"

A few weeks previously, a series of protests took place across Hong Kong after the Chinese government issued a ruling limiting those who could stand as a candidate in the upcoming general election for the next leader. Just like any controversial political ruling, activists were infuriated as they wanted the right to choose their own leader. The result meant protests not only paralysed parts of Hong Kong, but turned the beautiful city into a complete war zone, with riot police using tear gas and batons to disperse the protesters.

I'd seen the riots play-out on British TV, but I hadn't taken them all that seriously as London had experienced riots on a large scale three years previously, so ultimately, every country has its problems.

"I don't blame the people for protesting – I'd have done the same thing myself!" I confessed.

"I was a protestor...I belong to the Hong Kong Federation of Students – the organisers behind the protests," the girl confessed gently.

"Oh right..." I gulped, not anticipating her close-involvement.

"I don't really know that much about it if I'm honest." I stumbled, now watching my words carefully.

"Our territory has been ruled under a 'one country, two systems' method for some time, and with that, Kong residents have more autonomy and freedom than our mainland counterparts. The elective process is still partly controlled by China. This means that we can only vote for pre-approved candidates under Chinese law – and I believe in independence!"

"What was the outcome then?" I felt compelled to ask, even though I'd seen the fallout on the news channels at home.

"The protest was our last fight for democracy... we left our summer jobs, made signs and took to the streets. All we were initially fighting for was for our future, but in the end it became a fight for survival against the people that are supposed to protect us."

"What do you mean?"

"I'll show you..."

I watched intently as the girl pulled out her smart phone, opened her gallery and whizzed past tens of videos and pictures, until suddenly she stopped and passed me her phone.

The video showcased scenes I'd seen play out on the news. With a background of crowd noise and white smoke, I watched as an entourage of officers (armed with shields and batons) moved in on the protesters.

"We were being peaceful and it was a public road!" The girl implored over the noisy sound of her video.

The person filming spun the camera around and behind the girl and her friends thousands of protesters were marched on by the officers, before tear gas was let off into the crowd. There were people on the floor, people fighting – it was chaos.

"We felt betrayed at the Police for treating us that way," the girl confessed.

"It is hard to watch..." I passed her back the phone, viewing her with fresh eyes. Suddenly, she seemed like a force not to be reckoned with.

"Would you protest again?" I found myself falling back into my journalistic ways.

"The experience was scary, but I would protest for anything that I believe in. Having a voice is something that everyone should have!"

There was something refreshing about this girl; she certainly stood up for what she believed in.

"I have to get off now, but, please – spread what I have told you. If more tourists understood and boycotted Hong Kong in protest themselves, then maybe the government would listen." The girl proudly stood to her feet.

As an after-thought, as she descended the stairs I shouted: "Good luck!"

"Who was that Mummy?"

"Oh, just a nice lady..." I glared out of the window, pondering towards the girl.

Minutes later and as Summer was happy chatting to Carl, I welcomed a serious dose of escapism by putting one earphone into my ear and taking in the acoustic sound of Ben Howard's song, *'Keep Your Head Up.'*

Tapping my foot to the beat, I discovered the lyrics: *'I saw a friend a mine the other day and he told me that my eyes were gleaming. I said I'd been away, and he knew - yeah he knew the depths I was meaning...'* extremely well-timed, and I hoped that when the trip was done I too would have found my epiphany and my eyes would sparkle once more. I couldn't remember the last time my eyes had gleamed with the squabbles of ex-relationships, the constant traffic of thoughts about everyday life dramas, and the nagging to-do lists that seemed to forever plague my thoughts.

Seizing the opportunity to pick up a magazine sitting on the edge of a chair in front, I came across a column of horoscopes that took my breath away as I absorbed the words on the page.

Virgo:

Virgos live for adventure and love doing unusual things, so make sure that you dive into the deep end and do every adventure activity that you can possibly do.

Likewise, make sure that you keep your eyes on the sky as it might give you the inspiration to make a major change in your life.

The people you meet this year will have a huge effect on your life in the future. As a Virgo, you're a born communicator and this will help you in many situations as people are naturally drawn to your quirky manner making you stand out from the crowd. Say yes during any travels that you embark on. It will lead you to some of the most unusual and magical places in the world.

I couldn't believe the words, especially after the 'eyes gleaming' thought I'd just experienced. *What were the chances of reading a horoscope like that whilst sat on a bus in Hong Kong, five days into a backpacking trip around Asia and reflecting on those Ben Howard lyrics?*

Sadly, my 60 seconds of wonderment were soon snatched away when Carl began yelling that we had missed our stop. No more than a minute later and we were on a Hong Kong sidewalk, with absolutely no idea where we were…

***

Finally, we reached the gateway to Hong Kong's Big Buddha and Monastery site. *Little did we know that on this day fate would take an ugly turn…*

To get to the Buddha statue you had to complete a 20-minute cable-car ride across the mountains. Feeling ecstatic, I couldn't wait to scale the endless sky. (Unlike my travel companion who looked as though he was going to pass out on discovering this fact.)

"There is an option to hire the 'crystal cabin' which features a transparent, three-layer glass floor. Would you like to go ahead and book onto that?" the assistant asked as we purchased our tickets.

"Ohhhh, that sounds incredible!" I said with a leap of joy.

"Laura…can I have a word?" Carl tugged at my sleeve.

"I don't think a cable car is a good idea… being high off the ground and above dangerous terrain, the results of any accident can be particularly severe. I'm not just saying this because of my fear of heights – cable cars are by nature incredibly dangerous modes of transport!"

"Excuse me – what are your safety regulations here?" He suddenly spun to face the assistant, who looked no older than 18 and as though she could be anywhere else but at work right now.

"Errrr…" she looked at us blankly.

"When was the rope wire last checked, for example? Because ropeways are highly exposed to the elements - strong gusts of wind pose a major hazard."

"Ignore him - it's ok..." I smiled sweetly in the girl's direction.

"Carl, look at the size of the queue! All these people trust it! I promise you - it will be fine! Three for the 'crystal cabin' please." I smiled once again at the girl.

"Are you out of your crazy mind? You do know that in Singapore in 1983 two cable car cabins plunged 55 metres into the sea and killed seven people! Now you're telling me that not only do want to risk our lives by travelling in one yourself, but you want a transparent floor to watch the decent too?"

Despite raging internally so loudly I could barely think, I really was too tired to argue.

"Ok, ok! Three for a boring, concealed-flooring cable car please."

After a rather lengthy queue, we were finally in sight of a car. I looked at Carl as a deep, purple vein bulged from his forehead and he held onto the railing as though his life depended on it.

"Carl, we're not even in the air yet - why are you so terrified already?"

"Laura, we're about to travel across mountains - who knows how high up in the sky, and I have a fear of heights! This is the second time this week that you have done this to me!"

"Well you should have told me about your fear before the trip! I'm sorry but it's something that you're just going to have to get over, [expecially] as you're going to have to endure heights repeatedly throughout the next five weeks!"

I knew I had to take this stance because of the adventurous activities I'd planned. Thailand would be an absolute nightmare if his fear continued on this level.

"You mean 'especially' not 'expecially!'" he glared my way.

"I was raised in London Carl, where ultimately I have a different dialect to you! So yes we mispronounce certain words, but it doesn't mean that the word's meaning is any different." I spat through gritted teeth. I was starting to see a totally different side to the work Carl that I knew. If I was honest - he was really starting to annoy me...

Taking a deep breath, I instead focused my attention towards the view from the cable-car. The beautiful hills and the striking Buddha statue (that shone like a beacon from the distance) was like nothing I'd seen before.

The Buddha was so remarkable that I couldn't help but stand to take pictures and video footage of the 360-degree view.

"You're making it rock – please sit down!" my travel companion pleaded, rather shocking me to say the least.

Despite feeling agitated, I begrudgingly obeyed his request until the beautiful view of Lantau Island's valleys, Country Park and the South China Sea took hold of me once again; the incredible sight was enough to make me stand to capture 'just one more photo!'

We had finally reached the gateway to the sacred Buddha statue.

My inner-child took over and I found myself enthusiastically running alongside Summer as we climbed the 260 golden steps to reach the top.

Sprinting past Carl, we laughed at the hordes of boring people who were taking each step in their stride because of the blistering heat. *Carl being one of them!*

Arriving at the peak's 360-degree view (a tad out-of-breath) we marvelled as Kevin and Perry had when they stared at the biggest nightclub in Ibiza for the very-first time. I took a moment to absorb the enormity of Big Buddha's presence.

The Buddha looked gigantic as it rested on its three-tier podium at the end of the staircase, with Lantau's beautiful valleys and mountains peacefully surrounding it.

"The first podium showcases six statues that are named the Bodhisattvas…" I read from the guide book.

"Can you see them, Summer? The statues offer different items to Buddha such as a flower, incense, fruit or music to represent charity, meditation, patience and wisdom." I continued to read as we both stood motionless at the statues before us.

"There you are!" Carl bolted towards us. *He was back then!*

The second podium was home to a museum that described Buddha's life and teachings. The final podium was the incredible Buddha himself, who stood at 112-foot-tall making it the world's tallest outdoor Buddha statue.

Sat on a wreath of lotus leaves (which in Buddhism is a symbol of purity) the statue is said to overlook the people of China.

Leafing through my guidebook for a further fact, I discovered that every feature of the statue has a symbolic meaning of religious significance. The eyes, lips, incline of the head and right hand (which is raised to deliver a blessing to all) syndicate an awe-inspiring depth of character and poise to the Buddha.

Summer soon became dissatisfied with her VTech play camera and instead repeatedly asked to use my very-expensive DSLR camera. *Typically, my daughter – naturally having expensive taste and all…*

Reluctantly, I agreed and she endearingly made me laugh when she tried to be creative with her shooting by tilting the camera and zooming in at speed to create funny abstract images of Buddha.

"Is that wise letting her hold the camera?" Carl groaned.

"It's ok – she knows it's expensive and to be careful - don't you Summer?" I asked my shrewd daughter as she peered towards us both with the camera's strap safely nestled around her neck.

"Kids never truly understand the value of things."

Choosing to ignore him, I instead peered at the forceful Buddha towering before me.

Despite being unreligious and knowing very little about Buddhism, I could still appreciate the sight and see why people visited. It was to clear their minds, pray and reflect.

Swallowing several shallow breaths, I admired the statue, blocked out the crowds and drunk in the peacefulness it possessed. Until my motherly-duties kicked in that is and Summer slam-dunked her head deep into my stomach, complaining that she was bored.

"Ok, let's head to the Po Lin Monastery that is opposite." I compromised in that parenting way that you do.

"Although the temple is a popular attraction to tourists…" I read from the guide book whilst we headed over.

"It still maintains its crux and ethnicities and is frequently visited by its devoted followers…"

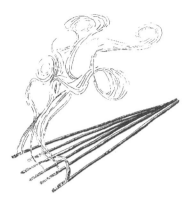

"What's that smell Mummy?" Summer asked as we ventured through the colourful temple's pleasant gardens.

"Yes, I noticed that young Summer. It is certainly an exotic scent." Carl peered around, as if for the first time.

"The smell is incense sticks – look around you – they're burning everywhere!" I observed.

We later discovered that believers lit the incense as a way of attracting the gods or to offer food for spirits that have passed.

"What are they doing Mummy?" Summer uttered as we observed a group of men making their wishes for the day by waving giant yellow joss sticks in the air, creating enormous puffs of grey smoke.

Just like Summer, I found the sight mesmerising. As we watched, more and more people lit incense sticks, prayed and chimed spiritual readings.

Catching my eye, people were burning a material-like paper into waste bins whilst praying.

"I wonder what burning the paper means?" I leaned into Carl.

"My guess is that they're burning it to represent good luck or fortune." He whispered into my ear intently.

"I'm really glad that we came here," I beamed as we walked out of the gated community, feeling inspired by the sacredness of the afternoon.

Remaining in silence, I immediately noticed something delicately blowing in the wind a few feet away.

"Look at that…" I yelled animatedly, full of wonderment as I bounced towards the flying object.

"Oh cool!" Summer skipped excitedly behind.

On closer inspection, we realised that the object was in fact a single piece of paper that had been burning at the monastery.

"It must have blown away as the people were burning them!" Summer hastily stamped her sandal onto the paper to stop it from blowing away.

Nobody would deny that the paper was striking. It looked as though it was made from cotton and was decorated in red and gold Chinese writing, shining like a shell that had been laid at the bottom of the sea for centuries.

"I think finding the paper means good luck!" Carl nodded intellectually.

"That would make sense…what are the chances of one landing at our feet? In fact," I continued to screech. "My horoscope this morning did say to 'keep my eyes on the sky!'"

Scooping the paper up carefully, I placed it inside my diary.

"Oh don't pick it up – it's just another thing to carry!"

"But you said it meant good luck? Plus, I hardly think that it's going to weigh the backpack down!" I giggled joyfully.

Continuing our walk back to the cable-car, we discussed the luck that the paper would hopefully bring for the remainder of the trip. We had experienced an incredible first few days already, so it could only get better from here on out.

Sadly it seemed our luck hadn't yet started, when we found ourselves queuing for over an hour for a cable-car back to the mainland.

The view on the journey back was as incredible as it was going. As the sun set over Buddha and the hills that nestled among the statue; I was in awe as I happily clicked away on my DSLR. (Arguing with Summer who wanted to have a go at capturing a perfect picture of the sunset just as much as I did.)

"Will the pair of you just sit down?" Carl screamed, taking me totally by surprise.

His fear of heights was obviously a lot worse than I'd initially realised and I started to feel more and more aggravated that he hadn't mentioned this so-called 'fear' before the trip had began.

As a gut reaction to Carl's scream, Summer and I somehow managed to stifle our giggles as we glanced towards each other, elevating our eyebrows. We were then, of course, good girls and took it in turns to share the camera.

Back at the mainland, we hurried to the train station as time seemed to disappear at an immense speed. We had paid

£100 for a boat cruise for that evening, so we were on a tight schedule to arrive at the boat on time.

Realising it would take too long to get the train and bus back to the hotel; we flagged down a taxi and decided to swallow the extra cost the journey would incur; if it meant getting back to the hotel in time to change for the boat trip that evening.

Looking out of the window with unmistakable delight, we were certainly in our home area of Aberdeen – *finally*! I did blow-out invisible vapour, however, when 10 minutes later we drove down the same street twice!

"I think the driver is lost...I recognise these streets from the walk we did yesterday. It will probably be quicker to find the hotel by foot."

"I don't think it's wise for us to get out of the taxi in a part of town that we know nothing about, Laura."

"Don't be daft! This is what backpacking is all about!" I asserted whilst indicating for the driver to pull over.

Immediately after, I watched with displeasure as Carl rolled his eyes tediously. *My laid-back nature must have been irritating him, just as some of his habits were starting to get on my nerves!*

Getting out of the taxi was a gamble that thankfully paid off. Within 20 minutes of walking, I had miraculously found our hotel. *I knew my photographic memory would help me out on this trip!*

Unfortunately, being late meant that we were left with a measly 25 minutes to get ready. With no time to waste we changed into our fancy evening wear and headed back to the city streets to flag down yet another taxi to take us back the very direction that we had just come from; this time heading towards the ferry port.

Strangely, for the first time since being in Hong Kong there were no available taxis in sight. Frustrated, we had to wait a whole 10 minutes until a free car was available.

Clock-watching, we finally arrived at the first of three tolls. Previously, all the journeys we had taken we were able to pass through each toll at speed.

My spirits fell at the speed of plummeting through the air on the Hollywood 'hotel' ride in Disneyland, when we were made to wait once again at the second toll booth. Brilliantly, we were then greeted by bumper-to-bumper of traffic. *Just great!*

Gazing at my phone out of boredom, we only had 30 minutes until the boat was to depart.

"Excuse me..." I coughed dramatically to get the driver's attention.

"Do you know another way? We have a boat to catch and if we don't get there soon then we will miss it!" I said with extreme urgency to my voice.

Glancing back towards me, the driver looked blank and confused. For the next five seconds a deafening silence filled the air.

"You're taking us to the ferry port?" I asked, nervous at his confused expression.

"Yes?" I repeated myself forcefully when he offered no response and instead began furiously tapping away at one of the many smart phone screens that haphazardly decorated his dashboard.

I exhaled like a deflated balloon and didn't hold out much hope of us arriving in time. Heck, I wasn't even confident that the driver even knew where we were heading!

After 10 more minutes of sitting stationary, the taxi slowly crept out of the tunnel to reveal a huge motorway flyover that was similarly decorated with an entourage of headlights.

Frustration soon turned to disappointment when our 20 minutes miserably dropped to just 10. Sitting back into my seat, sadness engulfed me as self-loathing rolled in like a fog....

It was a momentary sense of defeat, but with only 10 minutes until the boat was to leave I knew we weren't going to make the departure. In that exact moment, I was desperately trying to temper the rage-filled air that was permeating our small faded-red, Toyota taxi.

The clock soon struck our deadline time and my expression become as strained as a glass of skimmed milk. We had missed the boat and had only moved a quarter-of-a mile since leaving the tunnel. *Fan-bloody-tastic!*

As the taxi continued to creep forwards at a snail pace, I noticed an array of shops just off the flyover that promptly charged me up like electricity. I blinked hastily as my eyelids matched my heart rate from both the anger and adrenaline of clock watching for what seemed like forever.

"Can you stop at those shops please?" I excitedly asked the driver. It was a request that he was clearly not happy with as it now meant he had lost his huge fair.

Despite not understanding his language, his sharp and hoarse voice informed me that he was indeed very angry. Not only that, but I could see his eyes staring through my pupils like laser beams.

I smiled as if to compensate for his frustration, and swiftly fumbled for the correct fare as I mouthed to Carl to 'discreetly' jump out.

Following orders, Carl grabbed Summer's hand and the duo fled the car so quick it was as though they were trying to escape a kidnap attempt! *Did the word 'discreet' mean nothing to Carl?*

Hurriedly passing the raging driver his cash, he continued to scream my way from his torn, leather seat.

"What's the plan now?" Asked a straight-face Carl, standing on yet another unrecognisable street but this time all dressed up with nowhere to go. *The story of my life…*

"We eat!" I declared confidently, which was a statement that was clearly easier said than done.

It seemed the town that we had found ourselves in didn't cater for tourists as every restaurant's menu was in Chinese, leaving us with no option but to point to the 'random' symbols on the menu when ordering.

Summer found this task hugely entertaining and I felt immensely proud of all of us. *Talk about taking you out of your comfort zone!*

Sitting in my chair in the buoyant restaurant, I noticed Carl hovering awkwardly around the table.

"Can you swap seats with me?" he gawkily asked.

"Why?" I answered, slightly bewildered by the odd request.

"I can't sit with my back to the room so I must sit in your seat."

"Err – sure!" I said with a little laugh, before switching seats and placing myself with my back to the room and the restaurant's entrance.

"What do you think is going to happen to you, exactly?" I questioned, incredibly intrigued.

"If something was coming towards you then I'd scream so you'd know about it anyway?"

"I just can't relax and won't enjoy my meal. It's the survival caveman instinct in me you see!" he sipped his beer, oddly gloating at the declaration.

Staring straight at me, he then confidently declared: "If a man and woman were to share a bed, the man would always want to sleep closest to the door - wouldn't he?"

I was just about to ramble something about sexism, when Summer saved the dispute by interrupting.

"Mummy, I don't want to sit in my seat either!"

"Oh, yes you are – don't be so silly!" I grabbed the menu as a distraction tool, completely forgetting that I couldn't read it; instead, I digested a bunch of mixed-up symbols, triggering a childhood memory.

As a severely dyslexic child, the English language used to be something of a minefield to me. Words were merely symbols - just like these Chinese ones were to me now.

It was a Friday evening. The restaurant was heaving with city workers who were enjoying their end of a working-week drink. Seemingly, as well as being the only tourists we were also the only ones with a child.

Sipping my drink, I pushed the picture of the vile, rundown kitchen to the back of my mind in fear that it would put me off the very food that would soon line my stomach.

The concept of having the kitchen openly on display in a restaurant is to reassure the diner about the quality of the food and cooking, is it not? In this restaurant, they clearly missed that point. To say the restaurant was unloved would be an understatement; with the use of beer crates as a table to house the cutlery, and a floor decorated by sticky lino that lifted when you walked across it! The restaurant certainly did not look like the type of place that you would pick out of choice, put it that way.

Anticipation for what was to be served soon grew along with our appetites. By the time the food arrived, I was ready to eat whatever 'bush-tucker' trial food I was given.

My face was the picture of horror when the first dish arrived, and I scanned the four white dumplings that resembled an animal's ball-bag on the TV programme, '*I'm a Celebrity Get Me Out of Here.*'

Served on a bamboo steamer, the dumplings sat like eyeballs staring through my soul. Despite my hunger, I instantly lost my appetite.

Carl wasted no time in eating the not-so-appetising dumplings, with a look of curiosity stretched across his bony face.

"Wow! This is actually really good!" He licked his fingers in satisfaction after the first few bites. *Really?*

"What actually is that?" I asked with my mouth turned up at the edges, peering in disgust at the three balls that were left.

"It's a shrimp dumpling, wrapped in pork and translucent wrapper."

"Can I try one, Mummy?"

"Of course!" I placed a ball (I mean dumpling) onto her plate. To my surprise, she ate the odd-looking dish with absolutely no hesitation; equally commenting about how yummy it was. *Just me then?*

Thankfully, the dishes that followed looked just like those that would come from 'The Golden Dragon' on a typical UK high street. *You can't beat a good Chow Mein, can you?*

Being superficial the look of a restaurant was always a president to how good the food would be. *How misguided I now felt…*

Despite the student furnishings and the gamble of pointing to random symbols on the menu, we indulged (to our surprise) on some of the best foods we had eaten in Hong Kong. Equally, we learnt the importance of never judging a book by its cover (or in this case a restaurant by its furnishings.)

Even though we had lost the £100 we had paid for the boat trip, and had missed our last opportunity to see the magnificent city lit up from the liner; we couldn't help but laugh at our downfall and later triumph of finding that restaurant and its magnificent food.

Standing to leave, I noticed Carl re-arranging the condiments on the table.

"What are you doing, now?" I giggled.

I felt as though I had learnt so much about Carl and his bizarre ways already. I dreaded the thought of any 'new' things that would later crop up.

At midnight, I climbed into bed exhausted. Tucking a loose piece of light brown hair behind my ear, a wave of tiredness flooded over me. Yawning loudly, I toppled sideways and fell into a deep sleep.

***

Four:

The curse of the 'unlucky' paper

Waiting for the taxi to take us to the airport to leave Hong Kong, I sparked up a conversation with the reception staff.

"Before we leave can you tell me the significance of something?" I asked, feeling a stab of both anticipation and excitement at the receptionist's impending answer to my longwinded story about us finding the paper and calling it our lucky charm.

"But I'd love to know what it actually means." I rambled on in that signature 'Laura' way that I always did.

A confused expression spread across the receptionist's face as he politely asked to see the paper. As soon as I produced the mystical object from my bag, I watched in alarm as his face dropped quicker than an ice-cube melting on a blazing hot day. He turned to his colleague in disbelief as she placed her hand across her mouth aghast. With four eyes flaring in my direction, I gazed at them both in utter bewilderment.

"You do not want this!" he yelled as he snatched the paper from my hand, a rigid expression plastered across his face.

I stared at him in utter shock... *What had we done?*

"You shouldn't have taken it!" his voice elevated, before mumbling on repeat that we wouldn't want it in our lives.

"But what does it mean?" I asked, desperate for an answer. *What was wrong with these people? Could they drag this out any longer?*

"You do not want to know..." he stared awkwardly at his colleague.

"Please!" I pleaded, suddenly thinking - *how bad can it be?*

"I really do want to know - what have we done wrong?"

Looking at his colleague and then back at me, all his previous warmth had vanished and his eyes dwindled to dark, burning points.

"People burn these to send messages to their ancestors that have passed. By taking it, the message hasn't been received and the ancestors could haunt you..." he finally revealed.

Carl and I glanced at each other in surprise as we peered through the gloom of the early morning, contemplating just what was actually being said.

"You can't be serious?" I laughed nervously.

"It's true!" interrupted his colleague in a small voice, accompanied by a worried expression across her face.

Comically timed, a short man (who wore tatty jeans and trainers) strolled through the swing doors and announced that he was our taxi driver.

"Well I hope you enjoyed Hong Kong!" The male receptionist cheerily sang in an upbeat tone, as if erasing the conversation we'd just had completely.

"Enjoy Thailand and safe travels!" He scooped up our bags to carry them to the taxi.

Safe travels – was he for real? We were just about to board an aircraft after several had already 'gone missing' that year. Even worse, he'd just told us that we were going to be haunted by dead people!

Bewildered, we dubiously followed him onto the busy city street and took our seats in the taxi. Poking his head into the car, he told us not to worry about the paper, and that he would burn it to try and counteract any damage we had caused.

With a face full of worry, he ordered for the driver to keep us safe - a statement that made Carl and I exchange apprehensive glances towards each other. *Maybe there was some truth to this after all?*

As the taxi 'carefully' made its way towards the toll, we all sat in complete silence…even Summer didn't dare to utter a single word.

"Do you believe any of that?" I eventually asked Carl, breaking the stillness that had fallen between us.

"I know that you shouldn't mess with Buddhists!" he snapped, before asking me why I took the paper.

"I told you not to!"

"Don't blame me!" I yelled.

"If you really thought we shouldn't have taken it then you wouldn't have let us! It was you that thought it meant good luck!"

Remaining in silence for a further minute, I couldn't help but break the peace once again.

"Ironic that we thought it meant good luck though, isn't it?" I giggled.

"Don't laugh Laura, it's not funny! I'm genuinely worried now!" He quavered.

And deep down, so was I…

***

On the way to the airport, frustratingly, we got stuck in a mountain of traffic.

Pondering the last few days, I suddenly noticed a familiar pattern. *How had I not seen it before?* Bizarrely we'd had nothing but bad luck since encountering that 'mysterious' piece of holy paper.

"Call it coincidence," I analysed. "But look what happened the evening of finding that paper. That was the night we missed the boat! Then the next day on route to Disneyland we realised that we'd forgotten the admission tickets so we had to go all the way back to Aberdeen! Who does that?

We are organised, structured people. To forget something like the admission tickets is out of character for both of us. If you were to really scrutinise it, we've had nothing but bad luck since we took that paper - so being haunted would make sense!" I found myself rambling, penny finally dropping.

Carl held my gaze and said nothing, taking in the words I'd uttered. Screwing up his expression, he shook his head rigorously and looked out of the window to his right. He remained silent. *Was he now was starting to believe it too?*

Time passed quickly. We both started to panic that the bad luck could result in us now missing our flight to Bangkok. This would cause our entire itinerary to be thrown out as we had a connecting flight to catch two hours after arriving into Bangkok. Not to mention the fact that we were heading to the elephant sanctuary to be 'elephant keepers' the following day.

Watching every minute pass on my phone with intense frustration, I hunched my shoulders forcefully; no-doubt looking more like a sulky teenager than a mature mother. Exhaling rather-loudly, I broke the silence that had filled the car.

Like a scene from *'Home Alone,'* we later raced through the airport as though our lives depended on it.

With my face flushed my heart thunder-clapped as I stormed through the security gate.

Typically, the alarm sounded. *Of course it did!*

"Great!" I huffed as I was directed towards a creepy-looking lady who scanned me up and down with her 'magic' wand.

"Jewellery off!" She ordered.

Frustratingly (despite removing the little jewellery I had on) the alarm roared as I walked through the barrier for a second time.

"Shoes off!" the woman snorted, as if she'd done this ritual 100 times already that day.

Sighing out loud, I bent down and undid the irritating six-strap sandals that I of course was wearing. (This took far too long for someone that had a plane to catch!)

"Turn around!" She abruptly pushed me into a starfish position and patted me down as though I was an inmate in the prison programme, *'Orange is the New Black.'*

"I'm actually boarding the AIQ503 flight to Bangkok! And I'm so late!" I pleaded.

Falling on deaf ears, she ignored my petition and instead began talking to her colleague.

Several exasperating minutes later and I was thankfully allowed to move on. However, just when we thought the shining beacon of the departure gate was within reach, we realised that we hadn't filled out our immigration cards - nor could we find a pen. *Could this check-in process take any longer? If this bad luck continues, I may suffer the risk of complete coronary failure before the trip has even begun!*

We arrived at the gate just as the announcement for 'priority persons to board' blasted through the croaky speakers. *Phew! I can't believe we actually made it!*

Leaning on a nearby seat to catch my breath (*I must join a gym as soon as I return home.*) I sniggered, glancing towards the queue of priority passengers. People in wheelchairs – yes agreed, children – loosely agreed but as I had one myself I wasn't going to argue that point, and bizarrely - monks. *Why were they prioritised? I pondered in total ignorance.*

However funny it was, Carl and I both felt reassured when we saw several monks stand to board the flight. We figured no Buddhist spirit would attack a plane with monks on board. As stupid as the theory was, it was as though we suddenly had a reliable source of evidence that we would be safe (for now at least.)

***

Securely at Bangkok airport and waiting for our connecting flight, Summer excitedly ran towards an oddly-placed soft play area that was conveniently positioned at the boarding gate. Meanwhile, I was told off by a Thai mum for stepping into the soft-play pit with my shoes on. *I'm not going to lie; it was slightly embarrassing being shouted at in Thai for the entire gate to see.*

Taking respite on a neighbouring bench I fondly watched as Summer played. With Carl marvelling around the nearby book store, my mind raced over the events of the day.

Distracting me, three monks dressed in their distinctive orange-cloth robes parked themselves on the bench to my left. I propped myself up on my elbow and looked their way. With the sun keeping a paternal gaze over us from the hallway of windows we had found ourselves perched by, the sharp rays illuminated the monks and highlighted the fact that they were clearly talking about Summer.

I wondered what they were saying and took out my diary to write about it. Lifting my head several minutes later, I noticed all three monks had their heads down and their iPhones out. I looked at the trio in confusion, totally lost in creative thought. My mouth dropped. It would have made such a great photo! *What a contrast of times that image would have portrayed!*

I was told that monks believe they cannot be in two places at once. Therefore, taking a photo would be perceived as highly disrespectful as they would believe their soul was then in two different places. With our latest string of bad luck (and having already unknowingly disrespected the Buddhist faith) I didn't want to cause any worse feeling by then taking a photo of them. *A mature move? I must be growing up! Not only that, but surely my decision to respect the monks would score vital brownie points with the ancestors?*

Continuing to watch Summer play, I had my writing head on and suddenly felt very inspired to scribble random notes about Hong Kong.

If there is a single place on earth that epitomises an emotion, a spirit, a philosophy...then that place is Asia...

I wrote about technology and the fact that there are TV screens and adverts everywhere across the city: on the buses, in the taxis, even on the train station platforms! Even more futuristic, there were projector screens displaying commercials across the many high-rise buildings that populated the skyline.

In the UK, we're generally quite discrete about checking our reflection on our phones or taking a photo of ourselves for the latest social networking site; yet in Hong Kong they're certainly not shy about pulling out their phones and pouting into the camera. Not just young women, I saw people of all ages doing this – even a 50-year-old man!

There was one day when, with humour, I watched as two teenage girls sat next to each other with their lunch on the table. Unlike most girls, they were not eating, sat gossiping or flicking through magazines. Instead they were individually pouting into their camera phones in complete silence for an entire 10 minutes!

Continuing to write, I moved onto the subject of people staring at us.

It was inevitable that people would stare, but I wasn't prepared to have people holding their gaze at us for significant periods of time. *How unnerving!* There was one guy who cocked his neck to sneak a peek at us on the bus, but rather than move back to a normal seated position following a quick glance in our direction; he held his tilted head in that awkward turned position for several minutes!

Numerous topics passed through my mind like items on a supermarket conveyor belt. I wrote about the waiting staff in Hong Kong and how they didn't understand personal boundaries; especially on one occasion when three waiters stood over us at the table whilst we ate. They didn't talk or smile; they just stood in a line a few inches from the table's edge and stared blankly my way as I inelegantly swallowed my dim sum.

The most unnerving and bizarre situation, however, was when we were at the theme park: Ocean Park. Whilst waiting for the bullet train we noticed those around us nudging each other and pointing towards Summer. Word of her presence soon spread like wild fire and before we knew it we were surrounded by a crowd of 20 people who were cooing and smiling as they touched her hair. We were polite and smiled back (of course) but for Summer that was a rather intimidating and frightening experience. Especially when they started touching her hair!

When the train arrived (and filled as quickly as a London tube during rush-hour) Summer was treated like a superstar and was offered a seat, despite other children being forced to stand. Throughout the journey people continued to approach and ask for photos of her. Others were not so obvious and tried to discretely take a photo from the distance.

It reminded me of when I was aged 19, standing in a flea market in Mexico. Taking me totally by surprise, a group of men approached and asked if I was Britney Spears. *You'd have thought the London accent would have given it away?* I ended up attracting so much attention that I found myself walking quickly through the market in search of a taxi as a crowd followed, frantically calling out: "Britney...Britney..." It was a surreal experience to say the least. *I wouldn't mind, but I didn't really look anything like Britney!*

Likewise, we noticed a difference in behaviour towards us westerners. Whilst queuing for a ride at Disneyland for example, a boy of 18 used his leaflet to fan Summer down in the hot, humid heat. *Could you imagine a teenage boy doing that at a UK theme park?*

It seemed Summer's presence lifted a smile to pretty much everyone we passed in Hong Kong. She found the attention difficult at first. When someone spoke to her or patted her head, she would bury her face deep into my lap.

I told her that people were just excited as they weren't used to seeing girls that looked like her.

"You don't have to be scared or rude to them. It's just like if you were to see someone from the TV."

"But I'm not on the TV!" My shrewd daughter responded, sounding more 15 than five.

After that conversation, her confidence increased and she started becoming more sociable.

When we were at Disneyland, I innocently bought Summer the 'Elsa' dress from the Disney film, Frozen. What a bad move that turned out to be! Children and adults alike continuously approached to hug her and ask if they could have their photo taken alongside her. Suddenly I adopted the role of "mother of a celebrity."

Following this, I went on to write about the sterile nature of Hong Kong and how clean the city was. The MTR (that's a tube to anyone that's unfamiliar) had stainless steel seats and an outright ban on consuming food and drink (even on the platforms!) With a hefty £160 fine if you were caught.

What can I say about the traffic in Hong Kong? Being raised in London, I thought I'd seen everything there was to see with regards to traffic. Seriously though, Hong Kong was something else altogether. To say there was hostility between taxi drivers was an understatement! They continuously refused to give way to each other in any situation.

Just to give you a taste of how dangerous and crazy it can be on the roads in the city, annual road death figures were visibly displayed on the side of the motorway, and in 2014 they had 15,500 fatalities! To put that figure into context, according to the Office of National Statistics there were 1,713 people killed in reported road traffic accidents across the whole of the UK that same year.

Continuing to write, I moved onto the topic of Halloween.

We were in Hong Kong the week before the holiday and it seemed the city had gone nuts in celebration of the 'spooky' day. There were market-lined roads dedicated to the occasion, with stall upon stall and shop upon shop selling endless Halloween memorabilia. There were even people walking around wearing Halloween costumes and the holiday wasn't for another week!

I saw one woman wearing an outfit that resembled '*Where's Wally*' with a red beanie hat, red and white stripped top and blue trousers.

On that same day, I saw another lady who was wearing a black and red short devil dress with a matching Alice band. It was particularly bizarre as she sat casually alongside many formal-looking morning commuters at 8am on a Wednesday morning. Some people were even sporting fake blood with cobwebs etched into the cheeks of their faces during their morning commutes.

"Mummy, I'm bored!" Summer's voice interrupted my writing flow.

In a bid to entertain, I broke off from writing and instead we looked at the Mandarin language and how the shapes and symbols made up a word. I tasked her to make up her own words using shapes and symbols and to tell me what they meant; an assignment that she found absolutely hilarious. *Oh, to be a five-year-old again...*

I felt as though Summer was already learning small yet important aspects from travelling, such as taking things with two hands instead of just one when someone passed her something. (In China, taking an item with two hands is a sign of respect.) She had even began asking if it was ok to take a photo of something before she snapped away on her camera, indicating that she was starting to understand and respect the culture. *My Little Asian Summer* was coming on nicely!

As my close friends know, I am defined by how hard I had to work for my education. I was the class-clown throughout school and left high school struggling with dyslexia and with the attention span of a newt! Ultimately, this meant that I left school with very few qualifications to my name.

Maturing into an adult, I realised what I wanted in life and worked hard to turn things around. Consequently, I now apply that discipline throughout my entire life.

The fact that my five-year-old daughter was already learning so many life skills at such a young age; filled my heart with sheer glee and pride.

***

Our flight to Chiang Mai was quick and straightforward. Well, apart from Carl hyperventilating into a sick bag mid-flight that is!

To my surprise, we arrived at a tiny airport where our backpacks were on the luggage carousel and onto our backs within minutes of stepping off of the aircraft. We had no immigration to pass through and were greeted outside the terminal doors by a hive of taxi drivers all wanting to take us to our accommodation.

Summer instantly grabbed the drivers' attention as a hoard of them bent down to her level and pulled on her bears, joking that they were theirs.

Warming instantly to one of the drivers, I stared with astonishment as we confidently climbed into his surprisingly classy, white-Mitsubishi Freelander Sport and drove 10 minutes to our accommodation. The journey cost a total of £3, and for such nice transport - we were impressed!

Staying in a hostel dorm room is an experience quite unlike anything else. Unless you join the army or get evacuated to the local leisure centre during a natural disaster; it's unlikely that you will ever find yourself crammed into a room with a dozen strangers. I had experienced hostel dormitories whilst backpacking Australia, but with Summer now in tow I didn't think it would be safe to share a room with strangers. It was for this reason that for the first leg of our now 'rustic' journey, I opted for a double room in a hostel instead.

I watched with curiosity as the driver carefully negotiated his rather-expensive Freelander down a tiny rundown alleyway, narrowly missing shacks and those cleaning their motorbikes or hanging out their washing.

Observing that this was clearly a residential road and not a tourist one, I started to feel nervous about our first 'backpacking' accommodation. A vision of a street I once stayed on in the red-light district of Bangkok flashed through my mind.

I remembered opening my curtains in the morning and seeing an array of naked bodies as people washed their bare skin in dirty drums of soapy water on their balconies…I hoped there would be no naked washing on this residential road with Summer's little eyes in tow.

My thoughts drifting further, the driver stopped outside what looked to be a house which ended my flashback rather snappishly.

Creeping towards the wooden building, a shrine of Buddha memorabilia filled my eye-line. Nearing closer to the reception, I could see hundreds of candles as well as a line of shoes at the door.

"Wow…this looks, urm, interesting…" muttered Carl under his breath, edging closer.

Following suit, I kicked off my sandals and slowly entered the dim-room where a frail, teapot-sized, elderly lady sat at a desk.

The counter was so full of statues, ornaments and candles that amusingly she held a newspaper in the air as she attempted to read the day's headlines.

I gazed at the old woman before me. With a face full of lines and creases, it was like her skin no longer had a link to the skull underneath and was so fragile it could rupture even by the softest of touches.

In Thailand, the custom is to 'wai' instead of shaking hands. This is when you place the palms of your hands together as if in prayer, and raise them to the level of your face whilst bowing slightly.

Noticing my presence, I wai'd at the lady and her fine hair which balanced over a near-enough bald scalp.

"Sa-wad-dee-ka - we have booked a room." I lapsed into English after my initial greeting. *How the hell do you say the second half of the sentence in Thai?*

Less than a minute later and Summer had taken her shoes off and joined me in the reception.

Glancing towards Carl outside, I giggled at his expression. *He looked as though he'd just walked through a fish market!*

Still chuckling, I gazed down at Summer who innocently smiled at the lady, before greeting her with '*sa-wad-dee*-ka' and a confident wai. I was so thrilled that she had listened when I explained to her that we no longer said '*ni-hao*' to people (as we did in Hong Kong) and instead 'hello' was 'sa-wad-dee-ka.'

The lady reassured my hostel nerves by smiling at Summer. Her brown eyes were warm. Just like the taxi drivers she pulled at Summer's bears and claimed that they were hers.

Climbing the staircase to our room, we looked at our new surroundings and the many signs that warned us to be 'quiet at all times.'

The room looked like a motel from the 1970's and was very basic with just one double and one single bed; a side unit and a TV that had a bigger back than those you would find covered in cobwebs in the attic.

Knowing we had to start our malaria tablets that evening, we needed to tackle the alleyway and venture out in search of food.

The rough, cobbled lane that was as straight as a drinking straw, had a peculiar aroma to it; with a mixture of food, candles and sweat filling both the air and our lungs, it was certainly an interesting walk. Summer enjoyed taking in the sights of people washing their clothes in a bucket or cleaning their mopeds and bikes whilst they went about their everyday lives.

Finally reaching a main road that was full of bars, restaurants and many mopeds that whizzed past at reckless speeds, we plonked ourselves on the side of the street. Drinking beers that cost just £1, we amusingly watched families of four huddled closely on the passing mopeds. Tickling my humour even further, some bikes even carried multiple police officers and monks! I had to pinch myself and blink twice to make sure that the scene before me was even real.

Our extremely cheap £3 meals soon arrived. With my stomach shouting at me to eat, hungrily taking my first bite, an uninvited splodge of water landed in my drink. Feeling ravenous for my cheap food, less than a minute later and we were welcomed to Chiang Mai by a horrendous thunderstorm. *Had we brought the English weather with us?*

Under a cloud of boredom, I blanched as I realised that two hours had passed and we were still stuck in the confined and now-stuffy restaurant with the thunderstorm showing no signs of passing. No longer being able to 'just sit,' we had no alternative but to run in the storm.

I've danced until my feet were sore and blistered, sung until my throat hoarse, and drunk until I could barely stand – *surely, I could cross some puddles?*

Laughing and squealing with Summer, I found running in the rain rather liberating - until we hit the water-logged alley that was! With puddles so deep the alleyway now resembled a river!

"Oh, sod it!" Carl laughed as he nonchalantly walked through the first huge puddle. Wow! It was the first-time I'd ever seen Carl so laid back! *How refreshing…*

"What about us?" I yelled from the other side, laughing as I put Summer on my back and confidently attempted to jump over the pool of water myself.

Hurdling over the enormous puddles with Summer on my backside was fun until I nearly fell on top of someone's motorbike. Cackling loudly, I held onto the bike's handles for support whilst attempting to stop Summer from slowly slipping down my back. In unison, we giggled like school friends as I attempted to hold onto her and not break the bike at the same time.

Suddenly, I could hear people laughing. Glancing upwards in misunderstanding, a crowd of locals watched and giggled from the comfort of their dry balconies at my no-doubt, rather comical moves. *A little help maybe? Obviously not...*

***

It had just gone 9.30pm and we were late taking our first malaria tablet. Carl and I wasted no time in swallowing ours. What I didn't account for, however, was the drama I would endure trying to get Summer to swallow her two tablets. With haste, she immediately spat the first tablet onto the floor. Rather calmly, I gave her another and told her that we were on limited stock so she couldn't waste it and had to swallow it. Despite my warning, within moments she immediately spat the second tablet onto the floor. With a dramatic chorus of cries, she refused to take any more.

A feeling of apprehension ran through my body as the consequences of taking the tablet late ran through my mind. It was as though she was Captain Hook and I was the crocodile who was chasing her with the clock!

"Come on Summer!" I yelled, now with a tad of intense frustration in my voice I admit.

To my relief she reluctantly tried to swallow the tablet again; only this time she spat the whole thing into a full bottle of water, turning the clear liquid a cordial-yellow colour.

I had no choice but to force her to drink the entire bottle of yellow-water, and in doing so she repaid me by screaming at the top of her lungs in a hostel that proactively advertised its 'quiet policy.'

Pleading with her to stop crying once more, she completely ignored me and continued to scream full-pelt regardless.

"What a bizarre reaction to swallowing a tablet." Carl unhelpfully muttered.

"She's only five!" I snapped in irritation. *I wondered why he thought his criticism was helping.*

"Well, my children took vitamins every day from a young age so they were used to the consistency of tablets – that's the thing you see, you have left it too late!"

I glanced at him in added annoyance. *Is purposely 'winding people up' a sport of his?*

"Summer does take vitamins but they're chewable ones like sweets."

I felt an infuriation bubble in the pit of my stomach at his implication that Summer's reaction was somehow down to bad parenting on my part. *How dare he?*

"Gummy vitamins actually contain smaller amounts of vitamins compared to the pill form." He retaliated in a sneering tone.

"In order for the companies to make them taste like sweets, the number of vitamins and minerals contained within them is in fact 'rather minimal.' This means that the sugar-to-nutrient is blurred and the unhealthy ingredients often get the upper hand."

I stared at him blankly. *Could he be more irritating? He really was a 'Mr Know-it-all.'*

"Well something is better than nothing!" I huffed like a stroppy teenager. *Since when did Carl become so opinionated?*

Just over 30 minutes later and I had one empty bottle of what was Malarone-filled water, and one very-upset little girl.

In bed that evening, I thought about the drama of trying to get Summer to take the tablet. A feeling of dread washed over me as I envisioned having to endure that ritual every night for the remainder of the trip. *Each time with Carl's judgement, no doubt.* I racked my brains. There must be another way I could get her to take them? *Surely, I could come up with something?*

***

The next morning we skipped down the now-familiar alleyway at 6.30am to get breakfast prior to our pick up for the elephant sanctuary. The sky was powder-blue and although it was still early, we could feel the sun's rays burning our backs as we gloriously enjoyed the morning heat.

The walk was fascinating! Thankfully the evening's puddles had cleared and incredibly, we found ourselves sharing the rustic, cobbled path with barefooted monks who walked alongside us in single-file.

With the eldest monk strolling in front, I watched with curiosity as two others quickly followed; each monk gripping an empty bowl as they went door-to-door collecting food.

Summer asked why they had no shoes on and were collecting food, and Carl educated us both by telling us that many years ago Buddhist monks were homeless and begged for their food.

"Their only possessions were their robes and begging bowls." He intellectually declared.

"That's how monks have traditionally existed young Summer. Today many monks still rely on receiving gifts of food."

Giggling, Summer seemed genuinely excited to see the scene unfold before her fascinated, beady, eyes.

"Quick, walk faster!" she squealed, increasing her pace to see the monks' next movements.

With ring-side seats to the monks' morning ritual, we noticed how some people congregated on their steps, patiently waiting for them to arrive; whilst others had already placed food, flowers and incense sticks outside their houses so they could help themselves. I looked ahead impressively.

It was a true privilege to witness the symbolic relationship between the local community and the monks', and more importantly, it was a great way to introduce Summer to the world of Buddhism.

***

Five:

Crushing away freedom

When you think about Thailand, the vision of chaotic Bangkok or the turquoise waters of Ko Samui may spring to mind. This diary entry will open your eyes to another rather 'hidden' side to Thailand that was both mesmerising and extremely sad for all of us.

The official symbol of Thailand is the Asian elephant. Sadly, that doesn't seem to stop this incredible creature from being gravely mistreated by copious amounts of people in the very country that celebrates its existence.

When researching activities, I stumbled across the Elephant Nature Park in Chiang Mai. The conservation centre offered an educational programme where you could be an 'elephant keeper' for several days. At that point, I didn't know much about elephants or how they are treated by some in Asia, but I thought it would be something fun and educational for Summer to participate in.

It was 7.30am on our first day in Chiang Mai and we were picked up in a comfortable air-conditioned bus and met our tour guide, Bee.

Our group consisted of a diverse mixture of people from different walks of life: a Frenchman in his 60's (who was travelling around Asia on his own for a few weeks) a Dutch couple in their 40's (who didn't speak much English) a European lesbian couple in their 20's (who didn't speak at all) and an American couple in their 30s who we hit-it-off with immediately.

During the drive, Bee told us about the nature park and why it existed. At that time, the centre had 35 elephants that had arrived in various states of ill-health, either neglected, blind, or with disabilities from the constant and harrowing abuse they had received at the hands of both the tourism and logging industries. (For those of you who don't know what logging is, it is when an elephant is commanded to shift heavy logs from one place to another.)

"Many elephants have been hunted, chained, made to perform and beg for money on the streets of Bangkok... some are even sold to circuses in China." Bee explained.

That statement completely saddened and devastated all of the tourists sat on the mini bus. Not to mention haunting me for the duration of our time in Thailand.

Perhaps most shocking of all, Thailand is home to fewer than 5,000 elephants. This figure would have been an impressive 100,000 elephants a hundred years ago. Visualising this mass decline, I couldn't believe how unbelievable and depressing the statistic actually was.

To add a touch of humanity to an otherwise catastrophic tragedy, we discovered that the nature park was opened in 2006 by a woman called Lek Chailert; who was raised in a tribal village in northern Chiang Mai. At a very young age Lek magically formed a strong bond with an elephant, which continued into adulthood and developed her passion for rescuing elephants in need.

We learnt that Lek successfully rescues the elephants by paying the abusers to sell them directly to her. It was for this reason that we were a direct lifeline to the sanctuary, bringing in a vital income.

Pulling up at the striking green valley, we couldn't help but absorb our surroundings.

"This place is incredible!" said Carl in ore, drinking-in the never-ending row of magnificent mountains that were offset by a calm and tranquil river.

"Views such as this are what backpacking is all about!" I confidently spouted as I pulled my backpack from the back of the van and contemplated how undeniably beautiful the view was.

We were soon directed to a lunch hall where gigantic wooden tables were laden with a mouth-watering selection of dishes that looked and smelt so divine, I was sure even the furniture sighed with luscious anticipation.

With a plate of food that was piled high, we started talking to the American couple, Mike and Laurie, who we discovered were from Washington DC travelling around Thailand for three weeks.

Immediately after lunch we were introduced to our official guide, Apple, who was the epitome of a good host. With her charismatic personality, Summer instantly warmed to her. Especially when she comically flapped her baby's arms and made clucking sounds that resembled a chicken. It was lovely to witness Summer so comfortable around her.

When the incessant giggling was over, Apple handed us copious amounts of melon and directed us to the elephant viewing deck, which was a surreal experience.

"Feeding the elephants is really easy," she explained.

"Just delicately position the fruit at the end of the trunk, so the elephant can curl its trunk into a ball and you can put the food into its mouth."

Overwhelming is the only word I can use to express the sensational experience of feeding the entourage of elephants suddenly at our feet. It was an odd feeling having a throng of trunks continuingly swooping up and sniffing around your flip flops for their eagerly-awaited treats.

Much to my utter astonishment, Summer's initial enthusiasm for feeding the elephants quickly turned into pure fear; resulting in her clumsily dropping the fruit any time an elephant's trunk came close.

We were intrigued to learn that elephant keepers were known as mahouts and were forbidden to be women. Wow! In the 21st century it's hard to believe that a gender gap still exists in some countries. What did Emmeline Pankhurst fight for exactly?

"My son will grow up to be a mahout just like his father and grandfather," Apple proudly stated with a twinkle in her eye.

Eventually, it was time to check into our rooms.

Walking as a group, the French man started talking to Carl.

"What brought you travelling Carl?" I heard him ask.

"I needed to get out of the rat-race. I'm a fraud investigator you see, so I have a rather hectic job..."

Oh, here we go again... I was forced to endure another painful explanation of his job.

"I can imagine that's a tough job – very demanding!" muttered the French man.

"In England, we have the National Health Service - which is free, so there's always room for people to abuse it."

"Yes, I can imagine."

"Prescription fraud is a big one and has such a wide-birth. It can involve anything from people coming to the UK from overseas and claiming free treatment, to British residents claiming free prescriptions that they are not entitled to. People sometimes alter their prescriptions – such as adding figures to the quantity of drugs they are collecting. Then there are others who try to obtain a volume of prescriptions by registering at numerous surgeries. The list is endless and that's just one part of my role..." He was clearly off on one...

"Oh my!" the French man gasped. All I could do was roll my eyes.

"Here's your hut." Apple thankfully interrupted.

Our new home was on stilts and had a stone path leading to it. With dusky stained wood and exquisite flowers carved into the wood work, even though it was basic it certainly had a comfortable aura to it.

Climbing the stairs to the entrance, Summer erupted into a fit of giggles. I turned in confusion to see the sight of a familiar but oddly-placed ginger cat. With a soft but mature look, in the gentle light his colour looked captivating.

"Look Mum...we even get a free pet!" Summer giggled with that dirty laugh that she was known for.

Ruining the moment completely, Carl declared: "Summer! Whatever you do – do not touch it!" Boisterously balancing his arm out, he prevented Summer from stepping any closer to the cat. Talk about spoilsport!

Within minutes of being inside the hut, I noticed numerous holes in our mosquito net. Pondering about what to do, I surprised myself with my resourcefulness by using my hair clips to cover each hole. Admittedly, I was proud of my practicality at this moment in time - even if Carl didn't bat an eyelid at my triumph.

We were told to change into long sleeved tops and trousers and head to the cinema room to watch a 60-minute documentary about the park.

The film illustrated exactly what the term 'elephant tourism' meant. We learnt that logging was banned in Thailand back in 1989. Consequently, elephants quickly found themselves out of a job, leaving many to be sold to neighboring countries such as Burma. Not-so-surprisingly, this caused a rapid decline in the population of elephants throughout Thailand. Many of the remaining ones were then forced to work in the 'legal' tourism industry.

This shift in the law also meant that elephants were then seen as domesticated, with no strict penalty for abuse or mistreatment of the animal.

The film certainly opened our eyes to the grief-stricken lives of the elephants. Describing how horrific the programme was would be an almost impossible task. All I can say to you is that many people were forced to leave the room. Emotions ran high as some of the content was too distressing to take in.

I was keen for Summer to watch at least some of the film so she would be able to acknowledge why it was so important for the elephants to reside at the park; and ultimately why we were there to help care for them.

At home, Summer and I often had mature conversations. Regularly watching the evening news together, coverage of a story that I had organised and overseen the filming of at work would be aired, and I'd explain what happened and why; leaving her full of questions.

It was an absolute pleasure having such an inquisitive child, and sometimes it was difficult to remember that she was merely five years old.

The film soon introduced us to Lek, the owner of the park. We learnt about her childhood and the initial passion and enthusiasm she found for elephants.

At 16 years old, Lek had seen a man stab an elephant in the eye for daring to dismiss his commands. It was a moment that would change her life forever; as the visual image of the traumatic episode was so strong that Lek was haunted by the elephants scream for the rest of her childhood.

It was this single incident that compelled Lek to commit her adult life to protect any elephant that was mistreated. That life-changing decision resulted in the wonderful 'Elephant Nature Park' coming to fruition.

The film explained how fully-sized elephants are placed in tiny cages called 'the crush.' (The cage looked smaller than a box-room in a terrace house!) Inside 'the crush' elephants are shackled like slaves in a space that is so small, it is impossible for them to move even a centimetre to the left or right.

In this prison, the elephants are repeatedly assaulted: punched, poked, starved, seriously sleep-deprived and kicked. Even more disturbing, we learnt that torture such as this could go on for as long as a week, with numerous people collectively taking it in turns to beat the elephant. The goal of the human's actions (although human is definitely not a word I'd use to describe them) was to eventually break any spirit the elephant might have left and therefore see the human as its 'master.'

The film explained that by seeing the human as its master, the elephant would then conform to demands such as allowing people to sit on its back or perform tricks in a circus.

Suddenly, it all made sense. I'd always wondered how they managed to get elephants to do such acts, but I would never have imagined it to be by something as torturous as 'the crush.'

Unsurprisingly, it was at this point that I thought Summer had seen enough.

Making our way over the bamboo pathway, Summer was full of inquisitiveness. My ever-curious daughter fired a stream of questions my way about what she had just seen.

"Why were people hitting the elephant Mummy? It's mean to hit animals!" She was certainly displaying a touch of empathy that I hadn't seen from her before.

"Where was the elephant's Mummy and Daddy? Why weren't they looking after him?"

I can honestly say that an experience like this leaves a mark on you. From this point onwards, Summer and I saw the nature park in a completely different light. We had certainly encountered the 'ugly side' of humanity that was for sure.

Reaching the end of the bamboo pathway, the view was immensely breath-taking. Dozens of elephants roamed free across the 250 acres of grassland that sat against the awe-inspiring backdrop of the mountains surrounding us.

Glancing across the field, a young girl with dark, heavy hair stood comfortably next to an elephant. I stared at her with curiosity. On closer inspection, I realised that my eyes had deceived me. It wasn't a young girl - it was the owner, Lek.

I took in her frame dubiously. It was shocking how minuscule she actually was. Standing hardly the width of the elephant's trunk, she was certainly a pocket-sized figure as she gently stroked the trunk of the elephant.

They say first impressions count...in this case it couldn't have been more true. This lady seemed extraordinary! Watching her movements, decorated with a very broad and bright smile, I couldn't envisage her anywhere other than on that very spot with the elephant's trunk in her hand.

The experience of the upper deck was entertaining, especially when Summer and I felt an impulsive jolt which prompted us to glance at our feet. We laughed and gasped hysterically when we realised that an elephant was stood directly beneath us, and was scratching its back on the very floor that we were standing on. His movements were so powerful that the floor was literally shaking, causing us to giggle uncontrollably.

I was keen to use this opportunity to take a close-up photograph of the elephant. However, as I crouched down the lens cover of my camera plummeted through the hole in the floorboards and landed straight into the surrounding dirt; landing literally inches from the elephant's foot!

Thankfully, Mike and Laurie had returned from the cinema room, so I left Summer with them and frantically ran towards the elephant to retrieve the lens cover.

Sprinting like a mad woman, I weaved in and out of the crowds of people with great precision, dodging my way towards the beautiful creation in desperation to recover the lens before the elephant crushed it.

Approaching with extreme caution, I hastily grabbed the cover from the dirt and slowly backed away from the enormous elephant that was towering over it.

The sheer reality of its enormous magnificence hit me at that very moment. Suddenly, my mere 5ft 7ins frame seemed miniscule against the elephant's mammoth physique.

Glancing up, I noticed the elephant's weeping eye that was so bold it was as if his eyes could tell a passionate, soulful story of immense pain and misery.

"He's blind..." a voice behind made me jump.

Nervously, I looked over my shoulder and was greeted by a young man who had floppy hair and was wearing a top that displayed the word 'Volunteer.'

"Usually elephants with sight lock trunks with the blind ones and guide them around. His guide obviously got distracted," he laughed casually in an Australian accent whilst gently stroking the saggy-skinned elephant.

I nodded unobtrusively. "Well I better get off..."

Glancing behind me at the mammoth elephant's frame, my mind was stuck on its weeping eye. *I did think that it was striking and told a story before I even knew that the elephant was blind.*

"Mummy: we're going to the elephant hospital now!" an excited Summer screeched on my approach, leaving her mark in the air that surrounded us.

We soon arrived at an enormous concrete square, where a vet explained the procedure for nursing injured elephants back to health. He then demonstrated the tricks of his trade on a baby elephant, totally mesmerising an engaged Summer.

With the ground smouldering, creating a distinct haze, we trotted across the hot, dry land until we came to a brown river that housed a family of elephants that were bathing themselves. Wanting Summer to experience this endearing moment in all its glory, I pushed her bottom up a nearby dirt hill without a care in the world.

"Mummy, stop pushing me – I'm going to fall over..."

"Don't be so boring!" I teased, as if I was the child.

Watching the elephants play, I strangely found myself envying their ability to relieve themselves from the immensely, suffocating heat. *Boy! Even the grass stood still as if too tired to move!*

Viewing the impressive creatures tumbling back into the water like children playing, I began visualising the extreme torture and widespread tragedy that the beautiful animals had experienced in their previous lives.

Seeing how happy they were, made me wonder if they even remembered the past.

"It's fascinating how naturally entertaining the elephants are, isn't it?" I said to the French man as he slumped his body next to mine on the dirt.

"I know – they don't need to perform tricks in a circus! They could just do this!" He pointed to a baby elephant that had just fallen back into the river and was happily squirting water from his trunk.

Dirt pounding, we later saw two mahouts dressed in denim overalls with oversized straw hats and knee-high leather boots that were caked in mud. *It was just the way I imagined them to look.*

One mahout was perched by a small fire carving a perfect replica of an elephant into a slab of wood.

"Wow that's incredible!" I leaned over his shoulder to take in the detail of the elephant and in doing so clumsily blocked his light.

"Oh sorry!" I giggled, realising what I'd done and taking a quick step backwards.

Walking away, Apple told me that they sold the wooden elephants in the gift shop and that all the profits went to the mahouts' families. I thought it was remarkable that the centre helped support the families of the workers as well as the elephants. It was at this moment that I captured the sheer brilliance of the centre. It truly was a lifeline for the families and all the animals that resided there.

With the passage of time firmly etched into his face, I looked towards a mahout as he cooked himself a corn-on-the-cob over the naked flames of the fire. *It was certainly a native sight to place in our endless picture book of memories…*

Turning around from speaking to the mahout, I saw Summer holding Apple's hand as the two of them led the group further across the land. At that moment, I was astounded by the maturity of my young daughter.

She truly looked as though she was in her element working alongside Apple; providing details to everybody and instructing them on where to walk.

Soon, we arrived at a different part of the river and Apple explained that it was now our turn to bathe the elephants.

Summer was given the important task of handing out the plastic buckets to the group, something she was extremely enthusiastic about as it made her feel like 'a grown up at work,' she later told me.

"Mummy - here is your bucket!" she squealed, passing me the red, plastic container and working her way down the line of grown-ups.

Several minutes later, I held Summer's hand tightly as we made our way into the river.

Flicking the warm water with my hand, I clumsily sent droplets scattering over the surface like rain.

Following orders, we hastily scooped bucket after bucket of murky water onto the elephant's boiling back.

With the sun radiating through the clouds, I found it rather difficult to repeatedly fill and lift the water onto the elephant whilst it stood completely stationary; enjoying being cooled down in the sweltering Thai heat.

Stupidly, I decided to stand close to the elephant's head. It was a disastrous move as it prompted the mischievous elephant to squirt me directly in the face with his hefty trunk, leaving me completely drenched.

If one thing was for sure, the activity certainly made the group bond. We continuously splashed the elephants and ourselves, giggling in joyful unison.

Whilst everybody laughed , I glanced lovingly towards Summer and drunk in the image of her captivating, dimpled grin and infectious giggle. I felt like the proudest mother on the planet; looking on and smiling at her angelic, animated face.

Here was my five-year-old: taken completely away from her home comforts and thrown into unfamiliar surroundings...and the best part of all? She was having immense fun at the same time!

Backpacking with a child was turning out to be the best experience ever!

***

It was soon time for Summer to take her next malaria tablet. Whilst she continued to bellow, I suddenly had a light-bulb moment.

"Put the tablet in your mouth and then eat this biscuit." I ordered with authority.

"Are you crazy? She's can't do that!" Carl yelled from the other side of the room.

"Why not?"

"It's ridiculous!" he spat.

"What will she do for the rest of her life? Always eat a biscuit every time she needs to take a tablet? It's a joke. You need to instil into her at this age that she has to swallow it - not pander to the problem!"

I couldn't believe his reaction.

"She's a child Carl! I don't care if aged five she has to eat a flaming biscuit to swallow a tablet; if it means that she swallows the very tablet that will stop her from catching malaria!" I yelled. *Perhaps it wasn't prized-parenting at its finest, but inevitably if it stops her from catching such a deadly disease - who cares?*

I looked at Summer as a tear balanced on her lash before it hastily dropped onto her already stained cheek.

"She's eating the biscuit!" I bellowed loudly.

Within minutes, Summer had swallowed both tablets and the only sound that filled the room was the crunching of her Butter Flower, Hong Kong biscuit - my idea had worked!

I looked at Carl as he sat quietly, not uttering a word.

I was rather surprised at his reaction - *who was he to dictate what I did with my child?*

***

The next morning, we awoke to birds singing and the sun shining illuminating rays into our hut.

Opening our balcony doors, we were greeted by a family of elephants. The view was undeniably beautiful. The huge daddy elephant looked busy as he scratched his back against the side of a tree. The baby and mother elephant peacefully looked on ahead.

Immediately after breakfast, we began the morning by trekking across the dry land.

Luckily, it was still early so the heat was tolerable.

Summer's confidence had increasingly grown as she began demonstrating her independent side. She held onto Mike and Laurie as if they were her very own parents and remained with them for the duration of the walk. They climbed under fences, laughed and joked, discussing the exciting sights they could see.

Our first task of the day was to make the elephant's food. Inside the cook house we were greeted by mountain upon mountain of the tiniest bananas I had ever seen.

Apple told us that agriculture remains Thailand's largest source of income, and that the bananas were locally grown and delivered by the villagers daily.

We each tried a banana and they tasted so different to the ones in the supermarket at home. Summer loved the taste and continued to eat them throughout our time in the cook house.

We were split into three groups. Carl, Summer and I becoming our own group.

Summer loved getting dirty in the banana storage, playfully climbing over hundreds of bananas to find the right ones.

Apple made the atmosphere come alive by playing music on full-pelt, making me feel as though I was 16 and working in a restaurant kitchen again.

Feeling exhausted before the day had even began; we were instructed to meticulously peel each banana. I could retain enthusiasm for this section of the task for approximately 50 or so bananas, but after this time my excitement fizzled out as quickly as a sparkler on bonfire night! The peeling soon become a painstaking chore and made me feel as though I was actually at work.

Summer, however, was a complete natural at the food task and thrived as Apple's helper, being extremely efficient in everything that she did. As soon as someone said they needed a bunch of bananas, she was up and out of her seat, stocking them up on supplies. It appeared my daughter was becoming extremely popular among the group. Even Apple noted that she needed an assistant like Summer on a permanent basis.

The toughest and most testing task was mashing the huge basket of peeled bananas with our bare knuckles, and in particular racing against the other groups to finish first.

Out of nowhere, however, the mixture began reacting with a cut on my knuckle. Staring at my red knuckles in dismay, I had no choice but to drastically slow-down my kneading.

As my pace continued to decline, Carl became more and more agitated with his 'not-so-speedy' team mate.

"Surely you can withstand the pain? It's only a tiny cut!" he obnoxiously shouted over the music.

I turned to him with 'Carl' exhaustion written all over my face.

"Why are you taking it so seriously? It's only a game - it's not the winning but the participating that counts!"

"Oh - so you're one of 'those' mothers!" He cackled in an annoying and dramatic way, air quoting and all.

I immediately halted the little mashing that I was doing and stared at him puzzled.

"Excuse me?"

"You know the type?" he continued to rant into the sweaty, working air.

"Parents that think you shouldn't have a winner or loser at the school sports day, and instead 'everyone' should get a prize!" he air quoted.

"Oh what-ever!" I couldn't be bothered to even respond so instead turned my attention to my small daughter.

I loved watching Summer come out of her shell as she worked alongside the adults and followed the instructions that were given to us all. This was another one of those surreal moments, when it was hard to believe that she had only celebrated her fifth birthday four months previously.

The second part of the task was about to get more exciting: elephant feeding time! I was unsure of how this task would go as Summer was still scared whenever a trunk went anywhere near her.

Thankfully, her confidence had unexpectedly magnified. To my elated surprise she sturdily held her hand in the right place without dropping any food when an elephant approached. *What a proud mother moment!*

Likewise, the whole group cheered and congratulated her as they had repeatedly seen her scared of the elephants' trunks over the time we'd all been together. Best of all, she was extremely proud of herself.

Amusingly, the elephants didn't like our batch of balls. *I admit, I never have been much of a cook, but even I was surprised when the hungry and gentle giants turned their noses up at my cooking! Charming!*

With that in mind, Summer and I tried to discretely pinch the other groups' balls to feed to the elephants. Being discrete is not a quality either of us naturally has, so we failed miserably - much to everyone's entertainment.

Immediately after lunch, I saw an opportunity for some 'me' time. Leisurely strolling around the camp, I noticed articles from magazines and newspapers plastered over the walls in the dining hall.

Glancing closely, it seemed a wealth of journalists from across the globe had stayed at the sanctuary and went on to write heart-warming stories about each of the resident elephants.

Reading the emotive words, I couldn't help but feel moved and emotionally charged. It was at that moment that the significance of the Nature Park became crystal clear: it truly was a lifeline for the troubled elephants.

One story about an elephant named 'Mac Dta Keow' was particularly poignant.

Once a logging and trekking elephant, Mac was repeatedly chained and deprived of food and water. The article described how the former working elephant had both tusks removed by a chainsaw and almost died from an infection that was left in the holes.

Mac's back right leg was broken which meant she was unable to do heavy labour; alternatively, she was made to beg on the streets. After this, Mac was put in a breeding programme that meant at one point she was chained for three months solid and forcibly mounted 29 times! When she didn't become pregnant her owner sold her.

When Mac Dta Keow arrived at the Nature Park, she had heavy scarring to her forehead, a badly deformed back right leg, and heavy pigments on her upper trunk and brow bone. *How could any human inflict such pain onto a defensive animal?*

The life of Jokia was equally as turbulent.

Jokia was born in 1960 and rescued by Lek in 1999 after suffering from extreme abuse.

Traumatically, she had endured a miscarriage whilst pulling a log up a hill.

Despite this harrowing situation, Jokia was prohibited from momentarily giving up work to check to see if her calf was dead or alive. This decision caused extreme physical and psychological distress to the elephant.

Shortly after, Jokia refused to work and thus was deliberately blinded by her elephant handler who shot rocks at one of her eyes with a sling shot. On a separate occasion (to get her to work harder) Jokia's remaining eye was even destroyed by a deliberately-aimed bow and arrow shot.

I was astounded, horrified and completely disgusted by what I was reading.

How completely unethical and inhumane! How could somebody treat an innocent animal like that?

Suddenly, my mind drifted and I wondered if Jokia was the elephant with the weeping eye that I had been looking at the day before.

Fortunately, thanks to Lek all the elephants mentioned had been given the chance to live free from harm, malpractice, violation and negligence.

***

It was 9.30pm when I found myself sat with Laurie in the gathering darkness of the elephant sanctuary.

Summer was soundly asleep with her head rested on my lap, and her legs stretched out across the bench of the group's huge, wooden, family table.

We were sat inside the dining room with nothing but darkness and candles surrounding us. For the first time since being away, I felt truly relaxed.

"So, what made you bring Summer travelling?" Laurie asked, taking a sip from her can of coke.

"We live in a small fishing village that is mainly made up of white, British people. One day we were in a city called Manchester and she asked why a person was black in colour. It really shocked me. I didn't want her to be raised to think that everyone looked as she did. So, I thought I'd bring her to Asia and introduce her to another world of culture, religion, food and everything else that backpacking brings." I giggled.

"As a Korean girl that was raised in America, I can understand that…" she laughed.

"My dad died in a motorbike accident when he was 31…I was only seven, so I know first-hand how short life can be and that you have to live for the moment." I admitted, taking a sip of my own coke.

"I'm by no means your typical traveller Laurie. I am a single mum, I have a mortgage and debt to my name…but I wanted to break out of the 9-5 cycle (for as long as I could get off work) which is five weeks by the way," I sniggered, placing my coke on the table.

"What about you? What brought you and Mike to Thailand?" I asked inquisitively.

"My trip to Thailand is a healing one," she confessed.

"I suffered a major tragedy four months ago when my downstairs neighbour set fire to my condominium building, destroying everything that I owned. This included the lives of my dear sweet cat and dog that were trapped inside."

Laurie's words took me totally by surprise. *What a resilient lady…I'd never have known.*

"Oh Laurie…I'm so sorry. That's awful!"
I couldn't believe what I was hearing.

"Could you imagine watching your home and beloved pets burn to the ground?" She asked into the faint, evening air.

That exact moment quickly become one of those rare times when I felt totally speechless.

"I had lived in Washington DC for 10 years before I decided to buy. I'm a risk-adverse type of person you see. But I knew I had to stop wasting my money on rent. So, after a year of searching for that perfect condo I finally decided to bite-the-bullet and invest my life savings into one."

Laurie explained how one minute it was a regular day as she drove along her familiar residential road, and the next her heart was in her mouth as she was forced to abandon her car in the middle of the street with the keys still in the ignition.

On auto-pilot, Laurie frantically ran through the yellow police tape and watched helplessly, knowing that her cat, Lila, and dog, Smalls were trapped inside the burning building.

"I literally lost everything except for the clothes that I was standing in that day." Laurie continued, managing to suppress an abundance of emotions that threatened to escape within that very sentence.

"I couldn't even imagine." I shook my head in disbelief.

"So, where did you go? What did you do?" I asked with my heart firmly in my mouth, captivated and sincerely shocked by her story.

"The Red Cross put all the residents in a hotel for a few days. My sister set up a donation web page where friends and strangers generously donated everything from hair ties to toothpaste. Meanwhile, I locked myself away to make hellish-call after-call to everyone from work, to fellow residents, the insurance company, the Police – the list was endless!"

I looked at Laurie's tiny frame impressively.

As she continued to tell me her incredibly personal story, sadness engulfed me as I contemplated what she'd been through.

"What caused the fire? It was your neighbour, you say?" I stared at her in sadness as she took a large gulp of air.

"It wasn't a stroke of bad luck put it that way! It was a nightmare that turned into a criminal investigation. The explosion was caused by a resident who doused his home as a suicide attempt."

I paused.

"What people don't see, Laura, is that I didn't just lose my home and pets from his thoughtless actions - I now have to live through this stressful and heart-wrenching nightmare daily to try and get my home and assets back, whilst grieving for my lost pets."

I didn't know what to say.

"Unfortunately, the insurance policy for the entire block was seriously out-dated at the time (unbeknown to us residents) and this seriously under-valued the property by tens of thousands of dollars. This meant that we were all faced with the need to contribute to restore the entire building - as well as our own condos!"

I sat back in my chair and sighed at the enormity of the task that Laurie was faced with.

"Where are we supposed to find that sort of money?" She asked. To which I had no answer.

"So, four months on – where are you now living?"

"I live with Mike as I continue to pay the mortgage on a property that no longer exists. It has been an incredibly challenging time in my life Laura... So, Thailand is a way to unplug, recuperate, and take stock of my life again."

"And two weeks in, do you feel as though it is helping?"

"I do feel as though it is helping a great deal," she answered softly, before sighing heavily and glancing towards the sky.

"Travelling to Thailand has given me psychological space by removing me physically away from the drama of my condo and the death of my furry family. The elephant sanctuary has also been especially healing because I really wanted to honour the pets that I was unable to save, by giving to a worthy charity that saves suffering animals."

I looked at Laurie impressively once more. She really was an incredible person.

"Well... I think that you're truly remarkable. And I really hope that this trip gives you the clarity and respite that you clearly need." I touched her arm with my right hand and smiled.

"Thank you for sharing your story with me Laurie. I appreciate it must be tough to talk about what happened on the very trip that you're trying to forget about it." I finished.

Laurie turned, took another sip of coke and looked out into the darkness in deep thought.

***

I would like to thank Laurie for allowing me to share her incredibly personal story in this book.

***

The next day...

I woke the next morning feeling pensive, contemplating the enormity of what I had been told by Laurie the evening before. I had to push such thoughts to the back of my mind, however, as it was soon time to head back to the city.

As a group, we spoke about how humbled and overwhelmed we felt by the Nature Park.

Regardless of all the destructive and distressing events we had been exposed to, we all felt optimistic and full of peace and hope. We were safe in the knowledge that the elephants that were fortunate enough to have been rescued would live the rest of their days in tranquillity.

On the bus back to the city we laughed, reminisced and took a moment to appreciate our short adventure.

In true Laura-style, I managed to add a touch of humour to the bus ride by recapping the tale of the 'Hong Kong curse' to an audience of bus passengers who erupted into laughter with every line of the embarrassing story.

Irritatingly, Carl felt the need to repeatedly interrupt mid-flow, forcing my frustration level to quickly rise.

"So, we thought the paper meant good luck," I rambled to my captivated audience.

"You mean you did!" Carl predictably corrected.

"We both did!" I sat bolt upright in my seat.

"I said no such thing!"

"What a liar you are!" I cackled.

"Anyway," I turned back to face the group as the entire bus looked towards me to finish the story.

"My horoscope that morning..."

81

"Her horoscope said to 'watch the sky' which means it must be fate!" Carl mocked in a higher than usual tone, impressed with his new-found humour of intentionally mocking me to gain brownie points with the laughing audience.

Maintaining my calm exterior, I glanced towards Carl and laughed on the inside. *Had I ever encountered somebody so eccentric in my life before? At times, being on this trip of a lifetime with him in tow was proving to be extremely challenging.*

That evening, whilst Summer was tucked up in bed, I read a book to her that I'd bought in the gift shop of the sanctuary. It told the story of Lek as a small child, and together Summer and I learned about Lek's relationship with her grandfather.

"From a very young age, Lek's grandfather would often take her into the jungle," I read.

"Lek looks like Mowgli from The Jungle Book!" Summer giggled, pointing to the page.

"The end…" I smiled, closing the book firmly.

Looking up towards me, I watched as Summer scanned my face intently. It was as if she was deep in thought.

Thinking about how fortunate we were and what a privileged life Summer was experiencing, I pushed a strand of her light-brown hair behind her ear and kissed her forehead tenderly.

Final note:

If you are to take anything away from this chapter then please take this:

An immeasurable number of elephants in the world are forced to beg for money on the swamped, polluted, city streets, which is far from the environment that they were born to live in. This causes relentless stress, exhaustion, dehydration and malnourishment.

I will advise you of this: if you encounter an elephant in a city whilst on holiday - not just in Thailand but anywhere - please don't pay to feed it or take pictures with it. Instead, stay away.

If every single tourist worldwide boycotted such displays of cruelty, then the keepers would come to realise that they are no longer making a profit from the elephants and would not exploit and abuse them in that way.

In addition to this, there are numerous keepers who use elephants in trekking camps. Here, they are forced to carry people on their backs through dense jungles. If you are offered this opportunity whilst on holiday, please don't do it. *How would you feel if you were forced to carry a heavy weight on your back whilst walking through a dense jungle?*

Please do not think I'm not being patronising when I say this. I too would have been oblivious to the torture if it wasn't for my visit to the Nature Park.

So please, if given the opportunity: don't sit on an elephant's back and instead walk alongside it.

Miserably, some elephants are coerced into painting pictures with their trunks and made to perform circus-like tricks in shows. This is such an unnatural thing for an elephant to do. It's not a skill that they would willingly learn. Any elephant that you have seen doing this has clearly been placed in a 'crushing box' in which they are beaten, gouged with sharp nails and immobilised for long periods of time. Sadly, that cage is just the beginning of what becomes a lifetime of suffering for the elephant.

Let's not forget the elephant mothers who have been killed for their calves so their babies can be trained and sold in the elephant trade. Did you know that a baby elephant can generate as much as £20,000?

So, the next time you are on holiday and you see any of the above, please remember this chapter and everything you have learnt from it.

Not everyone will get to visit a sanctuary like I did, but if I and anybody else that visits spreads this message then eventually cruelty like this can stop. All we can do is be hopeful, and collectively act to stamp out this needless brutality.

***

Six:

Overwhelmed

Two hours and six stops later, it was eventually our turn to experience what would be 'home' for the next few days.

The bus came to a halt on a hectic road that was laced with restaurants and bars.

Staring towards a tiny, dull-white building, I felt perplexed as anxiety kicked in. Where was the entrance?

After backpacking around Australia for a year, it is fair to say that I've stayed in lots of weird and wonderful places during my life.

I'm now a strong believer that the best way to meet fellow travellers is to stay in dormitories. The biggest dorm I have ever stayed in slept 19 other people! With Summer now on-board, however, I had to think about her safety so instead opted for a family room.

To say the accommodation was basic would be a complete under-statement.

"Blimey! There's more furniture in a prison cell!" Carl shrieked as we walked into our new base. He said it just loud enough to ensure that everyone knew his opinion.

"You get what you pay for!" I backwards-dived onto the bed, quickly discovering the mattress was as comfortable as a park-bench.

"Trust me; this is reasonable compared to some hostels I've stayed in!" I sniggered, contemplating the idiocy of his statement.

"When I was in Brisbane I stayed in a hostel that was literally crawling in bed bugs!"

"That's gross! And you stayed there?"

"I'd already pre-paid for three nights. If that wasn't bad enough, on arrival at the dorm one of the girls said she had over 30 bites in just three days! Unsurprisingly, for the few days I tucked my body into my sleeping bag so tight in fear of being bitten alive."

"Why didn't you just leave?" He asked naively. Clearly, he hasn't suffered like the rest of us...

"Because I was penniless and it was all I could afford. I actually stayed on an extra night in return for working for free in the bag-drop room!" I laughed at the ridiculous memory. "That's how broke I was Carl! Blimey, I remember being so broke on one occasion I actually pitched a tent in the middle of a field. I remember waking in the middle of the night to wild kangaroos hopping around the tent." I giggled.

Predictably, he didn't see the funny side; instead he just awkwardly glanced around the room, staring from left to right between deep sighs.

"I don't see that story as humorous; I actually think you once again put yourself in harm's way Laura!" He looked me deep in the eye.

"You know that a kangaroo is essentially stamping its place to be the modern day T-Rex, don't you? I admit a vegetarian one... but it is Australia's fifth dangerous animal. They may look cute and cuddly, but I assure you they're not! Their powerful hind legs and sharp toenails are an incredibly dangerous weapon."

Ignoring him completely and suddenly feeling completely famished, we headed to a café down the road that was so small it resembled a one-fish goldfish bowl.

With an American man in his 60's sat at one of the tables, we plonked ourselves at the spare table and less than a minute after sitting the man began talking to us. Who invited him to dinner? It was bad-enough having to invite Carl!

In hindsight, I was probably too trusting. Within minutes this man had known who we were, why we were in Chiang Mai and where we were staying. The word stalker sprang to mind...

I had trusted him because he appeared to be an open-book; telling me about his life and how he had spiritually 'found' himself in the city.

He told us that when in America, he had fallen critically ill and the doctors had thought his chances of survival were slim. Unfortunately for him, at the same time his wife had an affair and left him.

"Oh...I'm sorry to hear that." I muttered into the faint, evening air.

"I defied the odds though! I then moved to Chiang Mai for a fresh start," he took an extra-large bite of his burger.

"I have two kids, but they're grown up now and have kids of their own – just call me Grandpa Jo!" He chuckled whilst thumping his huge chest in a gorilla fashion and disgustingly revealing a mouthful of food.

We later discovered that after several years in the city, both of his brothers had joined him and had married young, Thai ladies. He had confessed, however, that he was less fortunate than his brothers and remained single.

During our chat, a man came out of the kitchen and sat opposite the American, introducing himself to us as the café owner. As the conversation developed, we realised that a distinctive pattern was emerging. The café owner had also married a young, Thai lady.

At this point our waitress stopped serving us altogether and weirdly the owner took over, whilst still sitting next to us talking.

As a gut reaction (seriously needing a drink) I stood to locate our waitress. Conversely, in a nano-second the owner was on the case, but in an artificial and bizarrely over-efficient manner that was extremely short-lived.

A minute or so later, he returned from the kitchen only to inform me that the two drinks I had ordered weren't in stock. This made me feel awkward; almost as though I was being too selective. I literally felt as though I was in his house! So in the true British spirit I said I'd, "have anything."

Settling for a Baileys, I was typically served a diminutive shot over two ice cubes. Unsurprisingly this meant I then finished my drink rather quickly, but I felt uncomfortable ordering another. In all honesty, I started to feel as though we were encroaching on his home environment!

I also couldn't help but notice that numerous white, western men began arriving at the café and were over-familiar with both men.

In total, we were in the café for two hours and for the whole duration only white western men had entered. *Rather peculiar, don't you think?*

I noticed that Carl's attitude began to dramatically change towards the men as well. He began questioning them intensely (almost like an interrogation) and it was clear to see that Carl's initial friendliness had faded.

Back at our room, Carl was eager to know what I thought of the men.

"I thought they were ok." I paused, before questioning, "Why?"

"I thought they were distinctively odd and there was something very peculiar about them."

"Well that explains why you went into 'fraud investigator' mode with them then! But yes, I know what you mean as I thought it was strange that…"

"I have to say Laura, I felt as though you dangerously exposed us by telling both men way too much information within minutes of meeting them - especially the American!" He rudely interrupted me mid-sentence.

"No I didn't!" I morphed into that defensive mode that you do.

"You must learn Laura, that you cannot be too trusting with people. Not everybody is as innocent as they seem."

"It sounds as though you're telling me off?"

"You're a grown woman, I do not need to 'tell you off' Laura! Look, I dealt with a case recently that centred around a couple who were in their 50's. They seemed like the type of people who were so kind, polite, ordinary and trustworthy. But we'd received a tip-off that all wasn't as it seemed at their residence. After a full investigation, we discovered that the wife worked for the NHS and had been intentionally directing NHS funds to her marital joint account. In total, the scheming pair stole a total of £400,000! Together, the couple spent the money on lavish meals, shopping and expensive holidays."

Where is this going exactly?

"The wife was found guilty of fraud and was jailed for five years, and her husband was found guilty of acquiring criminal property after statements revealed the couple used the money to pay large mortgage repayments. He was later jailed for…"

"Ok Carl!" I shouted. "I get the point – not everyone is as they seem!"

As annoying as Carl was, in bed that evening I couldn't stop thinking about what he had said. In hindsight, I felt as though I could have almost jeopardised myself and Summer's imminent safety. The thought of placing her in harm's way sent a shiver down my spine... Maybe I needed to re-assess my actions? *Perhaps I wear my heart on my sleeve too much?*

Feeling as though I had learnt a valuable life lesson, I promised myself that I wouldn't be too trusting of strangers in the future because let's face it, not everybody is as friendly as they appear to be and you cannot expect other people to have the same values and morals of behaviour as you.

As I tried to sleep the conversation with the two men kept winding around my brain, capturing my thoughts and leaving me with a bad taste in my mouth.

One thing was for sure: I would need to watch my words in future!

***

In true cliché fashion, we found ourselves standing outside the hostel, representing the epitome of what it meant to be a British tourist.

There we were, swamped by a gigantic map; trying to make sense of our surroundings. Our saving grace was that a Tuk-tuk pulled alongside us and the driver politely enquired as to where we were heading.

To say that Carl was displeased about the sudden offer of a ride would be a genuine under-statement. In true Carl fashion, he assumed that I would politely decline because this is what his 'superior mind' would do.

So, when I started negotiating prices (like a barn-owl) Carl spun his head around at a 360-degree angle and yelled: "There's no-way I'm getting into that death trap!"

Soon coming to his senses, he climbed on-board, but old habits die-hard and less than a minute into the journey he gave a running commentary about the numerous traffic offences he had seen and how dangerous that mode of transport was. *Deep sigh!*

We arrived at a bustling city street that was lined with interesting-looking bars and restaurants. Embracing in a leisurely afternoon of good old-fashioned bar-hopping, I had the perfect opportunity to catch up on some school work with Summer. Not to mention the much-needed chill out time that I had been so-desperately craving.

Constantly changing establishments did have some obvious set-backs with Carl in tow. I had to change seats each time Carl expressed a dislike of the seating arrangements. Equally, it also meant that I had to consistently endure the laborious ritual of watching him rearrange the condiments at every table we sat at!

We discovered that various restaurants in Chiang Mai offered Asia's interpretation of western dishes. Comically a mouth-watering waffle which is famously served with ice or whipped cream in the western world was instead served with shredded pork mayonnaise! *Imagine my face when I bit into that?*

If you wanted to have a light soup, there was no tomato or carrot and coriander on the menu. Instead it was the likes of 'raw blood' which I was told was made from the blood of a pig and is mouth-wateringly topped with lime leaves and fried pork skin - you know, for that added flavour!

If that didn't satisfy your taste buds than slow-grilled pig boob was available. The chewy, fatty boob even had a milky taste to it, which was certainly enough to remind me of what I was eating and positively decline the remainder.

Maybe I needed something lighter? Displayed proudly on a chalk board under the heading of 'bar snacks,' was none other than the intrepid deep-fried frog skin. One thing was for sure - we certainly were not going to go hungry in Chiang Mai... *or were we?*

Completing spellings with Summer, the waitress approached and asked if we'd like another round of drinks.

In-between ordering, I asked Summer to spell a word.

"School work?" the petite, young, Thai waitress asked as she curiously leaned over my shoulder.

"Yes - there's no escaping it!" I giggled, before correcting Summer on her incorrect spelling.

"You know what would make you smart?" The waitress glanced at my curious daughter.

"We have pig's brain on the menu - it will make you very, very clever! Would you like me to order you one?"

I giggled, obviously assuming that she was joking. *I mean - who would take that statement seriously?*

"Yes?" she clarified when I did not respond.

"Oh, you're being serious?" I laughed awkwardly. "Sorry I thought you were joking!"

"Not at all! We mash the brain with curry paste and wrap it in a banana leaf, before grilling it. It really will make you smart!" She repeated as her slightly intoxicating brown eyes expanded as though she was trying to hypnotise me.

"Carl?" My eyes beckoned him into the conversation. I clearly wanted his help in politely declining her extremely serious question.

"Well - we all know that pigs are extraordinarily smart. Winston Churchill once famously said that 'dogs look up to man, cats look down to man and pigs look straight in the eye of the man and see an equal.' Not just that..." *Oh god, he was off on one...*

"Did you know that a pig can communicate with another? They have a range of oinks, grunts and squeals that extraordinarily have different meanings."

Leaning forward in his chair, he continued to rattle on: "They are smarter than a dolphin as well."

I looked at him stunned as he gave the total opposite response to what I was actually after.

Staring intently at him with one eyebrow slightly raised for several seconds, I responded to the waitress: "No thank you." I smiled for good measure.

Several Asian dishes passed our lips over the course of the afternoon, and something I quickly picked up on was that most of the dishes came with an added 'something.'

When I ordered some sticky rice and steamed vegetables for instance, the waitress asked if I would like a beetle chilli relish dip to go with it. Despite a look of horror stretching across my face, she then asked if I'd like it seasoned with an extra beetle to add a blue cheese-like flavour! *Of course, I didn't!*

Continuing to discover the local restaurants and cafés, with a distinctive waft of noodles in the air, I began thinking about the constant presence of Tuk-tuk's that evidently seemed to follow us everywhere that we went.

Regardless of where we were or what we were doing (whether that was walking aimlessly down the road, sat idly in a restaurant, or clearly perched on another Tuk-tuk) the drivers would sound their distinctive horns at us from afar.

The positioning of the public toilets in Chiang Mai was also a conversation starter to say the least. In one restaurant, the toilet was oddly placed in the kitchen. *I couldn't fathom why anybody would build a toilet in the kitchen? It seemed unethical and unhygienic.* The weirdest thing about this experience was that the wall encasing the toilet stood only five feet in height; thus, when standing you could clearly witness the chef cooking up a delight. You then had to use the kitchen sink to wash your hands! – Yes really!

In addition to this, some toilets didn't feature any toilet roll and instead opted for a shower head so that customers could 'clean their bottoms' with water. Unsurprisingly, this meant many toilets were literally swimming in water.

On the upside, visiting a variety of bars and restaurants that day enabled us to meet lots of Thai families with children for Summer to play with.

Carl spoke to me about his home life, and how much he still missed his wife. He told me about an occasion when he'd taken her away for the weekend to try and reconcile their relationship, and whilst away produced a ring as a token of them starting again. She rejected the ring and announced that she had been offered a new job and was moving to the other side of the country. Within three months she met someone else and within a year had controversially moved him in. That was five years ago and Carl clearly hadn't moved on, continuing to live alone in a small flat and dedicating his life to his career.

I could suddenly see why all Carl seemed to talk about was work. His life quite literally was his work.

He also confessed that he'd only ever done package holidays to Spain, and that the Asia trip was taking him out of his comfort zone completely. *I'd never have guessed!*

I had to admit, travelling with an uptight Fraud Investigator was both challenging and entertaining. I honestly felt as though I was travelling with a life insurance coordinator. Being such a carefree character myself, I was beginning to think that we were a lethal concoction together.

I found Carl's character extremely complex and insanely difficult to get my head around. I had truly never met anyone quite like him before. He was constantly correcting people, talking over-them as if their opinion was completely inferior to his superior way of thinking. He was full of peculiar and wonderfully entertaining (even if wacky) conspiracy theories; he bizarrely couldn't resist re-arranging table condiments whilst eating out, he had a foot that tapped to an invisible beat when nervous or bored, and this is only the beginning of a very long list of 'eccentric' character traits.

As irritating as I was finding Carl, however, I was now starting to understand some of the reasoning behind his peculiar behaviour.

He was a man that had been single for five years and had little contact with his children. He'd never travelled and by nature over obsessed about everything! Now he was backpacking Asia with a laid-back, single mum and a five-year-old who had a huge personality and quite frankly - he didn't really know.

Learning more about Carl allowed me to see him in a slightly different light. I almost felt sorry for him. I made a pact with myself that I'd try to be more understanding with him for the remainder of the trip.

Making me jump completely out of my skin, the driver of a truck began shouting through a mammoth speaker broadcasting a local fight to the various tourists that laced the surrounding restaurants.

Strangely, the man only conducted this broadcast in Thai, which seemed daft considering the amount of people from different nationalities that occupied the outdoor tables. You didn't have to be a brain surgeon to work out that most people were completely dumbfounded by what he was even saying.

Another alluring sight that captivated me was the local obsession with mopeds as a method of commuting. I had never seen so many makes and models in my life! Sometimes you would see whole families precariously balanced on one! Alarmingly, we even spotted several babies that were proudly balanced at the front as they whizzed past us at an uncountable speed.

One man even drove one-handed whilst his other hand was gripped to an enormous metal pole that spanned the length of two cars!

"There are plenty of signs that clearly instruct for helmets to be worn when driving, so why is everybody so blatantly ignoring the rule?" I asked Carl, suddenly sounding more like him than myself.

"I guess it is like the elephant situation. It is illegal to take an elephant into a city to beg, but people still do it and from what I can see the Police seem to do little to stop either rule from being broken..." Carl babbled in between bites of food.

"It's obvious why the Police don't get involved though..." Carl continued rambling whilst gulping his food in one and placing his index finger into the air for emphasis.

"Is it?" I quizzed. *Was I missing something?*

"It's a way for the government to slow the population down, of course."

With my eyes swivelling around in my head, I coughed on the seaweed that I was at that precise moment munching on.

"Oh Carl, you and your theories – you do make me laugh!" I sniggered at another one of his outrageous yet creative philosophies.

People-watching that afternoon was immensely gratifying and undoubtedly ignited my passion for travelling across non-westernised continents even more. However, with a crash back down to reality, the sheer volume of old, white, western men populating Chiang Mai became more obvious with every day I spent in the city.

They seemed to be very predictable in their behaviour as well. If they were not alone then they were instead accompanied by Thai ladies many years their junior.

I personally struggled to come to terms with the sheer quantity of them as they seemed to be spread everywhere I looked.

From an outsider's perspective, it was rather spine-chilling and sinister. Literally prompting me to tally the amount of white, old men I saw in the space of five minutes.

"Time!" Carl shouted, forcing me to violently throw down my pen and glance over to Summer who was happily playing with the owner's children to my left.

"Ok, I've got it!" I yelled.

"How many old, white, western men have I just seen in five minutes?"

Taking one last glance across the street, Carl looked me directly in the eye. Grazing his two front teeth over his bottom lip, he slowly answered: "30?"

"I'm actually stunned…and sadly cannot believe this figure myself!" I solemnly glanced down at my diary once more to double-check the figure.

"It's 52!"

I watched as an expression of astonishment swept across his face. Without answering he spun his head around like a barn owl to glance at the streets and people surrounding us. I did the same.

"Actually…" I said into the silent air. "I will retract my comment. On second glance, I can believe it!" I took a large mouthful of my drink and absorbed the sleazy-looking men around me.

Just to reiterate, that tally was 52 white men over the age of 50 that were either solitary or accompanied by a young, Thai woman.

It made me consider the café we had visited the day before. I couldn't help but remember the faces of the copious amounts of men who all seemed so familiar with one another. Men who were shamefacedly conjoined by, in my opinion, their sordid, sinister and seedy lifestyles. The thought of what those men could potentially be representing made me shudder inside-out.

***

The next morning, we avoided the café with a wide birth and eagerly took our seats in a neighbouring restaurant instead.

"Do you sell [expresso?]" I asked the waitress.

"E-x-p-r-e-s-s-o?" Carl laughed. "You mean espresso?"

"Oh whatever Carl!" I sighed deeply at yet another 'word-correction' from him.

Unsurprisingly, breakfast turned out to be an interesting twist on the 'Traditional English' with a frankfurter instead of a juicy butcher's sausage, and bread and butter despite it being advertised as toast.

On the advice of the weird-American we had met the previous night, we decided to visit the shopping centre he recommended.

We quickly discovered that the journey time was much longer than advised; leaving us painfully trekking through the stifling afternoon heat desperately trying to reach the 'awesome' centre.

I am being far from dramatic when I say that my face was literally melting from the intense sun. To make matters worse, Summer was endlessly complaining that her little legs were hurting despite walking for just 20 minutes.

Bizarrely, for the first-time since travelling around Chiang Mai, there didn't seem to be a single Tuk-tuk in sight.

Frustrated as we were, walking was clearly the only option. Suddenly, I caught sight of the illuminating and luscious colours of the remarkable street signs. The navy-blue backgrounds with their rich gold outlines were alluring and it was difficult to draw my eyes away from the neatly intricate detail.

"I cannot fathom the logic behind such luxurious road signs in contrast with the run-down road itself!" I looked around at the abandoned shop-fronts and filthy sidewalks that spoilt my eyeline. *Another comment that sounded more like Carl than myself...I hoped I wasn't morphing into a mini him?*

"Yes, you have brought us to what seems like the roughest part of Chiang Mai in search of none-other than a shopping centre!"

"Don't say it like that - you wanted to go as well!"

Progressing deeper into the neighbourhood, we spotted two Police Officers who were travelling by moped. The sight of the second officer clenching the waist of the first officer immaturely made me chuckle.

"Very childish Laura!" Carl gasped as I continued to snigger even minutes later.

In complete and utter contradiction to the hilarious sight I had just been exposed to, I lazily glanced in the direction of the opposite side of the road. I watched alarmed as a man casually strolled along with none-other than a rifle tightly gripped into the palm of his hand. My heart raced as I contemplated why he had a gun and what could happen next. It was such an alien sight!

In total contradiction to everything that a gun represents, surprising me further, a bare-footed monk calmly walked behind the man as peaceful as could be. Where else in the world would you observe such opposing opposites at the same time? *Chiang Mai certainly was a city of contradiction...*

Continuing to travel down the hot, dry road, a red pick-up truck pulled in alongside us. Intrigued, I peered into the vehicle curiously to discover an entire family packed tightly together in the front.

The husband was driving, his wife was sat comfortably in the passenger seat, a teenage girl was lost in a magazine whilst two toddlers chaotically climbed over all of them.

To our complete astonishment, we learnt that the family were offering a taxi service. In all honesty, my eyes twirled in the back of my head as I quickly mustered up our options.

"I'm not getting in some random truck just because the owners happen to claim they are operating some kind of 'taxi' service!" Carl air quoted before storming off further up the road.

"We are taxi!" shouted the wife as the husband crawled the van alongside us.

Glancing casually into the back of the truck, two Thai teenage girls sat happily chatting away.

When they said they were heading to the same shopping centre that we were looking for, it was enough to persuade me to take a gamble and jump on board - much to Carl's irritation.

"This is a stupid idea!" he hissed, reluctantly hopping into the back of the truck moments later.

Throughout the journey, I was in a great mood as I chuckled to myself about the absurdity of travelling in a quirky vehicle, with an entire family who offered lifts for a living.

A few minutes later and we safely arrived at the shopping centre and were thankfully not held as hostages and sold on the black, Thai market.

Trip in full swing, my daughter seemed to be blossoming more and more with each day that passed. Sometimes I simply forgot that she was just five-years-old! It was clear that being 'on the road' was ageing her mind and making her more street-wise. This became particularly noticeable when Carl and I were questioning something (for example, what direction to travel in) and Summer would confidently interrupt and offer her own opinion, or repeat thoughts we had earlier aired ourselves.

In all honesty, I had always encouraged Summer to have an opinion, as I wanted her to have a clear identity of her own. However, never had I noticed her airing it or getting involved in adult conversations so comfortably as she now was.

I loved her new-found confidence because it demonstrated that she was listening and had a rough understanding *(as much as a five-year- old could)* to this new world around her.

If we were talking to strangers we had just met and were telling them a story, she had started cutting us off mid-sentence and finishing the story herself. Normally I wouldn't condone this rudeness, but I could see her confidence growing and the excitement in her eyes when she told our 'latest new friend' a funny travelling story from the day before. *Gone were the days when she would hide behind my legs in Hong Kong!*

I loved watching the look of delight on the person's face when they experienced Summer's innocent, continuous babble. Sometimes, I would steal a quiet moment to myself to reflect upon her obvious developments in such a short period. Her vocabulary was clearly growing along with her confidence that had simply sky-rocketed.

The most astonishing thing about this was that the trip was only weeks (not months) in duration, and the transformation was so glaringly obvious already.

Considering this, I would disagree heavily with the various cynics out there who are too quick to put their hand up and state that there is no place for a small child on a backpacking trip.

In my mind, it was crystal-clear that there was every place for a small child on a travelling expedition.

***

We couldn't leave Chiang Mai without visiting the famous night bazaar. In the way that we humans always do, I tried to compare this to the 'Temple Street' night market in Hong Kong. However, I soon realised that they weren't comparable in the slightest.

This bazaar felt both safe and secure. I was particularly relieved about this as for once it meant that Carl was relaxed and manageable.

The single most memorable thing about the market was its gigantic size, stretching throughout various buildings and across numerous streets.

Walking aimlessly, we unexpectedly stumbled across various pop-up restaurants and a live band.

This turned out to be a great opportunity to indulge on some exceptionally cheap food and drink, whilst listening to the calming tones of an acoustic band. Uncannily, we were once again surrounded by an array of white, western men who were consuming dinner with their young, Thai females. One thought raced through my mind: Disturbing. Some of these women were young enough to be their grand-daughters!

When I reminisce about this part of the trip, a memory springs to mind of when I met a young boy who served us on his father's stall.

Haggling is common place in this country and considering this; I bartered to get a pair of boxing shorts for my nephew Sidney for £3. On agreeing the sale, the owner gave the shorts to his young son, who helpfully put them into a carrier bag and thanked us. As we walked away, I watched as the boy returned to his chair to finish his crisps.

My gut reaction upon seeing him do this was to glance down at my watch and absorb the fact that it was nearly 9pm.

"Don't you find it upsetting that a boy of nine or so is working on his father's stall at 9pm on a school night?" I asked Carl glumly.

"I suppose!" he shrugged his shoulders nonchalantly.

Rummaging around in my pocket, I found the 100 baht note that the boy had given me in change from the sale. In pounds, this amounted to just £2; which in retrospect was the same amount that I had just negotiated off the shorts! It was for this reason that I decided to give the note back to the boy.

"Rubes, can you go and give this to the boy that just served us?"

Following orders, Summer ran to the boy and I watched on as his dad thanked Summer but declined the money.

"It's ok, please take it." I shouted from afar.

"It's for the boy to treat himself with."

On Summer's return, she instantly questioned why I had given the boy the money. I told her that there wasn't a reason and that sometimes, it's just nice to show some love to strangers.

This conversation plagued my mind. The fact that Summer's innocent mind was unable to spot the obvious differences in her lifestyle and that of the boy's was disturbing me.

Summer clearly had a life a million miles away from the experiences of this child...her privilege was his depravity. *Why must the world be so cruel?* I knew I obviously had more work to do with exposing Summer to the lifestyle difference.

Wrapped tightly in my own thoughts like a cake sucked in cellophane, I only crashed back down to reality when I heard, "Sa-wad-dee-ka" almost as if in surround-sound.

Turning around in a flash, I noticed the boy excitedly chasing us down the road eagerly clutching a bag of sweets.

"For you!" he proudly declared to Summer as he enthusiastically passed her the bag.

I looked up and saw that his dad was now the one watching from the distance with a smile stretching across the contours of his face.

"You keep them!" I smiled at the boy.

He clearly needed no convincing. Within seconds he'd wai'd to us and devotedly ran back to his dad smiling.

"You know the likelihood is that these people aren't even remotely poor, don't you?" Carl obnoxiously declared, completely ruining the moment.

"Let me guess...do the government make them look poor so the tourists flood them with money?" I mocked.

"Yes! That's exactly it! See you're on my wave-length now!"

I couldn't help but respond with a belly giggle. *What planet was this guy on?*

***

The atmosphere at the night bazaar was intense; I could almost feel a current of electrical energy zapping through my body with every stall my crystal-blue eyes soaked up.

I scanned the area at a 360-degree angle to determine which direction to head in next.

I had been collecting oil paintings of my travels for some time. This is because I am a firm believer that the encounters you have make up the fabric of your life. You can now imagine my ultimate joy when we stumbled across a stall that was selling oil paintings. An intriguing oil painting always sets fire to my curiosity, making me feel like Alice in a conceptual wonderland.

I watched intently as a young girl (who was no older than 10-years-old) was meticulously and diligently painting on a huge canvas.

101

I was speechless – the paintings surrounding her were absolutely remarkable!

"My goodness- did she paint these?" I asked the husband and wife genuinely intrigued. *Surely not? They were incredible!*

Smiling, the couple giggled affectionately at my ridiculous question and declared that their daughter had not made the magnificent works of art.

I felt a little disappointed on discovering this fact; I'm not going to lie. Nevertheless, this feeling soon disintegrated when the wife stated that she was actually the incredibly-talented artist, and was teaching her young daughter how to paint.

In a sea full of alluring and appealing paintings, one instantly captured my attention: The Chiang Mai floating market.

I couldn't bring myself to haggle for such a unique work of art so I gave the full asking price of £30. When you compare this price to the £4 that I paid for an oil painting in Hong Kong, on reflection it was rather expensive for Asia, but it was worth every penny.

For a few brief moments, I watched the girl as she delicately stroked the canvas with the brush in gentle, rhythmic motions.

Tenderness took over and subconsciously I found myself spontaneously handing Summer another 100 baht note and asked her to deliver it to the girl, just as she had the boy.

The sheer level of genuine gratitude that was shown towards us that evening made me feel overwhelmingly happy and humbled.

I wish I could explain why I kept giving money away that evening. If I'm being honest, I am not entirely sure myself. All I can say is that motherhood changes your perception of the world and since having Summer I always find it so upsetting when I see underprivileged children living a life of constant hardship. They didn't sign up for that level of disadvantage - it was the hand that they were dealt through no fault of their own.

As difficult as this was to stomach, on reflection, the children I had come across that evening were the lucky ones. Their parents had their own businesses and were earning money - even if their standard of living seemed impoverished compared to ours in the western world.

In all honesty, I was completely restless knowing that there were thousands of Thai children spending countless hours 'doing their duty' on the family stall very late into the dark hours of the night (way past their bed time) instead of being comfortably tucked up in bed in preparation for a hectic day of schooling the following day. That is, if they were one of the very few lucky ones who were privileged enough to be educated.

It sounds weird talking about education as a privilege...because many children in the UK would describe school as a necessary chore - even a necessary evil for some of them, including me when I was at school! However, the reality throughout most of Asia is that education is indeed a privilege for the minority.

***

Sometimes the best laid plans go to waste...

I had stupidly forgotten to carry a business card stipulating our accommodation details. Consequently, four Tuk-tuk drivers were completely lost as to where they were supposed to be dropping us when we later wanted to go home. Eventually, more drivers joined the discussion to pin-point the hostel, but it seemed no one had a clue where it was. The night sky was growing later by the minute and sleep was tiresomely engulfing us with every frustrating minute that passed.

Despite my tiredness, I experienced a Laura light-bulb moment when I decided to load my emails onto my phone to try and locate a hard copy of the hostel address recorded on our itinerary.

Typically, just when you think you have found a great solution to a problem, your luck runs out. No phone signal whatsoever meant that my Plan B was completely redundant! *Why on earth didn't I save the itinerary as a picture to my phone gallery?* I grumbled in tired frustration.

Out of the blue, one of the drivers declared that he was confident that he knew where the hostel was. Naively, we eagerly jumped on-board but unsurprisingly 10 minutes later with an asleep Summer now on my shoulder - we were completely lost.

Not one for hanging around in limbo, I decided to take-action! Vaguely recognising our surroundings, I confidently turned to Carl: "I think I know the way from here."

His expression suggested that he was not convinced in my ability; further highlighted by a mocking toned: "Yeah right!" response.

Irritatingly he continued to question my decisions throughout the journey by constantly glaring at me with that smug, 'you have no idea where you are going' expression. As ever, I held onto my unwavering faith and I'm proud to say that it eventually paid off.

Out of nowhere and shining like a lighthouse from a choppy sea, in the distance I suddenly noticed the creepy café. *Thank god for that! That's one place I never imagined I'd be so happy to see!*

Breathing an inner-sign of relief, I took great satisfaction in relating this point back to Carl. At the end of the day, if you cannot beat somebody's arrogance sometimes you must join in!

As we jumped off the Tuk-tuk, it appeared my generous streak was catching when Carl surprisingly handed the driver a 200 baht note instead of the agreed 100. I honestly wish I could have captured the bewildered look that stretched across the driver's face at that very moment.

This still image was very intriguing. I had genuinely never seen a grown man look so overwhelmed (especially when you consider that the tip was so small.) I for one was not expecting to witness this layer of vulnerability on such a grown man.

That evening, I kept seeing the driver's smile flashing through my mind. The way he held the notes so tenderly reminded me of when Charlie discovers the 'golden ticket' in the film, Charlie and the Chocolate Factory.

The experiences of the evening touched the deepest corners of my heart and in hindsight; I wished we had given the driver more.

***

Seven:

Being intrepid and fearless and staying with locals that speak no English!

The next morning, we awoke bright and early ready to venture into the northern Jungle of Chiang Mai.

Whilst showering, anticipation and a skittish excitement shot through my veins with immense speed.

My mind wandered off…I was in a complete daydream as I conjured up wild plans about what adventures may take place during the next step of our travelling voyage; all from the dizzy heights of a tree house, nonetheless.

It was 8am when we found ourselves waiting for our host to collect us.

As a gut reaction and with great haste, I grabbed my backpack, violently pushed it to the ground and parked my agitated, sticky and weary body onto my man-made cushion.

"I wouldn't do that if I was you! Your bag will get filthy!"

Rolling my eyes irritatingly, I totally disregarded Carl's grating remark and instead pushed Summer's bag to the ground.

"Here Sum - take a seat." I patted the bag like a cushion.

With a smug grin across my face, 20 minutes later I watched with glee as Carl pushed his own bag to the ground and took a seat in the same motion as we had.

"I wouldn't do that if I was you - your bag will get dirty!" I sniggered like an evil hyena in the African Savannah.

Carl responded by snorting like a warthog and smiling a conspicuous, cheesy grin.

In the deepest corners of my mind, I couldn't help reflecting on my small but satisfying victory.

Over the minutes that passed, talk inevitably turned to our experiences in Chiang Mai and how the city was so different to the preconceived opinions that we held.

Personally, I had always been under the impression that Chiang Mai was a place of great spiritual enlightenment…possessing copious amounts of peaceful yoga and spa retreats. Sadly, I found that I felt far wearier in Chiang Mai then I had been in Hong Kong.

Sensing potential danger, my maternal instincts had taught me to sit Summer on the inside of a table when eating in a café or restaurant that was outside. To be completely honest, I hadn't even contemplated being that fiercely protective in Hong Kong.

Regrettably, I struggled to understand what was so impressive about the city. Nothing remotely special stood out for me – except for the people at the night bazaar that was; the people I met that evening had certainly left an impression that would glow a bright light in my memory for a long time.

"So, would you visit Chiang Mai again?" Carl interrupted my thoughts.

"I doubt it!" I responded in a tone more passionate than I had envisaged.

Almost as if on cue, a battered 4x4 pulled alongside us and a short, stocky man emerged (It was our host, John.)

What I knew of John from the emails we had exchanged was that he was a former architect from Cambridge and had initially travelled to Thailand to study.

Like a typical romantic love story, a Thai girl had captured his heart and thus he'd moved to the land of smiles to be with her.

"Good morning campers!" He shouted through his unwound window.

"Chuck your backpacks in the boot and jump in!" John patted the door of his 4x4 with his hand.

Following instruction, Carl jumped in the front seat whilst Summer and I hurdled into the back.

"We have a two-hour journey ahead of us folks, so make yourself comfortable!"

Summer eagerly rested her delicate little head on my hot shoulder and lovingly closed her eyes.

"So how did you end up with the tree house?" I heard Carl ask John.

"My wife introduced me to a friend of hers who wanted to build a tree-house in their remote village that he could live in with his wife, as well as let to holidaymakers. At first, I was providing them with information and advice on the structural design of the house; but slowly I morphed into their business partner. I was contributing rather heavily to the design features, and eventually my responsibility increased to the point that I'm now practically running it!"

"That's incredible! That's a lot like my role..." Carl couldn't help but say.

I rolled my eyes at what was coming – Carl talking about work again!

I was pleasantly surprised, however, as John completed ignored what Carl had said, and instead continued with his own story. (*I'm not going to lie, it did make me chuckle inside!*)

"Some things happen for a reason and become the path that we were meant to follow in life." John remarked insightfully as he slipped the gear stick into a higher number and forced the 4x4 to plough faster through the wilderness.

With the immense hive of activity we'd participated in since travelling, to my embarrassment my tiredness took over and I found myself nodding off onto the cold window.

With my dignity remaining not-so-much intact, the jeep pulled up sharp forcing my head to slam firmly into the window.

"Ouch! I felt that bang! Are you ok?" hollered John from the front.

Sleepily, I opened my right eye; swiftly followed by my left. Familiarising myself with my newfound surroundings, I rigorously rubbed my forehead and immersed the luscious, green forest outside of the 4x4. Smiling, I absorbed the captivating, awe-inspiring view.

"Yeah, yeah, I'm fine!" I gave an embarrassed giggle as I continued to rub my fingertips into my forehead to relieve the pressure.

"This is the Mae Ping River – known to the locals as the 'Lifeline of the Province.' It is here where you will embark on some rafting!" John beamed as we roared further into the jungle.

Blissfully stepping out of the air-conditioned 4x4 several minutes later, the fierce jungle humidity hit me like a tonne of bricks.

"Wow! How hot is it here?" I not-so-discreetly attempted to mask the level of uncomfortableness that I was suddenly experiencing.

Awkwardly, I proceeded to wipe sweat from my encased brow as I gulped the water from my bottle at an almighty speed.

"Summer, drink up!" I barked, tossing her a bottle of water.

Within minutes, my mouth was as dry as the Sahara Desert and I was finding it difficult to catch my breath.

Still rubbing my injured forehead, John directed us through a gravel pathway that was surrounded by overgrown woods of undisturbed farm land.

Gravel pounding, we soon approached a huge bamboo bridge that spanned the top of an immense, brown river.

As I looked on, the murky-water unfolded for what seemed like miles and miles.

Approaching the bridge with caution, I nervously surveyed the rotting wooden floorboards that were tentatively held airborne by numerous rusty pieces of wire.

Once again, Carl looked unimpressed.

With raised eyebrows he held my gaze for what seemed like forever.

"What?" I nervously laughed as I tilted my head to face him.

"I'm sorry about the height if that's what you're trying to say! I genuinely didn't know we'd have to cross a bridge like this." I laughed apprehensively as I intently watched the paleness and wrenched expression increase across his bony face.

"I am honestly as surprised as you!" I babbled into the now uncomfortable stillness that had fallen between us.

Strangely, Carl didn't answer and to my surprise was the first to step onto the bridge. But within seconds it was obvious that he was 100 per cent out of his comfort zone as he clutched both ropes so tight, I could see masses of blue veins bulging through his skin.

Dutifully following him, I took a few steps onto the decayed wood, but thanks to the whistling wind the footbridge swayed harshly from left-to-right.

I immediately reached for the rope to steady myself, but as it was only made from two threadbare ropes and a piece of wire it did little to stop the unforeseen swinging of the bridge.

"You are walking like an elephant!" Carl screamed as a noticeable blue vein violently protruded from his forehead.

"It's not me it's the wind!" I nervously giggled.

Being a person with a larger-then-life personality; I couldn't help but see the sunny-side of most situations, which evidently meant I often laughed at inappropriate times. It seemed on this occasion I was the only one laughing - well me and a certain five-year-old that is, when I glanced at Summer to find her inwardly giggling too.

Staring downwards; the murky, mud-brown river stared straight back at me as the enormity of our height suddenly ran through my veins. Looking up and across the bridge at the white smog of clouds above the mountains, there was no denying that it was a picture-perfect sight that I would no doubt hold in my memory for a lifetime.

We soon made it to the other side, which I thought was a victory given the heavy-breathing and panting that was coming from my now extremely pale, travelling companion.

Rather practically, hidden amongst the trees I spotted a toilet block; but unpractically it was officially the worst toilet of the trip as the cubical looked more like a cell in the TV programme, 'Banged up Abroad.' It had filthy cemented walls and floor, with graffiti splashed haphazardly across every square inch of the germ-infested square.

As I leaned across to look at the stainless-steel toilet, my eyeline was immediately occupied by thousands of bugs that were indulging on the infested seat. I had never seen anything quite like it before in my entire life.

"I'm not using that!" Summer screamed as she took in the horrendous sight and sprinted at the speed of a lightning bolt from an angry and thunderous cloud.

Despite knowing that I could find myself in a situation where she needed the toilet and there would be none in sight, I agreed with her.

"Come on!" I tenderly slipped my arm over her shoulders as we continued down the gravel path through the forest. As soon as we arrived at the coffee-coloured river, I noticed a miniscule, Thai man sat on a bamboo raft.

"Sa-wat-dee Kraup." I greeted the man, feeling proudly cultured at my marvellous language skills.

"Guys - this is Akara, he will be your guide for rafting. Just so you know, he doesn't speak any English." John laughed mischievously.

"Laura, I don't think this is such a good idea..." A petrified Carl whispered into my earlobe as we both stared completely speechless at the lack-lustre, make-shift raft that was made from what looked to be bamboo and string.

"I mean look at it!" he continued to rant as he pointed towards the raft that I admit, looked as though it could capsize in an instant.

Before I could even respond, the Thai man passed me a children's lifejacket.

"I agree the raft doesn't look the best," I fastened the jacket onto Summer. "But Summer has a life jacket, we can both swim and the river isn't fast-flowing so what's the worst that can happen?" I tossed my hands into the air, not really understanding what all the fuss was about.

He looked at me blankly.

"Well?" I pushed for an answer.

"I...I... can't swim, ok!" He looked me deep in the eye, taking me totally by surprise.

"What?... Really?... Why?" I babbled in confusion.

"I was never taught Laura. It wasn't a priority for my parents!"

Without answering I turned to the Thai man.

"Do-you-have-an adult's-life-jacket-please?" I dragged my words out slowly, pointing at Summer's jacket, aware that he couldn't understand English.

Surprising me, the man clearly understood as he immediately passed me an adult's jacket.

"Put this on!" I hollered to Carl as I tossed him his life-line.

"I'm not wearing this - I'll look stupid!" He threw the jacket to the ground.

I stared at him in disappointment.

"Well if you can't swim than you have no choice!" Screeching through gritted teeth, I tightened Summer's pony tail. *It really was like talking to a child, sometimes.*

Out of nowhere, the Thai man tossed me a second jacket. *He obviously understands more English than John thinks he does*, I sniggered to myself.

"Look - I'll wear one too." I spun to face Carl. "That way no-one looks stupid!"

"No it's ok. I'll just sit this one out..."

My inner thoughts were squealing, 'What a wimp!' But I decided that some positive (if slightly forthright) encouragement would be a better option.

"Come on Carl! You're in Thailand - on a once in a lifetime trip! Trust me you will regret it if you don't go. Now come on!" I tossed him the jacket from the ground unsympathetically.

Several minutes later, as I stepped onto the bamboo the raft immediately became overwhelmed with water. Alarmed, I looked to the water's edge but John did not look worried and instead continued to joyfully wave us off.

"I'll meet you at the end!" he shouted, oblivious to the now water-logged raft that was supposedly safe for us to travel on.

With a wooden bench rested on the raft, I carefully sat down and held onto Summer tightly.

As we took a seat, the man opened a cool box and passed us each a triangle hat that was made of bamboo.

I looked at Carl whose face was as pale as a ghost. His entire body looked frozen.

Deciding to travel on the raft had seemed like a good idea at first. However, I am the first to admit that I'm an adrenaline junkie who at times can get carried away. In retrospect, perhaps it was selfish of me to have put Carl through an eccentric raft experience. You only had to glance for a millisecond in his direction to witness the fear oozing from every morsel of his sweat-enriched body.

In a shameful bid to rediscover my kind morals, I tried my best to distract him by animatedly pointing out our surroundings. I desperately hoped that my enthusiasm would catch.

Without realising it at the time, I was talking Carl into an oblivion (masking the fact that I didn't really know how to handle the situation) and was babbling like a broken record on repeat.

Even though I felt genuinely pathetic for doing this, my tactic unusually worked a treat! Within a matter of minutes, we were all (including Carl) absorbed by the serenity of our surroundings as the forest's silence engulfed us.

Staring at the nothingness surrounding me, in the distant background was the faint sound of splashing water with the occasional bird chirping gloriously into the passing wind.

"I have never in my life been anywhere so quiet!" I broke the obstinate silence that so blatantly separated Carl and I.

"This is stunning!" Carl turned to face me, speaking for the first-time in ages.

To my utter astonishment his face no longer resembled a Madame Tussauds waxwork. Instead a huge grin that was as wide as a photo-shopped monkey, spread from one cheek-bone to the other.

"This is what travelling is about - isn't it?" Carl enquired. "Removing yourself from your comfort zone to truly 'experience life'" He positioned the palms of his hands into the air for emphasis.

"Sure is!" I beamed back.

Glaring into the screen of my smart phone in the way that Penny from 'Inspector Gadget' consults her watch for instructions to her next mission; the scorching temperature recorded at just over 40 Celsius.

"Look Mummy - it's like the Jungle Book!" Summer shouted as we all marvelled at an enormous black snake that was wrapped around a tree and glistening like a wet seal basking in the late, afternoon sun.

Knowing that deadly Cobras are found in jungle landscapes such as the one we were rafting through, I wondered if the striking snake was that of a deadly Cobra.

As I peacefully sat, I bizarrely had a vision of the raft sinking and us all being stranded in the middle of the unknown jungle - surrounded *by the* snakes! I suddenly thought, gulping hard. *As you do…*

"Thanks for pushing me to do this." Carl interrupted my crazy thought.

"I would never usually put myself in a situation where I'm not in control, so thanks for the impulsion - I'm glad that I came!"

"Carl, this entire trip you're going to repeatedly find yourself in situations where you're not in control!" I laughed bitterly.

"That's the nature of travelling, whether that's on a package holiday or backpacking. You can't control every situation: but that's part of the thrill! How you handle it shapes your personality for when you later return home to the 9-5, repetitive rat-race that we're on this very trip to get away from!"

"Since when did you become so wise?" he snorted, forcing me to chuckle.

"It's always been there, you just have to get through the humour!" I giggled.

Before long the rafting ended and despite my rather-odd disturbing vision, we thankfully made it safely back to the water's edge.

Climbing onto the dry land, we ascended a small hill where unexpectedly we spotted a freeway. In confusion, we glanced towards each other. Bizarrely, we were not in the part of the forest where we had boarded the raft.

In blind panic, we both instantaneously looked back towards the river, but the man continued rafting away smiling at us from now a considerable distance.

"Wait! I frantically yelled, tossing my arms in the air in the way that a desperate, desolate person making an SOS call might.

The man's reaction was to completely ignore me and continue peacefully downstream.

"Where the hell are we?" Carl yelled, quickly returning to his anxious, edgy self.

How ironic considering his soft declaration of 'thank you' only moments before. *Clearly his softness had been swept away with the faint breeze...*

"How the hell do I know?" I yelled.

Why did I have to always call on troubles door? Conjuring up sadistic visions of us getting stranded in the middle of the jungle? I thought.

"On the upside - we are next to a freeway!" I tried to retain as much optimism as I could.

"It's not as though we are in the middle of the wilderness as there is at least a road!" I continued pacing up the hill towards a concrete bench that sat deserted and lonely by the side of the road.

"I guess we should just wait here until John collects us..." I muttered over-confidently into the noiseless air, forcing both Summer and Carl to glance at each other not so confidentially.

"This is what backpacking is all about!" Carl mimicked in a perfectly pitched and precisely executed, mock-female, childlike voice.

So now, he had stooped so low as to openly mock me in front of my daughter! My blood boiled with internal rage.

Resisting temptation to be drawn into the obvious child's play; I somehow remained cool, calm and firmly voiceless. Feeling like the grown up, I made an executive decision that it would be best to simply let his obnoxious behaviour play its course until he got bored of the sound of his own voice, and the blatant lack of reaction from me.

"What? Getting stranded in the middle of the jungle?" He continued to rant, this time reverting to his usual stale, tedious and monotone voice.

"Having an argument about it isn't going to change the situation so you might as well save your breath!" I snapped in annoyance.

To make the time go faster by occupying the actual child in the group, I immediately turned to Summer.

"Rubes, shall we collect some leaves to stick in your scrap book?"

"And why exactly do you call her 'Rubes?'" He mimicked, arrogantly air quoting the nickname 'Rubes' in the most exaggeratedly-animated way possible.

"Erm - because her name is Summer-Ruby, so Rubes is short for Ruby." I explained, my rage clearly expanding at great speed with each passing second.

"Personally, I have never understood the whole 'nickname' thing. I think it is a rather dangerous game if you ask me..."

I was desperately trying to control the gobsmacked look of surprise from breaking out all over my face.

"Having a nickname could lead to the child having a split personality, causing them to adopt two separate identities..." he continued to ramble, despite the aggressive expression I was no doubt harbouring.

Carl's words fell into death's door with immense haste, forcing an awkward silence to completely consume us. I couldn't quite fathom what I had just heard and this caused me to glare at him venomously in utter dislike and sheer disbelief.

The voices in my head were bouncing up and down screaming, 'I didn't ask you, did I?' But I really didn't want to argue in front of Summer...With my cheeks glowing pinker, I stared from Carl to Summer. I couldn't help myself. I bit...

"Oh, for god's sake!" I found myself shouting so loudly, it was like listening to the agitated sound of my own voice in cinema surround-sound.

"Of course it doesn't! It is a nickname, which is a bit of fun. Stop over-analysing everything!" I yelled, feeling like I was about to totally lose the plot. *Boy, he knew how to push me over the edge!*

It was a terrible feeling knowing that he had so much control over my disposition. I needed to be the bigger person. As we all know, this is often more easily said than done...

"Mummy, stop shouting - I don't like it!" Summer demanded in the politest way possible. This made me feel instantly guilty and like I had just lost significant brownie points in my mothering role.

"You're right Summer, and I'm really sorry." I shamefully uttered, walking towards Carl to purposefully whisper into his ear.

"You and I are going to squabble on this trip, but where possible I do not want my child to witness it...agreed?" I hanged onto the rhetorical question that wasn't actually rhetorical at all; whilst simultaneously glaring at him into the centre point of his pupils. It felt like a stand-off in the African Savannah between an elephant and a rhino...neither of whom wanted to lose face.

Just short of 10 minutes later and with pockets full to the brim of jungle leaves, John pulled up in his adventurous-looking 4x4. I have never felt so utterly relieved. His timing couldn't have been better executed.

"Hey guys! How was it?" He leaned out of his window just as he had that very morning.

"Yeah good! Although Laura became a little apprehensive (thinking we were stranded) when you were not here to collect us." Carl lied, attempting to make friends through clearly mocking me.

"Women!" cackled John.

That little voice in my head reared its ugly vocal chords again; chastising the unnecessary sexism displayed by John.

I looked at both men as I mentally debated whether to say anything in response. I concluded that I couldn't be bothered and instead chose to speak to Summer about the leaves we had collected. *Honestly sometimes it is easier and more pleasant to converse with children than bear the opinionated views of adults.*

The last 30 minutes of the drive were wonderfully scenic.

We travelled to what seemed like the epicentre of the jungle itself; the 4x4 climbing precariously every step of the way up the steepest mountain.

So this is what the heart of the jungle looks like... I wondrously glared out of the window.

"Wow Mummy - look at that!" Summer peered at the scene, nose pressed firmly against the cold air-conditioned window.

The view was picturesque from the interior of the 4x4. With mist seeping idly across the jungle's summit; it was truly breath-taking.

"Here - take some photos." I passed her my DSLR.

"Wow! Thanks Mummy!" she gasped in glee, immediately focusing on the passing mountains.

Continuing forth, the road was almost vertical and the wind was fiercely turbulent. Every now and then we were met by the occasional goat or motorcycle that stubbornly blocked our path. With several sharp, blind corners, John had to continuously strike his horn to warn of our presence.

At times, I felt as though our 4x4 was being swallowed up by the dense forest, as thick, unbreakable grass carpeted the narrow, unspoilt strip of road; just like a scene in an exotic Disney movie.

Eventually, we arrived at the tree house which appeared to be sitting in the heart of a small, microscopic village. There were numerous shacks that winded down a dirt-encrusted road at the top of the mountain's edge.

"Just to advise you..." John warned as I eagerly climbed out of the 4x4.

"A Thai family of 14 are likely to still be occupying the tree house until late afternoon, but they're friendly people and won't cause you the slightest bother," he said sincerely, whilst grabbing Summer's backpack and slamming the truck's boot down with an earth-shattering force that could rival that of the 'Incredible Hulk's.'

Retrieving my own backpack, I found my mind becoming engrossed in the excitement of the 'unknown' as I crept towards the house in a slow but purposeful manner.

On approaching the entrance, we were swiftly instructed to take our shoes off; which we did with great haste.

Entering the tree house was both surreal and intimidating in equal measure, as numerous Thai faces started straight back at us, surveying our every movement. I had never experienced anything quite like it before.

Mirroring my apprehension, Summer reacted in much the same way; ducking behind the curves of my legs and morphing into my shadow.

I grabbed her hand tightly as I confidently strode into the main living area (masking any feelings of trepidation.)

Searching and scanning up and around the property in every nook and cranny, I instantly concluded that this tree house had complete craftsmanship. The property was truly unique in every way humanely imaginable.

The wooden wall of the house only stood as tall as my hip, and over the edge was the perimeter of the mountain's superiority. The view was like something you would see in the film, 'Planet of the Apes,' with elegant canopy trees as high as the skyscrapers that perfectly line the streets of New York.

Accompanied was a fresh, aromatic and lemony smell that was so incredibly inviting my nose wanted to follow the path of the sent without hesitation.

The family were spread out across the living room. Some were huddled together in an ensemble; others were idly lazing on bean bags and smaller proportions were swinging from one of the many hammocks that hung from the wooden beams.

Out of the corner of my eye, I noticed three men playing the guitar cheerfully whilst every member of the family unanimously sang a song in Thai that I desperately wished I was familiar with.

In the corner, two women were enjoying a massage whilst more cooked food joyfully on the open fire pit that stood in the middle of the room. Like intrepid travellers, the three of us stood and unapologetically stared on, completely intrigued.

Suddenly, one of the guitar players shouted over the singing, enquiring where Carl was from.

"Wales!" he bellowed, taking me totally by surprise.

"Wales?" I turned to him, confused as hell.

"Well, I lived there until I was 13 before my parents moved south," he shouted my way, competing with the chorus of music.

"I think they mean where do you live now?" I laughed. "Not your birth place!"

"Guys…" John beckoned us to the kitchen to introduce us to the tree house cooks.

To Summer's absolute delight, the couple had a four-year-old daughter called Ubon. Incredibly, despite not speaking the same language; the children instantly hit it off as they innocently tickled and chased each other around the tree house.

As Summer ran around like a free-spirited gypsy, the family later motioned for us to return to the living room. As we entered, the guitarists suddenly erupted into the 1965 hit, 'It's Not Unusual' to resemble both Carl's and the singer of the song, Tom Jones, hometown of Wales.

It was such a thoughtful gesture and immediately put me at ease.

I laughed and sang along freely as they bellowed the lyrics.

"It's not unusual to be loved by anyone…" we all sang.

"It's not unusual to have fun with anyone…

"But when I see you hanging about with anyone…

"It's not unusual to see me cry…

"Oh, I wanna die…" Carl and I sang in carefree tones as we looked at each other, giggling like school children on a term-time trip.

After the song, John directed us back towards the kitchen and ushered us to a wooden table that was at the rear of the property.

The table sat alongside another wooden wall that was the height of my hip and similarly had a drop that looked down the perimeter of the mountain's edge. A Thai man in his 60's was sat at the table and behind him loomed another open room where I could see several Thai teenagers sat idly gossiping.

As we carefully took our seats, John introduced the man as the owner of the tree house. Awkwardly the owner spoke little English, hence the uncomfortable strained conversation we had. Amongst a few obstinate silences, we were served a bowl of white, boiled rice and an orange each.

Placing the bowls in front of us, the cooks stood a few inches from the table with grins as wide as the jungle splashed across their faces.

"You tell us you like, yes?" The wife asked.

It was the first time we had been served food without being asked what we had wanted first. I immediately hoped we were served something more substantial then plain rice and an orange throughout the remainder of our stay.

"Of course." I nodded and smiled as I scooped a generous portion of rice onto my fork and into my mouth.

It soon became apparent that the rice wasn't as plain as it looked. The spice was so intense that after only several mouthfuls I could feel my lips tingling, my tongue burning, and my neck contracting from the intense heat increasing both inside as well as outside of my body.

"Rice ok?" The wife smiled towards us sweetly.

"Lovely, thank you!" I eagerly scooped another dreaded mouthful.

Swallowing hard, I glanced towards Ubon and Summer as they happily tucked into their bowls without an utter flinch... *Did they have a different batch?*

After lunch, we were introduced to Jaco, who was the only man in the village that spoke English.

Jaco was a tall, slim man who was in his 50's and had a short beard that accompanied his grizzled hair and big, beady, brown eyes. He wore a brown, nut-coloured t-shirt with faded jeans and wellington boots. Passing us each a bottle of water, he advised us to wear long-sleeved tops and trousers, along with sturdy shoes as unbeknown to us he was taking us on a three-hour hike through the jungle.

***

Before we ventured into the forest, John directed us to our bedroom at the top of the house.

Climbing the open staircase, a feeling of excitement at what the room would look like suddenly came over me.

With widespread-eyes and a huge grin, my expression dropped quicker than a penny hitting the ground.

"Oh-my-god..." was all I could muster.

"Well this is an anti-climax for you, isn't it?" Carl cackled as I spun my head from left-to-right taking in the bare room that consisted of three beds and one side table, absolutely no décor and instead plain, bamboo walls.

Immediately dumping my backpack onto the bed, I headed to the enormous square that was cut from the bamboo wall to make a window.

In disbelief, I leaned my head out of the makeshift window and looked out across the mountains. The hole was a scary prospect for any parent that had an excited, energetic five-year-old with them, so I warned Summer that she was to not go anywhere near the window throughout our stay.

"What an odd opening," Carl observed, looking down the decent with caution and instantly breathing heavy at just how high up we were.

"I assume this slides over the hole at night?" I picked up a huge bamboo square that had obviously been cut from the wall.

"Great: there are holes in it!" I griped.

"I now understand the importance of covering our skin throughout the stay as we will literally be sleeping in a tree in the jungle with little protection from the mosquitoes around us!" I squirmed.

"Laura – are you actually concerned about something for once?"

"What do you mean for once?" My tone deepened.

"Carl, I have a child to think about and we are in a malaria zone so of course I'm worried."

"I'm just surprised that's all…"

Continuing to root through my bag for the sun lotion, I could feel his gaze on me almost as strong as sunshine.

"What?" I hissed in annoyance to his stare, before being interrupted by the sound of Summer and Ubon running up-and-down the hallway.

"Girls!" I agitatedly called, making my way out of the bedroom and onto the landing that overlooked the main living area. The family were still singing and laughing with each other as I looked down.

Despite trying to be carefree, my eyes were on constant overdrive as I desperately tried to keep abreast of Summer's every movement as her and Ubon ran untroubled throughout the very-much open property.

"Summer - look around you please!" I shouted.

"Look at the low edges and sudden drops! And stay where I can see you!" I demanded before sighing out loud.

"I don't think this accommodation was such a good idea, was it?" Carl smugly remarked, appearing next to me in the hallway.

"Of course, it is Carl. I just need to keep an eye on her that's all." I challenged his remark through gritted teeth.

"If you fear everything then you'll never do anything!" I chirped in annoyance as I walked towards my backpack and continued to root through it.

"Hello…" Jaco hollered from the bottom of the stairs.

"We will leave for the trek in a few minutes: please remember to wear sturdy shoes."

Hunting for my trainers in the bag of washing from the laundrette, to my utter shock my brand-new cream, cotton blazer had blue dye all over it.

"Oh no!" I roared. "The laundrette must have put my Converse in with all the clothes and the blue dye has run from the denim in the trainers onto all the whites!"

"Now you know why there was no extra charge for washing the Converse - it's because the woman just washed everything together!" Carl recalled unhelpfully.

"God: you don't say!" I irritatingly barked before sighing dramatically to contemplate just how bad the stain was.

"So, the £4 load I was immensely impressed with has now cost me dearly!" I bellowed in annoyance before throwing the jacket onto the bed in aggression.

"I did tell you that it was crazy cheap and we shouldn't…"

"We both said that Carl!" I interrupted him mid-sentence, raising the decimals of my voice slightly.

"Why do you always have to do that?" I screeched. "It's so annoying."

"There's no need to be rude!" he whimpered.

Speechless, I simply rolled my eyes… *sometimes it is better to say nothing*, I sighed.

Converse on, we headed to the front of the house where Jaco and a boy (who was around 17 in age) were waiting for us.

Passing us each a bamboo stick, Jaco declared that we would need them for the hike - prompting us to exchange glances at just how in-depth the walk was going to be.

Setting off down the dirt track, I found myself walking alongside the boy in complete silence. I can't say I have ever been comfortable with silence, so I decided to try my luck and start a conversation.

"What's your name?"

"He doesn't speak English!" Jaco laughed at my stupidity.

As we walked, we passed several shacks that were made with bamboo and had tarpaulin as roof tops.

Summer looked to be in her element, joyfully leaning on her stick. Occasionally I'd even catch her swinging it in happiness as though she was Willy Wonka with his cane.

Taking a moment I absorbed her expression. She looked so content and as bright as a silver dollar. It made me laugh that something as simple as walking with a stick was keeping her so entertained. We weren't at Disneyland or in a soft play area, but were simply walking in nature. *This child clearly wasn't just for inner-city living*, I laughed to myself.

With the lack of people and the unworn trail we were embarking on, it felt as though we were exploring undiscovered land - making the whole experience incredibly exciting.

With no pathway to stand on, I excitedly clicked away on my camera to capture the surrounding overgrown trees and fast-running stream that flowed to the left of us.

"Laura!" Carl barked in front.

"Stay with the group!" He rolled his eyes just as a sulky teenager would.

We soon arrived at a wooden bridge that crossed over to a school.

"This is the school that I was told you wanted to visit?"

"Oh, yes that's right. Sorry Jaco, I didn't realise we would be doing that on this trek. Thank you!" I suddenly felt incredibly excited at the prospect of visiting the school.

Before leaving the UK, Summer and I fundraised for stationery and toys for a few schools and orphanages that I had planned to visit during the trip.

The courier company, Transglobal Express, had posted the boxes to the schools for free and two of the boxes were sent to a school local to the tree house, ready for us to hand-out during our stay.

Ban Ma Maeh School educates and provides a home for orphaned and underprivileged children in the remote hill country of the Chiang Dao district, which lies above the green slopes of the Doi Chiang Dao Mountain.

The school was initially started by villagers to give the local children an education; however, in 2002 there was a government crackdown on drugs which led to many families being torn apart. Parents that were found to be guilty by the courts were sent to jail and some were even killed. This led to many children becoming orphans, and left those that ran the school with no choice but to house the children that needed a home. (The controversial 'war on drugs' campaign was said to have left more than 2,200 people across the country dead in a three-month period.)

The school is remote and inaccessible by road and cellular telephone signals (hence us trekking through the jungle to reach it) and under the Government's Basic Education Commission, it runs on an allowance of just 30 cents per student - which clearly isn't enough to feed the students three-times a day.

Furthermore, as the number of students increase, the dormitories are running out of space. There are not enough beds for all the students, leaving some having to sleep on the cold floor which sometimes causes flu and other diseases. Additionally, the school is too far from the nearest hospital so it is hard for sick students to then seek medical treatment.

Over the years, the building has suffered wear and tear (with the roof leaking and walls breaking down) which has made living conditions extremely difficult during seasonal changes. Even more shockingly, there are 118 students to only seven teachers.

John informed me that the school relies heavily on donations. With the teachers working tirelessly to pull in enough funds for food, they can't even begin to think about starting on improving the living conditions.

After a year of fundraising and reading about the school online, the prospect that we would now visit it was both daunting and exciting; but most importantly, I was looking forward to making the children smile by giving them some toys and practical items for their classrooms.

**

A cemented square playground that had one extremely worn basketball hoop for entertainment glazed my vision as we crossed the bridge. I looked on as 50 or more children played what looked to be a game of tag. Tables were pushed together with the two boxes that Transglobal Express had generously posted a few months previous. The boxes hadn't been opened and it was nice to see them again.

"Look Mummy - there's our boxes!" Summer shouted in excitement, sprinting towards them as though they were long-lost friends.

"This is so cool!" Carl gasped. "Do you mind if I hand them out as well?"

Noticing our presence, the teachers greeted us in Thai and instructed the children to form a line.

With a look of anticipation and confusion in their eyes, the children wasted no time in forming two lines in front of the tables.

I wondered what they had been told about us. Looking at the expressions on their faces they had absolutely no idea who we were and why we were there.

Within minutes a neat line of boys and girls had been formed and the teacher introduced us to the children. Most of them waved enthusiastically, forcing Summer to duck behind my legs as her nerves took over. *Wow – she hasn't done that since Hong Kong!*

Discreetly crouching down to her height, I whispered: "Summer, these children don't have bedrooms with toys and a TV like you do, so that's why we collected all those gifts for them. Remember?"

"Yeah – I gave them my skates and books and…." she gloated.

"Exactly!" I cut her off mid-sentence, tenderly taking her hand.

"So, there's nothing to be afraid of is there? Now, I can't hand all these presents out by myself can I? So, are you going to be a big girl and help me?"

I watched as her spaniel-like eyes enlarged along with her smile. Nodding yes, I spun her body to face outwards towards the children.

Jaco, who was acting as our translator, told us that because it was a Sunday most of the children were at home with their families and the ones that remained were residents. It was a fact that didn't sit well at all with me.

Suddenly, I began to absorb the sight of the 50 or so children that stood before us. For obvious reasons, complete sadness engulfed my heart. I couldn't believe that every child before me was an orphan. It was one thing reading about them on the school's website, but quite another seeing just how many there were.

What would they have done if the school didn't exist? I shuddered.

"How sad that they're all orphans?" breathed Carl towards me as if reading my mind.

"I was just thinking the exact same thing myself. This just doesn't feel enough…" I glumly scanned our two measly boxes.

"Of course, it is! This will make their day!" He smiled encouragingly.

"Khx peid klxng!" The teacher shouted towards the children.

"She said, 'Let's open the boxes!' Jaco leaned in close.

Summer, Carl and I stood alongside the tables, handing each child a gift or two. Once they had an item, they joined the back of the queue until it was their turn again.

"Oh no!" I scanned the queue of children in front of me.

"What's wrong?" Carl leaned in.

"Look how many teenage boys there are in the queue!" I suddenly paused in alarm.

"There's hardly anything in these boxes for teenage boys! Most of the boys' gifts are for children; with bubbles, toy cars, pens and English-written books."

"You have tried your best Laura - don't fret about it."

"Easier said than done!" I squeaked in a barely audible voice, before dramatically sighing out loud.

"I can't give a 15-year-old a packet of bubbles!" I howled, feeling my skin turn a darker shade of pink from both the embarrassment and intense Thai heat.

"They will be grateful no matter what, I'm sure." Carl assured encouragingly, touching my shoulder gently and smiling. However nice the sentiment, for some reason it made me slightly uncomfortable. I am by no means a touchy-feely person, and I'm certainly not the type of person to openly cuddle another unless it is my child, family or partner. I was therefore shocked at the sudden 'touching of skin' from Mr Baines.

Handing out the gifts several minutes later, I was astonished when I gave one boy of 10 years old a Frisbee. Clearly, he had no idea what the round bit of plastic was that I handed him as he scanned my face suspiciously.

"Watch!" I instructed, even though I knew he couldn't understand English.

On impulse, I tossed the Frisbee high into the jungle air. The boy watched in ore as the plastic carelessly flew across the playground at an almighty speed.

With glee, I giggled as the boy chased after the plastic with such haste; it looked as though his legs could buckle at any moment.

Next in line was a petit young girl who looked to be close to Summer's age.

"Hello…" I bent down to her eye-level.

"I have the perfect present for you – wait here!" I enthusiastically shouted as I headed over to Carl's box and peered inside.

"Yes! They're still here!" I screeched in excitement as I pulled out Summer's skates. *You know, the infant skates that strap over trainers?*

Measuring the girl's tiny feet against the skate, she stared at me slightly bewildered.

"Watch!" I smiled.

With my hand inside the skate, I moved it back-and-forth on the concrete playground to demonstrate what it was, but the girl continued to look towards me confused. She clearly had no idea what I was giving her.

"Jaco!" I shouted across the playground, prompting him to run towards me.

"Can you explain what these are please?"

"I'm not entirely sure I know myself…" he giggled.

"You're kidding me, aren't you?" I teased in disbelief. "They're skates…"

"Oh right!" he analysed them closely, as if looking at them for the first time.

The next child in line was a teenage boy. *Dam!* I felt myself panic. *What could I give him?* He wouldn't want a toy car or bubbles, and all the Frisbees and yoyos had gone. I did have a huge supply of football kits but that wasn't something I could hand out individually.

Consequently, I had no choice but to embarrassingly and reluctantly hand him a packet of bubbles. Expecting a typical teenage expression that said, 'what the hell is this?' remarkably, and to my utter surprise, the boy put both palms into a pray position and bowed his head to 'wai' in thanks, as all the children had done each time we had given them a gift.

"Blimey…" I muttered under my breath.

Was it bad that I was expecting him to be ungrateful? What does that say about the western world? Or me? I thought glumly.

We had been at the school for only 30 minutes and already I could see Summer's confidence growing with every minute that passed.

At one point I looked across to her and with an arm full of pens and pads, she confidently approached a group of four girls each looking to be around 12 or so in age. Appearing incredibly self-assured, she handed each of them a pen and pad. It was crazy to think that 20 minutes prior she was hiding behind my legs!

For a five-year-old it takes a lot of sureness to approach a group of older girls like that, especially without being instructed and with no encouragement from an adult to do so.

A London football team had generously donated a strip to our fundraiser, which included 22 football shirts, tracksuit tops and football socks. I was overjoyed when the boys looked genuinely pleased and excited as they held up the tops and measured them against their chests, shouting "Futbxl!" to one another smiling.

"I take it that means football?" I asked Jaco, feeling humbled by their reaction.

"Yes - and 'Yĕn' means cool, so I think they like it!" he chuckled, observing the repetitive shouting of the word.

Staring towards the playground, I could feel myself feeling rather tearful and overwhelmed with the success of the day. Witnessing the sheer joy on the children's faces was absolutely priceless.

Shelving my thoughts, I suddenly noticed two boys around the age of 14 flicking through one of the children's books they had been given. I kicked myself that I hadn't included any Thai-written teenage books. *I bet they have no idea what they even say?* I thought in frustration. *How could I have not thought of that?*

Happily people-watching, most of the children were talking to each other and comparing what gifts they had been given: some were amusingly even swapping items!

The children were soon dismissed by their teacher so continued to run freely around the playground, but this time clutching their precious gifts.

I couldn't believe it when I saw the teenage boy I had given the bubbles to, running frantically across the playground laughing with his friends as they blew bubbles towards each other.

In the UK, when would you ever see a boy of that age running around genuinely content to be playing with bubbles? It reminded me of the boy at the theme park in Hong Kong who fanned Summer down in the blistering heat.

"K̄hx k̄hxbkhuṇ!" the children shouted towards us as we headed out of the playground towards the back of the school.

"They are shouting 'thank you!'" Jaco translated as we walked across the open space, glancing behind for a final time towards the excited children.

"That was fun Mummy!" Summer swung her stick in the air through happiness.

"I'm glad … more importantly; you did a nice thing, didn't you? Now all those children will have something new to play with!"

"Yep!" she simply responded, continuing to swing her stick as she walked.

Strolling through the grounds, we passed a boy of around eight who was sat bare-chested on a plastic seat whilst his head was shaved by an older man. Witnessing this moment made me feel increasingly uncomfortable - almost as though we were intruding, somehow.

"Why is he getting his hair taken off Mummy?"

Before I even had the slightest chance to respond, Jaco answered for me.

"Buddhist monks shave their heads and beard to show commitment to the Holy Life. As a rule, they should not let their hair grow beyond a certain length of time, so often they shave at least once a fortnight."

"Are you not a monk then?" Summer quizzed, staring intently at Jaco's curly and extremely-long, tangled hair.

"No Summer... I'm afraid not!" He giggled as we passed through the school's gate and back into the overgrown trees and jungle landscape.

With a tiny pathway to walk on, the adjacent drop to the left (which featured a fast-flowing stream) suddenly made the walk rather daunting for amateur walkers such as us.

"We are currently stood at a height of 2,225m," Jaco informed. "This is the highest peak in the area and the third-highest in all of Thailand!"

"Great!" Carl huffed, prompting me to laugh inappropriately.

Standing on the narrow plains of the limestone mountain, I looked out at the spectacular view and took in the sea of fog on the Chiang Dao side. It was truly mesmerising.

It was crazy to think I was experiencing this with a five-year-old in tow... I smiled to myself, consumed only by happy thoughts.

***

Eight:

Embracing my inner Indiana Jones

The walk through the jungle was challenging - it certainly wasn't a well-worn trail and definitely wasn't for the faint-hearted, especially with a five-year-old in tow.

Nevertheless, I tried to embrace my inner Indiana Jones and make light of our surroundings.

Carl's face on the other hand, told an entirely different story and instead looked as though it was frozen in solid-rock.

Not helping himself, he refused to let me take Summer and instead insisted on being in charge.

"Carl, I'm more than capable of taking her!" I repeatedly said.

"I'm stronger than you. I am fine!" He snapped unnecessarily each time.

Not being one for arguing in public, I therefore let him take the reins.

Whilst walking, I continuously stopped in my tracks to either take a photo or record footage on my action camera.

Unsurprisingly, this decision did not go down well with 'Mr Sensible,' who thought it was nothing but 'irresponsible.' Every so often I'd even catch him tutting in disapproval or shooting me an evil stare.

We soon reached a passage where we needed to pull ourselves through the crossing by holding onto passing vines. Needing both hands, I had no choice but to place all my gadgets into the backpack that Carl was carrying.

"Carl, chuck me the camera please! "I shouted after the climb. Complete silence answered me back.

"Carl!" I yelled.

"It is irresponsible Laura!" He glared towards me with a dark, disturbing stare.

"Look at the narrow path and the steep drop to your left!" He shouted. "It's just too dangerous! You can have it back when we are on an even surface!"

"Carl! I am a grown woman! I do not need you to tell me when I can - or cannot - have equipment that I have bought!" I yelled through gritted teeth.

"Yes, you're a grown woman Laura, but you can be incredibly irresponsible at times! Look at your decision to sleep in the wild with kangaroos! Do you know how many people die climbing Kilimanjaro a year? Now..." he paused at my muddled expression.

"I admit... this doesn't have a patch on that mountain, but my point is..."

"Your point is redundant as this isn't Killy!" I screamed with a built-up of heartfelt frustration. *So much for not arguing in public...*

"You're correct!" he puffed.

"This is not Kilimanjaro, but reliable sources estimate that between three and seven deaths occur each year on that mountain! Now...I acknowledge, the deaths are not all down to falling at a great height... some are caused by hypothermia and malaria, but my point is..."

"Carl!" I shouted, completely vexed by his annoying tone. "ENOUGH!"

"Laura - when you look back on this you will thank me."

I shot him a deathly, lingering stare that spoke volumes.

"How so?" I spun to face him.

"Because the risk of you falling to capture that 'must-have' image" ... he idiotically used his index fingers to create air quote-marks. "Is incredibly high... so you could say that I'm essentially saving your life!"

"Oh, for goodness sake!" I gasped, hunching my shoulders and stomping through the jungle, suddenly feeling more like a sulky teenager than a mature twenty-nine-year-old mother.

It didn't take long for the tension between us to become obdurate and no-doubt rather obvious to Jaco and his walking buddy.

There were plenty of awkward silences and huffing and puffing on my part. Nonetheless, I continued to power through the vast jungle in frustrated silence.

Although it was just over 30 degrees, the jungle was shaded which made the soaring temperature unusually bearable. Unfortunately, we didn't have the luxury of growing used to our surroundings as the landscape seemed to continuously change; sometimes we were at great height and other occasions low to the stream.

It certainly made the hike interesting, especially when we had to cross large, wet stones as well as mud. Some of the plants we were pushing our way through towered over Summer's miniscule height, so it was a strenuous walk for all of us.

Walking alongside the stream, you could suddenly hear the flow of the water rapidly picking up pace. Venturing further, Jaco and his friend wasted no time stomping through the knee-deep water as they crossed over large wet rocks that sat beneath the fast-flowing creek.

What struck me was that both men were walking through the river oblivious to the fact that we had clearly not done the hike before; we had a young child with us and we were not wearing wellington boots as they were. We were instead wearing impractical Converse, and the following day would be embarking a 27-hour journey across Thailand in those very shoes! The prospect, therefore, of continuing the hike and doing the following day's journey in wet footwear was for obvious reasons not ideal.

After a quick evaluation, I said to Carl that maybe we shouldn't continue with the hike to the waterfall after all, and instead we should head back to the tree house. Deep down I was gutted that we wouldn't see the waterfall, but with the stride of the river rapidly picking up pace suddenly the hike didn't feel as safe as it had earlier.

Although I am a laid-back person (and I was making light of the situation previously,) I did have Summer to think about. We'd only been hiking for an hour and already we were struggling to keep up; so, the prospect of continuing for another two-hours with not really knowing our exact location, or who Jaco and his friend were, suddenly made me re-evaluate the entire situation and not feel as carefree as I once did.

"Finally! Shame it took you so long to realise!" Carl hissed.

As we headed back, Jaco asked if we would like to go to his house as it was close to the tree house. He explained that it was a temporary shelter as he was building a permanent home elsewhere.

"There is even a shallow stream that Summer can play in," he smiled.

"Sounds perfect!" I thanked him for his kind offer.

"This is a parasitic flower." Jaco crouched down next to a weird-looking bud on-route to his house.

"Its survival tactic is it attach itself to vines before gradually zapping the life from them, so over-time they're literally starved to death. It takes nine months for them to then blossom - only for them to die four days later…"

"Pretty pointless task if you ask me!" Carl chuckled.

"But look how beautiful it is whilst it's in bloom!" Jaco tenderly caressed the leaves with his fingertips.

I admit the flower was striking. Nevertheless, it looked more like a star fish and was by far the oddest-looking bloom I'd ever seen!

"Summer: do you know what a parasite is?" Jaco asked, still crouching beside the plant.

"No!" Summer shook her head blankly.

"All living things need animals or plants as their food - agreed?"

"Yes!" Summer smiled broadly, looking immensely proud of herself for understanding the basic principle of this.

"Animals constantly go in search of food. But plants remain fixed in one place." Jaco tugged at the root of a neighbouring plant, imposing Summer to intriguingly bend down and analysis it closely.

"Some plants make their own food by using energy from the sunlight, but others
are unable to produce food so need to feed on other plants for survival. These particular plants are called parasites.''

"Can I take a picture of the parasite plant Mummy?" Summer stood to her feet.

"Of course!" I smiled.

"Carl, the camera please!" I said with attitude despite smiling. *Hu! Now you have to give me my camera back!*

A while later and we approached a landscape of dense, bamboo forest.

Patting my wet sweaty brow and sighing out loud, Jaco spun to face us. With his arms stretched wide and a broad smile to match, he shouted: "This is where I will be building my new house!" just as an excited child would when showing off the den they'd just made under the family dining table.

Jaco looked incredibly proud as he pointed to a part of the jungle that appeared to look no different to any other part we had already trekked through.

When Jaco said he was building a house, I assumed he had already started it. *How did he even remember where his plot was?* I glanced around at the empty land.

Staring through the trees, I heard a rustling noise in the bush. Completely startling me, out of nowhere John unexpectedly appeared.

"Where did you come from?" I snorted as he squeezed his muscular body through the overgrown bush.

"You're next to the tree house and I heard you guys talking."

"It all looks the same to us!" Summer laughed, making everyone erupt into fits of giggles at her wit at just five-years-old.

With John now in tow, we continued down the steep hill to where Jaco's temporary house resided.

His house was behind a picturesque stream that had planks of bamboo that were nailed together resting across.

Proudly spanning the bridge first, Jaco was greeted by two yapping dogs whose ear-piercing barks noisily warned of our presence; impelling a pretty, young lady to emerge from inside the house. This beauty turned out to be Jaco's extremely young and heavily pregnant wife who appeared to be in her 30s, despite Jaco being in his mid 50s.

Holding hands with Summer as we cautiously followed across the bridge, a galaxy of dragonflies fizzed through the beams of light in the magical space between the water and the air, leaving the mysteriousness of the place reminding me of nothing other than a Disney movie.

We greeted Jaco's wife politely, but as she couldn't understand English she smiled warmly, eagerly waving in our direction.

"My wife is very good at Thai spa," Jaco leaned in close, proud-as-punch.

"She does them for all the tree house guests. Would you like her to visit you later for one?"

I didn't really know what the spa entailed or how much it was, but I didn't want to look rude so in that very conservative British-way that you do: I reluctantly agreed.

The temporary house was simple but effective. The building was made of wood and the roof from corrugated iron. I was genuinely impressed at how the people in the village created houses out of the most basic of materials.

Barking uncontrollably, one of the dogs excitedly jumped up at Summer's chest. Within seconds she burst into a dramatic flood of tears, frantically crying that she wanted to return to the tree house.

"I just want to go back!" Her voice exaggeratedly echoed through the trees, punctuated by the occasional snort.

"Summer! Calm down now!" I shouted with authority; grabbing her arm and leading her away from the group and into a neighbouring bush.

"No! I want to go home!" She continued to yell melodramatically whilst tears cascaded down her now-puffy, slightly-tear-stained face.

"We're not going back, so I suggest that you calm down and be quiet right now!" I raised my tone in sudden embarrassment by her 'drama queen' outburst.

"We are in Jaco's house and the way that you're behaving is incredibly rude!" I hissed, inciting her to cross her arms and in a stubborn, powerful pose, she stormed off towards the bridge.

Just as I was about to follow, Carl swiftly appeared by my side.

"I don't mean to tell you how to 'suck eggs'" he air quoted.

"But it won't stop you will it Carl?" I crossed both my eyes and arms and raised my eyebrows in an accusing tone.

"Tantrums are a cry for attention and I'm sure you will agree that they're both a disruptive and a wholly-inappropriate way to seek an audience. When my girls were young myself and my wife set a precedent that we would always treat tantrums with some 'alone' time. This has taught both girls that 'throwing a tantrum'" he air quoted once more. "Is the fastest way to get ignored. Both girls now often voice their displeasure, but they do not throw tantrums or act up in order to do so. Instead they simply react to discontent with thoughtful discussion..."

I was so stunned by his shocking-speech that for a second, I couldn't fathom any words to respond with. Alternatively, I chose to hold his gaze in an aloof way. Then I bit...

"Carl - I don't mean to be rude, but you're not exactly a 'hands on' dad, are you?" I sarcastically and rather cruelly air quoted back, shamefully stooping to his immature level.

"I appreciate that your wife moved both girls far away so that is of no fault of your own, but being there every day compared to once every few months is a different thing altogether." I stormed off at the speed of lightening towards Summer, not even bothering to wait for his response.

The kinder side of my personality was cursing my cruel words - but it needed to be said.

Sensing tension in the air, John shouted from the distance to ask if we would like to go to the bar.

"The bar?" I bellowed back, confused.

"Come on!" He gestured for us to follow.

Walking through the passing trees, I tried my best to distract Summer by being playful. A pointless exercise, nevertheless, as she continued behaving in a spoilt fashion, irritating me further as it was the first time she'd behaved in such a way since we'd been away.

Glancing through the trees, I was astounded by what I could see. With all the hiking I'd endured, the bar simply loomed in front of me like a jewel on the top of a mountain's peak.

Inside the most extraordinary bar I'd ever experienced, sat wooden shelves full of glass bottles of various concoctions, and two bar stools that were perched against a wooden breakfast bar. There was even a wooden stage where a guitar sat in anticipation of its jungle punters…and all inside a tropical forest, nonetheless.

"Beer?" John hollered from behind the bar.

Whilst Carl and I perched on a stall, John occupied Summer by setting her the important task of drawing one of the many cats that the bar unusually occupied.

I'm not usually a beer drinker but as that was all that was on offer, I wasn't going to decline. For the first-time ever, the Chang beer went down mouth-wateringly well. At six per cent alcohol, the fizz was much stronger then Western beers; combined with the heat and dehydration that I was experiencing, the fizz instantly made my head feel fuzzy. *Drunk in the jungle, ay? What an interesting prospect…*

As I drank, Jaco told me that Dao (the district name of the jungle) meant 'star' in Thai.

"The mountains are at such a height that they're practically on the same level as the stars themselves," he insightfully explained.

"That's beautiful!" I sipped my beer peacefully.

"This place is astonishing – I just don't know how you remember your way around. It's like a gigantic maze!"

"Well this district of forest extends all the way to the Burmese border. If you can spare a few days, you can actually venture into our neighbouring country of Burma! John - you have done the trek to Burma haven't you?"

"I have indeed! The Burmese tour starts about seven hours north of here in a remote village called Mae Sot, in the west of Thailand. Mae Sot is unlike any place I've ever visited before and would have been remarkable for you guys to experience!"

"Really? In what way?" I took another sip of Chang, suddenly intrigued.

"It's untouched by tourism and one of the most culturally diverse places that I've ever had the pleasure of visiting.

"As you casually walk down the road you find yourself mesmerised by a mixture of bearded Muslims, Thai army rangers, Burmese men in sarongs; Hmong and Karen women in traditional hill-tribe dress - and foreign NGO workers. Where else in the world would you see such a collective mixture of people in one place?" he asked.

"Even the shop signs are in Thai, Burmese and Chinese - it's so ethically-diverse!"

"Oh...how irritating that we don't have extra time when we're so incredibly close." I shrugged in frustration, staring thoughtfully towards my drink.

"The trek takes you through the jungle and passes through other small villages, before rafting down the Umphang River - which is simply stunning! Then, whilst rafting you pass through waterfalls, areas of tropical rainforest and majestic caves! Honestly, it is such an adventure!"

"John - what are you doing to me? That sounds incredible!"

"It is!" he unhelpfully responded, before continuing to ramble about how 'marvellous' the trek was and 'what a shame it was that we couldn't embark on it ourselves.'

"You then camp in Thi Lo Su National Park, before touching down in Burma the next day. On the border, you get to visit a cascade of unforgettable waterfalls that are all set at various heights – the tallest being 300 metres, which is the highest in Southeast Asia!"

"Thank god we're not doing that then!" Carl muttered under his breath.

"This is the downside to a trip like ours," I explained to John, ignoring Carl's insensitive and selfish comment.

"We only have a set time off work so we are restricted by a timetable. It would have been nice to have suddenly travelled to Burma on a whim. But we have such a tight schedule already and have flights and accommodation booked."

"Ahh, I understand – next time!"

"Yes, next time!" I repeated his words, knowing that there most likely wouldn't be a 'next time.' *It wasn't easy to embark on a trip like this! I had to put my entire life on hold for three years to save for these precious weeks…*

Our conversation was soon interrupted by Jaco's wife, who thoughtfully brought over a dish of fried rice, served with pineapple that was wrapped in banana leaves.

"Help yourself!" Jaco proudly offered as he passed the dish around.

After several mouthfuls, I left a miniscule amount of rice on my plate and instead quietly finished my beer.

"Laura," John leaned in closely.

"Rice is difficult to grow, harvest, and is an essential ingredient in Thailand. It is for this reason that it is considered impolite and disrespectful to leave leftovers on your plate – even if it is a small amount. Sorry to ask – and if you don't mind of course, but could you eat the last of your rice before Jaco sees!"

"Oh," I looked towards him blankly. I wasn't entirely sure if he was joking or not.

"Are you being serious or is that a joke?" I quizzed at his silence and grave expression.

"No! I'm being serious!" He said with straight-eyes.

"Oh right…no problem at all!" I uncomfortably muttered into the faint, jungle air, before pulling my plate back in front of my stomach and scooping the remainder of the rice into my mouth at lightning speed.

"The guide books must have left that fact out!" I awkwardly laughed in-between bites.

"Well being married to a Thai, I learn new rules every day!" he giggled, before walking over to Carl and leaving me with my own thoughts for company.

Anxiously chewing the last of my rice, I overheard a snippet of John and Carl's conversation, which bizarrely seemed to be littered with the C words: children, credit crunch and catchment areas. The conversation soon moved onto politics and a debate about Thailand and the UK and how certain processes worked. It was all very doom and gloom middle-class neurosis - much like a David Hare play - but in such a bizarre setting…the middle of the jungle, nonetheless!

The conversation thankfully moved away from politics and onto a topic I felt much more familiar with - alcohol.

"If you like whisky - then you'll love this!" John jumped up from the stall he was perched at and immediately began pouring several shots of whisky from an unbranded bottle that looked as though it had seen better days.

"It's a local whisky that is made from rice." He pushed the shot glass towards me and, along with Jaco, downed his shot in one.

Being the impulsive person that I am, I followed suit in swallowing my shot in one. Unlike Carl who refused because he was "in the middle of a jungle with strangers who in reality were piling him with alcohol!" He later told me.

"A branded bottle of beer was one thing," he explained, "but an unknown local whisky? There is no chance I'm drinking that!" He winced when I queried why he didn't drink his shot like the rest of us.

Whereas me? I'm a person that endlessly strives to try something new and make an experience out of most situations - of course I was going to try the whisky!

Knocking the liquid to the back of my throat, the sharp taste of the malted grain combined with the soaring Thai heat hit my tonsils like a charged electrical bolt. It tasted unusually similar to that of rum, but with a hint of vanilla, herbs, citrus and oddly - toffee.

***

It was 7pm and thankfully time for dinner.

I hoped that we would be served something a little more substantial than rice for this meal. Mercifully, I certainly wasn't disappointed when endless plates of delicious dishes were placed in front of us. I literally wolfed the food down like an excited child devouring Cadbury's chocolate.

My tastebuds ignited at the pumpkin stir fry, along with the homemade chicken nuggets that were the best nuggets I had ever tasted - so much so that we polished off two plates! The satay chicken and homemade peanut dip was mouth-wateringly flavoursome and by far the tastiest satay I'd ever experienced.

Feeling satisfied, the atmosphere around the table was very comfortable. I didn't feel as though we were eating with strangers at all.

Summer and Ubon laughed and drew pictures as they ate; and thanks to John acting as the translator we were all able to participate in small talk across the table as we shared an entourage of dishes laid in from of us like an Italian family at supper time.

Even though we couldn't converse in the same language, we all laughed in sync at the same joke which created an atmosphere I found totally absorbing.

After dinner, Jaco and his wife soon arrived and asked if I was ready for my Thai spa. My feet were placed into a bucket of warm, herbal water whilst bamboo charcoal was smeared across my face.

Sipping a cup of herbal tea and sitting alone for 10 minutes, I watched Carl and Summer from a distance; they were chatting and laughing with John, Jaco and his wife; the owners, the cooks and Ubon.

Having a total out-of-body experience, I studied the scene before me and found it rather surreal. Here we were in the middle of a jungle staying with a bunch of people that spoke very little English (if any) yet despite the language barrier, you could still hear a room full of happy chatter and laughter.

This is what backpacking is about! Taking yourself out of our comfort zone and truly embracing other cultures… I smiled to myself.

Glancing lovingly towards Summer, I couldn't help but beam. Considering she didn't know anyone in the room, spoke a different language to the majority and had found herself in a tree house in the middle of the jungle, she had totally adapted to her surroundings. Blending into her environment, she was simply getting on with her day as she would any other. I was so proud of the person that she was already becoming.

Sitting alone, I considered my life at home. Like 99 per cent of the western world it was continuously dominated by the words 'rush, rush, rush'…with nagging to do lists governing even the supposed Sabbath day of rest.

Over the years, my life has been complicated and generally less romantic then the Disney films I expected it to mirror when I was a naïve adolescent wishing to grow older. Sitting for those 10 minutes allowed me the opportunity to take time-out to truly reflect – which was the most basic thing that I admit; I did little of at home.

After a joyous 10 minutes of 'thinking,' I was soon instructed to wash the charcoal from my face and apply a cleansing gel to eliminate any dirty skin that remained.

After cleansing, I walked down the open-aired staircase and for the first time noticed how dark it had become. The lingering light that was previously in attendance had quickly been taken over by the falling night sky. *How long had I been in the bathroom?*

Reaching the bottom of the staircase, Jaco's wife was sitting in the now-dark corner on a yoga mat praying. Unsure if to intrude, I stood frozen on the spot as I bit my lip and pondered my next action.

Lying flat on the floor several minutes later, I closed my eyes and exhaled deeply. *Time to relax…*

My face and head were massaged with soothing sesame seed oil and I started to semi-relax, but having Ubon and Summer chasing each other as they laughed and shouted carelessly in their own languages inches from my head, ruined it somewhat.

Attempting to unwind was once again short-lived when the children began running up the stairs, making my heart skip a beat because of the steep drop and darkness surrounding them.

The thunder-clapping of their feet on the stairs echoed in surround-sound through my ears. I blinked rapidly, eyelids flapping at a rate that matched my increasing heart rate.

I felt as though I was continuously calling-out asking the children to stay downstairs. *It didn't take long for no me-time to kick back in…* I breathed in and exhaled a large sigh.

Immediately after the 'spa,' I placed a blanket in front of the open fire and lay peacefully on the floor doodling pictures with the children.

The night sky was so dark that you could no longer view the jungle over the edge of the house; in fact it was as if a black wall was pushed against the bamboo's edge.

Whilst colouring, every so often I stopped and daydreamed as I observed the orange flames from the fire come to life. The blaze seemed to form a wild, flickering dance that projected shadows and hopped onto the furniture surrounding us; twisting and curling in obscure shapes before my mesmerised eyes. *This house has the same romantic feel as a castaway's shack on a desert island…* I dreamily thought.

Watching the fire gave me as much escapism as what a good book does, and the wilderness of the night actually resurfaced memories of an evening I had spent on a cattle ranch on the east-coast of Australia.

I fondly remembered the grandma of the head cowboy dishing out her legendary pumpkin soup as we danced around a fire in leather, brown cowboy hats. Reminiscing further, I remembered breaking away from the dancing and sitting around an adjacent fire, swapping tales with fellow travellers about how we had ended up at the ranch. The next day some treated the stay as a pit stop and left the ranch as I did, whereas others opted to stay on and work.

The memory made me think about John's story of trekking to Burma, and I instantly felt rattled that I was restricted by a timetable. *If only I could have got longer off work?* Or better still, just say 'to heck with it' and return to England when I truly wanted to.

I rubbed my head in frustration as I stared into the distance with endless possibilities flashing before my eyes. Unfurling like a rehydrated flower, for once my mind was free from the usual buzz and whirr of things to do and things left undone…*could I just forget my life at home and return home when I actually wanted to?*

***

"Anyone for a game of Jenga?" I casually asked whilst Carl, John and Summer sat chatting.

"What's Jenga?"

"Oh John! You have clearly lived in Asia for too long my friend!" I teased.

"Rubes, will you show John how to play Jenga? You can be his teacher!"

"Yes!" Summer punched the air, instantly giddy at the prospect.

By 9pm, we had all played our traditional travelling game of Jenga, and Summer enjoyed colouring in a wooden Jenga brick to represent the tree house stay.

The moon had now taken complete residence over the tree house and the darkness of the night swamped the property; broken only by the light of the fire and the mosquito-repellent candles that were dotted erratically around the lounge.

With blankets and pillows nestled on the chairs, I lined six pillows into a square on the floor and made Summer a bed by the fire.

As I lay side-by-side with my daughter, Carl and John sat at the neighbouring table chatting about life.

The relaxed atmosphere meant it didn't take long for Summer to fall into a deep sleep, allowing me to drink yet another Chang with the boys as we chatted endlessly about our dreamlike location.

"It's great that she sleeps anywhere!" John complimented as Summer snored on the floor next to us; Duffy bear firmly tucked under her arm.

"Well that's travelling for you!" I swallowed a large gulp of ice-cold beer."They learn to sleep anywhere!"

***

It was 10.30pm when John decided to hit the sack, leaving Carl and I chatting alone in the deserted tree house.

"When you were having your spa earlier, Jaco told me that it has taken him over four years to save to build his house, and he still hasn't got enough money!" Carl announced.

"He's an artist by trade but is working as John's guide because his paintings aren't consistently making enough money. He said it's going to take him a long time to save enough for the construction. He confided that he's worried about the baby being at his current house as the roof is leaking and the place is falling apart."

"I'm surprised that you believe him, what with your conspiracy theories about the poor people in the city?" I frowned.

"There's something different about him. I really like the guy. He is 100 per cent legit, I'm sure of it!" He took a sip of his drink, watching the fire.

Before I left the UK my sister-in-law's dad, Tony, had given me £50 and told me to use the money as I wished whilst we were away. I reluctantly took the cash but told him that I wouldn't spend it on myself and would instead use it towards whatever I saw fit whilst we were away.

"Shall we give Jaco some money towards his house?"

I watched as Carl's mouth turned down at the edges and he raised his eyebrows in sync.

"You want to give away more money?" He exaggeratedly giggled, whilst staring at me intently with an accusing, yet questioning look.

"What?" I shrieked.

"I'm only joking - that's what I was going to suggest actually!" he unexpectedly announced.

We didn't have a huge amount of money in our joint travelling account, and I had worked out a daily budget for the trip. However, it felt morally right to give Jaco Tony's money, and I wanted to make a difference somehow to his savings.

"My suggestion is that we use Tony's £50, plus give Jaco £50 from our own money."

"Sounds good!" Carl nodded, taking another sip of beer. "I will give it to him as the donation might be better coming from a man."

"If you say so!" I blew air out of my nostrils at his 1940s way of thinking.

***

At sunrise the next morning I sleepily opened my eyes and rolled onto my side. The room was illuminated by the bright rays that happily streamed through the cracks in the bamboo walls.

With the morning's silence engulfing the house, I peered through the cracks and absorbed the mountains that surrounded the tree house. It was incredibly peaceful as I intently listened to the sound of the birds chirping, along with the tree frogs that resembled the beeping sound of a digital camera.

Up and dressed, we later headed downstairs and sat on the now-familiar family dining table. At 7.30am and for what seemed like the longest moment, the three of us were motionless staring at each other in disbelief at the spread of food that had been prepared for us. With dishes that included noodles and chicken, at 7.30am it was a feast to say the least.

"Mummy - this is dinner food!" Summer implored with a small frown.

"Just eat!" I gave my daughter a darting look about her rudeness.

I admit, I found it difficult to eat noodles and chicken that early in the morning too, but I swallowed hard in fear of looking impolite.

After breakfast, the children took it in turns to swing each other on the hammocks that swung from the open-aired living room.

As I watched my daughter squeal with delight, I laughed at her excitement.

"Summer looks as happy as I would be if I saw a flash of Tiffany blue or Hermes orange right about now." I laughed to Carl as the two of us watched the children playing joyfully.

"What's Tiffany blue or Hermes orange?" muttered Carl with a confused look.

"Really? God our worlds are far apart." I giggled at my girly nature.

I couldn't remember the last time I had sat in a hammock. Amusing myself, I climbed into the adjacent piece of material that hung from the bamboo beam and squealed like an energized child as the kids pushed me with delight.

"Laura, I think we better start packing up." Carl yelled from the top of the stairs several minutes later, interrupting my child-like swinging.

"Summer, can you come with me please?" I stood to my feet.

"Why? I'm having fun!" she sulked.

"I know but I need to keep you in sight because of the low walls, so come on!"

Whilst packing, we heard an almighty bang and the sound of Ubon screaming in pain. On instinct, I immediately threw down the clothes I was holding and ran to the balcony to see that Ubon had fallen from the hammock and landed on the hard, unforgiving, wooden floor.

The fall obviously hurt and her tiny face was instantly stained and puffy from the steam of tears that were tumbling like a gushing waterfall from her delicate lashes.

As she struggled to breath in-between her sobs, I quickly made my way from the balcony to the stairs to console her. Stopping immediately in my tracks, I suddenly noticed the silhouette of her mother in the corner of the room.

Expecting her mother to pick her up and console, I watched as she instead yelled something to her in Thai. Slowly, Ubon raised herself from the floor and sat on the neighbouring bench as she sobbed in isolation.

Instantly feeling awkward about going to her rescue (not wanting to tread on her mother's toes by interfering,) I reluctantly headed back to our room.

"Is Ubon ok?" Both Carl and Summer asked as I approached.

I told Carl about what I'd seen and how shocked I was that her mother hadn't given her any affection to stop her tears.

"You remember what the guide book says - in Asia the children are taught to not show emotion. Why do you think they're all so tough? That's obviously their way of doing it."

Sighing out loud, I walked back to the balcony and looked down to where Ubon was still sobbing on the bench under the watchful eye of her mother. I still felt awkward about going over, but I equally felt wretched leaving her to cry.

"Summer - why don't you go and play with Ubon and check she's ok?"

"But I thought…"

"I know what I said but I'll be down in a second. Go and cheer her up!" I smiled.

Summer needed no convincing and immediately threw down the pile of clothes that she was holding and ran down the stairs as if her life depended on it.

"Walk - don't run!" I shouted.

A few minutes later and as I looked at the girls from the balcony above, I noticed Summer had her arm firmly around Ubon's shoulders comforting her.

*This was the start of Summer's great journey of independence as a human in this world...*I couldn't help thinking as a grin stretched across my face.

Just before we were about to leave, Jaco and his wife came to the house to say their goodbyes. We had 20 minutes to wait until John was to take us back to the city so I decided to take respite at the family dining table.

Despite obsessively covering my legs with backpacker harem pants for the entire time I'd been in the jungle, my legs burned and itched from the mosquito bites that had now taken residency on my legs. I couldn't help but scratch as hard as a coin on a scratch card at the pain that was constantly niggling away.

Jaco took a seat on the bench next to me.

"Are you ok?"

"My legs are killing me!" I rolled up my left trouser leg to reveal several rather-large red bites.

"They continue right up my thighs... I don't know why I have so many as I have worn pants the entire time I have been here!" I complained.

Without saying a word Jaco walked to the corner of the room where his wife had given me the spa the evening before, fetching a bottle from the shelf.

"I have something for you..." he passed me the bottle.

"It's a herbal cream that my wife made – It's very good! You need to apply it to your bites several times a day to stop the itching."

"Thank you, that's great! How much do I owe you?"

"Nothing!" he touched my shoulder; standing to his feet, he picking up my heavy backpack and kindly carried it to the 4x4.

We still hadn't given Jaco the money. I hoped that Carl would take the opportunity of it being just the two of them outside to give it to him.

"Summer!" I yelled some 10 minutes later.

"We are leaving now so come and sit on the toilet before we go..."

As we ventured to the toilet, Jaco took me completely by surprise by running towards me and placing a cotton painting into the palms of my hands.

"This is a present for you, Carl and Summer to say thank you for the kind gesture," he smiled.

I grinned as I absorbed the painting in my hands.

It was A4 in size, bright orange and displayed an image of a Thai god in black.

I was so speechless that I simply smiled and wai'd in acceptance.

Walking towards John's 4x4, Ubon, her mother; Jaco and his wife walked to the top of the dirt-lined road to wave us off.

"Nanny June said to give a bracelet to any friends I make on the trip - so here you go Ubon!" Summer excitedly placed the pink-and-purple beaded bracelet onto her new friend's wrist.

Despite them not speaking a word of each other's language, they had become friends, and to my delight had done nothing but laugh since the moment they had met.

Whilst driving to the city's airport, I sat in silence whilst gazing intently out of the window.

Smiling broadly, a sense of wonderment, adventure and exploration ran through my veins, exciting me about the next stage of the trip and what was to come. The trip was certainly touching us all in different ways, which was exactly what I hoped to achieve on this epic journey across Asia.

***

Nine:

27-hour cross-country slog

A few hours after leaving the tree house, we had found ourselves on yet another flight; this time we were heading to Bangkok to catch the sleeper train to the south islands of Thailand.

Mid-flight, I got chatting to a couple who (along with their three children) were moving from Nottingham in the UK to Asia.

The couple explained that they were moving to a remote area to undertake the challenge of writing an official language. (The region they were relocating to didn't have a written communication system.) *Cue - eyebrow raise!*

Nevertheless, with their three children in tow they were relocating to a remote area in Asia for three-years. The couple looked no older than 35 and their youngest child was barely out of nappies. They explained how they were travelling around Asia for four weeks to see the continent before they settled.

I couldn't help but think about how courageous they were. Their children would not only miss out on a free, western education, but they were voluntary uprooting themselves into a dearth town in Asia for three years! Volunteering for a month or two is one thing, but several years with three kids in tow - that takes some balls!

The flight was cramped, chilly from the air conditioning and slightly claustrophobic. *How had air travel become like a marathon bus ride? Where was the glamour?* I pulled my blanket (essentially a lump of fibre that was held together by static, therefore passing the test for a blanket) around my shoulders, drained the last of my coffee and leaned back into the compact, aircraft chair.

Glancing around the cabin, I thought about the variety of reasons that people decide to escape the 9-5 rat race and travel the world with only a backpack to their name. I had certainly heard a multitude of stories on my travels, that was for sure! *But moving an entire young family to write a language? Wow!*

"Look Mummy!" Summer elatedly pointed out of the small-oval window to what looked like a toy-town of sculptured Scalextric below. In unison, we squealed in a fever-pitch of excitement, attracting several stares from inside the cosy cabin.

"This looks so cool Mummy!"

And it really did…

***

After landing at Don Mueang International airport, we bought a train ticket to central Hualamphong train station to get our sleeper train to the south islands of Thailand.

"I can't believe that the ticket only cost 50p for an hour-long journey! How crazy is that?" I nudged Carl in disbelief, eye-balling the cardboard ticket in complete astonishment.

I watched as an anxious and troubled expression carpeted his face, causing me to break into a fit of inappropriate giggles.

"Hmmm…" accompanied by a sideways glimpse, was all he could respond to my childishness.

With 15 minutes until our departure time and no benches to sit on, we once again transferred our backpacks into temporary floor cushions. Only this time Carl showed no hesitation in joining us - much to my hilarity.

Squinting and sweating buckets by the sun's blazing hot rays, several men (wearing what looked to be military uniforms) held guns and patrolled the platform with great authority. Every so often I would even catch one staring chillingly in our direction.

I don't know what sort of train I was expecting in Bangkok (at a mere 50p a journey) but the one that arrived resembled a 1960's slam-door train.

I watched as Carl's mouth flung open in exasperation...

Inside, all I could see was an endless bed of silver... with the chairs, rails and doors all stainless steel, clinical looking and insanely unwelcoming.

Plonking ourselves into a bay, I instantly felt as though I was perched in a hot and sweaty tin can. *Still! It was all very exciting! Travelling like a local and all...*

Minutes ticking by, I could feel the abundance of stares from those surrounding us. This made me increasingly aware that we were the only westerners on-board.

"This must be cattle class - that's why it was so cheap!" Carl irritatingly whined into my ear.

"Who cares? That's what this trip is all about! Actually, travelling with the locals - not sitting in first class!" I grumbled, animating my mischievous face into an expression of childlike amazement.

As I spoke, I noticed a Thai teenage boy (who looked poster-boy handsome and around only 15 years of age) staring attentively in our direction.

Despite sitting on the furthest seat from us, I watched as the boy strained his neck to sneak a peak in our direction. After several minutes, I realised that for the first time since we had been away the boy wasn't staring at Summer- and was instead staring at me! Every so often, the boy moved seats further up the carriage and headed closer to where we were sat.

"Watch that kid behind me! He keeps moving closer and is staring at you." Carl barked with a protected look across his face.

I knew that Carl was an investigator, but it certainly amazed me that he had even noticed the boy as his back was facing him.

Since being in Asia, Carl had suffered with bad tummy pains and we were not sure what was causing them as we had all been eating the same foods and Summer and I were fine.

I assumed it was because his stomach didn't take too well to the Asian dishes and extra spice like ours had. I joked that he was a 'little Englander' and not as well travelled as myself, which was a joke his dry sense of humour clearly couldn't fathom.

Throughout the journey, my travel companion continued to groan about how sick he felt, the basic train I had booked and the driver's terrible breaking.

I admit the train did feel like a roller coaster because of the driver's constant sharp breaking. The sun bouncing off the windows and reflecting onto our faces wasn't helping either; not to mention the lack of air con. *We were backpacking - what did he expect?*

Nonetheless, it appeared as though it was all too much for him and in that moment in time Carl had truly had enough.

We had only been away for three-weeks, but it felt as though it had been several months because of the never-ending multitude of experiences we had already participated in.

It had been a long day, what with the two-hour drive to the airport, the hour and a half wait for the flight; plus the hour flying time. I feared that if Carl was in low-spirits already, then he would be a nightmare by the time the 27-hour journey across the country was done.

I watched with amusement as the teenage boy pulled out an I Phone and (like most people in Asia), checked his reflection. With stance, he proudly stood to his feet and picked up his bag. It was for this very reason that I assumed he was getting off at the next stop. Rather oddly, the boy instead travelled further down the carriage and loitered uneasily around our seats. I shuffled on the bench, eyes twinkling with interest at his next move.

When the train came to a rapid-halt the boy continued to loiter before peering his tiny head out of the speedy train's window.

Eyeballs expanding by the second, I gasped in horror…

"I have a really bad feeling that his head is going to get chopped off by a passing train!" I leaned in and whispered to Carl, whose response was to raise his eyebrows and sigh a heavy breath.

I thought he was about to tell me that I was being melodramatic, but instead he simply said: "Well it could happen…"

I blanched in fear. After a few shallow breaths I then spent the next few minutes mentally pleading with the boy to put his head back in the carriage.

A lady in a triangular bamboo hat thankfully broke my thoughts in half when she entered the sweaty tin-can carriage.

"You like spicy rice?" she leaned over us as she spoke.

Looking around 50 in age (and slightly dirty-looking,) the lady held a tray that was strapped to her neck and contained lots of tiny pots of rice, each sporting a single piece of cling film as its lid.

"No thank you…" I smiled. With no sales, the lady vacated the carriage but left the smell of spicy rice lingering in the air behind her.

I looked out of the window…the glass was cool on my finger tips even if the heat was scorching.

"Right! I need to get off this train at the next stop!" Carl yelped, jumping out of his seat so fast it was as if he'd been sat on razor-sharp pins.

"I can't handle that smell as well as the constant breaking Laura! We can get a taxi the rest of the way."

"I appreciate that you feel unwell Carl…" I tried to reason. "But we have been on the train for what feels like forever - so we must nearly be there. Getting off is totally pointless and a complete waste of money!" I felt my frustration levels reach boiling point. "And another thing…" I added. *I was the one on one now…*

"This is what the trip is about: actually travelling with locals and seeing the real Thailand." I threw my hands in the air in utter vexation.

Carl's response was to fixatedly stare at the teenage boy instead of acknowledging my words. *Was I speaking in another language? How rude!*

I guessed the boy's behaviour was putting him further on edge as he still hadn't sat down, and was continuing to gawp out of the window he was now perched at.

Over the passing minutes, I watched as Carl's left leg bobbed up-and-down and he constantly itched his ears and head. Clearly, he was irritated...

A familiar feeling started to build up in my stomach... *Why does he have to behave like this and ruin the 'experience' all the time?* I exhaled, totally lost in thought.

"What's wrong?" Carl unexpectedly asked. *Since when did he care how I felt?*

In all honesty, I was totally exhausted by his behaviour...

'My head feels fuzzy and full of the cotton wool that you continue to wrap us in!' I wanted to shout; but to keep the peace I instead muttered: "I'm just tired." And yawned for theatrical effect.

"I really don't like that boy's body language." Carl immediately reverted to his typical cynical self.

"Oh take-a-chill-pill! I'm sure he doesn't mean any harm!" I rolled my eyes in irritation.

Body remaining frozen, Carl's face abruptly studied my expression. It was as if he was trying to decide whether to respond or not.

"You will never learn, will you..."

Darting him a hard stare, I snorted a loud, heavy groan and glanced out of the window.

Moments later and the train came to an almighty holt, forcing Carl out of his seat without a moment to spare.

"Come on - let's go!" he yelled, flinging his heavy backpack over his bony shoulder and fiercely grabbing Summer's bag.

I exhaled in an over-exaggerated fashion and stood to my feet with sudden purpose. Flinging my own backpack over my achy shoulder, I protectively grabbed Summer's hand and headed towards Carl.

Yanking the door of the train wide-open, Carl spun to face me totally dumbstruck. Now *what was his problem?*

Peering over the door for a glimpse, an unimpressive dirt track was standing in the place of what would usually be a concentrate platform.

Ridiculously confused, we stared at the hordes of people that descended from the neighbouring carriage without a care in the world.

"It must be a legit stop if they're getting off!" Carl spun to face me.

"What – so it just has no concrete platform? Well - I'm not getting off onto a line Carl!" I grunted, before sitting back down sulkily and crossing my arms and eyes in utter frustration.

Continuing for what seemed like an eternity, eventually a ticket inspector entered the carriage.

"Excuse me – do you how long until we reach Hualamphong station?"

"30 minutes!" the inspector snarled, before venturing further up the carriage.

"WHAT? 30 MINUTES?" Carl stared with anger exploding from every contour of his face.

"I thought we had been on here much longer then half-an-hour Carl!" I retaliated to his fractious expression. *Maybe the journey felt much longer because of his irrational behaviour!*

Approximately five minutes later and the train came to an almighty holt, painfully forcing me to have to repeat the ritual of getting up all over again. H*ow many times will I have to go through this experience?*

Pulling the door open for hopefully a final time, Carl's fury blew-a-gasket when the door jammed.

"Getting off is clearly not meant to be Carl!" I slammed the heavy backpack from my sore shoulder onto the grimy floor.

"Seriously, let's just stay on!"

Without even answering and completely red-faced, Carl threw himself into his seat with sweat noticeably twinkling from his forehead. Anger and frustration were flowing through his veins at an almighty speed, just as carp would through water.

Reluctantly sitting next to him, I forced the laughter that was boiling up inside of me back down. *What must the locals think of the dizzy westerners repeatedly attempting (but failing) to get off the train?* I giggled as I looked across the carriage to the abundance of stares that we were still receiving.

"Why are you grinning?" Carl spun his head towards me faster than an owl.

"I'm glad that me being unwell amuses you…"

"Oh, Carl! Stop being so over-the-top! Imagine what we must look like..." A huge-grin spanned the width of my face and my childish laughter inappropriately filled the cabin.

"Well thanks for your support! I'll remember this next time you're feeling unwell."

The situation wasn't even that funny, but for some reason a fit of giggles took over my body. Childishly, I couldn't stop laughing. This of course meant that Summer also copied, even though she had no idea what she was actually giggling at.

"Great parenting – educating your daughter to laugh at someone else's misfortune!" Carl rose to his feet. In haste, he grabbed several of our bags and threw himself onto an alternative bench further up the carriage.

"Oh Carl, I'm not even laughing at you being unwell. I'm laughing at what we must look like to those around us!" I hollered down the carriage. *Why am I still laughing? Seriously Laura – just stop!*

"And you're still laughing! Just forget it!" He compellingly turned his back and instead opted to stare at the dirty, poverty-stricken Bangkok street that we were at that moment passing through.

I desperately wanted to take a picture of the carriage, so breaking the obstinate silence that had fallen between us over the minutes that had passed, I asked Carl to pass me the bag that contained my I Phone.

Old habits clearly die hard. When refusing, he remarked that 'there was no way that we were getting our equipment out on the train as we could get mugged and therefore would be asking for trouble.'

Carl not giving me the equipment caused further heated words between us, leaving me to exhale at speed like a deflating balloon.

His constant edgy nature seemed to pick up as often as the rest of us picked up coffee cups. I prayed that by the time we reached Cambodia, he would be more relaxed and not so weary of everyone and everything. *What a bad quality to possess...*

Fear has always been an unwanted companion of mine so his anxious behaviour was completely alien to me.

There's being cautious and then there's Carl...his attitude in front of Summer also worried me. Children are like sponges and consistently soak up what they see and hear. The last thing I wanted was for Summer to copy from his examples.

Despite me repeatedly asking him to not air the fact that he was afraid of heights in front of my impressionable five-year-old, for example, he selfishly continued and she had already aired that she was now afraid of heights. A few days ago she was happily hiking at great height! As a parent, I want Summer to be as carefree as I am. Until meeting Carl she had been. The trip was supposed to open her eyes to a new world - not make her scared of it.

The heat within the carriage had reached an unbearable stage and my face started to feel as though it was actually melting.

Urgh! Sweat lingering in the warmth of the bustling carriage along with a sea of revoltingly filthy feet... I suddenly wanted to projectile vomit.

As for Carl...I was irritated with him for not giving me the bag to take any pictures or video footage; whilst he was annoyed at me for purposely booking economy class, making him stay on the train, and for supposedly laughing at him - even though I wasn't actually laughing at him, but the situation. The only thing that broke the cabin's silence was Summer asking if we were there yet.

***

We finally reached Hualamphong train station.

Walking from the train with heavy bags fixed onto our backs, the young boy that had stared at me throughout the entire train journey walked at merely a pace in front of us.

I watched as he casually glanced back to catch a glimpse in my direction. His eyes glistened with excitement and an unexpectant smile crept across his face. Perplexed, I was unsure whether to smile in response or act as though I hadn't seen his expression towards me.

Before I could even respond the boy waved, smiled and set-off in the opposite direction. For a moment, I desperately tried to contain the smugness from erupting all over my face. But then I thought - 'what the heck!'

"Can I just point out how right I was!" I giggled cheekily to lighten the increasingly frosty atmosphere.

"Excuse me?" Carl snarled, continuing to walk at a pace.

"The boy! I told you he didn't mean any harm towards us, didn't I?" I smiled with a self-approving look as I adjusted the strap on my backpack and walked at speed to keep up.

"If I'm honest, I think he just liked the look of me Carl! And as a teenager with no doubt raging hormones pumping through his body... maybe he just took a fancy? You know - a boy fancying me wouldn't be the strangest occurrence in the world Carl!" I giggled at my super-funny joke.

"On this occasion, maybe..." Carl scolded as he instantly halted in his tracks and spun around to face us, making Summer and I abruptly stop in his path.

"But it could have easily been the other way around Laura!"

I knew the boy wasn't going to rob us, and his behaviour (although strange) wasn't threatening. It seemed that even at 29 years old, I was still learning new information about my own character with every day that passed. *In future: I'll follow my gut!*

***

Exactly three-hours and twenty minutes later, and we were sat on our backpacks in the middle of a very-hot and sticky train station that resembled London Victoria back in the 1970's.

Summer was busy playing 'count the monks,' Carl was listening to music and I was writing in my diary.

As I wrote, an almighty clock chime split into the core of my thoughts. Glancing from left-to-right, my ears pricked for interest. Around me everybody suddenly stood to attention. The stillness of the former busy station was somewhat absurd.

With my mind completely blank, my mouth dropped with a thud. It seemed the entire station had broken religiously into the national anthem. Simultaneously, images of the king appeared on the huge TV screens that projected his majesty across the station's forecourt.

In fear of offending, the three of us promptly stood to our feet and waited for the anthem to stop. It reminded me of a staged flash mob where everybody suddenly breaks into a dance seemingly out of nowhere. As soon as the song then finishes, the participants continue with their journey as if the event never happened.

It was an extraordinary thing to witness, and I couldn't help but admire the Thai people for their solidarity and loyalty.

Feeling hot and sticky in my super-cool but often unpractical elephant backpacker pants, I ventured to the toilet to change into some denim shorts.

"Two Baht!" a lady attendant barked as I approached the cubical.

"Oh, I didn't realise you have to pay. Sorry: I have no cash on me..."

"Two-baht!" She shook her head disapprovingly, allowing several others to pass in front. I grazed my teeth in angered frustration.

"Umm...Look...I only need to change into my shorts..." I wooed over the heads of the passing trade.

To my surprise (after all it was Thailand - where they charge for everything,) the lady let me through.

"Go!" she pushed my sweaty back through the carousel in an aggressive fashion.

Skipping around the corner, my expression dropped quicker than a tonne of bricks as I abruptly stopped in my tracks. I felt as though I had walked into the backdrop of a 1960's-horror film! Put simply, words cannot explain just how unpleasant the toilets were.

In fear of breathing in the stench of both urine and sweat, I held my breath as though my life depended on it!

Cautiously, I pushed open a graffiti-filled cubical door and held my glare at the dirtiest, most revolting paid-for toilet I had ever seen in all my years on planet earth.

My eyes scanned the huge puddle that swamped the floor, along with the filthy walls that accompanied. Urgh! *But what was the alternative? Changing in front of Carl?*

Stepping back from the cubical in hesitation, I checked the neighbouring toilet. *Deep sigh!*

Suddenly feeling as brave as the character Pita in the Denzel Washington film, 'Man on Fire,' *you know? When the gunshot sounds for her jump into the pool for the swimming race?* I took a large deep breath, stood tall and straight-backed, blinked a few times for courage and headed inside the horror-show of a cubical.

Balancing my feet unsteadily either side of the puddle, I pulled the pants to my thighs and slowly attempted to step out of one trouser leg and quickly into the shorts.

Not wanting to lean on the dirty walls or stand in the puddle of dirty water, I relied on the art of balancing. This was a good strategy until an enormous spider in the corner of the cubical caught my eye; forcing me to lose both my train of thought and balance!

As if pushed violently, my body brusquely fell with great speed into the dirty, graffiti-filled wall.

As I fell, my bare foot, short leg and trousers that I was holding landed in the puddle of dirty water that occupied the floor.

Peeling my sticky, moist back and arm from the filthy wall made me gag uncomfortably, and I fled the toilets *as* though I was trying to escape a kidnap attempt!

Great! Grimy, drenched shorts and trousers ahead of a 24-hour journey across Thailand was all I needed.

***

Ten:

Taking a step back in time on the pauper's Orient Express

I was like an energized child as Summer and I ran freely down the carriage of the sleeper train, eagerly peering into all the cabins trying to locate what would be our home for the night.

"Found it!" Carl shouted a few cabins up from the one Summer and I were nosing in.

My elated mood and broad smile immediately froze as I peered my head around the door of the cabin and stared at the tiny space blankly. The bubble of excitement that was in the pit of my stomach was instantly replaced by anxiety. Our cabin was rear-facing!

Being a migraine sufferer, the thought of travelling backwards overnight put me instantly on edge.

"Excuse me…" I asked the young, attractive attendant who had the youthful face of a TV presenter but wore an 'important' uniform.

"Can we swap our cabin for a rear-facing one please?"

The attendant stared at me totally expressionless.

"I'm a migraine sufferer you see…" I rambled to fill the void of complete silence; face animated as I elaborated my point.

With every sentence I blurted out the attendant jerked his head meaningfully, reassuring me that he understood and would help; raising my spirits considerably.

"So, if we could swap I'd be most grateful…"

Out of no-where, the attendant sighed heavily and thumped his paperwork with conviction onto a nearby surface. *How rude! Especially after I was so polite. I gave him my best telephone voice too!*

"Cabins sold out!" he declared.

"You have to ask the occupiers yourself!" *Great!*

I had already sussed out the other cabins so knew there were more rear-facing than forward facing ones available. My anxiety levels began to elevate beyond all control.

Ironically (or some would call it fate) the cabin next to ours was forward-facing. I just needed to wait for its occupier…

Just over 20 minutes later, a Chinese businessman boarded the train and headed into the 'deluxe' cabin that I so badly wanted and would do anything to achieve… I surveyed my victim in delight.

Before I even had the chance to say 'hello,' however, the man immediately locked the inside door which led to our cabin, and abruptly closed the curtain so we couldn't see inside.

As I shuffled apprehensively outside his cabin, Carl yelped: "Laura!" behind me like an irritating pet dog.

"He obviously doesn't want to be disturbed - it's embarrassing - just leave it!"

"This isn't a joke Carl." I found myself hissing indignantly.

"I'm a migraine sufferer and travelling backwards could set one off!"

"Everyone is a migraine sufferer these days…" he curled his lip and stared at the ceiling.

I instantly wanted to punch him in the epicentre of his moral compass!

"Carl, I take [pur-scrip-shun] medicine daily to stop them!"

"It's not 'pur'" he air quoted in an irritating fashion. 'It's 'pres-crip-tion' – there's an R and an E, it's not 'pur' like a cat!"

"Oh what-ever!" I growled, knocking on the man's cabin door, admittedly a little harder than I intended.

"Hello – umm, do you speak English?" I cleared my throat self consciously as he slowly opened the door.

Smiling warmly, the man nodded his head to indicate that he did. *Let's hope my kind personality transpires through the kindness of my smile…*

"I'm hoping you can help me. I suffer from terrible migraines that often result in loss of vision. I have been allocated a cabin that is rear-facing - and travelling backwards would most-likely cause a migraine..." I babbled in the best telephone voice I could muster… *I was using this a lot today!*

"I don't suppose you would be so kind as to swap cabins with me? I know it's a big ask, but I'd be extremely grateful…"

Why is he staring at me so blankly? Maybe he doesn't understand what I am saying? Maybe I was talking too quickly?

In desperation, I pulled the mother card out of the bag.

"Summer…come here please..." I hollered down the corridor to where Summer was perched.

"As you can see, I am travelling with a child." I smiled, firmly placing one arm around Summer's tiny shoulders.

"I must care for my child so I really can't be sick…"

Gawping sheepishly at the Chinese man, I tensed up inside as I eagerly anticipated a hopeful and positive response.

In a millie-second the man's expression suddenly changed from what was an unreadable blank, to a huge unexpectant smile.

"Of course!" he beckoned in an upbeat voice, before immediately packing up the belongings he'd already neatly displayed around his cosy cabin.

As the train started to roll from the station, that fuzzy feeling of foreign ground under my feet passed through my body like an electrical jolt. Summer and I looked at each other animatedly. *Who knew that travelling by train could be so exhilarating?*

***

It was just over two hours into the journey and I had already drawn several pictures with Summer, completed a selection of school work, consumed a tonne of Pringles and was officially bored with itchy feet.

"I'm just going to see what the other carriages are like…" I slipped on my shoes.

"Why can't you just sit still for two minutes?"

"Carl, we have a cabin so we are technically in first class. I want to experience what the rest of the train is like for the other passengers. Plus, there's a restaurant somewhere… Rubes, do you want to come and explore with me?" The excitement glistered from my crystal-blue eyes.

"I don't think that's a good idea!" interjected Carl, grabbing Summer's arm as she attempted to put her crocs on with precision.

"What do you think is going to happen to her under my watchful eye, exactly?" I snapped, wanting to bite his words in half.

"It's dangerous Laura!"

"How exactly?" I raised my voice and crossed my arms.

I shouldn't have shouted – I knew that! But I had bitten my tongue several times already with his continuous interferences and unwanted advice regarding my parenting skills. Inevitably, I was going to lose my cool eventually.

"Carl, what you do with your children is entirely up to you, however, this is my child and I'm afraid it is not up-to-you…Come on Summer, let's go!" I animatedly instructed as I looked at Carl with growing resentment, grabbed the action camera and headed out of the door… Summer's eyes gleaming at the prospect of our next 'mini' mother-and-daughter adventure.

Holding onto her hand tightly, we made our way through the train. Reaching the end of our carriage, I blinked furiously as I observed the large gap. The adjoining door to our carriage wasn't firmly connected by a joining galley, meaning you had to literally jump from one carriage to the next!

Watching the ground whizz past at an almighty speed, the opening between the carriages was so big that if Summer took a wrong step, her body could easily fall through the gap in an instant.

With a massive sigh of disappointment, I had no choice but to head back to the carriage. Carl loved this of course, I on the other-hand felt irritated to the core.

Attempting the gaps myself too many hours later, I felt as fearless as one of the brothers in the film: 'Slumdog Millionaire,' *you know the scene? When the two brothers jump across the train carriages?* Granted, the boys jumped across the roof tops of the trains and not a tiny gap between the trains, but considering who I was I figured my jump was on par!

Watching the boarding class drop with every approaching carriage I stepped into was fascinating. The first carriage reminded me of the slam-door trains from my childhood.

The next carriage was certainly an interesting walk. You still had bays of seats on either side of the aisles, but the seats were much smaller and had metal ladders that were positioned erratically in the aisle. The ladders lead to what I can only describe as a shelf on the wall that was full to the brim of people either sitting or sleeping.

I couldn't imagine being stuck on one of those shelves for 12 hours! I shuddered, squeezing between the sweaty people.

Stopping to take a large glug of water, I looked around the carriage. People were certainly packed in like sardines, and the tin can was deafening from the chatter amongst the many people it housed.

Pulling out my action camera, I turned the camera on myself and cheerily waved into the lens in that exaggerated tourist fashion that one does. *Cringe, but no one knows me so who cares?*

Noticing a member of staff, I asked how far the restaurant was. Annoyingly he advised that it was the other end of the train and it would be easier for him to take my order instead.

Talk about boring!

With the cloud of boredom now hanging over me, I disappointingly ordered three toasted cheese and ham sandwiches for the following morning, along with two coffees and an orange juice. I was left stunned when I was charged a whopping £20 for the delightful spread! *Was I in Paris or Bangkok?*

Back at the cabin, it was soon time for our first sleeper-train toilet experience.

I guess I was naive to assume the train would have western features such as a seat and flush, but the facilities couldn't have been further from a western toilet if we tried.

"Right!" I nodded, trying my best to sound as natural as possible at the disturbing sight.

The cubical had a hole in the ground and once again occupied a shower hose instead of paper. Of course, this meant that everything was wet. But not just by hose water, given we were on a rocking train...

As Summer absorbed the view of the toilet, she erupted into a theatrical flood of tears.

"I'm not using that!" she snarled, attempting to run out of the tiny, smelly cubical.

"Don't run off!" I grabbed both of her shoulders, mainly to hold my balance from the rocking of the carriage.

"Look - I know it's disgusting..." I pleaded. "But we are on this train until tomorrow Rube! There really is nowhere else to go..."

"But it's dirty and it smells...."

"I know..." I said in a childlike voice with a matching expression to try and poke fun at the situation.

"But at least there are no bugs on it! Remember that one in the jungle? Now that was a bad toilet!" I laughed to lighten the mood.

"I will lift you up so you don't have to touch anything other than me – ok?"

Like a stroppy teenager, I watched as my five-year-old huffed a deep sigh and through gritted teeth replied in a tiny voice. "Ok."

"At least you have someone to pick you up!" I giggled. "I don't! Unless you want to try and lift me?" I once again tried to be funny.

"Don't be silly Mummy!" she spat like a petulant teenager; reaching her arms in the air for me to lift her.

***

It was 11.30pm and our carriage now resembled a miniature motel room.

Carl was asleep in the top bunk and I was top-and-tailing in the bottom bunk with a forever-fidgeting Summer-Ruby.

Despite paying for three people, the cabin only slept two so we were only allocated two pillows and two blankets. Like most mothers, I drew the short-straw by having to go without a pillow or a blanket.

With the sound of Carl and Summer's snoring filling the cabin, I attempted to sleep as I used a towel as a blanket and a hooded jacket as a pillow. *Backpacking at its finest ladies and gentlemen!*

Sitting bolt-upright, I swiftly turned on the night light and rigorously rubbed my neck and achy shoulder. Watching the streets whizz past quickly, I put one earphone into my drum for company and spent an hour writing about the drama of the squatting toilet and the cattle-class shelf beds I had seen a few carriages along.

Unexpectedly the train suddenly reduced to a snail-pace, prompting me to look up from my diary.

Opening my eyes further, we were travelling through what looked to be the inside of a slum village. It was a peculiar sight to say the least! I could see people huddled together eating and cooking. We were travelling so sluggish I was sure they could see me as much as I could see them - after all, my face was illuminated by a night light.

Consumed by sleep several hours later, the clickerty-clacks of the train snappishly woke me. As soon as I opened my sticky, sleepy eyes, I felt the pressing of my jacket zip etched into the side of my cheek. Rubbing my sore face, I sleepily squinted out the window to a countryside of darkness.

It was 4.30am and the train sounded silent, unlike when I was awake and writing several hours before.

Feeling the aches and pains in both my shoulder and my back once more, I attempted to stretch my legs. Unfortunately

I was blocked by Summer's sleeping position where she resembled a starfish and took up most of the miniscule bed.

"Are you awake?" Carl mouthed into the darkness.

"What do you think?" I laughed in sarcasm at the fact that I had no pillow, no blanket, zip-marks etched into my face, and was of course sharing the tiniest bed known to man with my forever-fidgeting daughter. *Of course, I was bloody awake!*

"I'm on a train that has no suspension so I am constantly rocking from left-to-right, laying on what can only be described as a padded bench with a towel for a blanket and a jumper for a pillow – yes I'm awake!" I giggled.

"The rocking is horrendous, isn't it? Beds are sizeable though, aren't they?"

"For you maybe, but you're not sharing with a starfish! I really need a wee but I've been holding it in fear of having to squat! Jesus I sound like Summer!" I sniggered.

"You know, squatting is actually quite good for you. I read about a Japanese study that researched six volunteers who had their rectums filled with contrast solution and were asked to release the fluid from both a sitting and squatting position. Interestingly, the participants squatting had less abdominal straining! Did you know that if you strain excessively you are more prone to developing tears of the anal lining?"

"CARL!" I cocked my head up towards his bunk in alarm. "Seriously – it's 4.30am!"

After 10 further minutes of staring at the discoloured ceiling (and nauseatingly thinking about Carl's random story about the Japanese study,) I abandoned my not-so-comfortable bed in favour of a not-so-pleasant squatting toilet instead.

***

No time at all later and I awoke to the sound of the painfully-screechy trolley wheels that were speeding down the carriage walkway.

I tentatively opened one eye and peered around the cabin...my head felt fuzzy - almost as though I'd slept upside down.

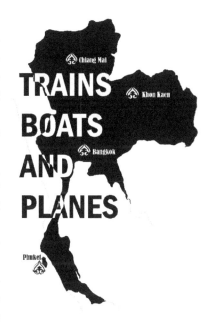

It was 6am and in true Western style, I awoke from the worst night's sleep with a bone-dry mouth literally gasping for a coffee...I couldn't wait to tuck into that toasted cheese sandwich I had pre-ordered.

As a wave of tiredness flooded over me, a bang on the door instantly woke me up...forcing my dreamlike image of breakfast to fizzle out almost as quickly as a sparkler on bonfire night.

Staring at my 'what-should-have-been' illustrious spread, I gawped at my morning coffee unimpressively. Disappointedly, the liquid tasted as sharp as rocket fuel and was so bad I heaved after just one mouthful.

Biting hungrily into the much-needed sandwich, I quickly discovered that the bread wasn't toasted and was in fact the cheapest, thinnest white bread possible. Not only that but it had clearly been made the day before as it was hard in places - and that certainly wasn't because it was toasted!

Alongside the sandwich sat a bed of parched green salad that had shrivelled to its core. Adjacent sat a blanket of warm fries that rested on the sandwich, making the cheap bread practically disintegrate before my eyes.

Not to mention Summer's juice, which was so over-populated by pulp and tasted so strong I was sure it had sat in an open-carton for numerous days...to think I had paid £20 for such a delightful spread!

It was thankfully soon time to vacate the train and delightfully we were greeted by two small cafes that sat opposite the station's platform. Along with the entire population of the train, we were told to wait in the cafes for our allocated coach.

Having left the last delightful breakfast, we ordered food in the rundown-looking cafe and swallowed with immense difficulty as it tasted only marginally better than the breakfast served on the train.

Waiting patiently for the toilet, I slowly cast my eye over the kitchen that we were queuing inside. It was like nothing I'd seen before and could rival some of the worst kitchens in the programme, 'Gordon's Kitchen Nightmares.' I therefore didn't hold out much hope that the toilet would be western or indeed hygienic.

Disturbing my thoughts, the cubical door came ajar and a man in his 30s with long dreadlocks and filthy skin stepped out. The man kindly held the door open for Summer; although appreciative, we were fixed upon holding our breaths for fear of dying an early death from toilet intoxication.

I expected the worst and it certainly didn't disappoint. Although gifted the luxury of a toilet seat and flush. The seat was swamped with urine, accompanied by a familiar human odour that nobody wants to smell when using a public toilet that early in the morning.

Commonly, there was a distinctive lack of toilet roll to even attempt to wipe the urine from the seat, leaving me with no choice but to give the muscles in my arms another workout as I balanced Summer's three-stone of body weight over the toilet.

For the third time since arriving in Thailand, I cleaned wee from the bottom of my sandals in the sink.

***

Within minutes of boarding the coach to the ferry port, it was clear that our driver was a fearless lunatic as he furiously sped down the highway as if attempting to lude a body of Police men. He was beeping his horn furiously at just about anyone that was in his way - even people that weren't.

An hour into the journey and thankfully the driver had no choice but to come to a halt when we were stopped by a red, seemingly life-saving light.

From the window, I watched with curiosity as an elderly lady strolled along the highway selling flowers that were draped in ribbon to passing drivers.

I scrutinised on as numerous motorists ushered the lady away like pesky flies. Of course our rather peculiar driver did not take this approach, and instead purchased a flower, put it between the palms of both of his hands, closed his eyes and prayed. *Seriously?* I stared on as several minutes passed and he remained fixed into the pray position.

Even after the traffic started to move the man was intent on not being interrupted.

I'm tolerant of praying and the need to fit this into a scheduled day, but I don't think that was the best of times. *Surely as soon as the traffic moves on, it's time to stop praying and get back to the deed in hand?*

As the driver continued to say his prayers, the cars behind beeped their horns in utter frustration as our huge coach blocked their ability to pass. Furious with their incessant beeping, the driver erupted into a chorus of rage as he screamed at the other drivers from the comfort of his protected window.

You can therefore imagine my joy to finally step off the death-trap of the coach and onto the ferry for the final leg of our 27-hour journey across the country, some 45 minutes later.

Slumping our fatigued bodies onto the ferry seats, we all felt exhausted from the long car journey from the tree house to the airport, the flight, the train journey through Bangkok; the three-hour wait, the sleeper train, the hazardous coach drive and now the ferry.

Considering the length of time we had been travelling, I was astounded at how well Summer was behaving. Literally, the only tears or tantrums I had experienced were because of the toilet - which was understandable.

Walking back to our ferry seats from the toilet, both Summer and I couldn't help but notice the boat happily dancing over the crust of the waves. Perched at the open back our hair ruthlessly blew in the fast-paced wind, making us giggle like sisters.

Looking out towards the islands in the distance, I stood behind Summer's tiny body and clenched her waist in fear of a possible clumsy fall. Balancing precariously with smiles as wide as the ocean, we admired just how beautiful the view was.

Feeling my protective touch, Summer lifted her arms out as though she didn't have a care in the world.

"This is so much fun Mummy!" she shouted over the noisy air; before the boat's edge hit the water dramatically and splashed us both in the face, prompting us to laugh mischievously in sync like school friends on a field trip.

"I love you!" I whispered into her miniscule ear.

"I love you too Mummy!" she squealed before the wind picked up great pace and forced us both back inside the cabin.

Finally arriving on the island of Ko Pha Ngan, a wave of tiredness flooded over me as I positioned the weight of the heavy backpack onto my sore back and walked to the ferry entrance.

"Excuse me," I attempted a conversation with a Thai man who was holding a sign that displayed the name 'Ballo.'

"You – Ballo?" The man asked.

"No Ballo!"

"More hotels - bottom of jetty…" He barked in a not-so-friendly manner.

"Great!" I grabbed Summer's hand and strolled down the incredibly long dock. At this moment in time, I didn't feel particularly up to the challenge of carrying two backpacks that felt double the weight they'd had the previous day.

Feeling like a thoroughbred horse that had just galloped through the finish line at Royal Ascot, sweat-drenched and desperate for rehydration, I guzzled an extra-large gulp of water and on impulse poured the remainder of the bottle over my sweaty head.

"Arrgghhh!" I yelped as I watched the drops of water sizzle on the burning pavement.

"What on earth are you doing?" hollered Carl from the corner of my eye.

Like my born partner in crime, Summer laughed in good measure at my action.

"Mummy - you're funny!" she lovingly wiped the excess water from my dripping face.

"I'm so hot!" I yelled breathlessly, laughing in unison with my side-kick.

Barely minutes later and we arrived to a car park of chaos as a cattle of people and a body of white vans flooded my eyeline.

"The hotel is down there..." The driver pointed across the street, arriving at the hotel's address barely minutes later.

As the van quickly disappeared into nothingness; we were left stranded on the sidewalk, staring down an intimidating gigantic hill.

I dabbed at my exhausted eyes and yawned. Widening them sleepily, I looked at the hill and omitted a mischievous giggle.

"At least it will be a laugh attempting to get down there with these hefty packs!" I said brightly.

"The quicker we get down it the faster it will be until we're sat with a glass of bubbly in our hand!" I began the verbal dance of being optimistic, that I knew all too well....

The hill was by far the steepest I'd ever tackled. With a 20kg backpack strapped to my body, Summer's10kg bag resting on my fatigued arm, wearing flimsy flip-flops and clutching the hand of a five-year-old; not to mention the fact that we had now passed the 27th hour of travelling continuously – the hill was certainly a challenge.

Descending with the sun toasting my bare skin, I found the weight of the bags forcing my legs to travel faster than my body could manage. Before I knew it, I felt my body begin to move at a speed I didn't know I was capable of achieving.

In haste, I let go of Summer's hand and instructed Carl to take her instead.

Shouting, I found my legs moving with such momentum that my torso almost couldn't keep up with the speed.

"OH MY GOD!" I yelped as I dashed down the hill so recklessly that I marginally missed the wall at the very bottom.

Carl's response was to stare at me in astonishment. *Thanks buddy!*

"Mum that was soooo funny!" Summer yelled behind me, holding onto Carl's hand and slowly making her way down the hill.

"Is walking over-rated Laura?" Carl teased.

"Well, I do have most of the weight Carl!" I shot him 'the look.' I was not in a mocking mood!

Venturing through the complex, the sun was forcibly shining through the clouds and the smell of sun screen filled the clammy air.

Blinking rapidly, the pit of my stomach bubbled with intense excitement. *Relaxation here we come!*

Stepping into the hotel's reception, our breaths were immediately taken away by a lustrous bar that stood on a secluded, miniscule beach.

"Wow!" We each stared in ore at the postcard-perfect ocean before us.

A toddler with beautifully shiny ginger hair and freckles that resembled scattering of sand from a day at the beach; interrupted my thoughts by running over my tired toes as a lady quickly followed in succession, calling out in a voice that bared the hallmarks of a British private-school education.

I watched like a fly on the wall as the lady passed the child to her male counterpart, and casually took a seat in the sun-dappled lobby of the upmarket hotel. She then proceeded to chat nonchalantly to what looked to be her friend over the rim of their champagne glasses.

With the waves creeping gently towards the ocean-front and drenching the golden sand, the resort looked as though it had been directly lifted from the canvas of a work of art.

The hotel was comprised across many levels, leaving rooms dotted randomly at various heights of the hill.

Walking into the open space of our room, my mouth fell wide-open in aghast as I studied the clear-glass walls that the strange room occupied.

"Are you kidding me?" I bawled, taking a moment to observe the clear-glassed wall that separated the bedroom from the bathroom and sat directly opposite (wait for it) a double bed!

"People by the pool and those on the beach can see straight into our room and no doubt into the bathroom!" I groaned in shock at our bizarre accommodation.

"Not to mention the fact that we will see each other go to the toilet and shower!" I continued ranting in the colour of red.

"Nature-is-nature!" Carl shrugged in a casual way.

I stared at him open-mouthed, completely dumbfounded.

"Carl, no offence but I don't want to see you naked…"

"It is just skin Laura, we all have it - don't we?"

Carl's response left me stunned beyond belief and totally lost for words. Unsurprisingly, his reaction was to babble even more.

"I have a back-to-nature philosophy, you see. The first human to ever set foot on planet earth was created unclothed after all…" he gazed in my direction.

I couldn't believe what I was hearing. *Was Carl a closet nudist?*

"Carl…" I turned towards him, staring in dismay.

"Are you a nudist?" I asked rather untactfully.

"Define 'nudist'…" he air quoted.

"Ummm…so you walk onto a beach and there's a sign that reads, 'clothes optional' what do you do?" I rested my hands on my hips to give myself a false sense of power. *I was enjoying this – I actually felt like Wonder Woman!*

"Depends who I am with."

"You're alone..."

"Then…I'd probably strip off!" he shrugged casually.

"Really?" my jaw dropped slightly as I began to giggle in that that uncontrollable child-like way. This took me back to 'sex education' when I'd laugh with my friends at the word 'condom.' Summer copied my actions falling into a fit of childish laughter.

"What's a [nudyiest]?" she interrupted.

"Someone who likes cheese very much!" I said over-enthusiastically in that mumsy-way when we think we are doing the best magician-style cover up. *What? It was the first-thing that came to mind.*

"Yes! Why not? I have nothing to be ashamed of!" Carl cleared his throat confidently, shifting uncomfortably from one foot to the other.

"I am happy in my own skin Laura… Clearly you are not!"

"Don't bring my constant need to diet into it Carl. I would never strip off on a beach regardless of whether I was a size six or sixteen!" I reached for my eyeliner and applied it thoughtfully.

"I can't believe you're a nudist!" I suddenly giggled into the empty air to lighten the mood, eyeliner pressed firmly onto my eyelid.

"I'm not a nudist!" Carl spun around, obviously vexed by my comment. "I'm just putting it out there that I have no problem with you or anyone else seeing me shower naked, that's all!"

"And toilet?" I threw my eyeliner into my makeup bag with conviction.

"Well…I'm sure you could go and sit on the beach when I need to use the toilet." He suggested in a tedious tone.

"Ok! I'm going to see if we can switch rooms as we only have one double bed anyway, and clearly we need two…"

Several minutes later and I was back from a wasteful visit to the hotel's reception.

"They can't change our room!" I cursed, backwards-diving onto the bed.

"I take it I'm on the sofa then?"

I closed my eyes as the feeling of the soft bed cushioned like a frame around my achy body that felt as though it weighed 1000lbs.

Rubbing my eyes sleepily, I yawned whilst glancing casually at the ceiling.

"What the…" my mouth flung-open for the second time in five minutes.

"What the hell is that?" I rasped, violently pointing to the huge mirror that spanned the entire length of the ceiling.

"Oh cool!" Summer marvelled, immediately jumping on the bed next to me to pull funny faces at her reflection.

Great! I huffed. *So, I'm staying in a kicky-ass room with a nudist who drives me insane. Could this trip get any stranger?* I giggled at the absurdity of it all.

Carl wasted no time in venturing to the toilet to get changed into his swimmers. Throughout which, my back was well-and-truly turned!

"We will meet you by the pool." I shouted.

"Summer - can you hold this towel around me please?" I attempted to change into my swimming costume in the bedroom.

"Mummy, are we going to have to do this every time we get changed?"

"I'm afraid so. As ridiculous as it is!" I pulled my costume up at speed.

"Look…" I pointed to a couple who happened to be walking past the window at that very moment.

"Carl - there are people right outside! They can probably see you…" I gasped.

"Who cares!" he oozed.

"I don't think he's bothered Mum…" Summer nodded blankly in a rather grown-up voice.

Raising my eyebrow I attempted to suffocate my giggles, of course I failed miserably.

"Just keep facing me Summer!" We laughed together in that endearing mother-daughter way.

A few moments later and nudeness aside, I was in my element as I marvelled at the feeling of baby soft sand between my tired, heavy toes.

It was the first-time Summer and I had experienced sand between our toes since our last British-summer beach days to the Witterings.

The feeling of the luxurious, cold sand as it touched the bare soles of my over-worked, forever-aging feet felt as rewarding as a luxurious spa day.

"Carl…" I yelled towards the pool.

"Come and feel the sand on your feet… it's amazing!"

"Oh - I don't do bare feet on sand!" he testified from across the way.

"What do you mean?"

I watched as Carl jumped out of the pool with haste, put on his trainers and slowly walked towards me.

"I have a condition called 'tactile defensiveness…" he leaned over us.

"What's that?"

"It means I am sensitive to touch-sensations…" he cleared his throat self-consciously.

Not knowing what to say, I simply paused.

179

"That's why I can't place my bare feet onto grass or sand."

I couldn't contain myself. I laughed.

"Very funny!" *Even after all this time together, I still didn't understand his rather-odd sense-of-humour…*

"It's not a joke… It started when I was a toddler and I have never grown out of it." He frowned.

"Oh!" was all I could manage as the feeling of guilt swept through every morsel of my being.

I instantly felt wrenched. I didn't even realise that was even a thing! How uneducated and insensitive of me to laugh. I felt like kicking myself.

"I'm sorry for laughing…I genuinely thought you were joking…"

I was sure I'd seen him bare-foot at some point? I racked my brain for evidence. *Hmm, explains why he always wears 'those' trainers!* I glanced at his unstylish clunky 1980s circa sneakers. I then wrongly pictured him naked with only his trainers on. *What? He openly admitted to being a nudist!*

"It goes another step further as well - I cannot wear socks that have seams in them…that one really sets me off!"

"You have a lot of things don't you Carl?" I giggled to lighten the mood.

"What do you mean?" he asked with a serious, questioning look.

"Oh, well… ummm…you can't sit with your back to a room, you have to rearrange all the condiments on a table in a restaurant - you're a closet nudist…" I snorted. "Now you're telling me that you can't walk on grass or sand, or wear socks with seams in them!" I giggled once more.

"I'm not a nudist!"

"Whatever! You know what I mean…"

"Well sorry that we're not all 'perfect' Laura!" He suddenly went all serious on me, air quoting and all.

"I didn't mean it like that. I just meant… well, you're a complex character aren't you Carl?"

Now I was the one to clear my throat self-consciously…

Laughing awkwardly and with a high pitch to my voice: "It's funny!" I giggled. "And endearing… you're unlike anyone I have ever met before that's all…"

Silence answered me back.

"Do you fancy taking Summer in the pool then?" I swiftly changed the subject.

"Sure!" he frowned.

Moments later and as I happily sat on the edge of the shoreline, the whiff of the salted-sea tingled my nostrils and the sand flowed onto my feet like a bed of blankets.

With my feet feeling incredibly sore and dry, the featherlike sand was a welcome relief and felt almost as good as a professional foot massage.

How could anyone fear putting their feet on this wonderful sand? I kept thinking. I *just didn't get it...*I was almost obsessing about the subject. That's the thing with travelling. You remove yourself from the mundane auto-pilot mode that life gives you, and you suddenly have an abundance of time to think.

Sitting on the shoreline, a memory of backpacking at 18 came to mind.

Like this trip, we travelled for hours to reach our first beach of the voyage. But calling it a 'beach' is a slight understatement as it was the largest sand island in the world and goes by the name of 'Fraser Island.'

Our group of ten hired a 4WD for a weekend of camping on the paradise island that is located on the east coast of Australia. Housing extraordinary freshwater lakes, crystal-like creeks and enormous sand dunes, the island is the only place on earth where rainforest grows on sand.

As the bath-warm water touched my feet, I reminisced about day two on the island when we reached Lake McKenzie after our first horrendous night of camping.

After an evening of giggling carelessly around a camp fire, our fun and fire was soon extinguished around 10pm after what we thought was a sudden downpour, resulted in an almighty thunder storm!

The rainstorm was so bad that our entire camp soon became dangerously water-logged, forcing us to spend the sodden night stood exhaustedly under a toilet block for shelter as we terrifyingly watched the lightening hit the 20m trees that surrounded us.

Reaching Lake Mckenzie the next day, with its perfectly clear waters and pure white sand, was a feeling like no other.

We felt as though we'd earned that experience of relaxation and excitement as the ten of us, shattered as we were, ran like animated children towards the water and backward-dived into the fresh lake still fully-clothed.

I smiled to myself as I remembered that childish wonderment feeling I'd experienced when ducking above and below the surface of that turquoise, dreamlike water. I remembered us all pushing and lifting each other's bodies into the air and squealing like children as our frames dive-bombed back into the mineral water.

I was immediately transported back to that feeling of trenching up the pure-white sand dunes immediately after being in the lake, as the exfoliating grains stuck to my body like glue.

Just like a child would, I laughed blissfully as I created starfish movements with my arms and legs (all the while teasing 'Barry White.') Barry was a fellow British camper who happened to have the whitest skin known to mankind. (Hence his nick-name.) Literally, when he did starfish moves in that flour-like sand all we could see were his eyes, mouth and hair! Bringing me back to the present, I giggled at the fond memory.

"What are you chuckling at?" Carl hollered from the pool.

"Oh nothing!" I cowered, choosing instead to keep the memory to myself.

As we later splashed in the pool, Summer accidently knocked over our cocktails that were perched on the edge. I cleaned up the broken glass and told the barman in case there were any small pieces I hadn't seen.

Minutes later and the barman approached armed with a hefty bill to cover the damages incurred. I was absolutely infuriated!

"It would be cheaper to venture to John Lewis and purchase a box of the finest wine glasses they stock!" I shrieked.

In bed that evening, staring helplessly at our reflection in the ceiling mirror, I once again couldn't sleep as Carl and Summer's snoring echoed around the room in surround sound.

Sitting upright, I drained my glass of water and sighed in desperation.

Looking out of the window at the beach, I suddenly longed to be outside.

Still in my pyjamas, I spontaneously grabbed my headphones and cardigan and ran to the beach.

Sitting directly outside my room with a clear view of Summer sleeping (maybe there was a benefit to having no blinds after all?) I looked out towards the noisy waves as they touched the shoreline. There was no denying that the beach was totally idyllic.

Listening to Coldplay's 'Yellow,' my thoughts drifted to home and family. Out of nowhere another de-ja-vu 'Australian moment' came sharply into focus.

I remembered staying on the Gold Coast and arguing dramatically with my then-boyfriend... in haste I ran to the beach for refuge.

Although I was in a totally different place, on both occasions I wanted to escape a small room that I was temporarily calling my 'home'...and in doing so ran to the largest space I could find - the beach.

Crying 11 years previously on that perfectly beautiful, golden shore in Surfers Paradise came sharply into focus. A memory of being interrupted by the arrival of two lads from Wales shot through my brain.

I knew the men as we were sharing a four-bed dorm with them at the time. I remembered them telling me about their dislike for my boyfriend, and offering for me to join them on their travels the following day.

"Come with!" I remembered them encouragingly suggesting.

As much as I would have loved to have thrown caution to the wind, ditched the argumentative boyfriend and joined the lads on their travels (what an adventure that could have been!) I remained sensible and declined their kind offer.

It was funny how even after 11 years, I only had to close my eyes for the briefest of moments and I was somehow transported right back to that beautiful Gold Coast beach.

You learn so much on trips like these... my hand drew meaningless lines in the sand as I glanced towards Summer's delicate frame asleep in the distance.

Leaning my head of my knees and closing my eyes, my thoughts suddenly switched to the present day as I attempted to absorb everything we had witnessed and learnt in the weeks since we had been away.

We had certainly seen both the ugly and good side of humanity… we had been cursed (I laughed to myself,) we'd already met some wonderful people…

I pictured the excited and grateful look on that teenager's face when I passed him that packet of bubbles at the school in the jungle. I then recalled the Tuk-Tuk driver's face when Carl handed him the $100 tip when driving back from the market in Chiang Mai. *Remember how he'd held the note in his hand like Charlie from 'Charlie in the chocolate factory' with his golden ticket?*

The endearing memories of those at the treehouse; followed by Bee, Apple, Laurie and Mike from the elephant sanctuary. As the minutes ticked by, I speculated about where Laurie and Mike could be in their travels. I then pondered if that receptionist in Hong Kong ever burned that paper for us!

A wave of tiredness suddenly dominated my thoughts.

Standing to my feet and brushing the sand off my bottom, I ventured back to bed; only 10 minutes later and I found myself staring once again at my reflection in the ceiling.

We were on such a limited time frame and I had scrimped and saved so hard for 'a trip of a lifetime.' I wanted to get as much out of every minute that we could. I'd had enough of the hotel and its petulant staff… quite frankly, I was ready to leave Ko Pha Ngan behind.

On impulse I scanned the internet on my phone, looking at the next island across - Ko Samui.

Completely overcome with frustration, I glanced at photos of the island and was ensnared by dreamlike images that claimed me inexorably as a black hole absorbs a galaxy. In haste, I found myself booking a swanky hotel for the following day on the paradise island.

I justified my spontaneously by figuring that I didn't have time to waste being unhappy on this trip. After all, there is no time like the present to change things.

***

184

The next morning I broke the news to Carl that we were moving from our love shack to a 5* resort instead.

There was a ferry departing that morning but it unhelpfully was docked at a different port to the one we'd arrived at and was located on the other side of the island. The pressure I felt at that moment was immense!

On route, the minutes ticked by almost as quickly as they had when we were in Honk Kong and were racing to get to the boat trip on time.

It was almost as though time was disintegrating through my fingertips and I was completely helpless to do anything about it – except hope that my guardian angel was watching over us. *Dad, if you're up there…*I mouthed to the sky.

It felt ironic that we were racing once again to meet a boat on time. I'd already decided that if we missed the ferry then it would be the curse catching up with us.

With only three minutes until the scheduled departure time, the taxi arrived at the port and we ran crazily towards the ticket office. Sitting comfortably on the ferry moments later, I pushed an irritating strand of hair out of my eyes and chuckled quietly to myself at my absurd new habit of blaming every bad experience on the curse.

***

Eleven:

Everything comes at a price!

Standing on the oceanfront listening to the soulful voice of Delilah through my earphones, I looked around at the spectacular beach surrounding me.

Ko Samui had been relaxing, but very quiet. We were practically the only guests at the hotel, and as the resort was in a secluded location we were rather cut off from society. Reflecting on our three days, I recalled us having a blast when playing football half-heartedly on a patch of grass inside the hotel. All was fun until Carl went and ruined it by kicking the ball so hard it crashed into an elephant statue and sliced through a singular toe knocking it clean off!

My eyes swivelled around as I registered what he'd done...

"Do not say anything!" I ran towards the elephant's stone toe that was shattered to pieces on the floor.

Scanning the area around me, I felt incredibly relieved when I realised that no one had seen. So, I did what most people would do: I balanced the toe back on the statue as if the incident had never happened.

Being his law-abiding self Carl of course wanted to tell the staff of the 'incident.'

I swallowed at the thought of what consequence a confession would bring. *The statue would clearly cost more than a few glasses around the pool this time…*

"I've balanced the stone on the statue so let's just stay out of this area for a while."

"Absolutely not!" Carl glared into the deepest corners of my eyes. "I'm owning up Laura, and if we receive a bill - then so be it!"

"Are you crazy?" I shouted in complete annoyance, biting my lip in distress.

"Do you know how much a statue like this will no doubt cost? That could completely wipe us out Carl! Don't talk absolute nonsense!"

I watched as his eyebrows drew together in a red-hot rage.

"Laura - I'm not like you!"

"What's that supposed to mean? Are you calling me an untrustworthy person? I'm not dishonest Carl. I'm simply using my common sense. I know that owning up will result in some almighty bill that could put an end to us travelling altogether! So, if we can get away with it…" I trailed off.

"Have you forgotten what I do for a living, Laura? Have you somehow eradicated it from your 'senseless' memory? I'm a fraud investigator - and you're asking me to be deceitful. Do you know how ridiculously ironic that sounds! This is criminal damage! I'm sorry but I'm owning up and that's the end of it!" His eyes stared through mine, darting me a look-could-kill sideways glance.

"Don't look at me like that or talk to me in that tone Carl!"

"Well a bit of respect wouldn't go a-miss!" *Was he completely out of his crazy mind?*

Clearly the build-up of tension, combined with forever treading on egg shells about each other's annoying habits, had finally come to the surface. *We were officially having our first fight.*

"A bit of respect? What are you even talking about? I'm telling you that owning up will land us with a debt that we haven't accounted for. No one saw what you did, so we should just leave it. Why put ourselves in a financial predicament abroad when we don't have to? It's common sense!" My anger levels reached boiling point.

"They charge £20 for a missing room service menu for Christ's sake. What do you think they will charge for a broken statue of that size? Think about it!"

"Stop it! Both of you!" Summer wailed.

Carl and I both paused, stunned and taken aback by the fact that we were clearly traumatising my five-year-old with our incessant bickering. I felt so embarrassed.

"Sorry Summer..." I said in a small voice.

"Look, I'm not going to argue with you in front of my daughter." I said in a calmer voice, rotating back to face him.

"Now come on..." I grabbed Summer's hand and headed off across the grass towards the beach, leaving Carl, the ball and the broken statue on the patch of grass alone.

***

I had read a lot about Chewang beach from my guide book, and my body was aching to sit peacefully on that charismatic shoreline surrounded by civilisation again.

We had decided to take advantage of the hotel's free shuttle bus to and from Chewang.

After an eye-watering 45-minute drive, I knew we were in Chewang when the bus stopped directly outside the 'golden temple' of McDonalds – how cultured I felt.

I could barely contain my excitement as the driver explained the departing time in the afternoon and where to meet.

Chaweng beach was jaw-dropping and by far the best seaside we had encountered on the trip. With its striking golden sand and luxurious turquoise waters, the beach had a lively atmosphere about it. With lots of upmarket hotel bars offering delicious cocktails and the ability to hire out powerful jet skis, the location was everything I wanted and more.

"Ahhh - civilisation!" I beamed at the vibrant atmosphere surrounding us.

Within merely minutes of relaxing on a sun lounger, I couldn't help but notice the hordes of people as they trailed the honey-comb grains selling sunglasses, scarfs and slices of melon.

Unsurprisingly, Carl was irritating me beyond belief! Once again, he wasn't happy and soon began to complain that the heat was 'intolerable!' *Yes, I agree - that is such a 'Carl' word!*

Consequently, he firmly parked himself onto a sun longer under a parasol, cranked it back to horizontal and refused to move.

With the sun shining through the faint and white fluffy clouds, and with a distinctive smell of sun screen in the air, I realised that Carl's non-involvement was actually a welcome dose of escapism.

Summer and I passed the time by engaging in some mother and daughter bonding-time in the tropical waters of an ocean that was the temperature of bath water.

The scene that unfolded before us was incredibly exciting as we bodysurfed in the gigantic rolling waves and laughed carelessly as I attempted to teach her how to snorkel.

As we perched on our stomachs at the shoreline and allowed the faint waves to smack our faces, we giggled hysterically. My mind travelled back to a few months previous when it was only Summer and I embarking on the trip. There would have been no stress and no other person's opinion or fears to contend with. I kicked myself that I had invited Carl as it certainly would have been a different trip without him.

Soaking in the sun, I looked around and to my surprise the beach seemed to be full of beautiful, young people. Strangely, despite the enormous amount of people within the square mile that I could see, for that moment the shoreline seemed completely silent. Soundless even... with a backdrop of elegant creatures who possessed perfect skin, directional haircuts and architecturally implausible bodies.

The occupants of the beach certainly made me feel self-conscious of my ever-growing body once again.

Despite how much effort I was putting into trying to eat healthily on the trip, and regardless of the never-ending walking and carrying of the immensely heavy backpacks, I could feel the weight rapidly creeping on with every day that passed.

My thoughts were soon disturbed by a young, glamorous blonde who was wearing a pure white bikini and screaming hysterically at her equally elegant-looking, tanned, muscular boyfriend as he chased her passionately through the water.

I watched as the man hurtled towards her and they exchanged a banter-filled minute of table-tennis splashing, giggling fondly towards each other. *God, it looks like a cheesy commercial…*I rolled my eyes, only slightly jealous of course.

Glued to the scene unravelling, the couple fell back into the warm, blue water as if it was a gym mattress. In that moment I longed for the closeness and intimacy of a relationship.

Although my eyes were very-much open, my mind was absent and transported somewhere else entirely.

At 29-years-old, I'd sadly had a lot of failed relationships under my belt. Some were serious and some were not, but I knew how hard it was to establish that 'connection' with somebody. I could get a boyfriend, that was never the problem, but I wanted more than to just be in a relationship with someone. To have that unforeseen first-love-like closeness was something to be treasured - if you are lucky enough to find it with another person that is…

Despite the endless list of relationships I could put to my name, I'd only really had that 'connection' twice, so I knew how rare it was to find.

I wonder how long it will be until I find that again…If ever… I pondered.

Sadly, my thoughts started to dominate my mood, but thankfully, Summer made me instantly snap out of it by splashing me with the warm, salty, ocean water.

"Let's play chase!" she squealed, promptly imposing a broad smile to spread across my formerly disappointed face.

Sitting bolt upright, I leant into the warmth of her body and delicately cupped her tiny, porcelain-like face into the palms of my hands.

"You're it!" I pelted my way through the crash of the waves, hysterically laughing in the way that a carefree sixteen-year-old would.

In that very second, my innocent daughter had made the negative thoughts about my increasing waist-line and failed romantic relationships completely vanish. We were eventually left mirroring the couple as we hurtled on top of each other like a stack of dominoes, laughing as we collapsed into the water as if landing on a mattress – minus the smooching of course...

***

We left the beach approximately three hours later where we strolled aimlessly along the main shopping strip of Chewang.

Like a dog picking up an irresistible scent, my nose twitched from the smell of freshly wet oil paint. An excitement buzzed inside of me as I observed a multitude of shops selling oil paintings.

Watching the artists' work as they dipped and flicked their brushes over their next masterpieces in the making was incredible.

In ore, I watched the flawless craftsmanship of the paintings come to life.

Astonishingly, there were many incredible reproductions of iconic works from the likes of Vincent Van Gogh, Andy Warhol and Pablo Picasso.

Many people may not consider reproductions of famous artwork to be 'real art,' but if you ever have the chance to witness just how defined and 'alive' the paintings are, you would certainly agree that the Chewang artists have talent.

I genuinely couldn't believe it when I watched one painter reproduce the famous Marilyn Monroe painting that Andy Warhol created. The Chewang painter's canvas looked identical! As did his interpretation of Warhol's famous Campbell's Soup painting that hung proudly on the wall behind where he worked.

I gave the painter a thought-provoking stare as I digested his floppy brown hair that every so often fell in a heap in front of his left eye, constraining him to repeatedly stop what he was doing and brush it back to a standing position.

The man wore light-blue denim jeans with a dog-eared, faded red t-shirt that screamed wartime, make-do-and-mend.

In contrast to his youthful face, the man had severely worn, dry feet that resembled the skin belonging to an ancient elephant.

Standing behind the painter, I intently watched as he applied a lively, vibrant yellow paint to Marilyn's distinctive blonde hair. A question was burning through the lining of my throat that I just had to ask…

"Do you sell many of these 'copy' paintings?"

"I do very well…I can reproduce anybody or anything…" he responded smugly.

"I'm not trying to pass my work off as an original, but it's an original copy," he remarked philosophically, before spinning around and rapidly adding: "Painting good copies requires a great deal of discipline and skill. It's much harder to paint a copy than to paint an original as there's no room for error. The skill is in the accuracy," he concluded in perfectly-pitched English.

Watching him intently, he turned back to his painting and flicked his bouncy brown hair back up to a standing position once again.

As he finished Marilyn's hair, I turned on my fake Havannas and stepped into his miniature gallery.

"Don't buy any of the re-productions!" Carl hissed into my ear like a snake spreading its evil venom.

"Carl! You were against me buying these fake Havannas because of your theory that they would 'deliberately' break and so I'd have to seek expensive medical treatment for loss of a toe or what-ever, and guess what? I've had them for just over a week and so far, no lost toe!" I grinned.

"I have a theory with these paintings - it's a government scam!"

I instantly laughed. Not again! This man is obsessed! *What does he have against the government?*

"Another conspiracy theory Carl? It's been a while since I've heard one of those…" I sniggered as I continued to marvel at the wealth of paintings surrounding us.

"Hear me out…the government pocket from these Marilyn and the like paintings, as they know that westerners will buy them… so they bribe the locals to paint them, but the government are the ones to profit from each painting sold!" He said, wide-eyed. *The scary thing was – he actually looked as though he genuinely believed what he was saying – a scary thought…*

"That cute little painter with the floppy, brown hair - the money doesn't go to him!" he continued rambling.

"Oh, for goodness sake! Just when I thought these theories couldn't get any worse Carl!"

I simply couldn't bear his level of mistrust in everyone and everything! *What a sad outlook to have on life!* I walked into a cove further inside the gallery just to get away from him.

"I can paint from a photo as well!" The floppy-haired painter suddenly appeared by my side from nowhere.

"I can see that! This canvas is fantastic!" I took in the finer-detail of a young girl that hung proudly alongside a Kodak photo of her.

Continuing through, I stopped by numerous pieces of fruit that were carved into various shapes on the counter by the till.

Making me jump, the painter appeared. *Was he following me or something?*

"Art comes in many forms – including edible ones…If you would like to learn a true 'Thai art' then we offer fruit and vegetable carving classes," he pointed to the basket of carved fruit.

I instantly laughed at the thought of unskilful me undertaking such a workshop…*it would be chaotic to put it lightly!*

"That would add some artistic flair to my dinner parties, wouldn't it?" I trailed off, sinking in awkwardness but laughing to cover the absurdity of the situation.

"You need to learn how to cook first!" Carl shouted almost as if in surround-sound from the other side of the gallery.

"Ha-di-ha-ha!" I sarcastically snorted. *How did he know I couldn't cook?*

Venturing further through the shopping strip, I was completely blown-away by the skill of the island's people.

Copious stalls stood before us, selling anything from leather, soap and wood carvings; to welded statues made from nuts, bolts, washers, wire and old car parts. It was hard not to appreciate the creativity and skill that went into the merchandise of Chewang. If I was honest, as a tourist it made me feel rather untalented.

***

After an exquisite day, it was soon time to meet the hotel's bus.

While the sun endlessly twinkling above the waves on the sea far behind us; we were unfortunately stood amongst a busy queue of people being burnt to a crisp by the sun's exceedingly hot rays.

As the time ticked by, hordes of people slowly disappeared leaving us deserted at the once-packed hotel's meeting point.

"We have been waiting for over an hour – don't you think it's weird that every other hotel's bus has arrived?" I fretted.

Shining like a shell that has laid at the bottom of the sea undiscovered for centuries, I suddenly noticed a Tourist Information Centre further up the road. Experiencing a complete 'Laura-light-bulb' moment, I had one of my 'great ideas.'

Peeling my thighs off the windowsill that I was perched on (leaving several layers of sunburned skin behind,) I confidently declared: "Watch Summer a minute whilst I go and see if I can phone the hotel. I'll be back in a minute!" Eagerly racing towards the centre, I was a woman on a loaded mission.

To my utter disgust, the hotel's receptionist was incredibly rude to me on the phone and said they were not running the afternoon shuttle bus that day. What infuriated me the most was that she didn't even apologise for the misinformation that we had been given by the driver that morning.

"Either way we were told by a member of your staff that the bus was running this afternoon, and because of that information we have stood in the blazing-hot sun for over an hour waiting!" I roared down the phone, making several people within the centre stare at my raised tone in alarm.

"Ok madam - we will collect you," she finally offered.

"I'm not waiting another 45 minutes for you to now arrive… that is ridiculous! We will get a taxi and you can cover the fare."

"No madam, we cannot do that!"

"Oh, you will!" I bellowed loudly, before abruptly hanging up.

In hindsight, I was rude to the lady. But her lack of empathy and customer service was what annoyed me the most, especially considering how expensive the hotel was to stay at. I stupidly expected more.

Slamming the phone back down, I spun around and thanked the man.

"Yes, yes," he said as I woefully wai'd towards him. Shockingly, as I lifted my head from my wai, I noticed the man holding the palm of his hand out to demand money.

"50 baht!" he snarled in the merciless tone of Dr C Law from Inspector Gadget, firing a dagger in my direction and piercing through my eyes brutally. I couldn't believe it. The words 'customer service' truly meant nothing in Thailand.

If a person was to step-foot into a Tourist Information Centre in the western world, I can guarantee that the centre wouldn't charge for the use of the phone.

Equally, the treatment we were receiving by our alleged 'five- star hotel' was also questionable. *What had happened to Thailand?*

When I had visited 10 years previously, the majority of the Thai people couldn't do enough to accommodate you, making you feel as though they genuinely appreciated your custom in their country. As saddened as I am to admit it, fast-forward 10 years and I genuinely felt as though many Thai people exploit the westerners as much as they can by squeezing out every last penny they can!

Arriving at the hotel an hour later, I informed the driver that the hotel was covering his 700-baht fare, and walked him into the reception to receive his payment. I knew it was a risky move in Thailand, but I was infuriated at the situation. I also felt sorry for the driver, who without knowing it had become 'piggy in the middle.'

"I think we should just pay the bill." Carl muttered under his breath whilst I waited impatiently for the management at the reception desk.

"At work, I often see cases where people haven't paid for their medical expenses, and..."

"Oh, for goodness sake Carl!" I blasted.

"That's hardly the same thing - for once just have a back-bone!"

How lovely it would have been for him to step-up and take control of the situation just once, so I could actually have some respite from having to do the confrontation all the time.

"Look…" I faced him in a slightly calmer tone.

"I know you have to be careful not paying your bills abroad, and I have no doubts that they would arrest a westerner for not paying up here, but sometimes you have to make a stand – and I strongly feel as though this is one of those times Carl…"

Despite me saying that 10 years prior the Thai tourist industry couldn't do enough for their customers, I did have one bad experience.

I had booked a boat trip in Bangkok to experience the floating market. Unfortunately, the market turned out to be one lady selling vegetables on her one-man boat. Unsurprisingly, when we returned I demanded a refund.

The company refused to take responsibility for the false advertising, so in protest I confidently stood on the jetty and re-directed any tourists that approached. They soon realised the impact this was having on sales so provided me with a full refund.

"I was lucky that they gave me a refund and didn't call the Police, but I stood up for something I believed in Carl…and every so often regardless of your location you have to do just that!"

"hmmm…" he glanced away flippantly, clearly not convinced.

Less than five minutes later and guess what? The hotel paid the fare.

Thank-god I have control of the money because if Carl did we'd probably have very little left…

***

Twelve:

Biting my lip in distress

I have a weird personality where at times I am the most confident person in the room and will always speak my mind, however, in stark-contrast I sometimes go into a shell and allow people to take advantage of me. Totally insane I know – *how can you be both people?*

I certainly wasn't gifted with a mannequin size body and doll-like physique – a fact that also made me rather shy about my body. It was for this reason that I'd only ever indulged in back massages.

Being an intrepid and fearless backpacker meant that (on this occasion) I was willing to sacrifice my body on behalf of all women in the world to truly identify if a massage in Asia really was as unique as its eccentric reputation.

Sadly, instead of feeling like a free-spirited gypsy as I immersed myself in the Asian culture, I instead was left feeling rather violated. *Yes! Violated!*

As I walked into the hanger-sized treatment room, I admired how fresh and well presented the area was. The play of light on the walls against the simple white furniture lent a calm and joyful air to the interior.

"Sa-wat-dee-ka." I greeted a lady that was all pearls and perfume and appeared to have most of her assets poured into a plunging, figure hugging, fuchsia pink dress. This distinctive character was the masseuse: Ning.

Standing a teeny 4ft 5 inches, Ning had a plus-size figure, a round cartoon-like face and an immense scary smile that immediately made me think of the joker from Batman (red lipstick and all!) To put it blankly, Ning was wearing enough makeup that she made coco the clown appear dull.

The comical tone of this massage was immediately set when Ning began pulling my top over my head, mimicking the way an adult would guide their child to get undressed. Then no sooner had she lifted the top, was she unclipping my bra!

"Lay down now!" She directed as my heavy breasts dropped abruptly from resting comfortably against the wire in my bra, to falling gruffly against my chest (taking my embarrassment level to its highest peak!)

Unsurprisingly, my usually-pale face swiftly turned a scarlet-pink colour.

Covering my bare breasts with the palm of my hands, I walked at speed towards the masseuse bed, quickly climbed on-board and placed my face firmly into the hole.

Closing the lids of my eyes, I allowed my mind to travel to a dream-like location…*that's what you do in a massage, right?*

Before I knew it, I'd been transported to a comfortable sun lounger with a luscious Pina Colada and a shiny copy of Elle in the tips of my fingers.

Suddenly, my sense of paradise disintegrated when (completely out of nowhere) my body felt weighed down by Ning's incredibly-heavy bodyweight. Sluggishly, she clambered on top of me without a care in the world.

Oh-my-god! I blinked furiously as my body absorbed the weight of what can only be described as a wheelbarrow of potatoes.

To make herself more comfortable against my rather anxious bottom, I felt Ning's body-weight shuffle robotically from left-to-right, forcing my eyes to expand in horror.

I exhaled deeply from the unexpected weight my body was now enduring. A motion that clearly prompted Ning to shuffle her bottom hastily once again; before finally coming to a resting position and relaxing her legs either side of my apprehensive frame.

In utter-shock I raised my head and like a barn owl, twirled it glaringly to my right. Instead of taking in the tranquil sight of the elegant treatment room, in its place was Ning's dry-skinned, flaky foot that was resting no more than an inch from my disgusted face!

Alarmingly, I crooked my neck to the left and as expected, Ning's other foot also harboured dry, broken skin as it rested inches from my horror-struck face.

As my lips curled up in distaste, Ning's hands pounded my back firmly in a robotic motion. The pain was excruciating and certainly wasn't what I'd call relaxing.

Within several minutes of being physically beaten, my body was comatose from the repeated blows I had agonizingly endured. I didn't even hear Ning's instruction to turn over. The first I knew about her wanting my attention was a hard jab to my head.

"Lady, turn over!" She thumped my head with her index finger.

"Oh sorry…" I apologised, being ever so British. *Hang on a minute: Why was I apologising?*

Lying on my back, I immediately felt self-conscious of my bare chest on show. I prayed that she would have to step away from her ultra-possessive position sometime soon. Thankfully, my prayers were swiftly answered.

With no time to spare, I sat up at a speed that would rival the outpouring of lightening. Fighting desperately against the clock, I grabbed a nearby towel and seized the opportunity to wrap my modesty away from view.

My mind was still baffled as to why (having paid for a back massage) I was required to lay breast-up?

Noticing my obvious change of position, Ning screwed her bowling-ball face up crossly, and stomped towards my limp body. *Gulp!*

Remaining silent, Ning pushed my agitated frame back to a laying position. Hastily removing the towel from my chest, she started preparing her hands for another massage instalment.

Gulping intensely once more, a further feeling of panic echoed through my body as I glanced at the product Ning was mashing between her fingers. Instead of harbouring an expected lotion or a massage oil, it seemed she was instead warming the Chinese ointment, Tiger Balm, between her fingertips.

Having regularly used the product to treat migraines, I knew how much it would sting if Ning placed the ointment anywhere near my eyes.

I watched in alarm as Ning helped herself to another generous portion of the ointment and rubbed it rigorously into my forehead.

Embarrassingly, my body soon burned to a fiery sweat - I gulped hard, body tensing at what was to come next...

Predictably, within seconds my eyes were stinging at a rapid pace as they filled with water. My body tensed in shock as Ning worked her way around my ears, pulling them downwards and causing a further nervousness to rush through my body at 100 miles per hour.

Suddenly, as my eyes experienced the after-effects of what felt like I'd cut 10 onions, thoughts of how I could escape the torture-chamber of Ning's salon ran through my head faster than a carousel at a funfair.

After several minutes of my eyes cascading with tears so heavily it was like an overpouring of water tumbling over the edge of Niagra Falls; combined with the stretching of my ear lobes as if I was the tangible toy, 'Stretch Armstrong,' Ning's voice brought me sharply back to reality.

"Sit up!" she barked.

Building up the courage (whilst trying to sound as natural as possible,) I leant forward and said: "Thank you. I'm happy with what you have done so let's just leave it there..."

"Not yet finished!" she boisterously hissed before pushing my body back down to a laying position.

"I will still pay the full amount if we finish now?" I tried to reason, leaning up on my elbow.

My desperate plea faded to dust as she looked at me with the blankest of expressions.

Did she enjoy inflicting this pain on me or something? Why was she insisting on seeing the hour through? Surely, she wanted to clock-off early?

My mind floated absently elsewhere, Ning launched herself at me in a move that replicated something straight out of 'NYPD.' At that moment, I could honestly vision her walking straight out of a Police training camp!

Ning's commanding action saw her force my right arm unnaturally towards my back, leaving me powerless to protect myself.

Despite being held in the awkward and hurtful position, I tried my best to use my left hand to hold the towel to my chest to cover my bare breasts, but before I knew it Ning let go of my right arm and hastily grabbed my left arm instead.

Almost in a robotic motion, I quickly grabbed the towel with my right arm. It was a move that clearly agitated Ning as she seized both of my arms at the same time, repeating the now pissed-off Police officer move on me.

"Interlock fingers!" she commanded before telling me to complete circular movements with my hands.

So now I was taking part in a gym class too? I was certain this was a warm-up exercise stolen straight from my Zumba class.

Doing just as I was told, I caught a glimpse of my reflection in the mirror...*Boy what a sight it was! Bare breasts dangling and all: I felt completely mortified!*

"Shuffle bum forward!"

Having no option but to play game, Ning hurriedly swung her body weight behind me. Sitting far too close for my liking, a little bit of me died inside. This was truly cringe-worthy.

Massaging my shoulders, I breathed out in complete frustration. *When was this nightmare going to end?*

With the eeriness of the room absorbing my uneasy frame, I tried my best to relax - for a few soundless moments, it somehow worked.

They say good things don't last forever and that was certainly true in this instance; less than a nano-second later and Ning pushed my head abruptly forwards making it brusquely fling towards my chest, just like a puppet on a string.

Shuddering, Ning's hands mechanically worked their way from the roundness of my shoulders to the very tip of my head.

Out of nowhere, I felt a harsh tugging on the elastic band of my pony tail. *What – the?*

Before I could even force a single word out of my mouth, my hair was colliding unnaturally and uncomfortably against my sweat-drenched back. Disturbingly, Ning began to stroke my curls tenderly.

My comatose body was soon brought back to life as Ning yanked my hair hard, constructing my head to fling back harshly, disturbing every neck muscle in my helpless body.

A tense silence engulfed the vast space surrounding us. Just then, I felt the bones from her knees plough deep into my back, forcing me to yelp in pain – a noise that surprisingly didn't even make Ning flinch! *Had I transformed into the product of a dominatrix film?*

Finally, Ning's weight elevated from the bed. As I slowly lifted my head up, I watched as she bowed her round, bowling-ball head, wai'd and left the room.

With the door safely closed, I jumped up from the bed like a rabbit caught in the glare of approaching headlights. Bewildered, I squinted at my reflection in the mirror.

What the?' My hair had been styled into a childlike French plait!

Completely bewildered, I dressed quickly and left the absurdity of what had just happened behind me.

My attempt at a quick exit was an epic failure when Ning suddenly appeared by my side like Houdini, armed with an espresso-size cup of Ginger tea. She then proceeded to usher me to the reception sofa before I could even attempt a polite decline.

Taking a seat in fear of offending (*what's wrong with us Brits?*) I inhaled the sizzling infusion as quickly as humanly possible. The liquid instantaneously scorched the back of my throat...but all I could focus on was making the swiftest exit known to man.

"Kop kun," I thanked, bowing my ridiculous French-plated head.

Skulking towards the pool dazed and confused, Carl immediately noticed my appearance.

Sniggering like Mutley, he declared melodramatically: "What the fuck's happened to your hair?" His eyes glazed over my childlike hair-style, forcing me to burst back into that 'signature Pauley laugh' – a marvellous, guttural, honkering wheeze, punctuated by the occasional snort.

I'd never heard Carl swear before…it wasn't really his style. His new-found normality was actually rather comforting.

"Oh, you'll find out soon enough…" I giggled manipulatively. "I've booked you in for a head massage!"

"It will be a cultural experience that you will definitely remember!" I trailed off, still giggling…

***

With the glorious sea swaying delicately behind us, one of the waiter's (who we'd got to know rather well) approached our table in the restaurant that evening and placed an alluring decorated basket before our pleasantly-surprised eyes.

"This is a Loi Krathong." Leap declared with a look of wonderment oozing from his tiny eyes.

The basket was hand-made from elaborate banana leaves that were held together by pins.

Eagerly glancing inside as if looking for treasure, my eyes scanned an incense stick, tealight candle and fresh flowers.

"Tonight, we're celebrating the Loy Krathong on the night of the full moon!" His hands perfectly depicted the curve of the moon and his eyes glistened with excitement.

"The Krathong festival originates from the 13th Century and is considered Thailand's most romantic and beautiful event, as Krathongs' are launched into rivers, lakes and the sea…Inside, a small coin is sometimes included as an offering to the water spirits… Little Summer…" Leap leant towards my enthusiastic daughter who was waiting in suspense for the arrival of his next word.

With Leap's eyes widening in sync with his spoken words (amusing me somewhat) he declared: "You are then granted a wish!"

"What does it mean though?" I asked, genuinely intrigued.

"The candle worships the Buddha with light, while a Krathong's floating symbolises letting go of all one's anger, violations and hatred," he paused, allowing his eyes to narrow thoughtfully.

"The Krathongs' are meant to remove all the sins of their owners, as well as any bad luck or unhappiness," he continued attentively, the most passionately I had ever heard anyone speak.

"To help their wishes come true, some equip their Krathongs with a lock of hair, a nail clipping or a coin as a symbol of letting go of negative thoughts and the past."

Sparks flicked in my eyes as I experienced another genius 'Laura-lightbulb' moment. A fantastic idea was emerging…

"It happens every year on this particular night in Thailand, on nearly every expanse of water - be it a river, lake or the ocean…" he continued rambling.

"Tonight, you will notice thousands of lights gliding across the water just like fairy dreams."

Wondrously staring out to the ocean, my hand gasped my mouth as I observed an array of alluring flickering lights extending far across the horizon.

Noticing my reaction, Leap smiled.

"Come!" he instructed, backing away from the table and running purposely towards the ocean.

Without haste we swiftly followed, and in doing so I whispered to Carl: "Did you hear what Leap was saying about getting rid of the past and any sins? This is like music to my ears Carl! We can finally stop the Hong Kong curse for good!" My pitch and tone increased in exhilaration, now resembling Leap.

"You have totally lost the plot!" Carl turned to face me head on.

"What is so funny? I am being serious!"

"I know – that's what scares me!"

Carl's comments aside, I seized the fresh opportunity by placing a coin inside the banana-leaf float.

Bending down to the water's edge, I closed my eyes...*because that is what you do when you make a wish...*

"I am sorry if we offended anyone in Hong Kong," I mumbled quietly in the most authentic voice that I could muster. "And my wish is that we are not cursed..." Standing to my feet, I faced my intrigued daughter with authority.

"It's your turn to make a wish Rube!"

Creasing her eyes together tightly, I watched as she exhaled deeply in an exaggerated fashion, before hastily pushing the float into the wider stream of the water.

The sun dipped below the horizon romantically and the full moon began to hover in the night sky. Grouped together, the Krathong slowly travelled away from us; flickering, dipping and dancing into the horizon with fellow floaters.

"Yes!" Leap punched the sky as he bounced onto the tips of his toes, making each of us look at him in baffled amusement.

"Let's hope that is the end of the Hong Kong curse for good!" I whispered to Carl.

In response, he raised his eyebrows dramatically and gave a condescending smile.

"The legend is that if the Krathong floats away from you, the coming year will bring good fortune," Leap interjected as we turned to walk away.

"But if it floats back towards the shore, then perhaps your luck may not be quite as you had wished after all..."

Spinning on our heels in an instant, Carl and I exchanged curious expressions...

"Well look at that – yours is floating away from you!" Leap cried excitedly.

I glanced at Carl, gulping hard.

Please don't float back, I repeated. *Please don't, please don't...*

Luck must have been riding down my street that day because what do you know – the float ventured into the darkness and certainly didn't return.

***

The next morning and it was time to leave the sunny shore of Ko Samui behind.

We'd had a relaxing time on the island, but after the craziness of Hong Kong, Chiang Mai, the elephant sanctuary, the tree house stay and the gruelling 27-hour journey across Thailand; we had been on the go continuously, so it felt unnatural to have quality time to relax, without a schedule in sight.

As enjoyable as the respite was, I couldn't wait to return to the chaos of backpacking and the excitement of the two-day jungle tour that we were about to embark on.

"Mummy, can I have one last run on the beach before we go?" Summer asked as we sat with Leap, wishing him well for the future.

I watched on from the distance as she ran across the beach like the looney five-year-old that she was, grabbed a coconut from the ground and eagerly ran towards me like a pirate who had discovered gold for the first time.

"Mummy, can I take this?" She breathlessly shouted.

"You can't drink that young Summer!" Leap sneered.

"When coconuts have fallen, they are not appropriate to drink!" he shouted, before immediately mounting a palm tree and ascending to the top to pick her the best quality coconut that he could find.

Scaling down like a professional, he enthusiastically threw a huge coconut to Summer's feet and shouted: "Young Summer - this will be the best coconut juice you will ever taste!"

Leap's enthusiastic tone reminded me of the Lost Boys in the children's classic, 'Peter Pan.'

"Do we have five minutes' Mum?" Leap hollered loudly, with that now-familiar look of childish wonderment elaborately spread across his face, reminding me of the child that never wanted to age once more.

"Sure!" I took a seat at one of the restaurant tables, watching on as he skinned the huge coconut from the neighbouring table.

"Here you go young Summer – for you to enjoy on your way to the airport!" Leap proudly passed over the meticulously skinned coconut that was accompanied with a tiny straw for her delicate mouth.

During our journey to the airport, we were greeted by an unexpected rain and thunder storm, which was rather daunting considering the narrow country lane we were driving down that seemed to be filling up fast.

With the rain thumping powerfully against the window, I continued leafing through a Thailand guide book. I stopped at a section about Ko Samui airport.

"The airport is described as rustic and rather like a shack!" I read the description out-loud.

"Great - as if I wasn't worried enough!" Carl barked.

"About what?"

"Flying…combined with this bad weather; now we're flying from a 'rustic' airport." He air quoted, jolting his leg nervously up-and-down in true 'Carl fashion.'

Thankfully, on arrival to the airport the rain had calmed.

"This looks more like an outlet shopping mall than the rustic shack that was described." I said in genuine confusion as we took our first steps into the building.

The airport had boutique shops, an amazing ice cream parlour, a few restaurants and a runway at the end.

Reaching the departure gate for Bangkok Airways, I felt as though I had stepped straight into a luxurious spa.

With soft jazz music playing faintly in the background, there was a computer suite, access to free wi fi, a children's play area; sofas featuring fluffy cushions, and the best bit – free food and drink! Cakes, pastries, popcorn and hot and cold beverages were on offer.

As I sat, a pleasant odour of lemongrass swept through the air. Despite planes taking off and landing within merely yards of the restful sofa I was perched on, I found the gate immensely relaxing. It was certainly the best airport I'd ever visited, and was the furthest from 'rustic' that you could get.

Glancing across the horizon of the runway, the rain was returning with a vengeance. The lounge was clearly prepared as electric blinds swiftly dissented from the ceiling as quick as the rain began to fall.

Glimpsing towards the glass roof sheltering me, I noticed an array of tiny colourful birds tweeted in sync with one another.

Elevating my knees towards my chest, I wrapped my arms around my legs and smiled. *How pretty!*

Striding towards the aircraft two hours later and I noticed the airline's strap line: 'Fly boutique, feel unique'. *Well I certainly felt that.*

Additionally, the airline's branding was distinctive to say the least. Running alongside the fleet were images of numerous cartoon toy aeroplanes that each had their own colour, name and personality.

"I want to be the pink one!" Summer joyfully screeched as we eagerly climbed five miniature steps to reach the aircraft. I couldn't believe how tiny the plane was, with only 100 seats or so it was by far the most miniscule plane I had ever travelled on.

"This is like a toy aeroplane!" Summer animatingly shouted; fellow passengers smiled and laughed endearingly.

Unsurprisingly, once on-board Summer and I were kept busy by leafing through the aircraft's brochures and marvelling at the descriptions of the toy aircrafts.

"Look Summer – it says: 'Each mascot has its own unique character. Sky is active, confident, and lively and fast; Sunshine is joyful, humble and cute; Rocky is reserved and strong; Windy is playful, courteous and talkative; and Daisy is naughty and playful...' Which one are you?"

"I'm cute like Sunshine so I must be Sunshine Summer!" she pulled her, 'let's-show-all-our-teeth' smile.

"Actually...I'd be Daisy too!" she quickly concluded.

"Why would you be Daisy - she's naughty!" I dramatized, gazing deeply into the pupils of her eyes.

"I like being naughty sometimes..." she said with a mischievous, dirty laugh.

Eagerly waiting for the plane to climb to great height, I had that familiar backpacking feeling of excitement in the pit of my stomach.

"Next stop Summer – the Jungle tour!" I blurted out with huge sparkly eyes.

Comically-timed, all the lights on the aircraft suddenly shut off and forced the cabin into complete darkness. *What the?*

"Cabin crew prepare for take-off." A voice announced over the speakers.

I was confused. *I'd never experienced a take-off in complete darkness before.*

I immediately felt as though I had been deposited straight into the British Army, during a time when we were sworn to secrecy; whilst fleeing a bomb-ridden Iraq!

The engines roar broke my thoughts completely in half, forcing me to look out of the tiny window with unmistakable delight. Within seconds, the aircraft's wings had grown, along with a whirling sound that resonated through the cabin.

Taking a generous glug from my bottle of Iced Tea, I peered at the raindrops on the cold, plastic window.

As the aircraft continued to soar through the evening sky, the howling wind desperately tried to burst through my dollhouse-sized window, causing the plastic to rattle a fierce melody.

The thunderstorm's voice seemed to echo around us every few seconds. I watched on helplessly as the dark-blue sky flashed a vibrant shade of silver with every bolt of lightning that greeted us with its intimidating presence.

I clung to Summer as we jolted up and down brusquely and the cabin lights continually flashed on and off, every so often forcing the cabin back into complete darkness.

"Mummy - what's going on?" Summer asked, confused.

"Oh, nothing..." I uttered in the most reassuring way possible, smiling at the nervous-looking lady who was distracting herself by staring in our direction.

"It's just a tiny storm, nothing to worry about. Just eat your snacks!" I forced a smile across my lips.

Noticing Carl's nervous disposition across the aisle, I smiled towards him.

"Not long now!" I mouthed encouragingly as I absorbed his cloudy white face.

Instead of responding, his expression remained firmly strained (staying eerily quiet for the Carl that I now knew.)

"Are you not eating your food?" I peered towards him.

"I can't eat when I'm anxious Laura!" He creased his eyebrows and took a dramatic deep gulp that communicated his fear.

I looked away and considered the Hong Kong curse... *Maybe it had finally caught up with us and that float meant absolutely nothing? Or perhaps I was just being stupid?*

Sitting paused in thought, I fixed my eyeline on Summer's drawing of the plane... suddenly, an almighty thud echoed through the essentially tin-can, triggering a sea of "oohhs," and an onslaught of confused chatter among the passengers.

Turning towards Carl, I watched as his leg bobbed up-and-down so quickly he resembled a nodding dog on the parcel-shelf of a fast-moving car.

The seat belt sign immediately flashed bright and a voice told us to put our trays away.

"That's not fair Mummy - I can't finish my drawing..."

Throwing my arm around her shoulder in protection, it was at this point that for the first-time (along with numerous other passengers – including the dude with the crazy hair, hippy clothes and humongous earphones) I clutched the arm rest so tightly you could now see the veins popping out of my skin, as Carl's had done several times since we'd been on our ventures.

Now I was the one that was extremely anxious. And it seemed: so were others! Even the 20-something British lads were mute, despite them being incredibly noisy at the start of the journey as they constantly laughed and teased each other.

Glancing to my right, I swallowed as if my life depended on it as I watched two strangers hold hands tentatively. I knew they didn't know each other, as they hadn't muttered a single word to each other for the entire flight. Their surprising closeness made me feel instantly apprehensive.

Less than 20 minutes later and it was thankfully time to land. Descending closer to the runway, I almost let out a huge sigh of relief. That was until a gigantic bang (that sounded like an engine backfiring) boomed through the cabin. Gossip suddenly cascaded as anxious passengers began speculating if the aircraft had hit the runway at touch-down.

As we cautiously rolled to a stop, the entire passenger fleet clapped the captain heroically.

I couldn't help but contemplate about the fearful curse – *had we escaped it yet again?*

***

Thirteen:

Life begins at the end of your comfort zone

It was 9.30pm when we found ourselves standing outside Phuket airport waiting for our ride to a local B&B.

After an exasperating wait, a 20-something Thai man approached in a sun-faded red car that looked as though it had seen better days from its endless decoration of dents and bumps.

As excitement buzzed through my body at our next 'home' for the night, the driver rather distinctively turned from the main road and instead began driving through neighbouring fields.

Alarmed, I looked at Carl with elevated eyebrows – *why were we driving through fields?*

Looking towards my travelling companion for non-verbal reassurance, he simply greeted me with a shrug of the shoulders that communicated his equal confusion.

Driving further through the fields, in the enveloping darkness I could just make-out the odd wooden shack. Evidently, the pitch-black darkness only made the fear of the unknown much worse.

Thankfully, my worries soon dissipated when to my delight the car came to a halt outside a building that was decorated with beautiful flowers and solar-panel lights that illuminated a bricked building.

Immediately spotting us, the owner approached and helpfully guided us to our room. Introducing himself as Bill, he was a British man who relocated to Phuket 10 years previously to run the B&B.

The room was incredibly basic but was certainly good enough for the night. Taking our malaria tablets, we soon hit the sack with the anticipation of the jungle tour the following day capturing our thoughts.

***

It was 6am when my eyes sleepily opened to the rock-sound of the 1990s Guns N' Roses track, 'Knockin on heaven's door.'

"What is this racket?" I drowsily pronounced as I glanced towards the wall that the music was blasting from.

"Oh, I used to love this track!" Carl reminisced, sitting bolt-upright and swaying his body gently to the music.

"Mama put my guns in the ground..." he carelessly sang as Summer and I uncontrollably giggled at our suddenly, slightly-more-relaxed travel companion.

"I can't shoot them anymoreeee...

"That cold black cloud is comin' down...

"Feels like I'm knockin' on heaven's door...

"Knock-knock-knockin' on heaven's door...hey, hey, hey, hey...

"Knock-knock-knockin' on heaven's door..."

"Knock-knock-knockin' on heaven's door…" Summer mimicked as she too swayed her body to the booming pelt of the music.

"Knock-knock-knockin' on heaven's door…" I sang in unison with my travel buddies, smiling gloriously through the lyrics.

Out of nowhere (and totally on impulse) I suddenly had the urge to jump onto the bed and mimic the moves of a guitarist. *As you do!*

Carl studied me for a while, before looking me up and down as though trying to decide whether to laugh at me or not.

"Oh, me too!" Summer grabbed my hands, spinning my body in dizzy circles.

With laughter and singing echoing around the cemented walls: "Knock-knock-knockin' on heaven's door…" we all cheerily sang.

At 7am, fully dressed and with our bags packed, I pushed open the patio doors; forcing the sun's sharp rays to burst through the room with force.

"Morning!" Bill shouted from the adjacent patio. "I'll bring you over some toast!"

Glancing to my right, I watched in alarm as our power-balled loving neighbour sat on his patio and downed shot-after-shot of whisky.

Apprehensively taking my seat in the early morning sunshine, Carl and I stared at each other in complete silence as we felt the eyes of our dodgy neighbour burn through our souls.

In true Carl fashion, he stared longingly towards the ketchup. I instantly knew what he was thinking. Clearly agitated by the stacking arrangements of the condiments, he switched the order of the ketchup, mustard, salt and pepper. Raising an eyebrow, I chuckled under my breath as I watched him with nothing but amusement.

"What are these lyrics?" I attempted to create conversation.

"Like a hot smokin' pistol on a Saturday night, you gotta go for the throat; you gotta fight for your life?" I raised my eyebrows.

Feeling eyes on me once again, I raised my chin and noticed that our neighbour was shooting a dark, hideous, evil stare towards me with every bite of toast that I consumed.

Literally, his pupils were expanding as if they were going to burst in disgust at any given moment; not only that but his eyelids were twitching in-between each whisky shot that was downed.

The man's odd behaviour instantly put me on edge. To my relief, breakfast was soon interrupted by a short, chubby, Thai woman who asked if we were booked onto the Jungle tour.

With absolutely no hesitation, we threw our bags onto our backs and left the power-balled guy to his whisky.

***

Sitting in the van, I realised how spoilt we'd been in the elephant sanctuary mini bus with its pristine seats, TV, drink holders and window blinds.

On the contrary, this bus was a beaten-up white transit van that had no seat belts and instead harboured grubby, stale seats.

"Laura - is this honestly our ride?" Carl questioned, taking a seat on the not-so-luxurious, murky bench.

"Unfortunately, yes!"

"There is absolutely no way this vehicle would pass a British MOT! It is just typical that they would use a van of this calibre."

I looked at him blankly.

"You know it's a massive loop hole for the tour operators, don't you?"

Glancing at him with conviction in my eyes, "Go on then, explain…" I gave him the platform he so badly wanted.

"The tour operators spend as little as they can get away with on their transport costs – and I'll tell you why! Think about it: you have already boarded the bus with no hesitation or fuss about the lack of seatbelts; therefore they cannot be sued if god forbid there was ever an accident on one of their buses. They could say that you 'happily' boarded it and continued with your journey with no seatbelts."

"Seriously! Where do you get all these absurd theories from?" I paused for effect.

"You don't actually believe them, do you?"

218

"Of course! Why do you think I have never ventured to exotic countries before? If the world of fraud investigating has taught me anything, it's that you just can't trust anyone or anything Laura!"

"Hello..." the chubby woman jumped into the passenger seat alongside the driver.

"Feet off!" she hastily snapped, pointing to my feet that were resting on the floor.

"But..ummm...they're on the floor?"

Nodding her head to indicate no, she vigorously pulled at the rug beneath my feet and tossed it aside.

Spinning in her seat to face us once again, she introduced herself as our guide and advised that the driver wasn't able to converse in English.

She didn't tell us her name, anything about herself (or our itinerary) unlike at the elephant sanctuary. Instead, she simply informed us that it would take three-hours to reach the jungle. The quality of her English wasn't great and she was hard to understand, which made Carl and I glance at each other every time she spoke to ask, 'did you get that?'

An hour into the journey and we were left puzzled when the van came to a stop at an elephant zoo featuring gigantic billboards advertising elephant rides, with pictures of westerners sitting on the backs of elephants. We looked at each other in confusion.

"You ride elephants now!" she ordered.

Carl and I exchanged confused glances towards each other. *We didn't know anything about visiting an elephant zoo.*

"We are going on a jungle tour? Yes?" I clarified after an extremely long pause.

"Later!" she snapped. "You ride elephants now!"

"We've actually spent time at an elephant sanctuary and have been educated in what comes with riding elephants, so we will pass thanks."

"I do not understand!" she harboured crossed eyebrows and a glum expression.

"We don't want to ride the elephants! It's cruel" said Summer, voice rather shrill. My mouth dropped at my suddenly outspoken daughter.

The driver soon roared the engine into action until we came to a halt outside a monkey cave. Jumping out of the van in anticipation, several monkeys eagerly jumped around our toes. All was great until minutes later and we were rather snappishly ushered back into the van. I instinctively eyeballed my phone. We had only been at the cave for eight minutes. *I mean, eight minutes?*

Our third and final stop was at an unimpressionable lookout, where predictably we were directed to jump out of the van for all of two minutes, whilst the guide took our happy 'dysfunctional-family' photo by a backdrop of glorious mountain edges on a grey and severely overcast day.

I'd booked for us to stay in Kao Sok National Park, which is home to the oldest-evergreen rainforest in the world; with mammoth limestone mountains; deep valleys, spectacular lakes; exhilarating caves and a vast amount of exotic, wild animals.

The advert described the accommodation as a wooden lodge nestled within the National Park. The images that accompanied displayed a row of wooden accommodation blocks that were perfectly lined in front of an enormous, rather-stunning lake.

Excursions were said to include a day and night canoe ride, a 200-metre zip line, a trek through the jungle to see wild elephants; a visit to an astounding waterfall and watching eagle-eyed monkeys nestled within a monkey cave. All meals were said to have been provided at a tranquil riverside restaurant. *Sounds incredible, right? Who wouldn't book it?*

As the rattily-old van continued to venture through the heart of the jungle, my mind was occupied by thoughts of our next home for the night - the idyllic wooden lodge... *Bliss!*

With my head leaning on the sticky window, listening through my earphones to the vibes of, 'As the rush comes' by the band Motorcycle, the lyrics were firmly printed in my mind. The tone couldn't have been more perfect. Smiling, I settled my thoughts to the tranquil and spectacular wooden lodge that we were yet to discover in the depths of the National Park.

*Travelin' somewhere, could be anywhere...*I tapped my foot to the lyrics.

There's a coldness in the air - but I don't care...

We drift deeper, life goes on…
We drift deeper - into the sound…feeling strong…

I felt immensely relaxed with every beat that struck a chord within the song. Suddenly, my attention was drawn away from the lyrics and instead focused on an approaching wooden shack that had a naked boy playing outside.

Continuing to absorb the song, the vision of the boy remained vibrant in my mind. I even found myself comparing him to the man-child, 'Mowgli' from the Jungle Book. I honestly felt as though we were crossing enchanted land and could almost feel a magical fairy-tale wilderness unfolding before my very eyes.

After a gruelling three-hour bumpy drive, the van finally abandoned the main road for a secluded turn-off.

"We are here!" the guide shouted as the van came to an abrupt stop.

I looked out of the window and was rather confused.

"Follow!" she ordered, marching at a speed my legs struggled to keep up with as we clambered out of the old, worn van.

Trailing behind, we ascended a flight of stairs to a wooden hut that was full with plastic tables and chairs. One table was occupied by four Russian 20-somethings that were eating.

"You eat now!"

Feeling confused, we took off our shoes and lined them up with the Russians. Sat at a neighbouring table, we exchanged muddled glances. *Riverside restaurant? Definitely not!*

"This doesn't look anything like the picture!" I anxiously whispered.

"Are you saying this isn't what you booked?" Carl looked as puzzled as I suddenly felt.

"Excuse me," I politely asked the table of Russians.

"Is this Kao Sok National Park?"

Ignoring me, they continued with their conversation. *How rude!*

Spinning back to face the table, a foot-long Esox fish was plopped on a plate in front of my repulsed face. I don't even eat fish fingers, let alone an olive, creepy-looking fish that looked as though it was swimming in the river only minutes previously.

Several bowls of white, boiled rice; sweet and sour chicken, spring rolls, greasy chicken balls and noodle soup quickly followed.

"Excuse me," I looked up towards the waitress's tiny frame.

"Is this Kao Sok National Park?"

The woman glanced at me blankly as if I had asked the dumbest question on earth. With a raised eyebrow she nodded her head to indicate that it was not.

"I knew it! We are in the wrong place!" I stood to my feet and stormed towards our guide, who was standing with a group of people on a patch of grass outside, casually ticking names from a list.

"Hi... I think you have brought us to the wrong place. I booked a two-day jungle safari tour to Kao Sok National Park," I said ever so politely (considering the circumstances) followed by a welcoming smile.

The guide looked at me expressionlessly – something that I was quickly getting used to in Asia.

"You go to Kao Sok tomorrow!"

"We are supposed to be sleeping at the national park though - we're not doing a day trip there. I paid for accommodation within the park."

My confused and slightly disheartened explanation was returned by a fake giggle, being told to finish my lunch (in a tone usually addressed to a young child by their parent,) and being advised that she would find me once she had finished with her group.

"I'm not too sure about eating this food," Carl shrieked with a questioning look as I returned to the table moments later.

"I know it's early but we don't know when we'll next be fed or what it will be, so it's best to eat whilst we have food being offered."

Honestly, I was starting to feel like his parent too...

"You have said there is something iffy about this place though. Now, I do have a theory..."

"Go on..." I took a mouthful of rice, mischievously chuckling inside at what was to come.

Every time Carl pitched one of his whacky theories to me, my reaction was to laugh and totally dismiss it – which was something that he never seemed to pick up on. Instead, he would continue to spill his garbage-ridden theories regardless of my lack of interest and every time he did, he would act as though it was the first theory he'd ever told me. Hysterically, each one would be delivered with such enthusiasm and animation it would amuse me even more.

Although he did drive me insane, Carl's creative mind and absolute passion for what he believed in was something that I certainly admired about him.

"Imagine this…" he rambled to my now rather amused expression.

"What if the guide was to give us food poisoning on purpose so that she could take us to a treatment centre that would of course be run by her friends or family; and in doing so, we would then claim on our health insurance – meaning they would profit from it!!"

I smirked.

"Now Carl, that theory could actually happen…" I bit into a chicken ball with attitude.

"Mmmmm yum!" I teased, taking another greasy bite.

"Poisoned?" Summer questioned in alarm, clearly ear-wigging our very 'grown-up' conversation.

"He's joking – eat up!"

We were just finishing our last mouthful of food when I spotted the guide climbing into the busy van. In blind panic (thinking that she was about to make a rather convenient, swift exit) I hastily flung down my cutlery and ran at speed towards the van, desperate to catch her.

"Hello!" I shouted.

"Oh - hello - your room is ready now, come!" she stepped out of the van and marched at what felt like 100-miles-per-hour ahead of me. *Was she purposely trying to lose me?*

We came to a stop next to a man who looked to be in his 50's. He wore flip flops complimented with blue shorts and had a distinctive enormously hairy stomach that rested over his shorts.

"I have to take the other group back to the city so he will now be your guide." She stated before making a quick exit.

"That is your room." Our new guide broke into my thoughts, pointing towards a single wooden cabin that was elevated by stilts and sat next to a brown, murky river that screamed total disappointment. It certainly didn't replicate the picture in the advertisement that was for sure.

"Err ok. Do you have the key?" I asked, totally bewildered by what was unfolding.

"No keys – remains open," he spat, before yelling something in Thai to a boy that was weeding on the opposite side of the field.

I turned around totally dumbfounded. With anger on his face, Carl was storming towards me with Summer in tow.

"Look at that: our backpacks have just been carelessly dumped on the ground!" he barked in distaste.

"Sod the backpacks! We have much bigger things to worry about..." I nervously scanned the property, apprehension building by the second. *Where the hell were we?*

"This place is so weird Carl!" I tried to think of my next Laura-lightbulb idea.

Inside our hut, I griped at the unembellished room that contained two double beds with mosquito nets that were littered with holes.

The bathroom was the size of a small cupboard and (true to form for Thailand) featured a wall that was merely the height of my 5ft 7 inches self, no toilet roll whatsoever, and as a feasible replacement: a shower that stood above the toilet.

Struggling to hide my dismay, I bit my lip and peered around the empty room.

Catching my eye, Summer plonked herself on the terrace bench and squinted out towards the murky river. Taking a seat alongside her and putting my arm around her shoulders protectively, we remained silent whilst we analysed our newfound surroundings.

Disturbing the peace, a red truck halted below our cabin.

I watched intently as a mid-twenties blonde man jumped out of the truck and went below our feet to a shed underneath.

"Are you ready to canoe?" he tilted his head and shouted up towards me, tying string around the red canoe on the back of the truck.

"Who me?" I stared down blankly.

"Of course, you! I have it down that you're canoeing: yes?"

Without saying another word, the man jumped into the driver's seat before yelling at Carl to sit at the back of the truck with a Thai man and the canoe.

"You guys can come inside with me," he patted the seat next to him.

I roared with laughter when at 60mph, the truck climbed a steep mountain's edge as Carl clasped the side of the canoe as if his life depended on it.

Throughout the drive, I learnt that our driver was from Germany and had arrived as a backpacker three years previously. He said he was 'so in love with the place' that he decided to stay. *Really?*

The conversation transported me right back to when I visited a hippy village in the hills of the east-coast of Australia. There were rumours flying around that many backpackers had joined tribes in the mountains to 'find' themselves and never returned to their original lives back home.

I looked at the guy with his surfer-blonde locks, muscles and deep tan, and sniggered about how out of place he must look against the village folk he now lived amongst.

We soon arrived at the top of a long-grassed steep hill, where Summer was given a lifejacket and we were instructed to make our way down by foot.

At the river's edge, the Thai man jumped inside the canoe and the blonde guy quickly left without saying goodbye. I have to say, I thought that was rather rude given the conversation I'd just had with him. *Whatever happened to having a connection with someone?*

Within minutes the four of us were huddled inside one extra-long canoe where we stayed on board for just over an hour.

Throughout the journey Summer marvelled at two iguanas and was incredibly excited when, peering through the nearby forestry, we spotted a shiny black snake with bright yellow crossbars that was wrapped around a tree.

"Wow - look at that snake!" she triumphantly yelled.

"Where?" I shrieked in high-decimal horror, thinking it was on the canoe.

"No Mummy! In the bushes!" she giggled hysterically at my sudden panic.

"That's an 'Ngu Sam Liam' – otherwise known as a 'Banded Kraits," the Thai man leaned over the canoe's edge.

"Those snakes can measure about the same height as your mother!" he teased my young daughter.

"They are lethargic during the day so the snake is most likely asleep now… but they're extremely poisonous so should be avoided at all times!"

Continuing to sail along, I suddenly noticed our hut from the distance.

"Come…" the man ordered as we carefully climbed out of the canoe and trudged across a patch of grass that sat opposite our hut.

The space was so small that I instantly noticed a zip line that ran from one side of the 'garden' to the other.

"You go on zip wire now – you get one turn each. Who is going first?" he asked in a military-style fashion.

The zip line was fun but over within a measly 15 seconds.

"This can't possibly be the one they advertised," I sneered afterwards.

"They said it was 200 metres, which is the equivalent of four lengths of a full-sized pool. This looks more like the length of a typical garden in a terrace house!"

"Maybe they meant 20 and the extra zero was a typo." Carl giggled. *Wow! A joke from 'Mr Serious?'*

"You know what? I think that's the funniest joke you have ever told!" I sniggered (genuinely meaning it.)

"What now, Mummy?"

"Good question…" I gazed around the vacant land glumly before venturing on a mission to hunt down our guide.

Heading into the restaurant, I found him perched at one of the tables watching TV. He was still bare-chested with his enormous stomach proudly balanced over his shorts. *Urgh! This was not a sight that I wanted to consume with my unprotected eyes…*

"Excuse me… I'm sorry for keep going on, but we have paid for a two-day jungle safari to Kao Sok. This clearly isn't it!" I asked extremely politely considering how tired I was of the tedious situation we'd found ourselves in.

"I tell you…national park tomorrow! Today canoe and zip line!"

"We have just done both activities and it's only 1.30pm - so what do we do now?" I could feel my cheeks growing hotter and redder with frustration.

"You have free time until sauna at 6pm!" he turned his back and scratched his bare, sweaty stomach.

I screwed my face up in total disgust.

"Free time? We have paid for a tour therefore it's up to you to keep us entertained and give us activities to do throughout the day. You can't now tell me that an hour in and that's all there is to do – there's nothing else here!" I snapped. As an afterthought I then shouted: "And where are all the other people? This is supposed to be a tour and we are the only ones here!"

I must have seriously pushed his irritation button when out of nowhere, the man stood up, drained his drink, slammed the glass onto the table in a fit of rage; and muttered something in Thai before storming through the double swing-doors that led into the kitchen.

"Come on: let's go back to the room," Carl sensibly suggested as we were left standing in the deserted restaurant.

Feeling useless and extremely unsatisfied, I had no choice but to follow.

***

Sitting on the terrace drawing pictures with Summer, I looked at my watch feeling insanely bored.

"Carl - it's only 2pm! We've only wasted 30 minutes. I can't sit here any longer. I'm going to find something for us to do!" I raced down the stairs and back towards the restaurant like a mad-woman on a mission.

Bouncing across the gravel path, I looked around the deserted property and noted that we were still the only tourists there. I couldn't even see the Russians anymore. I just didn't understand what was going on. *Where were all the people?*

Trudging up the stairs to the restaurant, I arrived to an empty room.

Seeing that the guide wasn't there, I headed towards the hut he had been in previously.

Out of breath from my incessant marching, I peered through the window to an entourage of clothes that were draped over every available space. The guide was lazily slumped on the sofa.

Hmmm…a familiar theme of bone-idleness…

"Hello: anyone there?" I called.

Making me jump, the guide and his vertical bed-hair immediately appeared through a washing line of clothes that hung diagonally across the room.

"Oh…you made me jump!" I smiled as warmly as I could.

"I'm sorry to bother you again…but we can't just sit on our balcony until 6pm with nothing to do. I have an energetic child with me you see!" I giggled awkwardly, even though the situation wasn't at all funny and was actually rather uncomfortable.

"Follow me..." he rolled his eyes in an agitated fashion, sighing heavily. Immediately marching across the land, we arrived to a severely worn, blue door.

With a smug look across his face (as though he was doing me a favour,) he announced: "This is the sauna – I can put it on for you early if you like?"

"We have a five-year-old with us so we can't have a sauna, and anyway…" I trailed off, peering my head into the room.

"Where's the temperature gauge? In fact - there's not even a handle on the inside of this door!" I took a huge step back from the accident-prone room.

With his brow creased, the man looked infuriated as he gave me the worst death stare I think I'd ever endured in my entire life. I was clearly annoying him but what did he expect? I wanted him to resolve the situation. Instead, I found he was as useful as a chocolate teapot and his lack of empathy was actually adding insult to injury.

Looking at my phone, I couldn't believe it when the screen screamed that it was only 2.15pm. *To hell with being polite!*

"Look at the time!" I barked impulsively as I furiously waved my phone in his face.

Glaring into the soul of his eyes, my death-stare directly challenged him. I swiftly followed this with: "You need to give us something to do!"

"Dinner will be served at 7pm in the restaurant. All other activities are tomorrow!" His voice elevated into an angry grasp. My heart raced as anger throbbed like a knife to the chest.

"We cannot sit on the balcony of the room for five hours! There must be somewhere we can go? An activity locally, perhaps?" I thrust my hands into the air in exasperation.

"I can take you to a fish cave but you have to pay me 300 baht!"

"Of course – there's always a cost in Thailand isn't there?" I shrilled.

I was beyond desperate for something to do that I agreed to meet him five minutes later to take us.

Gravel pounding, I raced up the stairs to our hut and shouted to Carl and Summer that we were going out.

"A fish cave? You don't even like fish! If it's anything like the monkey cave, we will no doubt be back here within 15 minutes anyway!"

I wanted to scream: 'Have you got any better ideas Carl?'

"Look, it's an activity for us to do so let's just go…" I instead politely encouraged.

"This man will take you." The guide grunted after an irritating 10-minute wait for him.

"And you need to pay him," he groaned, instantly walking back towards his hut. *No doubt to finish the important lunchtime siesta that I had so-rudely interrupted*!

The man spoke no English and directed us with his hand to a white Toyota Hylux pickup truck, where we were ushered into the open-aired back just as sheep would be herded in preparation to be shaved.

For the first few minutes the drive around the mountain's edge was rather enjoyable; and I couldn't help but chuckle like a toddler when the wind blew hastily past my ears like a musical flute.

Waving gaily into Summer's camera, a flicker of cold rain ran down my back. Glancing my head towards the sky, pellets of water cooled my sweaty face as an enormous grey rain cloud consumed my vision. Within minutes we helplessly watched as numerous depressing clouds raced across the sky, carrying a charged energy they were clearly desperate to release.

What started as huge drops of dampness soon turned into a bizarre 60 seconds of downpour as the rain fell in crazy chaotic drops, catching us completely off-guard.

Even though the rain lasted for less than a minute, by the end of the downpour we looked as though we'd completed back-to-back goes on a theme park log-flume ride.

Completely drenched, I looked at my travel companions and laughed.

"I think we are doomed adventurers!"

Minutes later and we arrived at the 'much-anticipated' fish cave.

As the truck's engine roared to a finish, I heard an outburst of birds chirping from the beautiful trees. Against the clear blue sky it was as if the rain had never been.

Despite the wet clothes, we remained in high spirits grateful for an activity to occupy us.

We followed the Indian man as he approached a table that was stacked high with fish food. Without uttering a word, we were each passed a bag and quietly followed him into the cave.

Entering the dark gloomy cavern, I watched my shadow dissolve into the surrounding darkness and paid close attention to the quiet sound of distant, dripping water.

Continuing through in silence, I looked on at our ancient surroundings and admired the jagged and uneven stone walls as they smoothly curved to the floor. It was like nothing I'd ever seen before...

Innocently following the driver's path, I noted a flickering of light in the distance. It was lighting up the tunnel and bathing the cavern into a flickering orange glow.

Taking a few steps forward, I looked on and to my utter disbelief an elderly cross-legged monk dressed in a distinctive orange robe, rested on a stone pillar surrounded by candles in the far corner.

My eyes scanned his body as I paused for action. I wasn't entirely sure on my next movement. *I didn't want to intrude...*

The monk wore no shoes and had both hands resting on his crossed knees with his palms facing towards the ceiling of the cave. His eyes remained firmly closed.

I looked at his blanket that was full of various pots, dotted between the many candles that illuminated against the concrete cave walls.

Carl and I exchanged raised eyebrows. We certainly wasn't expecting to see that when we entered the dark (what looked to be) deserted cave.

I tapped Summer on the shoulder and placed my index finger across my lips to warn her to be quiet; but her pintsized beady eyes were transfixed on the monk and his orange cloth.

Tip-toeing past ever-so slowly, the monk sluggishly opened his eyes, lifted his left four fingers up and beaconed for us to approach. *Oh-my-god!* We looked at each other in total surprise.

Walking towards the monk at a snail pace and totally mesmerized by his presence, I looked at our driver as he continued towards the pond, oblivious to us stopping behind him.

I took a huge no doubt rather noticeable gulp in my throat; and with my palms resting on Summer's shoulders we slowly approached the monk totally miffed as to what exactly was going to happen next.

Standing in front of the monk, I watched with surprise as he touched Summer's hand and pulled it towards his knee. Carl and I exchanged glances once again. Summer's piercing eyes widened as she looked towards me in astonishment.

The monk left Summer's hand resting on his knee whilst he produced a weaved bracelet from a china pot that sat alongside him. The bracelet was threaded with pink, orange, yellow and blue cotton.

Stunned, I watched as he tied the bracelet around Summer's tiny wrist and picked up a stick of wood that was resting on the many pots that sat on his blanket.

With his eyes closed and reciting a chant, the stick of wood was whirled inside a pot of (I guess) 'holy water' and flower petals. Harbouring a serious expression, the enchanted liquid was trickled onto Summer's forehead; a sensation that forced a giggle to erupt from her mischievous mouth.

The monk grabbed both mine and Carl's hands, repeating the process.

When the ritual was finished, we looked at each other astounded by what had just happened. I wasn't entirely sure of what to do next...

Wai! I suddenly thought in inspiration.

To totally dissipate our uncertainty the monk smiled broadly. Taking the deadpan air as a departing greeting I was just about to spin on my sandal and head towards the fish, when a cloth covering one of the pots was lifted.

A rush of excitement buzzed through every vein in my body as I leaned forward on the tips of my toes to peer inside. *What will captivate us now?* My eyes gleamed at the thought.

Deep inside the perfectly-sculptured ceramic pot contained none other than...wait for it...money!

Oh! My expression fell to a small frown. *What an epic disappointment!*

With a questioning look, I produced a 100 baht note and reluctantly placed it inside the pot.

Confusion and dismay filled the air surrounding us. I was under the impression that receiving such an unexpected blessing from a random monk in a cave was an incredible experience. After all it was totally unforeseen and was the sort of experience I'd hoped for on this trip. However, the fact that the monk only did it for money simply summed up my impression of Thailand – everything seemed to be about money! *Where had the country's charm and endearing, engaging people gone?*

My moral compass was totally put out: I didn't like the thought of paying the monk solely for his blessing. Somehow it seemed totally unethical.

Carl didn't agree and thought it was only right that we had paid him. A part of me understood (as monks survive on donations.) However, at the same time it was a religious blessing, and anything religious certainly shouldn't be in exchange for cash. If he hadn't have asked, I'd no doubt have given him a donation anyway!

Continuing through the cave, our driver was perched on a rock as he carelessly threw stones into the stream that flowed between the caves and led towards the highlands of the mountains.

"Do you know of anywhere else we can go?" I asked the man 10 minutes later when our fish food bags were empty.

"Market? Shops?"

The man nodded his head from left-to-right to rigorously indicate no.

I breathed a deep sigh. We had only been out for 30 minutes!

"Food?" I tried again.

The man used his fingers to draw a square and nodded his head to indicate yes.

I didn't understand the square but was relieved for the opportunity to visit somewhere else.

"Brilliant!"

Taking a seat on the van's rather rain-sodden bench, I felt stupidly-excited at the prospect of visiting a shop. It was as if every former-mundane encounter was suddenly an adventure!

Exactly three minutes later and the van stopped outside a convenience store that was next to what looked to be a car garage.

Outside, a woman was selling stir fry and there was an energetic atmosphere surrounding her. Approaching, we noticed the chatter amongst the locals abruptly stop as all eyes unexpectedly surveyed our every movement.

Noticing a line of shoes at the door of the shop, we slipped off our sandals and headed inside.

The shop was the strangest convenience store I had ever visited. The owners were clearly not used to seeing white folk as they stared intently towards us and analysed our every movement as though we were aliens that had just landed from outa space.

"Found anything interesting?" I sneaked up on Carl several minutes later, arms full of sugary snacks.

"No not really...although, it's almost as though these raspberries are going through puberty with all these little hairs, don't you think?"

I stared at him blankly. "Is that a serious question?"

"Yes – I've always thought it."

"Well I have never thought it – although I will now!" I giggled. *He was so random!*

"Pass them over anyway. The health benefit of those raspberries can outweigh the evil of all this sugar!"

"Oh no you can't buy them! Not out here anyway. Raspberries thrive when grown in a cooler climate. Thailand is a pretty harsh environment for them to harvest in, so I'm amazed that they have managed to grow the produce full-stop! I definitely wouldn't trust any batch grown out here – I guarantee that some kind of chemical has been pumped into them to make them grow!"

"Right!" I nodded, totally expressionless.

Pushing an irritating strand of hair out of my eyes, I approached the counter with an arm-full of useless sugary snacks and no 'mid-puberty,' chemical-ridden fruit.

Noticing my presence, the cashier jumped up from her chair, bumped her leg on the table and in doing so spilled green tea all over the counter.

Studying me for a while, she stood motionless as she stared my frame up and down as though she was trying to decide whether to serve me or not.

"Sa-wa-de-ka..." I smiled to calm her nerves.

Bagging up my items around the puddle of tea, the lady didn't remove her eyes from my face for a single second - even when shouting something towards the room behind her.

Seconds later and an older woman peered her head around the door, before three other people suddenly appeared from the back office. I stood motionless as the group gasped and nudged each other in horror towards me. *I suddenly felt as though I was an inmate on the run from prison! Had they figured out who I was?*

Within 10 minutes and we were back on our balcony, less than an hour after we had left for the fish cave.

Summer enjoyed herself as we decorated an elephant in her sketch book, played Russian Roulette with the unfamiliar snacks we had bought, and drew the animals that lived in the wild. *I have to say, it was quite a cool drawing task against the jungle backdrop.*

A hour later and like children at Christmas, we had devoured every last morsel of our Asian treats.

Sitting on the balcony, Summer and I talked about Hong Kong and the city's skyline. We even devised a story about aliens invading and drew the aliens nestled amongst the high-rise buildings and mountains.

Having quality time with my endearing five-year-old was something I yearned to have back home, so as silly as the story was the fact that we even had time to invent one meant a lot to me.

"Summer…" I stopped in my tracks as we later walked across the land.

"Do you know what this walk reminds me of?" I said, before bursting into an onslaught of the children's song: 'We're going on a bear hunt.'

Singing and marching towards the water's edge, to our surprise we discovered a man-made swing that was securely balanced on a thick branch.

"How exciting!" Summer ran at speed towards the simple but effective piece of play equipment.

Consequently, we spent thirty minutes leisurely playing on the swing without a care in the world. Sadly, the fun was soon put to a stop when another burst of rain pounded down on us as hard as nails, forcing us back to our unwelcoming balcony.

Despite trying to make light of the situation (and engaging in any activity I could think of to entertain a certain five-year-old,) a part of me felt incredibly frustrated. I had spent three years saving for this once-in-a-lifetime opportunity, and with limited days left time shouldn't have been wasted. In that very moment - that was exactly what we were doing.

The blow of our circumstances rapidly took the wind out of my sails somewhat. My frustration was also heightened by the fact that we were isolated with nobody to share the experience with. The unfriendliness of the staff was also adding to my sense of distress…nothing seemed to add up, making me feel constantly on edge.

The most-shocking part about the 'tour' was that they had a pet Gibbon that was placed in an unshaded cage that was far too small for a monkey of its size. It had no space to swing and for the entire time we were there, we hadn't seen the guide feed it, give it water or even let it out.

Next to the gibbon was another cage that housed an un-kept rabbit. The floor of the cage was wire, so the rabbit couldn't move around at all. Equally, it had no shade and was given no entertainment or food whilst we were there. *That's animal cruelty, surely?*

By 6.30pm we had exhausted every activity available. I'd even wasted an hour using every hair grip I owned to cover the holes in the mosquito nets. We had simply (and rather painfully) ran out of things to do! The length of our stay loomed ahead like a prison sentence.

With half-an-hour to wait until our evening meal, we decided to head to the restaurant (again, a term I will use loosely) early to try and kill some time.

On-route, we stopped momentarily at the cages of the gibbon and the rabbit. I immediately felt a wave of sadness sweep over me. The poor care they were receiving was completely devastating.

On our approach, the gibbon excitedly swung (well, the one swing that it could) to the side of the cage we were approaching from. Thrilled, he immediately placed his hand through the wire to touch us.

I was struck by the gibbon's love, affection and level of trust, given the circumstance he was in.

"Look Mummy - he's putting his hand out to try and shake my hand!" Summer screamed in exhilaration as the two of them held hands.

"Why is the rabbit's fur all matted Mummy?"

I peered at the rabbit. Its fur was a car crash of mangled hair interlaced together and connected by thick knots.

"It looks as though they have never brushed or washed it Rube." I said in a glum voice.

Leaving the neglected animals, we headed inside the restaurant. I felt instantly awkward when the guide and two ladies were sat on plastic chairs (watching a vintage big-backed TV) hysterically laughing at a Thai version of the talent show: 'The Voice.'

Noticing our obviously inconvenient presence, the guide exasperatingly rolled his eyes at one of the ladies before breaking into a melodramatic laughter. My interpretation of him was negatively clouded by the vision of Matilda's cruel slob-of-a-father from Roald Dahl's iconic film, Matilda. *He could play that character so well!* I thought, cautiously taking my seat.

"How long do you think these dishes have been prepared for in the kitchen?" Carl whispered after being served our first dish of the evening.

"I dread to think – let's just stick to the rice and avoid the chicken like the plague." I warned over the trio's hysterical screeching of laughter.

"I wonder what he's saying that is so funny?" I asked as the judge delivered feedback to a singer on the show.

It was such a strange and uncomfortable atmosphere; I felt as though I was in a prison and being kept forcibly against my will. I had clearly pissed the guide off (the eye-rolling indicated that his female companions were informed of this.) We were clearly not welcome. *Christ! We didn't even know where we were. It certainly wasn't Kao Sok National Park, that was for sure!*

"Mummy, I don't want my pineapple so can I give it to the monkey?"

"Good idea! In fact, let's take all the fruit and give it to the gibbon and rabbit." I immediately began wrapping the fruit into napkins and placing them discreetly into my bag.

I have never been a soppy animal person, but the trip was steadily revealing emotions I was unaware I had towards animals.

"Dinner has only wasted 30 minutes!" I blew air out of my nostrils like Puff the magic dragon as we clambered disappointingly down the stairs of the restaurant, back towards the animals.

Excited to see us (*At least someone was!*) The gibbon immediately placed his arm through the wire cage. With his palm extended, we carefully positioned copious chunks of pineapple and apple into his eager hand.

Being extra cautious, he slowly retracted each piece of fruit through the wire of the cage. It was as though he'd dropped food on many occasions; and just as a human would think, he was desperately trying to not drop the occasional feed that he was now receiving.

It made me think about how I had felt only minutes before. Alongside us, this monkey was also a prisoner to the guide. In contrast to us, however, his fate had no expiry date. Depressingly, the ugly side of humanity was rearing its ugly head once again.

Glaring deep into the monkey's eyes, he looked awfully dejected. *This was no life for any animal... he should be in the jungle roaming free...*

"Wow - look at those people!" Summer animatedly yelled, pointing towards the river.

To our admiration, we watched on as local people crossed the river in the most unconventional way possible.

Armed with a simple piece of string that crossed from one side of the river to the other, we watched as three men and one child balanced their bodies onto a plank of bamboo and pulled themselves along using the string. It was so simple, yet mesmerising and incredibly resourceful.

***

It was 10pm and feeling incredibly apprehensive, I paced the wooden cabin unable to sleep.

We were in the middle of god knows where with people that didn't like us, in a room that didn't lock; and next to a river that anyone could cross.

The fact that we were in a tourist ghost town, combined with the fact that our guide didn't have a kind bone in his body, unnerved me. I'd also concluded that we'd clearly been conned by the tour company: so, did I feel safe to sleep? *Did I heck.*

Pacing up-and-down the cabin's creaky floor boards, I desperately tried to get a signal on my phone - but it was impossible! We had never been so cut-off from the world...

"I'm going on the balcony to see if I can get a signal!" I flung the door open and frantically waved my phone in the air... to which it made absolutely no difference.

"Laura: come back inside!" Carl shrieked quietly to not wake a sleeping Summer.

"They could do anything to us!" I yelled through the door, tossing my useless phone in vexation.

"The jungle tour was supposed to be the highlight of the trip!" I sighed feeling hurt, conned and massively cheated.

Looking out across the gloomy land that was illuminated solely by the moon, my chest tightened as I shuddered at just how petrifying the place was.

Gazing angrily at the moon, a nervous quiver ran through every microscopic part of my body. It was enough to make me swiftly move back inside the hut. I very rarely felt scared, so it was an odd feeling for me to experience.

"We are such an easy target to them Carl. They have seen us use all our electrical gadgets. What is stopping them from mugging us? We are a kidnapper's dream!"

"Well what would you like to do?"

"Why are you asking me that question as though we have so many options available Carl?" I shrieked, totally defeated.

He looked at me vacantly.

"I'll just call a taxi and ask them to pick us up shall I? Or actually, let's check into the hotel up the sodding road!" I shouted when he didn't respond.

Confused and dumbfounded about what to do, I unfairly directed my annoyance, irritation and bad-temper onto Carl.

Experiencing a complete 'Laura light-bulb' moment, I grabbed each of our backpacks and barricaded them against the door.

"What are you doing now?" Carl asked in total exasperation.

"I'm putting the backpacks against the door so the sound of the bags falling will wake me up if anyone tries to get in."

"You're mad!" he leafed through his book, seemingly unconcerned.

"Are you not worried? I don't get it? During this entire trip you have over-analysed and worried about everything! And now – when we could actually be in real danger, you don't care?" I asked, totally bewildered.

"Laura…If they were going to do anything to us then they would have done it by now. Just go to sleep and what will be will be!" He said in a *here-we-go-again* voice.

I suddenly felt as though we had switched roles - and I didn't like it.

They say that silence is powerful in the face of adversity, so, I didn't respond and instead lay next to a sound-asleep Summer; but no matter how hard I tried to sleep I was wide awake.

I kicked myself for not trusting my instincts earlier. We should have left as soon as I realised that we had been mis-sold the tour.

"Do you want me to come and sleep in your bed?" Carl asked, completely out of the blue.

I have always been a strong-willed person who didn't need a man, but at that moment in time I totally lost my head, swallowed my pride and said 'yes.' *Laura! What are you doing?*

***

Fourteen:

The magic of watching the moon shine from the other side of the world

The next morning I awoke to the sound of the birds chirping, which was pleasant until I opened my eyes and remembered where I was.

Throwing on some clothes with sleepy dust still resting in my eyes, I went on a mission to find the guide.

With hardness, I banged on his door to warn of my presence. After several minutes a dark shadow emerged. It was him.

Standing sluggishly in a pair of flimsy shorts that displayed his belly slumped over the waist band, he looked mystified to see me standing on his door step at 7am. *Surely, he wanted shot of me as quickly as I wanted to be shot of him?*

"I want to go back to Phuket this morning!" I ordered with meaningful expression buried into my eyes. I was a woman who meant business.

"That's not possible – we are going to the national park today - like you wanted."

"Absolutely no way! You have already wasted enough of our time! There's no way you're wasting another day of it!"

With a frustrated sigh, he leaned into my 'private' space.

"Ok! Someone can take you to the city - but it will cost!"

"Are you kidding me? You have already conned us out of hundreds of pounds and now you have the cheek to try and squeeze more money out of me!"

"Well if you want to go…" he belly-laughed. "Then you will have to pay…"

After 10 minutes of arguing my case I knew I had no choice but to swallow my pride and admit defeat. *He had me where we wanted and he knew it.*

"Fine - I'll pay!" I frustratingly yelled, cursing myself inside for having to give in.

"Your driver needs to stop at an ATM - and I want to go in the next five minutes!"

"No, no, have some breakfast first!" he declared with an ever-so-fake smile. *Was he for real? What was he playing at?*

"I don't want your breakfast! I just want to go back to Phuket!" I yelled with my pitch significantly loud, causing his eyes to widen with further amusement.

"No need to get so upset, we are all friends here!" He gave a cunning smirk, before hysterically laughing (which in turn imposed his enormously-large belly to wobble in sync.)

Prick! I stormed towards our hut with rage oozing from every pore in my body.

"See you soon lady!" he shouted across the field through the roar of his evil laughter.

"Where have you been?" Carl enquired as I speedily arrived at the hut, very-nearly buckling over my own feet

"To see the guide…"

"Whilst we were sleeping? I thought it would be nice for us to all wake together for the first time. I was worried…" *First time? What's he talking about?*

Distracted by both determination and infuriation, I began picking items up from the floor at an immense speed, carelessly throwing them into the backpacks.

"We are going to Phuket in five minutes so hurry up and get dressed!" I yelled, shoving three garments into my bag in one sweep.

"It's also going to cost around £80, but right now I'd pay double to get the hell out of here! I know its money that we haven't really got, but I'll play around with the figures and see if I can shuffle some other activities around to reclaim it."

Exactly three minutes and 45 seconds later and we were stood on the drive with our backpacks on, waiting (not so patiently) for our designated driver.

"Oh, the Gibbon!" I suddenly thought, sprinting towards its cage.

"Where are you going now?" Carl sighed.

Without hesitation, I swiftly snapped photos of the monkey and its tiny cage on my phone.

"Bye little man..." I put my hand into the cage and absorbed his thoughtful eyes for a final time.

"Where did you go?" Carl asked several minutes later.

"I'm going to track down a Gibbon rescue centre and send them pictures of the monkey and the condition it's living in."

"Laura, you're the last person I'd expect to do something like that. You don't even like animals!"

"I don't dislike them! I just can't bear the thought of that monkey being left behind. It shouldn't be living in that condition Carl! If I could, I'd take it with me now!"

He shook his head violently. "You are a walking contradiction!"

My mouth dropped. *Can't a girl show some compassion? How rude!*

Waiting in the engulfing silence, I breathed a deep, frustrating sigh and looked towards Carl.

It was starting to irritate me that I always had to be the one to sort all our troubles out all the time. I had confronted our initial guide to find out what was going on; followed by arguing with this guide non-stop to try and resolve the situation we had found ourselves in. I had organised the fish cave visit, then the shop visit. I was also the one to barricade the door in last night, and I had to organise an escape route this morning. It had all been me!

I'm not saying that I needed a man to take charge, but it would have been nice if I could have taken a step back and Carl had taken control just once.

***

The three-hour drive to Phuket was more intense and nerve-wrecking then the latest roller-coaster ride at your favourite theme park. At least with a roller-coaster there is an element of trust with the park. You know the ride has been safety tested countless times and others have been on it and emerged safe, so the odds are on your side. The same, unfortunately, could not be said for the drive we terrifyingly had to endure.

With the driver speeding into blind corners on the severely steep slopes of the mountain's edge, combined with repeatedly overtaking numerous cars at the same time, the drive was so petrifying I had totally lost my ability to speak.

I cannot even label myself as a nervous passenger. Speed is my middle name and I love nothing more than to get my adrenaline pumping. However, this was a nervous, intense feeling that I didn't like. Especially as my child was in the car.

Concluding that the sensible option was to stop looking ahead and instead glance out of the window to my left, I couldn't believe my eyes when the driver suddenly moved the car into the hard shoulder without indicating. In doing so he marginally missed a motorbike that was travelling in that very spot!

What was even more surreal was that the driver had no reason to go onto the hard shoulder. No sooner had we entered it, did he move immediately back into the main road again. *It was as if he wanted to knock the man from his bike?*

Excessively wiping my now rather sweaty brow, the car rolled to an unexpected stop in the middle of a forest. I scanned the area around me. I felt totally on edge.

"ATM!" he barked, impatiently pointing to the bushes on the left.

Exchanging tangled glances towards each other, we fixed our gazes in the direction of the bush. Staring closely, oddly positioned between the trees stood none other than an ATM machine - *right there in the middle of the jungle, nonetheless.*

"I refuse to withdraw cash in the middle of the jungle!" Carl spoke for the first time. *Was he finally taking charge of something?*

"I therefore request that you take us to a 7/11 store...please." He added for good measure.

Staring expressionlessly towards us in confusion, I sensed trouble brewing from our driver.

"You pay now!" he demanded in a higher, more abrupt tone than he previously spoke.

Glancing towards me, Carl groaned out loud as an indication that I needed to step in and take control once again. *Well that lasted long!*

"Take us to a convenience store and you will get your money!"

Devoid of all emotion, the man reacted merely by staring through my eyes.

"Look - we are not going to withdraw money here!" I snapped.

After an hour of sitting in complete silence as the car chaotically roared through the jungle, I huffed a deep, noticeable sigh.

"ATM!" The driver finally announced as the car came to a halt at a petrol station's forecourt.

Nestled safely inside the station's shop, I watched the driver from the window with suspicious intent. *How much were they paying him to do this somewhat uncomfortable six-hour round-trip, I wonder?*

Taking our seats back in the vehicle, the driver immediately placed the palm of his hand towards me in a commanding position to request the money.

"I don't think so!" I spat with venom pouring from my mouth.

Unsurprisingly, the driver responded with a deathly stare that communicated a thousand swear words towards me, I was sure.

"YOU PAY NOW!" He growled in the deepest tone I had ever heard come from such a tiny man.

"No! it doesn't work like that – you take us to our accommodation and we will pay you on arrival." I said, surprisingly calm.

With sinister intention, the man began uncontrollably laughing. "hahahahahahahahahahaha!" he sniggered into the silence of the air.

I held onto Summer tightly. Moments later and the laughter stopped.

"Lady, I call the shots and you need to pay me now!" He looked through my eyes as though I was totally transparent.

"In the UK, we pay when we arrive. As you can see, I have the money." I waved some notes in the air. "But I'm not paying you until we're in Phuket."

"Why?"

"Once we have arrived safely we will pay you the money."

The man's laughter cut through every word of my sentence.

"Safely?" he repeated with a hint of sarcasm to his voice.

"Why? Are you scared?" He disturbingly chuckled, displaying a row of missing teeth. *How had I not noticed that before?*

At a snail-pace, he moved his head closer to mine.

"Don't be scared!" he said in a calm, unruffled voice.

"Why would I be scared of you?" I remained expressionless with one arm still slung protectively around my daughter's shoulders.

Summer clearly felt the tension by involuntarily tucking her head deep into the depths of my body. It was a moment that every mother would hope that they would never have to endure - witnessing their child scared and anxious. *This was certainly not what the trip was about, how dare he!*

Holding his gaze purposely, I refused to back down.

Meanwhile Carl continued to sit peacefully, acting as though nothing was happening at all. True to form, I felt as though it was only me against the man.

"Look – it's just the way we do things!" I said in a gentler tone, attempting to smooth things over.

The driver held my gaze for several seconds before turning to face the steering wheel.

With suspense in the air, he thankfully roared the car back into action.

An hour later and thankfully the van pulled into a road that was positioned against a glorious golden beach.

Relief engulfing me, I climbed out and smiled as the sun blinded my eyes and the salty smell of the ocean filled my lungs.

Dumping our backpacks on the grainy sand, we ran like children towards an ocean that resembled a rippling blanket of brochure-blue.

Comfortably, I slumped my body to its knees on the soft blanket of the powdered-sand. The sea song of the waves instantly soothed my haggard body. With the disastrous jungle tour well and truly behind us, I was looking forward to living in an enchanted beach hut for some much-needed respite.

My stomach rumbled like fierce thunder as the smell of cooked breakfast rapidly filled the air. Looking behind, a couple were eating their morning eggs.

The smell made me appreciate just how famished I was. Like a good advertising campaign, the vapour of the well-done breakfast guided our noses towards the café for a much-needed feast. We were greeted by a petite and pleasant-looking lady who looked to be in her early 30's.

"You check in?"

"We're going to eat first and check in after." I hovered over a white-plastic table nestled in the sand.

"No – check in first!" *What was it with bossy people in this country?*

The 'beach hut' was a far-cry from the inviting picture on the company's website. *This was becoming a regular occurrence in Thailand!* I thought as imaginary vapour blew out of my ears.

Online pictures displayed a hut that was sat directly on the beach, with its doors opening perfectly opposite the jewel-blue sea. Unfortunately for us, our hut was located at the top of a flight of unsightly stairs, situated on the roadside.

"The sea might as well be a million miles away. Honestly, if we hadn't just seen a glimpse I wouldn't have even known the ocean existed on this road." I groaned, stepping into the straw square that was the size of a miniscule garden shed.

Stepping my 5ft 7 body into the confined cabin of the beach hut made me feel like a giraffe attempting to stand in a human house without blowing the roof clean-off!

Attempting to walk to the other side of the room, I heard the crackling sound of the straw with every step that I took.

"Oh god: I don't think this will even take our weight!" I confessed, standing as still as a statue.

The tiny square was overwhelmed by the occupancy of a double mattress that was laying on the floor, leaving a space of no more than 10 inches resting between the mattress and the wall.

"And there's only one bed!" I suddenly noticed.

"That's ok – I don't mind top-and-tailing!" Carl smiled (a little too pleased at the prospect.)

"Well I do!"

On the back wall of the hut, a square was cut that pushed open. Feeling comparable to Alice in a conceptual wonderland, I pressed the square and stepped out to the mystery that awaited me. Looking out across the concrete platform, to my despair I absorbed the misery of a toilet and accompanying shower hose.

It was a western toilet, granted, but it had a shower hose resting above that was connected to a neighbouring tap. Glancing around, I could clearly see the toilet and shower to both huts that stood either side of ours.

We all looked around in bitter disappointment.

"Well, let's just eat and we'll talk about it after." I attempted to reassure my travel companions.

Taking a seat at a plastic table that was burrowed under palm trees; the café's seating arrangements felt unobtrusive and peaceful. Instead of soaking up the menu (as I thought I would) I instead tilted my head towards the golden sun and closed my eyes, yawning heavily. *What a mad couple of days we'd had. Backpacking was certainly about taking the rough with the smooth, that was for sure.*

Lazily yawning without a care in the world, I absorbed the rays in the sun that were beaming hard onto my face. Sleepily yawning for a second time, my moment was immediately snatched away when a fly flew abruptly into my mouth! Chocking dramatically, I sat up sharply and coughed.

"That was funny Mummy!" Summer chuckled, eyeballing my dramatized coughing state.

Fully recovered, we ordered a Thai version of a 'full English' (frankfurter sausages and bread) something that I still wasn't used to. *Oh, how I missed juicy butcher sausages, buttery toast and ketchup that didn't taste as though it had a pint of vinegar brewing inside the bottle.*

Despite the breakfast tasting sleeper-train bad, it was a race to inhale the nasty food before the flies took over.

Causing a further distaste in my mouth, a pack of stray dogs wagged their long, wet tongues as they stood inches from our table, licking their lips at my vile tasting eggs, cheap hotdog sausages and bread; which was now nestled amongst a copious amount of flies that seemed to be enjoying the breakfast more than I was.

"It's crazy, isn't it?" I slammed my cutlery down with force.

"If I was to capture a photo of this postcard-like view, you would be blown away by the tranquillity of the scene: wouldn't you?"

"Of course."

"In reality - the beach is full to the brim of flies, stray begging dogs and terrible food."

"A lot like a social media photo then? The picture looks great, but when you see beyond the photo you actually see a different scene altogether."

"Very insightful Carl - I like that analogy!" I giggled.

When I thought about it, the beach reminded me of the coastline they film the soap opera, 'Home and Away' on in Australia.

A memory of when I visited the 'Home and Away' beach on my last backpacking trip flashed through my mind. I remembered how the sand was grainy and hard. Likewise, the beach was so full of flies it was impossible to eat my ice cream, or even sun bathe! Yet, on TV it looked like paradise on earth.

Sitting in my British garden the summer before the Asia trip, the thought of staying in a beach hut in Thailand sounded idyllic. But after the disaster jungle tour, lack of sleep, no shower, a three-hour hellish drive and generally feeling run down; all I wanted and desperately craved for was a bit of western hospitality and normality for Summer.

"I think I saw a hotel at the top of the road as we drove in." Carl confessed, taking a huge sip of coffee and immediately spitting it back out - just as I had on the sleeper train.

"God this is ghastly..." his upper lip stiffed up as he placed his coffee cup back on the table.

"Look, I know how much you enjoy all this adventure stuff, so I didn't dare suggest the hotel," he laughed. "But if you want to – it is an option..." My travel companion's sudden normality actually made me giggle in sync.

"You know me – I'm always up for a laugh Carl! And I'm sure staying in the hut would be just that! But, this hut is far too small for us anyway, and when you consider the disaster jungle tour we've just endured I feel as though we deserve a treat..." I tried to justify another extravagant hotel purchase.

***

Less than 10 minutes later and the three of us were standing outside the 5* hotel complex with a look of wonderment and excitement glazing across our eyes, just as children would outside an adventure playground.

The resort had several pools, a fancy-pants restaurant and swanky pool bar.

"This is so exciting!" Summer screeched whilst running with Carl towards the luxurious pool that had a magnificent view of the ocean in the background.

Stepping into the deluxe fresh-flower reception, I looked out of the window at the grounds with unmistakable delight. The glass was cool on my finger tips even if the heat was scorching.

Out of nowhere a surprisingly sharp index finger was prodded into my lower back. Spinning around in surprise: it was Carl.

"You ok?" he held my shoulders and gave a warm smile, cocking his head to the right as you would to a young child. *Why was he acting so weird? And what was with the close body contact all of a sudden?*

"Erm, yes," I said, rather taken aback.

Attracting a few stares from inside the reception, I immediately felt like Julia Roberts in the film, 'Pretty Woman.'

In the film, the character Vivienne visits an upmarket store in the wealthy area of Beverley Hills. Wearing a skimpy outfit from her job as a prostitute, her appearance makes everyone in the shop stare intently at her with a look of disapproval.

Clearly, I wasn't dressed like a prostitute, but I was wearing casual backpacking-esque clothes, had unwashed greasy hair, grubby skin and nails, and could feel the eyes of several well-presented holiday makers and the odd staff member staring at us…they were no doubt thinking that we were in the wrong place.

My eyes scanned the room and came to a stop by a sea of gigantic sofas that featured huge, fluffy pillows, clearly inviting me over. I was in sofa-heaven! I had never been so happy to see a settee in all my life!

Carl and Summer obviously felt the same as we all made a beeline for the biggest couch and giggled uncontrollably, shoving each over as we fought over the almighty space.

"Oh, this is most definitely more us!" I closed my eyes peacefully, absorbing the warmth and cosiness of the fluffy cushions surrounding me. My body instantly relaxed as the cushions moulded themselves to my frame. I had truly forgotten just how good a sofa felt! When I thought about it… I couldn't even remember the last time I had even sat on one.

"Can I help?" a receptionist peered over us, no doubt thinking that we were a strange family who had never showered or sat on a sofa before.

"Oh hello…" I said in my posh telephone voice.

"Do you have any spare rooms?"

Directing us to a nearby desk, the lady checked her computer screen.

"Would you like a cranberry juice and a hot flannel?" Another receptionist with a captivating dimpled grin approached, carrying a tray.

I swallowed the refreshing juice in one purposeful gulp, relaxing back into the fluffy, inviting chair.

"And your flannel madam…" she passed me a royal-blue flannel that was wrapped in red ribbon.

Placing the steaming-hot flannel on my dirty, greasy face, I no longer cared that I was sat at a reception desk. In fact – I suddenly felt unbelievably stress-free and content.

Somehow, I had managed to turn my brain completely off and instead focused on absolutely nothing other than the soothing sounds of the reception music; the delicious smell of the fresh flowers, and the concoction of various sun creams that were wafting through the hotel's open doors from the pool-side.

I know this sounds a complete over-reaction to having a hot flannel on your face, but in that very moment I felt immensely soothed.

For every second that I breathed the warmness of the flannel in, I could feel the pollution; dirt and grease that had been absorbed into my skin completely vanish from my face. Swirling my head from left to right, I rubbed my neck with my fingertips.

"Madam! Hello, madam – are you awake?"

Exhaling in-and-out dramatically, I almost felt as though I was in labour and zoning out from the voice of the midwife.

Swiftly, I could feel the stretch of a smile spreading across my now sparkling, un-toxic face.

"Madam – hello?"

Then she did it! Out of nowhere I felt a tap on my shoulder and I was instantly brought back to life.

"Who me?" I panicked, abruptly sitting up and allowing the flannel to fall gruffly onto my lap - ending the unbelievable trance I had found myself in.

I scanned the room for Carl and Summer…

There they are! I glanced towards the pair as they hovered by the pool's edge, taking in the incredible view. *How long had I been 'spa-ing' for?*

"Madam – do you want to book the room?"

The hotel was £200 a night, which was £170 more than what we had paid for the beach hut. Not to mention the fact that we had just paid for an extra night at the hut because we had arrived a day early. Combine that with the £80 fair we had paid for our death-trap-taxi ride from the jungle; the money we had given Jaco at the treehouse; and the change of accommodation in Ko Samui - our money was starting to drastically decline.

"Carl…" I ushered him over for his opinion.

"Well Laura - you are aware of the current state of the finances – what do you think?"

***

Fifteen :

Washing the grime of daily life from our souls

Within minutes of paying the £400 fee for a two-night stay at the hotel, we were each presented with another glass of cranberry juice and a nutty-filled pretzel.

"Western hospitality is clearly back." Carl mumbled as we surveyed the pool with obvious joy.

The hotel offered to drive us to the beach hut to collect our belongings. Arriving at the reception of the hut in a van that was completely plastered in the hotel's branding was embarrassing and awkward, to say the least.

Climbing out of the people-carrier, the petite lady from check-in immediately approached.

"Is everything ok?" she asked with a genuine look of concern.

Obviously, I felt incredibly uncomfortable about the situation. However, when you are completely immersed in exhaustion I'm sorry to say that I wasn't as tactile with my words as I could have been.

"I'm sorry. We have come from the jungle so we just need a good shower, a comfortable bed and a full night's sleep."

The lady stood motionless as she blinked in my direction, clearly lost in thought.

"I have brought you a spare pillow for your child." She smiled sweetly as I stepped out of the hut several minutes later, backpack firmly wedded to my back-bone.

"No, we are leaving," I seethed, a little too stern than intended.

"Is everything ok? What have we done wrong?" she wailed in alarm, as if we hadn't just had this exact conversation only moments before.

Dropping my heavy backpack to the floor, I exhaled in an outburst of frustration.

"You have done absolutely nothing wrong! This place is lovely!" I smiled with my arms outstretched.

"We just need something more..." I hesitated. "Comfortable..."

"Buttttt - I don't understand!" her pitch elevated, just slightly.

"Laura! Let's go..." Carl yelled from the van.

"I have to leave - I'm so sorry!" I picked up my heavy bag and balanced it on my achy shoulder.

"Please don't leave!" she yelled after me as I walked away.

"We are a small business - just myself and my husband. Just like you, we have a small child." She continued to bellow towards my turned back.

I couldn't believe her reaction.

"We don't want a refund!" I spun to face her.

"Keep the money and let the hut to someone else - then you will make double!"

Speeding down the road, I looked out of the van's back window and to my disbelief I watched as the woman stood distraught on the pavement watching us speed away as she gripped the pillow motionless. She remained static as the van faded into the distance. I felt wrenched.

***

Arriving at the new (slightly more extravagant) hotel, butterflies were churning in my stomach at a rapid pace. *Please live up to the excessive price tag!* I toppled out of the van.

We were immediately greeted by a receptionist who handed me an envelope with the room keys.

"I'm sorry madam, but we had no standard rooms left after all so we have moved you to a junior suite."

I looked at her confused. *Oh-my-god…the finances!* I suddenly squirmed. *We can't possibly pay out more money! Nor can we now go back to the beach hut!*

"How much extra will this be please?" I bravely asked, swallowing at the disastrous thought.

To my delight she responded with my three favourite words: "No extra charge!"

The apartment was out of this world! It featured a locked front gate, its own private garden, a miniature swimming pool; living room and one gigantic bedroom. We were speechless - it was truly breath-taking. The only downside was that the toilet and shower were once again outside.

"What is it with Asia? Why do they insist on putting their showers and toilets outside?" I peered my head into the garden.

"Don't you think it's ironic that we've left a one-star beach hut that had an outside toilet and shower, ventured across the road to a five-star complex to end up with the exact same thing – an upgraded version nonetheless, but the toilet facilities are still outside!"

***

It's not until you take away the simple things in life that you truly appreciate them. That night (whilst Summer slept) Carl and I watched a film on the sofa, drunk pre-mixed cocktail cans and ate far too many overpriced Pringles from the mini fridge.

It was a far cry from the previous night when I was frantically climbing in and out of the mosquito net as rapidly as I could. I then couldn't sleep a wink in fear of being taken against my will and sold on the black-Thai market! *Now that would be a twist to this tale!*

"Laura, can we talk?" Carl broke into my wandering mind.

"I just want to say: I know I am a massive pain in the ass sometimes, but I really appreciate you for persuading me to break out of my comfort zone to participate in activities that I never felt possible before. Your energy is infectious! The thrill seeking, the forever chasing dreams…"

I smiled. *I certainly wasn't expecting that from Mr Know-it-all.*

"You're more than welcome!" I propped myself up on my elbow to glance at the contents within the transparent fridge.

"We are out of cans so shall we crack open a bottle of red?" I pointed to several bottles of wine that were neatly stacked above the mini fridge.

"Why not?" Carl looked like the cat that got the cream.

"You know? The fact that we are even drinking out of a wine glass is a luxury…" I giggled.

"When I backpacked Australia, we used to carry around the 'wine in a bag' and would gulp the warm drink from the tap when on the go!"I giggled fondly at the memory.

"You're kidding?" Carl looked absolutely aghast.

"You're not as fussy at 18…" I laughed at how insanely different my two backpacking trips were. *Being a grown up now and all! Oh how I've matured…*

Three hours later and the pair of us were reminiscing about the trip so far.

"I love the way you confront situations Laura!" Carl drunkenly gulped his wine.

"As I'm sure you're aware, I am a person that never hides from confrontation…"

I suddenly wanted to burst out laughing – *was he for real? I was the one and only spokesperson in our travelling pack! Summer was more of a spokesperson than him!*

"However, with you I have allowed you to take the reins to have 'your moment!' Which, I have to say..." he continued to guzzle his wine. "Is very rare for me…"

"What do you mean by your moment?"

Ignoring my question completely and instead choosing to guzzle his wine, something destructive in me made me approach the question again.

"Well?" I pushed for a response.

"You women: I know at times you need to feel as though you're in complete control. I could easily confront people myself, but it is nice to allow you to have 'your moment' to shine. I deal with hostility every day at work Laura! So, it's nice to have someone else handle it for a change."

I instantly wanted to punch him in his scrawny-little face.

"Are you for real?" I drunkenly exclaimed, leaping from the sofa.

"Carl, I'm a press officer! Dealing with conflict is a major part of my day-job! Do you not think I need a break from it myself? If it wasn't for me, then god knows where we would be and what we would be doing now. I have had to do all the confrontation because if I left it to you, we would never get anywhere!" I paused to collect my thoughts.

"You can be very patronising at times; do you know that Carl?" I continued, clearly rattled.

"I'm sorry − are you upset with me? My words sometimes get jumbled up. I didn't mean to offend."

"Really? You could have fooled me! Offend is all you ever seem to do, Carl!"

He bowled his head as if to communicate the feeling of disappointment.

"I know we bicker Laura... and believe me when I say that you drive me insane at times! I mean, the way you handle things is incredibly senseless... You can be messy, you're a sloppy decision-maker, you're opinionated; and a little too lenient on Summer if you ask me! Although she is only five years old, you speak to her as if she is an adult! You give her far too much information all the time! Worst of all, you are the most unsympathetic person when it comes to other people's fears...."

"Well I'm sorry that I'm such a disappointment to you Carl." I cut him off mid-sentence.

"Luckily for you; it won't be long and you will be shot of me for good!" I paused to down a large gulp of wine. Allowing it to hit the back of my throat with force, I looked him directly in the eye.

"You have absolutely no ties to me whatsoever, so why are you so bothered?" I said as an after-thought.

"I'm sorry. What I said was not intended to be hurtful...this has all come out wrong. I am not trying to be critical. What I was going to say was... despite all your negative traits and how crazy you drive me... I think...(I don't quite know how to say this)...I...ummm...well, Laura – you know me - I'm an assertive person, and, ummm, well...."

"Oh, spit it out Carl!"

"Oh, what the hell! I'll just show you..." he rambled before leaning in and grabbing my left cheek with his cold, scrawny left-hand. To my utter shock he attempted to - kiss me! *Well I didn't see that one coming...*

"What the hell do you think you're doing?" I shrieked as I pushed him with force and in turn sent both him and his wine flying.

"Laura – you have spilt red wine all over my shirt!"

"I don't care! What are you playing at?"

"I..umm...I mean, it was a gamble but – I thought you felt the same way?"

"Are you for real? Carl, all we ever do is argue and drive each other crazy!"

"Clearly, I miss-read the signals..."

"What signals?" I yelped, confused and stunned.

"Well, last night you asked me to sleep in your bed."

"I did no such thing!"

"You did..."

I glared at him completely dumbfounded. Racking my brains...suddenly a memory flashed through my mind.

"At the jungle tour? Oh, Carl! I was scared shitless and you offered so I stupidly agreed, in which I felt really silly for the next day. In reality, we both slept in our clothes and I was cuddled up to Summer on one side of the bed and you were 'way' over on the other side. What could you possibly like about that?"

"I found it endearing that you needed me for once." He shrugged his shoulders.

"I did not!"

"Well, I took it as a sign that you did. On top of that, you decided to book this romantic hideaway. Swiftly followed by you cracking open a bottle of wine - can you see where I am going with this Laura?"

"Coming here was your idea! And we ran out of mini-bar cans - opening a bottle of wine doesn't mean I fancy you Carl!"

A wave of stupidity completely submerged me. *That comment this morning about us waking up together 'for the first time,' the over-familiarity from him in the hotel's reception…What had I done inviting him on my 'once in a lifetime' trip?* He had driven me completely bonkers the entire time we had been away, and now he was trying it on with me!

"Carl, I'm going to bed! When we wake tomorrow I want absolutely no mention of the last 10 minutes!" I snapped decisively, climbing onto the bed and tucking my body under the covers tightly, still fully-dressed.

And breath!

***

At the start of our second evening on the island, we were informed that the hotel's entertainment would be traditional Thai dancing.

As we ate in the hotel's restaurant, the dancer swiftly entered the room. I nearly choked on my lemongrass when I realised who it was.

Of all the people…

Mouth aghast, I looked awkwardly towards the beach-hut owner as she sat on the floor a stone's throw away from our table. Cross-legged, she clicked her fingers to the rhythm of the drum that was beating a healthy tempo behind her.

As our eyes met, she gave me a hard stare. I flushed slightly as I uncomfortably shuffled in my seat.

"Why did we have to sit at the front?" I hissed as the woman's eyes burned through the inner-most depths of my soul. Her presence made me feel dreadful with every minute that painfully ticked by.

After what was easily the most uncomfortable meal I had ever endured, we left the restaurant and headed in the direction of much-needed cocktails.

The pool bar was decorated in happy, bright-orange colours and had a cosy seating area that was full of the liveliest fake grass I'd ever seen, scattered with a rainbow of brightly-coloured bean bags.

It was a welcome relief to break away from backpacking and feel as though we were on holiday again. I loved the contrast that the trip was offering.

Calmly sipping my bright-green, party-infused cocktail (consisting of a concoction of citrus vodka, coconut rum; basil and lemongrass,) I glanced at the pool that was spectacularly illuminated by orange spot lights; complete with the serene golden-beach that was nestled cutely behind. It looked like paradise on earth.

"Laura, can we talk about last night? You have avoided me all day!" *Correction, it was paradise on earth until Carl spoke!*

"There's really nothing to say." I attempted to walk towards Summer who was happily playing Jenga with a Scottish girl of her age a few feet in front.

"I find it infuriating that you won't even talk about it!"

"Talk about what exactly?" I yelled, making him look at me gormlessly.

"Come on – don't ruin the trip." I echoed dimly when he didn't respond.

"We are colleagues and now travel companions and that's it - there really is nothing more to it Carl!"

"So, we are not even friends now? Great, thanks Laura."

"I didn't mean it like that! Of course we are friends." *Since when did he become so sensitive?*

"No, it's ok. At least I know where I stand now."

"Look – please don't turn this into something it's not." I pleaded.

"We are not a couple and never will be. We are work colleagues and - friends – yes, so please: just drop it!"

Within the hour, we had somehow managed to brush over the awkwardness and found ourselves chatting to a German couple called Freddie and Emilia.

"Have you much planned whilst here?" I asked Freddie as we sipped our cocktails.

"Well," he stringed his shoulders, looking to the ground glumly.

"Obviously we want to relax and do some swimming, sunbathing and have a few meals out... but..."

I watched as Freddie took a deep breath, followed by a long sip of his drink. (It was almost as if in confidence.) I paused in total anticipation.

"In 2004 I was visiting Phuket with my family when the Tsunami struck," he said in a tone that was so quiet, it was barely audible.

"Oh, I'm sorry to hear that. Please don't feel obliged to tell me your story if it will make you feel uncomfortable." I gulped, feeling almost guilty for intruding already.

"I was with my Mum, Oma – erm that's my Grandmother, and two sisters," he continued regardless.

"My parents had recently divorced and as such, Mum was in a bad place. Being that it was Christmas both her and Oma thought it would be incredibly spontaneous – which they never were – and surprised us with a trip to Thailand. To evaporate her troubles, I guess."

With every detail that passed through Freddie's lips, my mouth went dry, the hairs on my arms raised further and I immediately felt worried about what had happened to his family.

"My Mum and one of my sisters died... so I like to come to Phuket to feel close to them because it was the last place that I saw them alive. This holiday (if you can call it that) well, it's is like a double-edged sword really. Looking at how they have rebuilt the place – it's incredible! However, I detest the fact that they have rebuilt it because it's as if the Tsunami didn't happen - but it did happen: and my family felt the full impact of it!"

"I'm sure that your Mum and sister would be extremely proud of you for coming out here and enduring that pain to keep their memory alive. That's a huge weight you must be carrying around with you." I looked into his mournful eyes.

"I was 15 years old and had to step up and be a parent to my other sister, so the weight is more like a tonne of bricks!"

A tornado of sadness whirled around my mind before wrapping itself around my insides tightly. I couldn't begin to imagine what that experience had done to Freddie's life.

Taking a long, hard sip on my drink, I glanced longingly towards the ocean. The same scene no longer looked like paradise and I felt incredibly wretched by what I'd just been told. It made me ponder about the multitudes of reasons why people leave their lives behind and head abroad. There's so much more to travelling than meets the eye.

***

The coastline was truly magnificent and it was liberating being able to walk along the water's edge with the sea creeping up slowly, tickling my toes with every step that I took. The sand was red-hot, making the cool ocean feel like a welcoming relief of lotion on the soles of my forever-tired feet. I now knew, however, that for some people this iconic coastline was etched in sorrow – never to be considered in the same way, ever again. The Thai government reported a total of 4,812 confirmed deaths, along with 8,457 injuries and 4,499 missing individuals after the 2004 tsunami, and two members of Freddie's family were sadly among those statistics.

As Carl and Summer raced ahead, it felt like the perfect moment for 'that song.'

Pulling out my phone, I connected the head phones and switched on the seamless song for that moment - Pure Shores by the 90s band, All Saints. As the song is the theme tune to the film, The Beach (which was ironically filmed on one of Phuket's neighbouring islands,) I was waiting for the perfect moment to play the track, and at that moment in time I wanted nothing more than to hear that iconic song.

Listening to the words and gazing meticulously towards the Phuket ocean, a vision of Freddie and his family came sharply to mind.

His Mother must have been going through hell with the separation to his father, to want to escape abroad over Christmas. For the Tsunami to strike at that exact moment and wipe out half the family, was totally unthinkable. I just couldn't imagine what life must have been like for Freddie, his Grandmother and the sister that survived. The cruelty of the world never ceases to amaze me.

The family's tragic story raced through my mind with every step that I took... *How long after did Freddie stay in Thailand for? Did the authorities ever find their bodies? What must it have been like to eventually return home? Where did Freddie and his sister live? With their Gran or dad?*

It was a story I would have loved to of heard more about, but I didn't intrude further than what Freddie had openly told me.

The level of empathy and sorrow I suddenly felt was immeasurable and Freddie's story made me think about my own childhood.

I was seven when my dad was knocked off of his motorbike and killed, right outside my school.

I remember my mum taking myself, my ten-year-old brother Lee and five-year-old sister Kylie to Greece sometime after his death. She went with her best friend Marie, and Marie's 10-year-old daughter, Hayley (who happened to do the illustrations for this book.)

My mum no doubt took us to Greece for the same reason that Freddie's mum took them to Thailand. Thankfully, we didn't have any disasters or further tragedy, but imagine if we did? As if we weren't going through enough...

Summer interrupted my thoughts by playfully hitting me on the bottom and trying to push me into the sea. *You could definitely tell that she was my child!*

With one ear-phone still attached and the song sadly coming to an end, I picked up her miniscule body, lifted her as high as I could manage and ran into the sea giggling.

"Don't throw me, don't throw me!" she yelled as I felt the cool water rise from my feet to my calves.

Stopping to catch my breath, I gave Summer's cute little face a gigantic kiss and told her that I loved her. In that very moment, I felt incredibly blessed.

When we venture away from home, we never really know what could happen whilst we are away. In that very moment I felt extremely lucky that the disasters encountered on this trip were minimal. The jungle excursion was significantly displeasing, but not life-threatening. Even with my constant low-level whining and my insistence that the Hong Kong curse was trailing behind us, we were incredibly fortunate that the trip was running as smoothly as it was. If this trip had taught me anything, it was that anything could happen at any minute…so live life for the moment and never take anything for granted. Life in itself is precious.

***

Throughout our time at the hotel numerous guests had told us how they had initially booked into a beach hut themselves, and like us had later checked into the hotel instead. I felt as though this news completely explained the owner's heartbroken reaction when we checked out, despite the fact that she wasn't going to lose any money. *Maybe she was just desperate to hold onto her guests?*

Tucked up in bed later that night, I felt as though I had one Phuket ghost that I needed to lay to rest before I left the island.

In deep thought, I searched online and eventually found a monkey conservation centre that rescued and cared for defenceless Gibbons. I attached photographic evidence of the Gibbon and its dire living conditions to an email, and hoped that the centre was as good as the Elephant Nature Park and that they would indeed rescue the monkey.

Completely on impulse, I then researched the safari tour. By the time the moon had finished its shift on our side of the world, I had discovered that the company was operating under a variety of titles and had tonnes of negative reviews. *How had I not seen any of this before? And how long have I been awake?* I glanced at the time in early-morning horror.

***

Sixteen:

Welcome to Bang-cock - no pun intended!

The departure lounge at Phuket airport was interesting to say the least. With no air con, I instantly felt a headache brewing from the extreme heat and masses of sweaty bodies that populated the small room.

With the boarding gate officially open, we stood to our feet and joined the queue.

After what seemed like a lifetime of waiting, I had lost all of my glamour, slumping my sweaty body onto the dirt-lined carpet and resting my head helplessly into my hands.

Patience never was a quality I naturally possess; venturing to the gate's book store to kill some time, I was astounded to find '50p' UK newspapers locked away in glass cabinets with hefty £4 price tags. I was even more dumbfounded that every

267

book and magazine within the store was sealed. *So much for sneaking a peak!*

Not only that but every 'Best Seller' appeared to be either the story of a western traveller being banged up in the notorious Bangkok Hilton prison, or was a tale of childhood prostitution on the grimy Bangkok or neighbouring Pataya streets. *How sad that so many of the 'Bestseller' books told tales of negativity and ugliness. Surely the country has more about it than this?*

Leaving the store several minutes later, my emotions took a turn for the worse. Bright green with envy, I looked on at the many passengers who were sat in the Bangkok Airways private lounge.

Thoughts drifting, I began to reminisce about the luxurious treatment we received when flying with the airline. That spectacular array of free food and drink that was on offer – the mini canapés, the popcorn machine that was nestled amongst the many comfortable seats, not to mention the computers that the lounge also exhibited...

Reaching an even darker shade of green, I shoved a huge stab of jealousy down brutally and stormed back to my not-so-indulgent queue; slumping my clammy body back onto the grimy carpet.

***

Following a swift plane journey to Bangkok, I immediately found myself on yet another toilet run.

Noticing that I had a small child in a rather lengthily queue, a cleaner pointed me in the direction of a neighbouring disabled toilet.

"Kob kun." I gratefully pushed Summer inside the cubical.

What I didn't expect to find, however, were two men inside as one charmingly lent over the sink whilst the second man (*how shall I put it?*) pounded the other with some force from behind!

In total shock, my eyes scanned the immediate area whilst my mind raced. With my mouth frozen wide-open like a goldfish in an expression of stunned surprise, the man that was (*double-cough*) inflicting the pounding, leapt in the air as if a firecracker had gone off; darting me a look with eyes like laser beams. His counterpart stayed as still as a statue, his face stuck in a disbelieving expression.

Swiftly spinning Summer around, I quickly ushered her out of the cubical and hoped that she hadn't registered the alarming sight that we had just seen. *I mean, how would she know?*

"What were they doing Mummy?" She innocently questioned as I remained silent, trying to bide time to answer that 'loaded' question.

"I need a wee!" she complained when I pushed her back into the original prolonged queue.

Gathering my thoughts quicker then Usain Bolt moments from the finishing line, the cleaner noticed me from afar and looked me up-and-down rather puzzled.

"There's someone in there!" I mouthed.

Raising her eyebrows, she screwed her face up like a bowling ball and headed straight into the cubical.

Oh-my-god! I blinked in haste, knowing what scene was about to unfold before my very eyes.

Within seconds the bossy cleaner emerged as she pushed both men dramatically out of the cubical with her bamboo broom, voice elevated to an angry crisp.

Making me giggle, the muscles in my neck instantly relaxed. Opening the cubical door widely, with a big smile on her face and a large noticeable gulp, the cleaner waved us into the cubical with her broom.

Letting out the deepest breath, I had to momentarily gather my thoughts.

"Summer - do not touch anything!" I barked.

Welcome to Bang-cock! I thought; no pun intended!

***

Our first morning in the capital and unsurprisingly we were eager beavers to explore the vibrant city streets of Bangkok.

Despite following a map, we soon found ourselves muddled as we looked on for the 'recommended' MBK shopping centre.

Not one to be defeated easily, I checked the map for a third and final time.

Clueless and frustrated, I gave in and asked a passer-by for directions.

As she attempted to answer, a man stopped in his tracks and bizarrely took over the conversation. The enthusiastic man was clearly Thai, looked to be in his 30s and was neatly presented in trousers and a crisp-white shirt.

After speaking, he screeched: "You understand me?" in the highest pitch I'd ever heard a man communicate.

"Yes - very clearly," I smiled infectiously.

"Wow this is remarkable! Have you got five minutes to spare? I can tell you lots of wonderful places to go?" he remarked in a tone that was desperate for further conversation.

Every so often his voice would break into a loud, punctuated squeal and he would question: "You can still understand me? Yes? This is incredibly pleasing!" Followed by an over-enthusiastic punch in the air; prompting us to inwardly giggle.

A few minutes later and as the conversation was coming to an end, I decisively stood to my feet to head down the station steps.

"And anyway, MBK isn't even open yet!" he continued to ramble as he followed in my path like a dark shadow trailing behind, before eventually flagging down a passing Tuk-tuk.

"Take these people to the International House of Fashion!" He impulsively instructed the driver; bundling us into the tiny automobile like sheep.

Sitting aimlessly in the heavy Bangkok traffic, I wondered how anyone in the city got anywhere. It was absolute mayhem! Noticing my brown, leather bag slung across my chest: "No wearing bag like that!" the driver snapped from his torn, leather seat.

"You put it between your legs or men on bikes will snatch as they drive past!"

In true dominant Laura style, I argued my opinion that I thought the bag would be more secure attached to me than on the floor, but the driver was rather insistent that he wanted the bag to go between my legs.

"He's correct…" Carl declared over-confidently.

"I am a Fraud Investigator in the UK you see…" he began to ramble the repetitive and unnecessary story of his boring life to the driver. As mind-numbing as it was, it was entertaining to watch the vacant, confused and unexpectant face of our clueless driver who could barely speak English. *Boy, it really hadn't been long enough since I'd last heard this spill…I wonder if it is getting on Summer's nerves yet?*

Eventually we arrived at the House of Fashion. Almost immediately we were greeted by a man who was dressed in the shiniest grey trousers I have ever seen, accompanied with a neat, white, crisp shirt.

With great haste, the man ushered us into the building and directed us to a room at the back of the store.

Curiously wandering through the space, I gazed in ore at the mountain-upon-mountain of fabric that littered my eyes. Politely entering a side room, we were ushered onto a grey leather sofa and passed a catalogue of clothes to leaf through.

As expected, the size eight, glamorous Thai ladies were pictured in designer coats, suits and dresses.

"You pick what you would like and I will make for you," the man offered (as if doing me a favour,) before simply standing back and resting his arms neatly behind his back.

"I'm sorry, but we are not interested." I placed the catalogue on the table in a defiant manner, standing bolt upright in a confident and commanding stance.

"But I make nice designer suit that will even fit your size!" The man obstructed my path, looked my not-so-slender frame up-and-down and widened his palms apart to indicate my size as 'big.'

"Honestly - I don't want a suit." I attempted to squeeze past him. *I'm also not offended at all that you have just implied that I'm fat!*

Clearly desperate for a sale, the man picked up the catalogue and frantically flicked through the pages at an almighty speed.

"We have Armani…Gucci…" he pointed out random garments on the page.

"What about you, sir?" he swiftly turned his attention to Carl, clearly realising that he had hit a concrete wall with me.

"I wear a uniform to work so I don't need a suit either;" Carl grabbed Summer's hand and attempted to lead her towards the exit.

"But we have lots of different colours and materials..." The man continued on a blatant failing mission, clearly not listening.

"I make you scarf?" He turned to me. *He had persistence (I'd give him that!)*

"No thank you, I'm fine. We really must be leaving now," I attempted to squeeze past him again.

"Everything ok here?" enquired a smartly-dressed, middle-aged man.

Equally as eager for a sale, this suited and booted salesman rammed his flawless and well-practised sales pitch down our exhausted throats.

"We are leaving I'm afraid - and we won't be purchasing a suit," said Carl assertively. *Go Carl!*

"You will get the best suits from across Bangkok here!" The man continued to push for that all important sale.

"We don't want a suit: OK!" Summer yelled with such a force that her tiny, yet confident voice echoed around the room. In unison, Carl and I erupted into a bed of laughter.

As a gut reaction, I desperately threw my hand to my mouth; I don't know why I found myself laughing so hard, but all of the sudden I couldn't stop. Tears gathered in the corners of my eyes as I attempted to suffocate any further laughter. Reaching the pavement outside, Carl and I burst into a fit of giggles at the little person that she was becoming.

In Asia, you need to be able to hold your own and fend off the pushy salesman; it seemed even at a mere five-years-old, Summer was already adapting and doing it herself. Welcome - my Asian Summer.

***

Lost down a side street in Bangkok, a sign advertising a coffee shop caught my eye. It looked as though it was inside a tall building that was nestled behind the advertisement.

"Look: a coffee shop! Let's get a drink and decide on our next movements." I suggested positively, already crossing the street towards the building.

Inside the double-glass doors sat a long, windy staircase.

Strangely, the building quickly declined in its decor and started to oddly resemble a derelict building site, with empty boarded-up shop fronts and absolutely no human life.

"I really don't think it's wise taking a child into a derelict building, Laura."

"Well, I didn't know it was going to look like this, did I?" I grumpily screeched, spanning my head around the staircase. *Why was he always so ready to criticise me all the time?*

"Oh look – a Nescafe poster! It must be here somewhere..." I continued pass the artwork, ascending the last series of stairs.

Seriously out-of-breath, we reached the top floor where three elderly ladies were perched at a table talking.

"Café?" I asked.

They looked at each other perplexed. One of the trio shrugged her shoulders and nodded her face to indicate 'no.'

"Nescafe?" I tried my luck again. Nodding her head to indicate no for a second time, we were left with no choice but to head back down the staircase.

"Well that was a waste of time!" I huffed.

"Fortune?" a woman's voice bellowed behind me.

"Pardon?" I stopped in my tracks, noticing one of the ladies at the top of the stairs.

"Come, fortune telling..." the wrinkly, old lady smiled in a friendly manner.

Within a flash I sprang to life; feeling incredibly curious.

"Laura - you're not serious?" Carl grabbed my arm a little too tightly.

"Come on, it will be a laugh!" I shrugged off his touch and instead grabbed Summer's hand.

"Sit..." The lady instructed with a radiant smile stretched across her face, exposing several missing teeth.

Marvelling at the woman inquisitively, I was eager to discover the wonders that were about to unravel.

"Mummy – lap!" Summer lifted her bottom onto my thighs.

I mouthed to Carl to sit down. However, in true Carl style he irritatingly ignored me and instead stood behind my frame like a bodyguard.

Just like an expert Vegas croupier, the lady produced a pack of cards that she splashed across the desk at lightning speed.

"Select five cards with your left hand..." she instructed, displaying her missing teeth once again.

I watched intently as she flicked over my choices and stared at the cards carefully.

"Mmmmm..."

She looked completely mystified...

"Meat is diminishing your power!" she soon declared in a passionate, soft voice.

"What?" I laughed, slightly bemused at the reading. *What does that even mean?*

"Sorry, I don't understand?" I smiled rather awkwardly, glancing towards Carl who rolled his eyes as if to say, 'what a load of crap!'

"Eating meat is making you weak - you must stop at once!"

My memory wandered back to many years previously when I was in Bangkok to celebrate the Chinese New Year. I recalled wandering through a busy city street that was proudly decorated in carnival gear. With the community out in force and minimal tourists around, I recalled the feeling of sickness as the scent of multiple cuisines stewed alongside each other, mixing further into the air along with the sturdy fumes of pollution.

I remembered breathing out of my mouth as an attempt to block the smell from entering my nostrils. I shrieked when the disturbing image of people queuing earnestly for a slice of pig's head (that was neatly displayed on a silver platter) flooded through my mind.

Firmly placing my hand across my mouth in disgust, I remembered spinning my body away at speed. Unbeknown to me, however, a man was standing directly behind me as he took an almighty bite from his delicious slice of Pig's brain.

With his mouth instantly stained (and seeing his teeth chomp down hard on the grit) I rotated my body again, but when I did a line of dead chickens filled my immediate eyeline as they swung lifeless from a rope by their ruined necks. I squirmed at the memory of projectile-vomiting into a side-street. *How lady-like! It certainly wasn't my proudest moment!*

It took an entire year before I was able to indulge in meat again after that episode.

Bringing me back to reality the lady touched my arm, looking me directly in the eye.

"Your two-tone eyebrows are an indication that you have a strong sense of right and wrong. This is telling me that your life has witnessed a series of peaks and valleys, but soon there will be 'big' changes..."

I went to speak; but she beat me to it.

"And..." she leaned in close. "This man is not right for you..." she darted Carl a mean, thoughtful stare.

"Good!" I laughed nervously, glancing towards Carl with his straight-face watching us in ore.

"You're a good person, but you need protection!" her eyes expanded.

This revelation silenced my laughter. *Protection? Now she had my undivided attention.*

I scanned her movements with my eyes. Watching intently, she stood to her feet and slowly walked to a nearby counter. Grabbing a pen and pad, she began attentively scribbling.

Observing in sheer silence, I glimpsed towards Carl as he rolled his eyes like a slot machine, exhaling a large, obvious puff of air.

"You need to go to the Wat Bang Phra temple for a scared Sak Yant..." the lady passed me a piece of paper displaying its name.

"You have spiritual Thai tattoo to offer you protection..."

I looked at her, taken aback.

"A tattoo? No that's not really me..." my voice dropped earnestly.

"It's magic!" The lady enlightened me with her immense and bulging eyes once again.

"It bestows a blessing of strength, luck, lifelong success; and protection against bad luck and evil spirits..."

I looked at Carl. *Was she talking about the Hong Kong curse? Could she see something that I couldn't? An upset ancestor perhaps?*

Suddenly - I panicked.

Flicking her hand with umpf, she declared: "A monk will be your master...he will bless the tattoo and breathe life into it! Your head is the most sacred part of your body. The further down the body, the less sacred. With the holy tattoo, you will follow rules to give yourself a clean life, but failure to do so will invalidate the power of the tattoo..."

Just when I thought that she had stopped talking, she pessimistically snapped: "NO MAGIC!" clapping her hands in front of her face, making Summer and I jump in unison.

"Ok - thank you..." I anxiously gulped, standing to my feet feeling somewhat confused by her jumbled reading. *Should I pay her?* I gulped, mind racing.

Uncertainly passing her several notes, she smiled in the most obscure manner, followed by a wai. She then took the money from my sweaty hands.

"Mummy - are you getting a tattoo? Can I get one too?"

***

Sometime later and we were still aimlessly wandering the streets of Bangkok.

"Do you even know where you're going?" Carl asked with a crumpled brow, agitation rising by the second.

"Of course I don't! I know as much as you do - but [of't'en] it is nice to walk without a purpose and just see where you end up!"

"You mean 'of-en'"

"Sorry?"

"You know the 't' is silent in the word 'often'?" he irritatingly air quoted.

I looked at him speechless.

Continuing to stare at him with fixed laser beamed eyes, I was just about to bark something witty in response when (like a firework going off in the background) I suddenly noticed a street laden with designer stores and shopping centres. With a Harrods pop-up shop, a Selfridges-style food court, an incredible gourmet market (which resembled the Selfridges food store) and a plethora of pop up restaurants for just about every international food chain in existence. It was certainly a contrast from the run-down building we had found ourselves in only 10 minutes previously.

I couldn't believe how different Bangkok was from when I had visited the city 10 years previously.

Curiously wandering between the high-class centres, a man with only one arm and one leg and no toes lay faced-down on the hard, dirty floor. I watched in astonishment as he clutched a money bucket in front of him.

The most shocking thing of all, however, was not the man's absence of body parts, but the copious amounts of sleek suit-wearing commuters and shopping-laden visitors that were literally stepping over his body as if he were a bag of rubbish that had been dumped on the sidewalk.

When I visited Bangkok previously, I witnessed sights such as this on every corner. After a few days in the city, the view (sadly) appeared to be a normal occurrence. *But you would never ignore and step over a person, surely?*

I had noticed that on this visit to Bangkok, the sight of people begging was much rarer than 10 years previously. It still happened (don't get me wrong) but it was absolutely nothing in comparison to how it had been, as the Police now move most of the beggars on.

"Why is the man on the floor Mummy?"

Before I even had a chance to answer, she fired me another question.

"Mummy - why doesn't the man have any toes? And why are people stepping over him?"

It was difficult (and heart-rending) to have to explain inhumane examples of injustice to a child. At this point, I stopped walking and bent down to Summer's eye-level.

I explained why some people needed to beg and what it meant, but I struggled to explain how the man had ended up on the floor. It was sad to think that his nearest relatives or 'friends' had put him there, as he certainly hadn't got there himself!

No sooner had I narrowly escaped that hurdle and I was soon faced with another.

Turning the corner, we were met with another beggar, but this time it was a middle-aged woman who appeared to have half of her face hanging off.

Both of the lady's eyes were missing and the loose skin on her face sagged down as far as her shoulder. I immediately distracted Summer by pointing out buildings on the other side of the street. Letting her see the man was one thing, but I genuinely feared that at only five-years-old the woman's face would inevitably disturb her. To my relief I distracted her well, but sadly the woman's image stayed with me for some time.

***

The next time I glanced at my watch it was 10pm. I couldn't quite believe that we had been out for 12 hours. It reminded me of when I was a kid and my Mother and Nan would take us shopping to Kingston for ten hours straight. Literally, I'd find myself in the likes of John Lewis for an entire day! (Being a greedy teenager, the Pizza Hut lunch always enticed me back the following week, I have to admit.)

My eyelids felt as heavy as my feet and my body was screaming for a hot bath and comfortable hotel bed.

Stomping heavily down the last of the subway steps; I exhaled an almighty yawn and stared straight ahead exhaustingly.

Looking on in confusion, a young girl (who looked to be no older than 10 years old) caught my eye. Sleeping on the bottom step and clutching a small dog, her dark-haired head balanced on a sign that warned of a 200 baht fine if you were caught begging. My heart dropped rapidly in sadness. *Surely not?*

Nearing closer, I watched as a man came out of the shop opposite and aggressively shook her tiny body to wake her. Alarmingly, he then hit her across the head with his hand and yelled at her to move on.

With a blank expression on her face, I watched helplessly as the girl sleepily stood to her feet, scooped up her dog and walked further up the street.

Unfortunately, we had to walk the opposite direction to the girl; along with Carl and Summer I found myself repeatedly turning back to watch the girl's next move.

Turning the corner, we noticed a lady sat on the dirty pavement cradling a baby of no more than six months old.

278

That evening as I tucked my extremely lucky, clean, pyjama-wearing daughter into her luxurious hotel bed, my mind was plagued with the image of that little girl and her dog. *I wished I could have brought her back to the hotel. I hoped that she was safe.*

***

Seventeen:

Experiencing life outside of the ordinary

"I can take you to a big market that's only 15 minutes away if you like?" An opportunistic Tuk-tuk driver interrupted as we openly discussed on a side street how to spend the rest of the afternoon.

"That sounds decent!" I said brightly, turning to Carl.

"Another market? I'd rather go back to the hotel and relax around the pool if I'm honest."

"Ok, well I'll take Summer to the market and meet you later."

Faultlessly weaving through the traffic moments later, like a broken record on repeat the driver asked if I would visit several shops that we were passing on the way. He wanted me to pretend to look around, and in return he would be given fuel vouchers from the store owner for taking a tourist there.

Despite my defiant 'no,' the driver shamelessly continued to pest me anyway, until eventually and thankfully we arrived at the market.

Full of excitement at the prospect of doing an activity with Summer alone, I ventured down the street towards what I believed to be the market entrance. Nearing closer, it appeared that the timber and iron roofs I'd seen from a distance were not market stalls after all... *are they – shacks?* It quickly became clear that the driver knowingly hadn't taken us to a market and in fact he'd dropped us at none-other than a city slum.

Hesitating and suddenly feeling incredibly anxious, I shuffled like a schoolboy with his shoelaces tied as I absorbed the community before me.

Abruptly filling my eyeline stood two-storey shanties that were made with copious amounts of scrap materials. Rusty pieces of plywood, timber and iron were held down with rocks, cloth or just about anything the inhabitants could find by the looks of it.

Peering further into the community, narrow alleyways lined the shanties that were literally dripping with humidity (and no doubt bacterial ferment.)

Scarily-skinny children (that were so dirty they looked as though they had never been washed or fed,) innocently played in puddles of raw sewage, whilst a swarm of flies hovered over their playground.

I turned to glimpse back towards the driver, but terrifyingly he had disappeared.

"Shit!"

"Oh Mummy - you said a bad word!"

"Sorry Rube." I gasped quietly, directing her out of the slum and heading north towards what I guessed was the city.

Moments later and a railway line blocked our pathway... worse; it was littered by a group of small children who were using it as their playground. Pausing to collect my thoughts, a man with waist-length, horse-like, black hair shouted at the children.

Undeterred, they simply stepped off of the track seconds before a train deafeningly chuckled past - less than an a few inches from their frail, undressed frames.

Hurrying over the line, Summer's eyes glowed as we passed the children who were happily skipping back onto the railway now the train had passed.

"Oh, that's so dangerous! Children must never play on a railway!" I hissed as we crossed over the steel tracks dubiously. A moment later and we had unexpectantly arrived at an enormous rubbish tip that had people delving through mounts of filthy waste.

"Look Mummy - people are cooking!" Summer pointed to an elderly lady working on top of a dirty heap of rubbish.

Against the backdrop of the sticky tropical heat and complemented by the rotting odour of the city's sewage system, I certainly wasn't experiencing the 'Land of Smiles' that Thailand advertises to its tourists.

Passing cautiously, I felt on edge. It was clear that we were not in a pleasant part of Bangkok and as tourists we stood out like a sore thumb. Of course my heart truly went out to the people on the tip. This life seemed so inhumane and that was no existence for anyone.

To remove ourselves from the edge of the dump, we crossed over a flyover footbridge to reach the other side of the street. Reaching the top of the closed-in bridge, I instantly wished we had stayed on the street as it quickly resembled what I imagined a crack-den would look like. A dirty, spray-painted, rusty timber frame housed several people that were huddled under sleeping bags on the grubby concrete floor. It was unpleasant to say the least.

Trying to conceal the wide-eyed look of horror from breaking out all over my face, I spontaneously scooped Summer's tiny body up and passed through the timber tunnel at a speedy pace.

Hurrying down the steps, a Thai man (who was kicking a beer bottle against the frame) loitered at the bottom of the staircase. Picking my pace up further, I continued to hold Summer's body tightly. I gulped forcefully with every step that I took.

"Oh look - that must be the city!" I tried to sound as natural as possible, thankfully spotting a series of high-rise buildings in the distance.

"That looks a little like the Hong Kong skyline that we drew - remember the aliens invading Summer?" I tried my best to distract her dutifully whilst struggling to hold her immense body weight.

Shining like a lighthouse beacon in the distance, I suddenly recognised the sign from the hotel I'd stayed in 10 years previously. Relief swept over me as if someone had wrapped me in an excessively large comforting blanket, prompting me to put my 'mini-elephant' down.

Peering below the street moments later, I suddenly spotted a canal. Just like a bustling bus stop, there were people waiting to board the next boat.

"Follow me..." I breathlessly led Summer to the canal's edge.

The smell of sewage was so insanely overpowering that it hit the back of my throat like poison, making me instantly gag.

"Mummy! It absolutely stinks and is making me feel sick!" My daughter echoed my thoughts precisely. *We were already so alike!*

"Breathe out of your nose to block out the smell - that's what I'm doing."

"I'm five Mummy - I don't know how to do that!" she cheekily sneered.

Within minutes a wooden canal boat (that looked as though it had seen better days) stopped. Several people stepped off.

"City?" I asked the crowd of people who simply stared at me as if I was an exhibit in an art gallery.

"Mummy!" Summer whined, pinching her nose in a dramatic fashion.

All of a sudden, I experienced a flash-back to the how the city's odour had smelt 10 years previously. No matter how much you scrubbed your skin back then, you just couldn't get rid of the stench! *Pollution mixed with cooking!* I painfully recalled, eyes lightening at the memory.

When I returned home after a year of backpacking (with Bangkok being my last stop,) my mum politely pulled me aside to inform me that I 'absolutely stunk' in her words. *Thanks Mum!*

It took several baths and showers to get rid of that Bangkok stench. Yet on this trip (thankfully) the city had lost that gruesome smell. *Well it had at ground level anyway...*

Pavement-pounding with determination, Summer spotted a dishevelled boy who looked to be the same age as her. He was begging with a takeaway coffee cup.

Sitting inches away, a lady was holding two small children. She had an identical cup placed by her feet, leaving me to assume that she was the boy's mother.

"Mummy - can we give the boy some money?"

Passing her a small note, I watched as my plucky daughter courageously stepped towards the boy, placing the note into his cup. Walking away, Summer was full of questions.

"Whilst you're busy playing with your friends at stage school, attending gymnastics, swimming classes, Martial Arts and the endless birthday parties that you attend; some children are not so lucky. Their day sadly consists of sitting on a flyover, holding a cup and asking people for money over and over again. Do you know why they do that, Rube? To no doubt buy a small snack that will only fill their tummies for lunch. These children may not be fortunate enough to fund another meal that day."

I raised my eyebrows towards her engaged face. She looked at me in deep thought.

Less than 30 seconds later and we passed yet another young child who was spending their afternoon begging.

We watched helplessly as the petite young girl tucked a dirty Barbie doll into an old rag.

"Look Mummy - she has a Barbie doll!" Summer's eyes widened with familiar astonishment.

"Well they're just normal children like you - they still want toys."

I hoped that whatever emotion Summer was feeling at that moment in time, stayed with her for a lifetime. Generosity and appreciating what you have in life were certainly two qualities that I wanted my young daughter to harbour, and the trip was certainly proving to achieve that.

***

In the fading November light, we had found ourselves in the bedlam of China Town.

The roads were full of an abundance of food vendors, locals and tourists, who were all trying their best to claim the 10 inches of floor space that was available. It was hard work trying to avoid the passing Tuk-tuks and motorbikes that screeched past our feet at such a speed, I feared the loss of my toes at any given moment.

Amongst the mayhem of the crowd, I glanced down to Summer and to my disbelief a man with no legs balanced on his hands next to her. It wasn't the fact that the man was walking on his hands that shocked me, but that he was attempting it in a crowd as big as the one we had found ourselves in.

Transporting me back to a memory of backpacking at 18, I began to have positive flash backs of a courageous 24-year-old Scottish girl I had become friends with in Melbourne. She had no legs (and like the man) was able to mobilise largely by use of her hands. What a remarkable person she was! Totally undeterred by her circumstances, she was determined to independently travel the world just like any of her peers; once again illustrating that anyone can travel if they wish. It just takes courage and determination.

Unsurprisingly, Summer noticed the man and was full of questions. The trip was certainly turning out to be an education and slice of life for her miniscule five-year-old mind that was for sure.

***

It had just passed 11pm and we were shattered as we completed the train station to hotel trail back to our room.

Despite feeling tired, the atmosphere between the three of us was jubilant as Carl and I took it in turns to carry Summer on our backs, laughing endlessly about our day and the sights we had encountered.

Bouncing our way down the final train station staircase, our mood suddenly changed when we came across a sad and familiar sight: It was the orphan girl with the dog. Parental instinct kicked in.

Approaching, we passed her several notes and continued to walk on by; yet something felt incredibly different with the girl to all the other children we had seen. The three of us couldn't help but continuously look back in her direction as we tried to walk away.

"Shall we buy her some food?" Summer suggested, staring glumly at her tiny frame propped up on the dirty station step; dog firmly wedged under her arm just as Summer carried her precious Duffy bear.

Crossing the road to the nearest 7/11 convenience store, Summer took great pleasure in selecting only the very best snacks for the little girl.

"I'm so excited to give the girl her treats!" she animatedly screeched, walking towards the child at speed, bag swinging merrily in hand.

As per, Carl immediately deflated the atmosphere by providing us with a lecture about 'how to pass the treats to the girl in the most discreet manner.'

"Laura, I have to say - I don't think it's a good idea allowing Summer to give the girl the treats. Her keeper could be watching and may not approve. I think it's best if you both wait on this corner and I instead pass her the bag."

Before I could even say anything he snatched the goodies from Summer's fingertips in an authoritative manner, and marched at a pace in front. In frustrated agreement, Summer and I exchanged irritated glances as we looked on at his fading-frame in astonishment.

As Carl carefully placed several notes into the girl's pot, he subtly passed her the bag of treats at the same time. A smile instantly beamed across the girl's heart-shaped face as she eagerly opened the bag, wasting no time whatsoever in rummaging through its contents.

The girl's reaction made my irritation towards Carl instantly vanish. *It was about the girl – not him.*

Surveying her movements, I wondered how long it had been since she'd last had the opportunity to indulge in a mouthful of food, let alone treats!

Within seconds, we watched as she hastily opened the pink box of teddy bear biscuits and ate them three-at-a-time without even taking a breath.

Approaching the end of the road a minute later, I turned to face the girl for a final time. With her dark-haired head remaining down, she ate like she'd never eaten before.

That night as I lay in bed and chilled to the song 'Funeral' by the band, 'To Kill a King,' I found myself glancing out of the hotel's window towards the Bangkok skyline. Knowing that the girl and her dog were still no-doubt sat below those very lights that glistened in the corner of my eyes, the view of the city's skyline somehow had lost its shine and didn't seem such a magical sight after all.

If I was being honest with myself, the people of Bangkok hadn't drawn me in like they had the first time I'd visited. Thai people (with their distinctive culture) ultimately define the city that much is true. However, I felt as though over the ten years since I'd last visited, the city had been swallowed up by globalisation. It still had pockets of cultural distinction (don't get me wrong) but it seemed that everything was consumed by the concept of money, and less about the people and culture that it once did.

My thoughts suddenly turned to the slum that Summer and I passed through. In haste, I decided to look online to figure out if it even was a slum. It was so close to the designer shopping centres, that I found it hard to believe that an area of such depravity could be situated so close to such wealth.

Scanning Google on my phone, I stumbled across an article that seemed to perfectly describe what I'd seen. *Surely not?*

'Google imaging' the slum's name from the online feature, I found a plethora of images that transported me straight back to that familiar railway track. Many of the images showed exactly what my eyes had seen that day. Feeling choked, I suddenly couldn't breathe. The article was in a magazine called Accent and was written by a man called Phil America. It read:

The Klong Toey slum in Bangkok is inhabited by one hundred thousand migrant workers and families from Southeast Asia. An eyesore to some, a home to others, and a liability to everyone, it is no sanctuary for the weak-hearted.

Klong Toey, which takes up two square miles in area, has gained notoriety throughout the world as a hub for the Thai mafia, with a high concentration of violence and gangs. Cutting through the centre of the slum are the polluted waters of the Klong Toey canal, and parallel to this runs a railroad. Homes lining the tracks all but touch the passing trains, full of passengers and goods.

Nearly a third of all people in the urban world live in similar conditions, but stepping inside Klong Toey feels like there's no place like it on earth. Naked children gather to see white skin, something closely associated with wealth in much of Southeast Asia. Their eyes are glued to me as I duck into one of the shacks to meet a family.

"We have no fresh water. We never know what tomorrow will bring. We used to be fearful, but now we just try to survive," one local told me.

'Home to the Thai mafia?' *No wonder people were staring at us. Why on earth did the driver tell me it was a market and drop us there?* The danger he could have knowingly put us in! It made no sense what so ever. *Maybe he took me there in revenge because I refused to go in the shops, so he thought he'd get his own back?*

Continuing to scan. I stumbled across another article. This time by a lady called Peewara Sapsuwan who was writing for a magazine called Borgen and had published the article only six months before our visit. Once again, the exact wording is below:

BANGKOK, Thailand– Only a few metro stops from Bangkok's luxurious malls and five-star hotels of the city centre, one arrives at Klong Toey, where Bangkok hides its slum in the same district with luxurious malls, expat bars, high-end hotels, parks and its Stock Exchange.

Located on a plot of land belonging to the Port Authority of Thailand, the Klong Toey slum, one of the country's 5,500 slum communities, covers an area of around a square mile and is home to around 100,000 people.

Around 20 percent of Bangkok's residents live in illegal squatter settlements all around the city. Dating back from the 1950s, Klong

Toey is one of the country's oldest and most well-known slums. Many inhabitants originate from the country's poorer northeast who have been attracted by the work opportunities of the district's river port. Aside from poverty, drug addiction is a very pressing problem among the slum's youth. Methamphetamine and crystal methamphetamine are the two most common hard drugs. Furthermore, basic amenities such as water and electricity are always in short supply.

In Klong Toey, an average household earns only around half of the national average and only around one-third of the income an average Bangkok household. Moreover, the living condition within the slum is also truly appalling. Against the backdrop of the intense and humid tropical heat of over-urbanized Bangkok accompanied with the putrefying odour of the city's sewage system, the residents of Klong Toey experience murders, abuse, petty and serious crimes, drug addictions, unmanaged waste, unemployment and grinding poverty on a regular basis.

As many inhabitants lack the skills and the recognized qualifications necessary to achieve social mobility, breaking away from the vicious cycle of poverty is incredibly difficult. To make matters worse, in Thailand (one of the global centres of human trafficking and the sex trade) many residents of Klong Toey find their livelihood in the informal sector, some of which are illicit.

If you look online and search the slum name 'Klong Toey,' you will see images of the community that I described – the shanties, the narrow railway line, the dump!

Feeling completely stunned at what I had just discovered, I finally decided to put the Hong Kong curse to bed. If we were cursed, then stumbling into the community of the Thai mafia could of had drastic consequences. If anything - luck was certainly on our side that afternoon.

***

Temperature soaring, I stood motionless as I contemplated the epic hustle and bustle of Bangkok's largest market, 'Chatuchuk.'

Certainly unique, this market was like nothing I had experienced before. It was hot, crowded and vibrant; playing home to more than 15,000 stalls that stretched over 14 hectares.

"Mummy, I need a wee!" Summer complained as we stood in yet another huge toilet queue, sweating buckets.

Cheering me up, I erupted into a bed of childish giggles as I watched a roll of tissue paper pass awkwardly down the queue of people. My childish side surfaced as I intently admired how some ladies broke off tiny pieces, and others took far too much paper for a quick wee.

Turning around, I chuckled even more when I noticed that Summer had also been captivated by this commotion and was too laughing – *like mother like daughter, it seemed.*

Finally reaching inside the toilet block, we were greeted by a foul smell of sewage, prompting me to switch to breathing out of my mouth (something that I was quickly growing used to in Asia.)

Pushing Summer inside the smallest toilet I had ever endured, to my relief there was no hole in the floor. As I gave my arms the familiar backpacking workout by holding Summer's increasing body-weight above the seat, I experienced the shock of my life when I flushed the toilet and out of nowhere it rapidly started to overflow.

Staring in disbelief as the water discharged from both the base and the tank, I stood immobile for several seconds registering the sight.

"Mummy!!!" Summer yelled in her typical drama-queen fashion, tears instantly cascading down her face.

"Stop crying – It will stop in a minute!"

But seconds later and the water continued to pour at a rapid speed. The cubical was so small that we were already standing in a fair-sized puddle with water hastily drifting into the neighbouring cubicles.

Lifting a screaming Summer, I attempted (with great difficulty) to step over the flowing toilet. Entering the sink area, I stood Summer firmly on the base to clean her legs and feet.

Weirdly, the Thai women didn't seem fazed by the water at all, and instead were continuing to use the cubicles despite them filling up with water.

Out of the corner of my eye, I watched as two women pointed at Summer's tears and giggled at her reaction. Their un-nurtured persona pissed me off to say the least. *How could they laugh at a distressed child?*

Although childish, I retaliated by shouting: "Funny, is it? Seeing a child cry?"

As predicted, I was greeted by scores of stares.

Attempting to frantically remove the toilet water from our feet in the sink, a cleaner approached as she frantically yelled at me in Thai.

For a split second, I must have looked completely clueless. I genuinely had no idea why she was so irate. Eventually giving up, eye-balling me she assertively pointed to the last cubical at the rear of the toilets.

For the very first time on our Asian adventure, I was overjoyed to see a squat toilet and adjoining shower head. Grabbing Summer, I carried her into the cubical.

"I don't want to squat!" she wailed a bed of cascading tears.

"You're not going to squat! I need to shower the toilet water off our feet and legs!" I shouted, profusely sweating from the immense bathroom heat that was over-powering my body.

"Everything alright?" Carl asked on our return several minutes later.

"Perfect!" I smiled back. I couldn't be bothered to explain what had happened.

"Why are your legs wet, Summer?"

"Don't ask!" she rolled her eyes towards me in an overly adult fashion. She really was so endearing; showcasing her vibrant personality with a touch of humour. *Obviously, she couldn't be bothered to talk about it either! What a little character she was becoming.*

***

If you are excited by inexpensive vintage clothes, then Chatuchuk is the place to go! It has an entire section that's dedicated to Levi's, retro tees, Converse and Doc Martins. Even more exciting: they even stocked items in western sizes!

I learnt something fascinating and quite shocking too! Who knew that it is considered inappropriate to buy a Buddha statue for decorative purposes?

We saw an array of signs and protestors throughout the market that were screaming at the tourists: "Only buy Buddha if you believe – it is not a decoration!" There was certainly no shortage of alternative souvenirs. With carved wooden figures, Thai handicrafts, bamboo table ware; jewellery and silk scarves on offer.

Every few steps, a food or beverage stall was placed, offering anything from exotic meats on cocktail sticks, to fresh fruit smoothies, choc-dipped bananas and endless fried snacks. The best food we indulged in, moreover, was the coconut ice cream that was even presented inside an authentic coconut shell! I'm easily pleased!

With lustrous green grass, enticing swings and a climbing frame to die for, the children's playground just outside of the market was certainly a great way to end the day.

It was 8pm and the sun had dissipated, making way for the darkness. Protectively standing over Summer like an over-protective bodyguard, we watched as she weaved with precision in and out of the climbing frame steps. In stark contrast, I glanced ahead to see a western couple lying indulged in one another, kissing passionately on the ground as their three-year-old son entertained himself on the climbing frame.

I was quite speechless having witnessed this, and instantly questioned my own parenting skills. Thoughts whirling around my head like a waltzer at a funfair, I wondered if I was being over protective by standing over Summer as she played. Was I wrapping her up in perhaps too much cotton wool?

Pushing the thought to the back of my mind, I sprinted to the top of the slide where Summer stood grinning at me from ear to ear.

"Let's have a race to see who can go down first!" I shrieked like an excited infant.

***

My heart instantly sank when on-route back to the hotel; we were met (once again) by the poverty-stricken girl who was sitting in her usual place at the bottom of the train station steps.

With a KFC in the adjoining Terminal 21 shopping centre, we walked-back on ourselves to get the girl a meal. Despite only being gone 10 minutes, however, the girl was sadly nowhere to be seen on our return.

"Where is she?" Summer asked gloomily, clutching the meal in her hands.

"I have no idea!" I exhaled miserably, before suggesting that we walk to the next footbridge in case she had been moved on.

Walking at a speedily pace, we saw a Policeman shouting at a man to stand to his feet.

Disappointed and anxious to know if the young girl was safe, we walked back to the hotel in a sombre mood. As dark thoughts crossed my mind, I needed to satisfy myself that the girl was unharmed, somehow.

Staring intently at Summer, I gulped in the acknowledgment that she too was feeling my pain. As a parent, this was hard to absorb. You never want to witness your child feeling sad and right now that's exactly how she looked!

"I know that it's upsetting that we can't help the girl." I tenderly brushed her hair behind her ear with my finger-tips. "But we have to use the energy that we have to help someone else, as there are lots of people that need help, isn't there?" I tried to sound casual.

Studying her face for a response, she looked at me blankly. "Let's give the meal to someone else!" I smiled.

***

As it was our very last night in the country, later that night Carl headed to a convenience store to pick up some of our favourite Thai teddy bear crisps, whilst I packed our bags.
"Please look out for the little girl..." I pleaded.

On his return he noted that he hadn't seen the girl, but instead he saw another child around the same age sat alone in the girl's spot.

This vision didn't sit well with me. The sheer intensity of poverty in Bangkok was rife, and too many innocent children were dragged into it. *It was 11pm for Christ's sake! No child should be alone on a city street at that time.*

"What was even sadder..." described Carl as he sat at the dressing table and slipped off his shoes.

"When I bent down to put money into the girl's plastic cup, I caught a glimpse of what looked to be her Mother sat nearby, drinking a can of beer and staring in my direction…"

"Wow! I have no words…" was literally all I could say. And I really didn't.

***

Eighteen:

Replacing the fear of the unknown with curiosity

A whirlwind dash to the airport left me feeling dizzy and dazed. Honestly, the three of us could easily have imitated a scene out of the film, Home Alone. The moment my bottom hit the airline seat, I exhaled an overwhelming sense of calm. *Despite waking up late we had somehow made it onto the aircraft.*

Summer was blissfully tucking into a can of ice tea and peanuts that she ordered. She really was five going on 15!

Stretching my arms out wide, I looked out towards the quietness of the cabin and found myself unfurling like a rehydrated flower.

Catching my eye, Carl was firmly griping the arm rest and rigidly breathing out of his nose, almost as though he was in labour.

"Why couldn't we have stuck with the bus idea..." he groaned.

"Because when I was researching the bus, some said the seven-hour drive took more than 20 hours to complete! We just don't have that time to waste Carl!" I rolled my eyes in his direction.

With the fuzzy feeling of foreign ground under my feet, I excitedly stared out of the window at the 30,000-foot decent and smiled a wide, contented beam; toppled sideways and dreamily fell asleep.

**

Sleeping soundly without a care in the world, I felt a hard jab hit my arm. It was Carl.

Opening my heavy, stinging eyes, I sleepily glanced around the cabin.

"How long have I been asleep?" I drowsily scratched my head.

"What the hell have you booked now?"

"What?" I glanced at him confused.

"Cabin crew - prepare for landing," the familiar voice of the pilot greeted us in surround-sound.

Curiosity pushed me to lean over Carl and gaze out of the window; a murky green and brown swamp that had houses stamped firmly in between filled the tiny cabin window.

"Where are all the roads? It looks as though it's all dirt tracks around here!"

"Siem is next to the largest fresh water lake in South East Asia you plonker! Have you never heard of Tonle Sap Lake? That's probably it!" I giggled.

Carl clearly wasn't getting it as his face resembled a map of confusion.

"Siem is built up - I promise!" I shook my head in total disbelief at his inability to be reassured.

"Do you think we are going to rock up and pitch a tent in the middle of a swamp or something?" I teased, awash with sarcasm.

"You never know with you!" he sniggered with an air of anxiety to his tone.

"Just live a little – it's exciting!"

Stepping out of the aircraft, the blazing heat immediately hit us full-force in the face. With the sun keeping a paternal gaze over us, we made our way past the noisy aircrafts, into the airport terminal.

Waiting calmly in the immigration queue, a small Cambodian man (in a teeny navy blue hat and official uniform) grabbed my arm and quickly ushered me into a neighbouring queue that was double the length of the one I was in.

"I'm British - I need to be in that queue!"

"No, you queue here!" he continued to shuffle my reluctant body away from my travelling duo.

Clutching Summer's passport along with me own, I ushered her over to stand with me. Less than a minute later, the man returned to my side. This time he took both passports from my hand, glanced at the pictures and gave Summer hers to hold.

I looked at him completely dumbfounded.

"You separate and she go to the desk before you!" he stormed into a side office where he watched me intently from a clear-glassed window.

Outraged, I looked at the lady standing behind me. I needed to air my opinion out loud to preserve my sanity.

"How odd!" I gasped towards the woman.

"He has moved me into a larger queue, and is now telling me to let my five-year-old pass through immigration alone!" I spouted in disbelief. "Is he for real?"

Laughing in surprise, the lady simply shook her head as if to say, 'crazy.'

"You're not going to be happy…" Carl declared, waiting for us at the luggage belt 10 minutes after passing through.

"That suitcase that we bought only yesterday – they have broken it!" he grounded his teeth in frustration.

Gawking at the case, it was a sorry sight. In addition to a missing wheel there was a large hole that revealed the foam, grey lining.

"The flight was an hour-long - how could they have possibly broken it?" I picked at a loose piece of plastic and sighed.

"Well I told you not to buy one!"

"I had to buy one Carl! We have acuminated so much stuff; it wouldn't all fit in the backpacks - which you well know!"

"Well, there is a simple solution to that – STOP SHOPPING!"

"The airline accepts no responsibility," a member of airport staff declared in an automated computer-style voice as I stood in his hanger-sized office, complaining several minutes later.

"You have to claim it on your insurance!"

Frustrated, we left the airport with one broken case, and some no-doubt rather useless paperwork that I couldn't even read as it wasn't in English.

Getting a taxi from the airport was incredibly easy and resembled an Argos queue where you are given a ticket, and patiently wait for your number to be called.

The best bit? The taxi cost a measly £5 for a 20-minute journey, much of which was spent trying to politely turn down the driver's offer of being our chauffeur for the duration of our stay.

With my nose firmly pressed against the window, the drive to the hotel was fascinating to say the least.

Speeding down the dirt-lined road, we passed many folk on bicycles, motorbikes and Tuk-tuks; whilst others stood on the side of the road selling cans of fizzy drinks or fixing their push-bikes.

Behind the coke sellers perched shoddy-looking huts that were strewn on the dirt. Inside artists were selling the most colourful and striking paintings of anything from tropical fruit, to the ochre of a monk's robe, to vibrant sunsets. I admired each painting like a child gawping through the window of a sweet shop.

Already having bought paintings in both Hong Kong and Thailand, I felt excited about what piece of art I could buy to represent Cambodia.

Nearing closer to the guesthouse, the dirt-lined roads suddenly turned into gravel and instantaneously the town started to bear a resemblance to a more western-feel.

"Wow! This is miles apart from the bird's eye view of the swampland, isn't it?" I optimistically pointed out to a very-quiet Carl.

"hmmm..." he nonchalantly continued to marvel out of the window.

Dumping our bags, we decided to eat in the guesthouse restaurant before we ventured into the unknown world of Siem Reap.

"Let's eat crocodile to really kick off the Cambodian adventure!" I squealed, spotting it on the menu.

Once you got over the idea of eating something that once had the ability to eat you, the crocodile was actually rather tasty; and I was ecstatic that even Summer was happy to give it a go.

"It tastes like chicken!" she bleated loudly after her first bite, catching the attention of a man who was sat at a nearby table.

"She's cute!" he howled, before standing to his feet and slowly walking towards us.

"I'm Tom - the Manager," he tenderly held out his hand for it to be shaken.

Tom looked to be in his early 30s and told us that he was from North London and had lived in Cambodia for four years.

"Is this your first time in Siem?" Obtrusively, he pulled a chair to our table and took a seat.

"Let me give you some advice," he instructed, before reeling off an unwanted list of 'dramatic' guidelines.

"Do not give any local children money as they're most likely part of a gang and it only leads to them being sent out to beg for more cash, or worse their parents use the money to buy drugs or alcohol."

I mentioned the fact that we were visiting several schools in the country, and Tom immediately put a dampener on the idea by explaining how some 'orphanages' were not what they seemed and were in fact businesses.

I had built up a good relationship with the two Cambodian schools that we were visiting, so I didn't think that they were 'businesses,' but Tom's words did make me slightly weary about what I was getting us into. I was taking Summer to these places after all. I had even booked for us to live in one of the school's for five days' later in the week.

Tom proceeded to tell us about some of the artefacts in the Angkor National Museum. He did such a good job of selling it in fact, that an hour later and curiosity took over when we found ourselves pouring over the very objects that Tom had described.

The modernised building felt peculiar against the thousands of ancient artefacts that stood proudly throughout the building. Additionally, this extravagant construction seemed almost out-of-place considering its poverty-stricken surroundings.

Immediately after entering, we were instructed to watch a short film about Angkor Wat. We learnt that the temple sat in the same class bracket as the Egyptian Pyramids, Machu Pichu and the Taj Mahal!

Before the film, the only thing I really knew about the temple complex was that parts of it featured in the Angelina Jolie film, 'Tomb Raider.' Suddenly, I felt incredibly stupid! Still, this trip was an educational one - for all of us!

Regardless of Summer's embarrassing tantrum throughout the first two minutes of the three-minute film, I learnt that at its height the complex dated as far back to the 8th and 13th centuries. Unbelievably, it was also home to over one million people - spreading out across 40 miles of Siem Reap.

Some of the temples had been successfully restored, while others remained shrouded in the surrounding jungle landscape. As you can imagine this gave the ruins a unique look, as the trees grew wildly through the ancient site.

"That explains why it was used for films such as Tomb Raider..." I whispered to Carl in a knowledgeable tone. My travelling companion was clearly oblivious, given the execution of his flippant stare.

I'll be honest, I'm not one for history and never have been, but I really enjoyed learning about the different temples and the meanings behind them.

As the film came to an end and the lights brightened the pitch-black cinema room; a statue of Angkor illuminated in a dramatic-fashion in the centre of the room, forcing the audience out of their seats as they absorbed every detail of the model that was shining brightly in front of them.

Glancing towards Summer, I couldn't believe my eyes when I realised that she was fast-asleep. The film was only three minutes long! How the hell could she be consumed by asleep already?

"Rube..." I hissed into her ear, in that irritating way that a mother does.

"Wake up babe. The film has finished..."

Blank response.

"Summer!" I raised my pitched a smidgen louder when she continued to dreamily snooze.

"Summer!" Raising my voice once again, I hollered as natural as possible given my quiet surroundings.

"Mummy - NO!" she screamed in a fit of rage.

"Don't shout at me like that!" she bellowed loudly, before storming off to a corner and crying that 'all she wanted to do was sleep'.

Children and 'adult' museums clearly didn't mix, let alone museums in Asia where children are taught to not show emotion.

"Laura, calm her down please. This is embarrassing!" Great! So now Carl was adding to the drama – as if it wasn't stressful enough?

"What do you think I'm trying to do?" I cried out, clearly agitated.

"Summer, if you walk calmly for 20 minutes then when we leave here, I promise I will find you an ice cream and we will do something fun!" I said, causing a nearby woman to look at me as though I was the worst mother in the entire world. She obviously had an issue with my bribe tactic as an attempt to alter Summer's behaviour.

Despite the offer of ice cream, Summer crossed her arms tightly, creased up her mouth (resulting in a huge frown line forming across her forehead) and dramatically sobbed. She was definitely over-tired!

Without wanting to be heard bribing for a second time, I breathed out a whisper of words that were so hushed they were barely audible.

"If you behave I will also get you candy floss!"

I watched as her eyes glowed at the mention of those two 'magical' words, just as the model of the temple had illuminated after the film, minutes prior.

"Ok! Candy floss it is and I'll walk for 20 minutes!" my smart, head-strong, five-year-old accepted the trade.

I had no idea where I would find candy floss in Cambodia. Surely it can't be that hard?

Walking at the pace of speedy Gonzales to catch up with Carl, we entered a gallery that displayed over 1,000 Buddha images.

Studying the various Buddha's, each one was individually illuminated. Some were made of metals, others wood; several were even draped in spectacular jewels.

Noticing Carl staring at a statue of a Buddha lying down, I bounced over to read the description that accompanied it.

"Hey Summer…" I called out after reading the first sentence.

"Do you see that this statue is lying down? It's because a man placed himself over a river to act as a bridge, making a perfect pathway for Buddha. That's cool, isn't it? Why don't you draw it in your book?" I was desperate to keep her mentally occupied.

"No that's boring! I want candyfloss!" she crossed her arms rigidly like a spoilt brat. I mentally kicked myself. I'd created a monster!

Slightly shame-faced, I followed Carl through the gallery where I noted how most of the statues only featured half of an arm.

"Why on earth do they only have half an arm?"

"I've no idea." Carl shook his head, similarly with no clue.

Overhearing, a man (who looked to be in his 50's and had an American accent) interjected.

"Every detail represents a different meaning. I'm not sure what half an arm means but I know that a long arm signifies generosity. Likewise, slender fingers symbolise mindfulness and purity."

"So maybe this model is instead greedy and impure?" I cheekily giggled.

"Who knows?" The man mirrored my laughter.

"What do other things mean?" I was suddenly incredibly inquisitive and alert.

"Half-closed eyes show a state of meditation; the elongated earlobes hear what's needed in the world. The hand gestures also have different meanings, such as teaching or protection.

"A dot on the forehead brings wisdom, and a third eye is to see unity. A full mouth indicates eloquent speech. Round heels represent an even temperament and fine webs between toes and fingers signal interconnectedness."

I looked at the man speechless.

Eventually, I blurted out: "Wow - someone has done their research!"

In a humorous tone, I then declared: "I suggest you find out the meaning of half-an-arm then, because otherwise it will be the missing link in your chain of knowledge!" The man chuckled, gazing confidently towards Carl.

"She's a keeper!" he simply smiled, walking away.

"I can tell you a fact as well!" Carl proudly spun to face me.

"Did you know that Angkor Wat faces west, which means death?"

I sniggered as I took in what he'd just revealed. Honestly, he came out with so much crap I never knew if he was serious or not!

"That's not true, is it?"

"It is actually!" The American man interjected from a distance, forcing me to raise my eyebrows in both disbelief and curiosity.

"Wow!" I raised my eyebrows impressively.

"So you believe him, but when I say it - you question it?" Carl's mouth dropped.

I flushed slightly.

"Of course not! Oh come on, Carl!" Jesus, someone is touchy! I screeched in a bored tone.

Continuing through the gallery, I stopped at an intriguing statue of what can only be described as a human's body, severely distorted by additional arms and none other than an elephant's head!

Curious, I read the description of the 'Ganesh.'

From what I could figure, a goddess named Parvati wanted to bathe. With no one to watch her house whilst she did, she made a boy out of sandstone (called him Ganesh) and assigned him the task of guarding the entrance to her bathroom. Now that is a proactive woman!

When her husband (Shiva) later returned, the Ganesh wouldn't let him in. In a fit of rage her husband killed the Ganesh by chopping his head clean off! Seeing what her husband had done, Parvati was inconsolable.

305

Angered, she made him find a head from the first living thing that he saw - which happened to be a dying elephant, explaining why the Ganesh is a boy's body complete with an elephant's head. Although I was still incredibly clueless as to why the statue featured extra arms. Hmmm...

Miraculously, the elephant's head brought the boy back to life. Nowadays, the figure symbolises wisdom, and gaining the knowledge of learning through reflection and listening. As Ganesh's role was to act as Parvati's protector, people now place statues of the Ganesh facing their doorways. This is believed to keep out the unworthy.

Now - how's that for history? It seemed that even I was learning on this trip. Could I rediscover my formula and actually return to the UK with a love of history?

Leaving the museum feeling somewhat wiser, my final task of the afternoon was to somehow track down a bag of candy floss. How hard could that be?

"Of all the things...why did it have to be candy floss that you offered her? That's got to be one of the hardest things to find here!"

With determination, we dipped in-and-out of the passing shops and tried our best to describe the fairground sweet to the shopkeepers. Having epically failed in our mission, we headed back to the guesthouse.

Approaching the doors a few steps ahead of us, I watched as Summer instinctively kicked off her Converse and walked through the lobby in her socks. 'My Asian Summer' was adapting well to the culture, I brimmed with pride.

***

Thanks to the Khmer Rouge regime and the long civil war, 30 per cent of the population of Cambodia are now living below the national poverty line. This leaves a wealth of children vulnerable, with sadly many families unable to care for them.

Whilst back in the UK, I stumbled across 'The Cambodian Children's House of Peace,' who offer a home and educational programme to those very children.

Just like the school in Thailand, I posted the 'House of Peace' a charity box and organised to visit when we were in Siem.

Sat on a Tuk-tuk with Tom's weary words running through my mind, the sky fell dark... matching the unwanted gloom that was darting through my thoughts, I gulped, staring at the barren street we were passing through.

Making our way down a dusty, beige road that was lined with alluring green trees; we suddenly pulled up outside a gated house. Our driver (otherwise known as 'number two') informed us that he would pick us up three hours later, and before we knew it we were standing in the middle of an unknown residential road.

Fear crept in. Tom had warned me about fake children's homes. The vile scam was common throughout the country, apparently. Anxiety and worry spread through my body like an electrical current running through a magnetic field. I prayed with every inch of my body that the school would be genuine.

Thankfully, my anxiety was eased less than a minute later when a boy (of approximately 16 years old) approached the gate and politely asked who we were. Remarkably, his English was crystal-clear. He told us that he lived in the house and had been a resident for many years.

Travelling through the gates, in the faded light I could see a part-wooden, part-concrete building that was significantly rustic, but looked homely with its brightly painted walls of yellow and powder blue.

Approaching the building, we were greeted by a long, wooden table where five or so boys sat chatting to an elderly lady. Immediately spotting us, the lady politely shook our hands and instructed for us to take a seat. She later returned with a pot of tea and poured us each an espresso-sized cup of a Ginger and lemon concoction.

Soon after, the manager was introduced and (over tea) we discussed why the house existed.

"We have 30 kids that range from the age of 6-18, both boys and girls. Many are from nearby remote villages or the countryside where their parents are extremely poor and survive on merely growing vegetables."

My eyes scanned the boys as they played football. Watching them kick the ball around nonchalantly, it was hard to imagine the harsh reality of their life at home.

"Because the families are poor, often they don't have enough money to eat – so they certainly cannot send their children to school. The children are then made to work by either growing vegetables or in nearby factories."

Gulping, I struggled to digest what the manager was saying. In my world, slave labour was a demon from the past – a Victorian concept. It was hard to think that across the world this still exists today...to the very children who were playing around us at that very moment.

My heart was full of sorrow as I tried to absorb the reality of the situation: these children were being robbed of their childhood...thank goodness the 'House of Peace' had stepped in.

"We are a non-government organisation that relies on donations. We provide the children with an opportunity to go to school and learn English. We regularly take the children back to the villages to see their family. To supplement the student's education, we teach them English, Khmer, maths, history and geography." I eyed the grounds surrounding me.

"We provide them with nutrition, health care, shelter and cultural and spiritual support. Our aim is to arm them with the knowledge to become productive, independent, confident people.

"In their free time, the children learn traditional Cambodian dance and often perform shows for the community. We do this with the purpose of raising funds to sustain the orphanage." I looked at him full of admiration, totally lost in thought.

During our conversation, it was clear that the children's health and wellbeing was the house's first priority. The manager was insistent that their happiness was the singular most important thing. If the children were too tired or they didn't want to perform a show for the community one evening, then they were not forced.

Just as the manager finished his sentence, the boys joined us back at the table. I watched them fondly as they poked, teased and made fun of each other in the way that siblings across the world do. Laughter, songs and endless teasing echoed around the cemented walls. I propped myself up on my elbows as I took it all in.

"We are a family and all our children think of each other as brothers and sisters!" The manager hollered loudly above the boy's infectious laughter and excitement that captivated the air around us.

I broke into a warm smile. The bond between the boys was electric, and genuinely nice to see…it actually reminded me of home.

"After graduating from secondary school, we help find the children an internship or college placement to further their studies. However, it is not all about learning. We want to create a peaceful and non-violent environment, with a family-like atmosphere. We aim to function as a surrogate family in every aspect of their lives."

The manager sat forward in his seat: "We give the children a reason to smile everyday and that is the greatest gift."

I beamed as I locked eyes on a sea of happy, contented faces.

"Would you like to go upstairs and meet the girls? I think they're getting ready for the community show!"

To scared to answer, my shy daughter simply nodded her head towards the manager to indicate yes.

Taking her hand, I led her up the steep, narrow, wooden staircase that was painted a peaceful sky blue colour.

Reaching the top of the stairs, a row of shoes lined the door frame. Almost on instruction, Summer and I kicked off our shoes in anticipation and pushed open the door. Inside sat five giggling teenage girls that were gossiping whilst applying makeup. Noticing Summer's tiny frame and doll-like features, the girls immediately screamed.

"Oh wow - she's so cute! I have never seen a child look like her before. She looks as though she's straight out of the television!" The girls squealed in what sounded like an American accent, eagerly jumping to their feet.

"What is your name?" A girl asked Summer in perfect English.

Suddenly shy of the limelight, Summer hid her body behind my legs.

I confidently crouched down, placed my knees on the hard floor and sat Summer on my thighs.

"Everyone - this is Summer and she is from England and is five years old. Is the make up for the show?" I asked the room, which led to the girls spending the next few minutes talking us through their make-up routine.

"I cannot believe how good your English is!" I proclaimed to one teenager, totally in ore.

"I couldn't speak English before I came here. I have been at the house for a few years, plus I learn it at school so I get a lot of practise!" she laughed, understanding her capabilities.

"Do you get to go home often?"

"Yes all the time. School holidays and stuff like that. I love it here though and have lots of fun!" She enthusiastically applied blue mascara to her friend's luscious lashes.

It was incredibly inspiring listening to one of the girl's describe how in three years, she had fluently mastered the art of English and learnt to dance.

"Well thank you for letting us into your bedroom!" I stood to my feet with Summer still clinging to my legs like a Kuala bear to a tree.

"We better take our seats for the show. See you soon!" We waved energetically, peacefully closing the door behind us.

Sometime later, a white lady with short, chestnut, bobbed hair (appearing to be in her early 30s) took a seat next to me.

"Hey, I'm Laura and this is Carl and Summer!" I smiled.

The woman introduced herself as Marie and said that she was German but lived in London.

Marie was visiting both Cambodia and Vietnam, and was taking two weeks out of her trip to teach the children at the house.

"The children are wonderful - they just soak up everything you teach them. They're so inspiring!" She broke into a heart-warming smile.

Watching Summer's reaction to the show was priceless. I simply wanted to freeze time altogether and capture the radiant image of her expression as she watched the children's performance in awe. Failing that, I wanted to box up her twinkling, almost majestic eyes and keep them as a tangible personal anecdote.

The quality of the music that the boys produced from their xylophone and drums was impressive. Likewise, the dancing was fault-less and as professional as the five-star show I had experienced at the hotel in Phuket.

I found the traditional comedic dance (Chhayam) extremely entertaining, and couldn't help but giggle at the boys fancying the 'beautiful' girls in the storyline. Each scene was so precisely-planned and was executed to perfection.

I laughed along with the boys as they giggled and poked fun at each other on stage, clearly teasing their brothers as they tried to be serious in character, but failed miserably by the laughter of their friends. The interaction between the children was truly electrifying.

After the show, the children pulled us onto the stage where we danced around like Looney Tunes characters without a care in the world. Tenderly, the children created a circle and took it in turns for one of them to dance in the middle.

Summer seemed totally captivated when a young boy of similar age, began confidently break-dancing inside the circle we had formed.

The girls' demonstrated how to bend your feet and hands into malleable positions when performing the Khmear classical dance, and I'm not ashamed to admit that we of course had been plagued by 'western inflexibility' when we tried to give it a go. I slipped my arm over Summer's shoulders and pulled her in close to me, smiling from ear-to-ear. What an adventure we were having.

***

The next morning, Summer couldn't praise the children's performance enough and insisted on making a 'thank you' card for the children.

"Mummy - can I give each girl one of Nanny June's bracelets?" She ruffled through her backpack to retrieve them.

I was delighted that the children had created such a monumental impact on Summer. They had certainly tapped into her emotion that was for sure.

I was in love with the 'Old Market's' laid-back charm, striking streets and buildings, reminding me of Paris. As appealing as the town was, however, I found the shop keepers, market vendors and drivers to be incredibly pushy. I would even go as far as to say that they were even worse than those in Thailand! You only had to walk past a shop and the keeper would come charging out, forcefully requesting for you to go in.

You could aimlessly be walking along one minute, and the next Tuk-tuk drivers would heckle: "Do you want a ride?" and would drive alongside you at a snail pace continuously asking. They would then ask Carl (who too would decline) and as a last resort they would then start pestering Summer!

Then there were the people with obvious disabilities or those that had limbs missing. They would spot you in the crowd and cross the road to be significantly close to you – many even went as far as to display signs that explained their disability.

If it wasn't that, then shop keepers would approach as you browsed and point out certain items. They would even tell you when a "handicapped person made it." Others were slightly more obvious and instead displayed signs that said, 'Made by a handicapped person.' It was all very odd.

Summer was in her element when we stumbled upon a bakery called, 'The Blue Pumpkin.' Inside we were served our treats whilst we lay in clean white-linen double beds. I certainly wasn't expecting that in a country that resembled a swamp from the skies.

Cambodia was certainly astounding me at every opportunity.

***

Nineteen:

Facing your fears to overcome them

The Kampong floating village was a place that tapped into the deepest, most innermost corners of my mind; opening a plethora of emotions.

Firstly, I felt considerably uneasy in the knowledge that I was travelling in a wealthy boat through murky, lifeless water that appeared to characterise a world of poverty.

Travelling north, dozens of wooden houses aimlessly floated on a brown, gloomy river.

"There are Vietnamese and Cambodian camps within the village," our guide, Atith, shouted over the engulfing roar of the engine.

"When the season changes the water is too high to stay, so as a sign of solidarity both communities move together."

In a curious mood, I leaned over the boat to stare deep into the door of the river. Surprisingly, an array of trees rested just below the surface.

Gliding further through the village, Atith pointed to a floating school. Peering inside, a teacher was writing on a blackboard to an audience of engaged children.

"Look Rube..." I said in childish wonderment. "Imagine going to school on a boat!" I enthusiastically shrieked, hoping this would be another experience that would open her eyes to a world outside of her own.

Atith told us that the life expectancy of the villagers was shockingly only 54 years. Even more upsetting, 12 per cent of the villager's children died before reaching just the tender age of five.

"Sadly, I have to tell you that one out of two children is malnourished as the annual income of a typical inhabitant is just $500!" Atith continued to inform as the boat crept towards a rundown hut.

The further into the village that we travelled, the more astonished I was by the individuality of the community. There were stilted houses, chicken coops and pig pens that were built on stilts.

The small children looked incredibly happy as they back-flipped into the grimy water, cooing and chuckling with their neighbours.

I watched as the elders made their way around the village via canoes completing everyday tasks. It all seemed very calm and peaceful.

The boat stopped at a floating shop full of the same souvenir merchandise that we had seen repeatedly throughout our trip. I was all for seizing an opportunity, but the concept of a 'village' gift shop didn't sit well with me. It made the community seem less authentic and more commercialised somehow.

Walking through the store, I bumped into a small lad of approximately 14 years old. Rather-bizarrely he held a miniscule snake that was casually wrapped around his neck.

Peering closer, a plaster rested haphazardly across the snake's eyes and mouth. *I'm no snake fan but prohibiting the reptile's movements and restricting his vision seemed almost cruel?*

"You want a picture?" the boy glared deeply into my eyes.

Ummm…hmmm…did I want a picture? Was it cruel? I guessed the picture would be good for memory's sake…and that is thoughtful of the kid, for thinking of me…

"Thanks. A picture would be great!" I smiled.

Pulling out my phone, I captured a single shot.

"$1!" he suddenly placed his palm out assertively to collect the bill, followed by a serious and prolonged stare that took me completely by surprise.

"You asked for the money after I took the picture!" I confidently announced.

"I don't have it, so sorry!" I sneered in irritation, forcing the boy to tut under his breath and storm off in a fit of rage.

In retrospect, I could have kicked myself for taking the photo in the first-place. My gut instinct had told me that the boy was being cruel to the snake.

Following his movements with my eyes, I watched the boy as he placed the snake into a shoebox-size crate and tucked it away under the counter. For the next five minutes the boy retrieved the snake whenever a tourist entered the store, completing the same ritual by exploiting the snake for none-other than a profit.

I was all for helping the locals and giving them donations, but I didn't like the way that the boy went about it. *In fact – I didn't like his whole demeanour!*

Entering the decking area, a group of people were peering into a small square pen. Inquisitively, I leaned over the edge to see what all the fuss was about.

To my shock, a small pond had six large crocodiles crammed together. I was astounded that the crocodiles hadn't hit back and escaped, or that no one had fallen through the gap into the crocodile pen. There were even holes in the wood that a fully-grown adult could fall through!

I left the shop with my curiosity well fed but an unpleasant aftertaste lingering in my mouth. With both the snake and the crocodiles - it was all very odd!

***

We were soon guided onto an enormous boat where we were swiftly served a buffet of Cambodian cultural delicacies along with a – wait for it, free bar!

Sitting on the top deck, time appeared to stand still altogether. Staring out across the blazing, burnt-orange, yellow and pink sunset, every last word had been stolen from my mouth. I was totally consumed by the stunning spectacle of the pumpkin-sunset.

"How are you doing?" Atith approached from behind, making me jump from my dreamy daze.

"Not too bad thank you. I was just admiring this tiny village. It's so different from my world at home; it's surreal to think that people live like this..." I confessed my true feelings.

"It's not actually that small. There are 160 villages with 80,000 inhabitants! However, I understand what you mean when you say it's different to how others live! I once dated a girl from this village and moved in with her family for two years. When I lived here, I tried to educate the locals about the hygiene of the water..." he shook his head in clear frustration.

"They would empty their toilets into the river, clean their pigs it and even bathe in it! Even worse, they would clean their teeth, drink and cook in it! That's why the life expectancy is so low!"

"You're kidding?" I gasped in disbelief.

"I wish I was! The villagers - they don't know any different, they just laugh it off when you try to explain the tragic consequences of living like that."

Forever curious, we were talking about the topic for so long that the deep sunset soon morphed into a pitch-black sky, swallowing our luxury boat in one.

"Time to head back folks..." Atith officially declared to the group; indicating for us to climb back into the wooden boat we had arrived on.

Making our way through the still and silent water, the village suddenly looked rather creepy from the threatening night sky. We were absorbed by nothingness; totally surrounded by the unknown - except for the odd wooden house that had electricity, that is.

"Mummy I'm scared!" Summer clung to my leg like I was her one and only lifeline.

"There's nothing to be scared of." I calmly passed her my phone and illuminated the torch. Unsurprisingly, like a magnet, she was glued to it.

"Maybe shining a light isn't the best idea…" Carl raised his eyebrows at a mountain of insects that were at that very moment, clambering around our feet and the sides of the boat; making Summer yelp and jump onto my lap for comfort the second she then spotted them.

With sleepy eyes, we eventually arrived at the familiar pier that we had departed from hours earlier. Attempting to make our way to the mini bus, a crowd of young children bounced around our feet.

"Please ignore and keep walking!" Atith raised his voice in exclamation in a here-we-go-again voice.

"$1, $1!" the children shouted like a choir in chorus as they boisterously pulled at our clothes.

Running a maze around our bodies, I felt as though I was securely pinned to the middle of a spider's web.

Suddenly, a girl of around just seven grabbed an Australian man's waist from behind. Completely startling him, on instinct he pushed the girl abruptly off as he yelled "no." Storming ahead, the man tossed his empty can of coke into a nearby bin and walked on politely.

Summer and I watched in astonishment as the girl and her friend impatiently ran towards the bin and rummaged through the mountain of rubbish looking for the can.

Despite the fact that the children were harassing us non-stop; my mothering instinct kicked in. I wanted to pick the girls up, give them a huge hug, feed them incessantly and provide them with a never-ending pot of gold.

"Why are the girls going through the bin, Mummy?"

"Ummm – well…do you remember those coke cans that were made into model Tuk- tuk's that we bought at the Kao San Road market in Thailand?"

"Oh yes…"

"Well, the people out here are really clever and can make things out of rubbish to sell on, so maybe the girl just wanted to make something out of the man's can?" I tried my best to sound optimistic.

"That's what I'd do!" Summer laughed innocently.

"Me too." I chuckled, glad that I didn't have to open a can of worms and delve into a more painful picture of deprivation.

On the bus, Atith told us about cat and dog napping in the country and how it's particularly bad in the area that he now lives in.

"If you see a restaurant that's advertising Special Meat - never order it! 'Special' means cat or dog meat!" he declared dramatically, making everyone stare at each other; completely silenced in stillness.

"You mean people actually sell their pets for meat?" someone gasped.

"No – they are stolen! One minute you could be walking your dog along the road peacefully, and the next someone swoops by on a motorbike and steals your dog right from under your feet!"

Atith told the group how some locals truly believe that if you eat the meat of a black dog (or drink its blood) than any internal illnesses you have will be cured.

"But this theory changes based on who you're talking to..." he explained.

"More dogs go missing in the winter months as it is much colder in the winter; many believe that a dog's meat heats the body up. A lot of construction workers will want to eat dog after a hard day's work to heat their body up." He kept the facts coming.

"Oh my goodness..." everyone implored as lots of mini discussions took place.

"Dogs have a high profit margin here, and with poverty the way that it is...that leaves people open to stealing them."

Staring at Atith in utter bewilderment, "It's a crazy world out here, hu?" the guy sat to my right broke into my thoughts.

The man's name was Simon. He looked to be in his mid 50s and told me that he was travelling with his wife, in-laws, 20-something daughter and her boyfriend.

Simon revealed that the family were on a two-week tour of Cambodia and Vietnam, and that they often took adventure holidays to break up the beach ones.

"We had a few free days in the city, so we thought we would visit the floating village and the circus."

"I actually remember reading about the circus," I effused, rather too animated considering my age.

"Is it the one that trains village children in the town of Battambang? I really wanted to visit but we didn't have enough days to travel that far," I sighed in disappointment.

"They have a circus in Siem as well. The bus is dropping us there this evening for a show. Why don't you come with us? I have one spare ticket as my daughter's boyfriend has a stomach bug today, so he stayed at the hotel. You're welcome to it!"

"Thank you – that's really lovely of you." I smiled.

"Carl - this is Simon. He has a spare ticket to the circus so said we could tag along with his family this evening," I excitedly span my body to face Carl who was sat behind with Summer.

"You just so happen to have a spare ticket?" Carl embarrassingly questioned my bus buddy, in a tone I wasn't entirely happy with.

"Yes, he does!" I eyeballed Carl's irritating expression and rudeness.

"No offence.... but we don't know you 'Simon'" he air quoted.

"I get it!" Simon interrupted, putting his hand in the air for emphasis.

"Look, I'm here with my wife Pam. She's sat in the front with her mother Maureen. My daughter, Violet, is also over there."

Sitting in the front row, a content-looking brunette turned to face us, waving enthusiastically in our direction.

"That's my father-in-law, Trevor, who is sat behind you."

I watched as a rigid expression clouded over Carl's face for what seemed like an eternity, fixing his gaze towards Simon.

Why was he being so rude? I suddenly wanted the ground to open and a crater-sized hole to swallow me up. I had never felt so mortified in my entire life.

"If you don't want to come, then that's cool. It's only that your girlfriend was saying…"

"I'm not his girlfriend!" I blurted out desperately - *could you imagine?*

"Either way, myself and Summer (my daughter,)" I leaned over and patted Summer's leg affectionately. "Would love to come! And my 'friend'..." I said a little too loudly. "Can decide if he would like to join or not."

Just like that our plans swiftly changed.

Jumping off the bus with a spring in my step, I walked the short distance to the circus entrance and confidently leant close to Carl's ear: "Never embarrass me like that again please!"

"Laura, I have told you before that you must stop being so trusting all the time."

"Carl - look at that huge tent in front of you. It's a circus, not a torture chamber! If we had arrived and been met by anything else, then I would have questioned it."

"Here's your ticket guys!" Simon interrupted, bouncing towards us.

"Thanks again, that's really nice of you." I kindly accepted the ticket with genuine gratitude.

"I'm sorry if I was a little off with you on the bus," Carl looked at Simon.

"I'm a fraud investigator so naturally, I question everyone."

I instantly shot him an aghast stare at yet another job-reveal.

"You wouldn't believe some of the things I have witnessed and continue to witness on a daily basis," he rambled.

"Ok, well Simon doesn't need to hear all about it when he's about to head into a 'fun'" (I air quoted) "circus..."

"It's ok!" Simon interrupted. "I was with in the navy for 35 years, so I understand."

Hahahaha – gutted Carl!

"Oh! What rank?" My travel companion predictably questioned.

I shot Carl another evil stare.

"Anyway... enjoy the circus guys!" Simon completely ignored Carl's question, turned on his sandal and walked back towards his family.

"So much for tagging along with the family - you scared him off!" I eyeballed Carl crossly.

"CANDY FLOSS!" Summer excitedly yelled, thankfully relieving the tension.

"I told you I'd find you some candy floss didn't I?" I sarcastically and smugly nodded my head to Carl, grinning in 'told you so' pleasure.

Yes I knew I was stooping to his level...but I just couldn't help myself! *The best bit – it felt brilliant!*

***

'Phare' the name of the circus, is not a clown and animal-act type of circus that you know from your childhood. Instead, it's a mixture of modern theatre, music and dance, with some great stunts and even better slapstick humour. What makes the show even more humbling is the reason for its existence.

During the performance, we learnt that the show was commissioned on behalf of the Phare Ponleu Selpak Association, a non-governmental association set up in 2004 by eight young Cambodian ex-refugee artists; with the aim of breaking the vicious cycle of poverty from reoccurring.

By teaching vulnerable children and young people how to perform; they provide each student with valuable work skills to avoid the poverty trap.

From start to finish the show was a ball of energy, featuring impressive juggling and balancing acts, trapezing, acrobatics and activities involving fire.

Purely through entertainment, the show opened my eyes to a hidden Cambodia that we wouldn't necessarily have witnessed as tourists visiting suggested tourist hotspots. If I had learnt one thing about the Cambodian way of life, it was that life is exceedingly tough and you need a bucket-load of resilience just to survive.

At the end of the show, the performers invited the audience onto the stage. Unbeknown to me, Summer had been captivated by one of the teenage actresses. With her newfound travelling confidence, she independently made a beeline for the young actress... wanting to meet her in person and have their photo taken together.

Watching Summer's independent movements personified the beauty of the evening and backpacking altogether. One minute you could find yourself casually sitting on a bus, and the next minute you subconsciously befriend a fellow traveller who enriches your experience by changing the shape of your day.

Being completely honest with yourself, when was the last time you allowed something like that to happen? In the western world, suspicion replaces spontaneity. News headlines leave us continuously scare-mongering ourselves into believing that everyone has a motif. Just ask Carl!

But maybe, just maybe…someone wants to offer you a free ticket to the circus – with absolutely no strings attached… Terrible pun - I know!

***

Twenty:

When a pursuit for an education saves your life...

There are few places in the world that give you that excited untouched feeling, Angkor Wat (one of the largest religious monuments in the world) is one of those places.

Looming impressively on the roadside like a jewel glittering effortlessly at the bottom of the sea, this majestic, religious monument looked nothing but immense.

Edging closer, the outer-structure seemed overwhelmingly breath-taking.

"The craftsmanship that has gone into each detail of the walls is incredibly skilful," remarked Carl in the pompous and intellectual tone of 'Carl.'

"Yes, it's very Indiana Jones-esque!" I not-so intellectually responded.

Whilst inside a narrow, dark and imposing hallway, Summer unexpectedly ejected a high-pitch screech that forced me to stop marvelling at a carving on the wall, and instead spin to face the ledge that she was perched on.

"Mummy! That monkey just jumped on me!" she wailed breathlessly, pointing at the erratic monkey that was bouncing on the wall like it was a pogo-stick from the 90s.

As a direct result of Summer's rather-loud revelation, we might as well have been on a Hollywood red carpet as a sea of cameras immediately surrounded us. It seemed those around us were desperate to capture a shot of the mischievous, bouncing monkey.

Venturing deeper into the dark hallway, a gloomy cave blocked our path.

Intrigued, we made our way through the shadowy cavern and were greeted by a man who handed us each an incense stick. Eagerly, he pointed to a shrine further inside the illuminated shelter.

Making our way further into the engulfing darkness, the man followed in our footsteps.

"This is a prayer for good luck," he said before reciting: "This is for your mother, your father, your sons and daughters."

Following this, the man indicated for us to gently place the palm of our hand onto a statue that was draped in a rainbow cloth and surrounded by tealight candles.

Stepping backwards, the man hastily revealed another colourful strand of fabric. Precisely at this moment my heart sank to the floor. Untastefully (just like the 'sacred' monk blessing in Thailand) a humongous pot of shiny gold coins stared straight back at us.

I paused.

"$10!" he snarled.

Great! Another scam! I rolled my eyes passionately.

After leaving what I will now call 'uncultured blessing number two,' we found ourselves alone at the back of the temple as we perched amongst a jungle landscape with the sun tumbling over the stone-carving in the distance.

Removed from the bustling body of tourists, we absorbed the beautiful and quiet surroundings of the tomb-raider ruins. I felt immensely-relaxed...

"Don't forget to draw every single step!" I peeped through the cracks of my fingers to gaze at Summer's developing drawing of Angkor.

"Mummy – my drawing is a surprise! No cheating!"

"Sorry!" I giggled, promptly closing the gaps between my fingers to obscure my view.

"Hello..." a small girl confidently declared, exhibiting a tray overloaded with magnets.

"$1!" she hastily stepped into my 'personal' space.

"No thank you...we have lots!" I attempted to remain polite but firm. *I've got this!*

"$1 for magnet" she yelled in a pitch that was fit for shaking window panes.

Rather awkwardly, the incredibly young sales girl remained extremely persistent and stayed in our company even after several minutes of us declining her sale.

Predictably (irrespective of already buying two that morning) I bought the magnet several minutes later just so that she would go away.

"See how lucky you are that you're not forced to work like that little girl? She should be in school, not selling fridge magnets!" I reminded my fortunate daughter sternly.

As the sun slipped down out of sight, three men sat in a bush delicately carving into sandstone.

"Let's go and have a look!" I eagerly edged closer to the men for a sneaky peek.

Entering the hibernation of the shaded trees, all I could hear were the crickets chattering away in surround-sound. Glancing around, I eagerly investigated my surroundings. The men's workstations were dressed from head to toe by a profusion of sculptors, pots and ornaments that were all intricately carved. I stood in awe, captivated by their fine craftmanship.

Standing like an alluring temptation before my eyes, I suddenly noticed it. With absolute flawless detail, standing right before me shined a squared block of sandstone that showcased a deep carving of Angkor.

"Are you selling?" I cheerily asked, inspecting his flawless masterpiece.

"$10."

My mouth dropped. *What an absolute bargain!* Needless to say, I snapped up my much-desired purchase within seconds.

Hunger pains soon dictating our thoughts, we headed to a café opposite the ruins.

Like a bad shadow, a young boy approached within seconds of our bottoms touching the seats.

"You buy?" he waved his $1 postcards around.

Despite our decline, the boy stood beside our table even when the waiter took our food order. He was completely undeterred. *There's no way I'm giving in to this one!*

During the 15 minutes that we waited for our food, the boy continued to hover around our table repeatedly interrupting our conversation.

"Why you not buy?" he shifted from one foot to the other, clearly offended.

It would have been so easy to buy the postcards just to get rid of the boy, but I'd already done that with the fridge magnet only that morning. I couldn't do it with everything…so I stood my ground, for now.

***

As it was our last afternoon in Siem Reap we decided to spend it relaxing around the guesthouse swimming pool. My first point of relaxation: a massage!

After the peculiar massages I'd endured in Thailand, I wasn't going to take my chances again. Sensibly, I did what most people would do – I opted for a foot massage. *What could possibly go wrong?*

Clutching a cheesy chick-lit novel, I was instructed to lay on my front.

Aimlessly reading, the lady massaged deeply between my toes and I started to feel my body soothing with every second that passed.

With tranquillity literally absorbing my mind, I tossed the book to one side, soothingly closed my eyes and breathed out a deep sigh.

With my eyes suddenly feeling as heavy as my feet, I began to nod off onto my arms. Relaxing further into the moment, the feeling of the masseuse's hands leaving the heels of my feet and working their way up to my ankles made my thoughts return.

Gradually reaching my calf muscles, my legs felt weighty and tender. With a skilful degree of pressure applied, the unexpectant leg-aspect of the massage was actually rather pleasurable. *Maybe there is a bonus to the 'extras' after all?*

Breathing a soulful sigh once again, I chuckled to myself. *What was it with Asia? You always got more than you paid for when it came to massages…*

The fact that the woman was massaging my legs as well as my feet was initially rather comical (not to mention immensely relaxing!) That is until the woman's hands started to creep further up my thigh that is, forcing me to abruptly and alarmingly open one eye like a crocodile detecting a presence.

I was completely lost for words when the woman's delicate fingers worked their way towards my bottom. Worse - with absolutely no warning whatsoever, the woman began mechanically kneading my bum in the fashion that a baker would his morning loaf.

Within seconds, her thumbs began creating circling motions on the surface of my skin, slowly pressing on the inside of my 'sensitive' thighs.

Forcing my head to spring up like a jack-in-the-box, she did the most unexpected and uninvited thing! *Oh-my-god – did she just touch my 'lady' bits?*

Immediately turning a dark shade of pink, my mouth went Sahara-dry. I didn't know where to look - I was completely mortified! All I could think about was how I'd found myself in that uncomfortable situation once again! *Id ordered a foot massage for Christ's sake! Surely that is the safest of all massages a person can have?*

Why does this keep happening to me? I screamed through the minefield of my internalised thoughts as a strange Asian woman pulled my body into shapes it had never created before – not even in Thailand.

***

Early the next morning and it was time to leave the guesthouse for the final time. Noticing our presence, 'number two' ran from his Tuk-tuk to help carry our bags. This time, however, we were not using his services and instead we were boarding a bus to the south of Cambodia.

"You sit on the bus and I'll load your bags," he bouncily smiled with a spring in his step.

He was such a charming man, but sadly he worked tirelessly for an absolute pittance! (Honestly, sometimes he would wait up to four hours for a measly $10 fare!) And yet here he was with the broadest beam dressed across his face - even when he had no fare to gain from us! He was still being as helpful as ever.

Ascending the first step of the bus, 'number two' gently touched my shoulder.

"Be lucky!" he declared with that warm and sincere smile that he was known to us for.

"You too!" I energetically spun to face him.

"Hey…" I said as an after-thought.

"You never did tell me your name..."

"Heng!" he grinned proudly.

"Well, it was lovely to meet you Heng. Take care of yourself." I gave him a hug and entered through the excessively-large bus door.

Taking our seats, Summer and I waved at Heng from the window.

Without a constant traffic of thought or nagging to do list plaguing my mind, I stared into space feeling a haven of calm. For once I had absolutely nothing dictating my thoughts…*How refreshing!*

Heng came to mind. What a lovely man he was. It suddenly occurred to me that most of the Asian people we had met revealed a meaning behind their name.

With absolutely nothing to do and free wi fi, I decided to search online…

'What does the boy's name 'Heng' mean in Cambodia?'

'Search results: Heng is a Cambodian boy's name, meaning "lucky."'

"Be lucky!" That's what Heng said when he touched my shoulder…

***

Passing through Siem Reap, I felt compelled to absorb the sights of the city for a final time.

"Look Carl!" Summer pointed to a man who was driving his motorbike, complete with a young woman and her miniscule baby who was clutching behind (hair erratically blowing in the wind.)

"It is incredibly dangerous not wearing a helmet isn't it, young Summer? I do hope that you wear one when you're on your bike. The amount of people that try and sue…"

"Carl!" I interjected before the story could go any further.

***

Two hours into the journey and thankfully it was time for the first toilet break.

The bus came to a holt on a scorching-hot, red-dust road. I felt extremely grateful for the opportunity to stretch my legs and expose myself to the deliciously hot sun-rays.

Experiencing the vulgar toilets, however, was enough to make me want to sprint back to the bus at an electrifying speed.

With the realisation that she would have to squat, Summer threw an almighty tantrum in front of the entire queue, storming into a neighbouring paddy field.

Instead of having sympathy, it seemed the other passengers were horrified by her over-the-top reaction, and reacted simply by glaring towards us as if we were featuring in a prized soap-opera.

"Summer - come back!" I frantically ran across the dry field after her.

"Don't you EVER storm off like that - do you hear me?" My pitch rose to a loud 85 decibels.

"We don't know this area! What if there was a hole or a swamp in this field, and you fell through it?" I continued to shout, experiencing a mixture of parental fear and anger.

"I mean it Summer! Don't you ever do that to me again!"

She lowered her head but glared up to slightly expose her increasingly oversized, sad eyes.

"Mummy, you don't understand! I DON'T WANT TO USE THOSE TOILETS!" she bawled, before a melodramatic tearless cry ensued into the quietness surrounding us.

"Well..." my mind raced quickly.

"You're going to have to go in the bush then aren't you?"

Huffing loudly, I pulled her into a neighbouring shrub and prayed that no-one saw. *What if it was an offence? Or a major sign of disrespect? My thoughts raced.*

"Mummy no!" she screamed at my solution.

"Summer - you have no choice! Now, hurry up! Everyone is back on the bus and is waiting for us!"

"Oh no!!" she bellowed as another no-tear, outrageous cry followed.

"What now?"

"I've wet all over my trousers and knickers!"

"Oh Summer! Right..." I paused to think for a second.

"Pull them up!"

"No they are wet!"

"You have no choice! Just pull them up and I will get you some new ones when we're back at the bus!"

To say the situation was easily rectified would be a blatant lie. Frustratingly my backpack was quite-conveniently stuffed at the back of the storage compartment with a dozen or more bags slumped in front and on top of it.

"What's going on?" Carl predictably appeared by my side several minutes later.

"Summer has wet her clothes when going to the toilet. I need my bag to get her some clean ones."

"What do you mean? She's five years old Laura!"

"It was an accident..."

"A child of five should not be wetting themselves! We had an incident when Molly was three and..."

Here we go again – Carl was fixated in master-preacher-mode as he attempted to trail off into a whirlwind of inappropriate bull.

"Carl, no offence but I really don't need to hear about how 'Molly repeatedly weed herself and you analysed a pattern of behaviour'…"

"We delved into the situation - yes! And when we did it became abundantly clear that she was worried about an issue at nursery. Perhaps Summer is anxious about something too?"

"Summer…" Carl bent down to her level.

"Is there anything you would like to talk about?"

"Carl!" I yelled, totally irritated by his outrageous manners.

"The only thing that's wrong with her is that she's currently standing in wet clothes and needs changing. She accidently wet herself from squatting in a nearby bush – it was an accident!"

A couple that were loitering within ear shot darted me a foul look of disgust, making me feel as though I was going to receive first prize in the 'worst mother of the whole universe' award. *Bloody wonderful!*

"Your bag," the driver thankfully interrupted…

***

The road between Phnom Penh and Siem Reap resembled a forgotten world. Tuk-tuk's and the odd coach were the only visible vehicles on a road that was decorated with wooden shacks and rice paddies.

What an extraordinary sight – witnessing the world go by from a vintage earth that is totally unfamiliar to the technology-advanced lifestyle that I am accustomed to back home. I guess it was what you'd call 'true Cambodian country life.' With push bikes instead of cars, and grubby, half-naked children chasing each other whilst they played in the dirt.

Bizarrely, some people were even gutting fish on the side of the road. Not to mention water buffaloes and the skinniest cows I had ever seen that were laying less than a foot from the traffic.

"How funny is that barber shop?" I chuckled to Carl as we passed none other than an open-aired barber shop that was perched on the side of the fast-moving road. I honestly couldn't help but laugh as I watched a man sit in a 60s Belmont leather barber chair on the makeshift pavement as he got his hair trimmed.

"They even have a red, white and blue striped barber pole!" I giggled like an excited child at Disneyland.

"I can tell you an interesting fact about a barber's pole." Carl proudly declared, spinning to face me.

"During medieval times, barbers performed surgery and tooth extractions on their customers. The pole's colours are from an era when people went to a barber not just for a haircut or shave - but also for medical procedures. During the Middle Ages Monks cared for the sick. A procedure they would often carry out would be to cut open a vein and allow blood to drain from it... given a barber's skill with sharp instruments, they often provided assistance."

"Really?" I looked at him stunned.

"Red represents the blood whilst the white stripe symbolises the bandages that were used to stem the bleeding. The pole itself signifies the stick that a patient would squeeze to make the veins in their arm stand out for the procedure..."

With an over-active imagination, I never knew whether to believe Carl. Whilst we had a quiet moment (a rare occasion with Carl in tow, I know) I discreetly looked online, and what do you know? Carl was right!

The road was certainly a hive of activity that was for sure.

***

Four hours into the journey and thankfully it was lunch time.

Walking down the bus steps onto the dusty street, 10 young children blocked our path by requesting a dollar bill. My gut felt wrenched as I fell into sympathetic mum-mode, absorbing their misery and depravity.

Squeezing Summer's hand tightly, I followed the crowd into the café and stopped to acknowledge a sign that read:

> '*Please do not give money to the children. Their parents send them here to beg for food and money instead of sending them to school. They are regular kids who have homes in the village. They are not homeless or from an orphanage.*'

Every child was grimy and caked in mud. Some were even shirtless and the ones that were dressed; looked as though their clothes hadn't been washed for some time.

Ascending further into the café, I watched as an American man offered the children his lunch, reinforcing the kindness of humanity.

Out of nowhere the kids aggressively snatched the food from the man's hands faster than he could pass it to them. Bewildered, I raised my eyebrows.

"Laura?"

"What?"

"Can you..." Carl waved his hand in the air to indicate for me to move seats. *Could he not see that I was watching something?*

Patiently waiting for our food, I looked across at the adjacent table's plates and suddenly didn't hold out much hope for a mouth-watering lunch. *The food looked sleeper-train bad! Deep sigh...*

Taking rambling detours and digressions, Carl annoyingly filled most of the vacant time by sprawling about an incident at work. Smiling awkwardly in his direction (but secretly staring into space) it was as if my guardian angel could tell what I was thinking at that exact moment. In a bid to make his pointless story stop, a giant insect landed hastily on his head!

"OMG! OMG!" I shouted in panic, absorbing the hilarious sight.

"Don't freak out - but there's a huge (I don't know what) crawling on your head!" I backed away from the table cautiously like the Pink Panther creeping out of the door in a calculated and meticulously planned out way.

"It's a Flying Mantis!" someone shouted from the next table along as those around us pulled out their camera phones and snapped away as if they were in a competition to capture the 'most dramatised' shot.

"Well don't run off - get it off!" Carl screamed in the highest pitch I'd ever heard his voice reach. I couldn't help but release that awkward 'Laura laugh' that I always did when the most inappropriate times surfaced.

"Don't laugh Laura! Help me!" he bellowed, shaking his body and wiggling his head and neck as a desperate attempt to release the bug. Uncontrollably, Summer and I erupted into a fit of giggles that I was desperately trying to hide, but I couldn't for the life of me help but expose.

"Seriously! This isn't funny!" he continued to dance around the café like a man who truly had ants in his pants.

The size of the Mantis was incredible! It had a triangular-shaped head; bulging eyes, four legs and wings. The best bit: it clung to Carl's hair as if its life depended on it.

Roaring with laughter like a fierce lion, I eventually plucked up the courage to whack the Mantis with a menu. Unfortunately, it seemed the insect was rather fond of Carl's hair and didn't want to let go - suitably entertaining the café's occupants even further.

After a third more successful whack with the menu, the Mantis finally released its monster-grip, but I'm afraid to say that it took some time to stop the laughter – and I'm not just talking about from me this time.

Back on the bus and once again I wished I hadn't sat at the front. We now had front-row seats to the terrible visibility that the driver was battling with, thanks to the enormous red-dust cloud that we were driving through.

There were several times when (gripping the armrest) I gulped helplessly as I watched a car or fellow bus plunge towards us out of nowhere.

Bumping through the deserted marshland, it was 4pm and I was entertaining myself by listening to Adele's, 'Set Fire to the Rain' track.

Blissfully nodding my head to the lyrics, I noticed something out of the window that immediately captivated my attention. From a distance it looked just like the swamp we had seen from the plane. A line of wooden houses rested comfortably in the water, with wooden bridges connecting each house together.

Mystified and doused in curiosity, I gazed past the houses and beyond. Tilting my head to the right, a lone teenage boy caught my eye. Sitting silently in the deserted marshland, he looked like a statue as he sat on his knees and looked out across the swamp as the 4pm sun glowed in the remoteness.

With Adele's voice echoing through my ear drums, I sat back and pondered what the boy was thinking…. *maybe his thoughts were that the view was all his life would ever amount to? The stark, inescapable realisation that 'this' was his life and the longer he remained there, the fewer opportunities he would be presented with?*

Of all the Cambodians I had met, they had all given me the impression that they were determined, resilient and strong-minded people that knew a better life existed elsewhere: *they just had to obtain it.*

Take the waiter Leap for example. He had travelled from Siem Reap in Cambodia to Ko Samui in Thailand to get a job, and was regularly sending money back to his family. Or look at all the children in the 'House of Peace' who had left their families in the country and headed to the city to make a better life for themselves – despite being just children!

It was almost as if the boy was the titanic and the marshland was the iceberg that was stopping him from progressing – would he stay frozen and drown, or find an opportunity to escape?

Or maybe I was completely wrong? Perhaps the boy had a happy life and was simply taking in the striking view with its unbelievable sunset? Whatever was running through his mind at that exact moment in time, I found it truly mesmerising to watch.

***

Descending the steps of the bus into the bustling city of Phnom Penh, we were met by an array of Tuk-tuk drivers that were in our faces as they enthusiastically tapped on our shoulders and chatted away. *No prizes for guessing what they were saying?* Like a broken record on repeat, I heard a sea of voices that were suggesting their restaurant for lunch, or a ride on their Tuk-tuk.

"Madam – Tuk-tuk?" one of the drivers bent down to grab my backpack.

"Too many bags!" I smiled apologetically.

"We will need a taxi."

"Taxi? We have no taxi in Phnom Penh madam! Only Tuk-tuk!"

"We will never fit all of our bags on that!" muttered a stressed-looking Carl as the driver began loading our belongings onto his tiny vehicle regardless.

Three minutes later and we were screeching through the vibrant city streets, surrounded by a mountain of luggage which totally submerged Summer's miniscule body. I giggled fondly at her resemblance of a gleaming beautiful rose hidden in a field of thorns.

Moments later, in the shadow of a bustling city street, our three-wheeled poor substitute for a taxi stopped outside a brown wooden gate that was located down a side-alley.

Rather excitedly, we had arrived at Seametry Children's Village where I had booked for us to stay for five days.

The owner was a lady called 'Muoy You' who had built a guesthouse inside the school. Charging £50 a night, she offered guests breakfast and board (with the fee contributing to the upkeep and running of the school.)

I had engaged in email conversations with Muoy for several months (and like the other schools) I had shipped two boxes of gifts to the children. I felt truly elated to finally arrive at the school.

Approaching the bottom of the staircase to the guesthouse, we customary removed our shoes and placed them neatly on the rack alongside countless others.

Proceeding up the wooden, polished staircase; a surprising array of art work decorated the walls; some of the pictures even depicted famous interpretations such as the much-loved and renowned Mona Lisa. Each masterpiece was exceedingly unusual and original, in that it featured offbeat (yet creative) fragments of string.

Taking a few steps further, in awe, I spotted a huge wooden sign dangling from the ceiling. It read:

'Welcome to my house. Please be respectful of my paintings – I lived and died for them.'

My eyebrows creased as I contemplated the words. Deep in thought, I continued to climb the stairs feeling as though I was in a museum that was steeped in precious history.

"Muoy has asked that you join her in her home shortly," the receptionist instructed, after knocking on our door.

"This is your thing," said Carl as he closed the door tightly.

"Take Summer and I'll see you after."

"Summer - you're to be on your best behaviour whilst we're in the lady's house. Do you understand?" I warned with parental fierce eyes.

"Yes!" she said in her most sarcastic voice to-date. *Hmm…She was growing up way too fast for my liking!*

With slight apprehension running through my veins, I climbed the next flight of stairs to reach Muoy's floor.

For what seemed like the longest moment, Muoy and I stood motionless staring at each other as she opened her front door. *Why was I so nervous?*

Luckily, as soon as I drunk in Muoy's petite frame and welcoming smile, my nerves completely vanished.

"Hello and welcome to Cambodia and to my home," she opened her arms in a gesture of genuine kindness.

Regardless of Muoy's tiny body, I could already tell that she was oozing with charm and had an enormous, captivating personality.

Making our way through the hallway and into the sitting room, I couldn't help but marvel at an enormous oil painting of parents and their children that took prized position on the main wall of the living room.

"This is my wonderful family many years ago."

"You have a lot of paintings, don't you? I couldn't help but admire all the ones on the staircase." I admitted a little shyly.

"My late husband was a painter and architect. His paintings were his world."

A vision of the wooden sign by the staircase suddenly made sense… *Welcome to my house. Please be respectful of my paintings – I lived and died for them.'*

"Would you like a fizzy pop, Laura? Perhaps some juice for you, Summer?"

"Oh, yes please. That's very nice of you." I attempted to relax on the sofa in her sitting room as Muoy headed to the kitchen for our drinks.

Taking a seat in an armchair opposite, Muoy pointed both palms of her hands to the ceiling in emphasis as she proudly declared: "Welcome to my house!"

I smiled.

"Let me start by telling you a little about me. I was born and raised in Cambodia. My father was a bicycle repair man and my mother a street vendor who sold coffee - I was not from a privileged background."

Muoy seemed fixed on those words and clearly wanted to draw my attention to the fact that she wasn't born with a golden spoon falling from her mouth.

"We lived in a squatter's shack. I had little education, but found that I was inspired by the books that I read; they really opened my mind and made me dream..."

My mind drifted to an image of Roald Dahl's fictional character Matilda, who had to fight hard for her education and found that reading books fired her imagination. *Muoy was like a real-life Matilda!*

"When I was a teenager, I astonishingly won a scholarship to study in France. Cambodia was governed by the French, you see..." Muoy further explained, disturbing my 'Matilda' thoughts.

"Chillingly, two years into my scholarship and the Khmer Rouge violently tore my country apart, driving the entire population of Phnom Penh into the countryside to meet their unavoidable and unpleasant fate of becoming slave labourers. Regrettably, this included my family Laura." Muoy's words sent an icy-cold breeze sweeping down the vertebrae of my back. My entire body shuddered as I swallowed hard.

Muoy described the moment she watched the nightmare unfold on her television screen in Paris.

"I was totally helpless and powerless to reach my family." She bowed her head, lowering her voice to a deflated, painful whisper.

I had researched the Khmer Rouge before the trip and understood that after the takeover, the Rouge ruled Cambodia for four years and was single-handedly accountable for one of the most horrific mass killings of the 20th Century; taking the lives of up to two million people!

Under the instruction of the leader Pol Pot, the Rouge tried to steer Cambodia back in the direction of the Middle Ages by forcing millions of people from the cities to work on farms in the countryside. Innocent civilians endured prolonged starvation, diseases, torturous forced labour and unthinkable executions.

"I was locked out of my own country, Laura."

It was clear to see that the brutality and injustice inflicted would remain with Muoy forever, like a lead-weight pulling down on her shoulders. I admired and appreciated her for trusting me with her story (and later letting me publish it.)

"I have lived in Africa, Europe and the Middle East raising my family and teaching children. We even lived in Tottenham in London! You're a Londoner, yes?" Muoy enthusiastically questioned; reminding me of my childhood home and making me smile affectionately.

"I could tell by the accent," she nodded her head in respect, flashing her cheeky grin.

Muoy explained that five years after the Khmear Rouge, she had received a letter from her sister detailing that she was living in a refugee camp in Thailand. Worst, the letter detailed that most of Muoy's family had died in the ordeal.

"The letter dealt with lots of unanswered questions (of course) but it also opened a void inside of my body that will always remain." Muoy's voice fell to an inaudible hush.

Whilst in England, Muoy worked in a children's day nursery and trained in Montessori care.

"The Khmear Rouge had finally finished. I'd visited Cambodia but not resided in the country since my teens. In 2003 I decided that I needed to return to Phnom Penh to help the children." Muoy leaned her elbow on her lap and looked me directly in the eye.

"It's very important that you understand that very few Cambodians have the chance to receive an education, Laura. It was my pursuit for schooling that ultimately saved my life! Consequently, I wanted to give the same educational prospect that I was blessed with to other Cambodians…but…" she placed her index finger into the air for emphasis.

"I don't want to 'just' teach the children to read and write. I want them to become impressive artists, writers and professionals of our future!"

After 31 years of living overseas, Muoy sold her British property, bought a small plot of land featuring a run-down hut in Phom Penh, and over time converted it into 'Seametrey Children's Village.'

"My school wasn't like a traditional school. I didn't even have tables and chairs when I started out!" she giggled mischievously.

"What the school did have, however, was a lady with a remarkable vision! Sadly, no children came at first and I thought it was a disaster," Muoy somehow managed to suppress the sigh that threatened to escape at any moment.

Listening to Muoy speak so passionately about her vision for bringing about positive change in a country drowned in injustice and corruption, allowed me to see just how remarkable she is.

Inwardly, I smiled broadly. Muoy was certainly one of life's rare givers that was for sure. There clearly wasn't a selfish bone in her body.

"We have a mixture of poor and wealthy children at our school, but you would never know who is who - which is just how I like it. I don't want my children to be stigmatised because they went to a certain school. At Seametrey the children are all the same!

"The wealthy families pay full school fees and the poor families pay whatever donation they can afford - if any. Some pay as little as $10! If the children are receiving an education and I can feasibly keep the school afloat – then that's all that matters."

"I had absolutely no idea that wealthy children attend the school as well." I confessed, genuinely stunned.

"I'd simply assumed the school was a saving-grace for the not-so fortunate children of Phnom Penh! Forgive me for asking…" I leaned forward in my seat. "Why did you involve wealthy children? Surely, they have lots of opportunities to get an education elsewhere? Or was it for financial reasons so their fees could keep the school afloat?" I nosily enquired.

"The upper classes are more likely to dictate the laws governing our future and become our leaders. By educating the wealthy children and expanding their vision of the world, I could potentially change the face of this country in the future!" Muoy stretched her arms out wide for emphasis.

"The problem at the start was that the poor families didn't see us as a 'traditional school' and the rich families wanted their children to go to established schools and not mix with the poor. As you can imagine, we had a challenging mountain to climb.

"We had managed to enrol eight local children at this point, but I wasn't charging for their schooling. This meant that there was no money in the pot and I was scared about the future of the school and whether I had been too ambitious.

"Then, after only three months the children began speaking English, which impressed their families and the local villagers. Before we knew it, we were at full capacity! With the income, I decided to rent the house next door and expand the school."

"That's incredible!" I remarked, genuinely impressed.

"It's important for you to understand that we have children from dirt-poor villages, urban slums and wealthy Phnom Penh families. But the key is that they're all treated the same! A poor farmer's son is often best friends with a rich rice-merchant's son, and they will run around all day laughing and playing - which is practically unheard of in Cambodia; where unfortunately we still have a huge social divide between the rich and the poor."

I was intrigued to know how the guesthouse had started in the first place. Muoy recalled that after the death of her husband, she decided to turn their four-story home into guest accommodation.

"The income from the guesthouse helps towards the running costs of the school." Muoy explained before taking another sip of her no-doubt extremely cold tea.

Listening to her gentle, self-deprecating observations; I was impressed by her survivor-warrior 'game face' attitude. She seemed to be the epitome of determination.

Being raised by a poor family in a country that is easily as war-torn as Afghanistan (but being educated in Paris) is certainly a mix that defines Muoy. There's no doubt that she is a smart, intelligent woman, but above all she has a survivor spirit that is incredibly admirable.

The conversation soon moved onto the present day, where Muoy explained about the financial struggles of the school.

"Because of our central position in the city, the overheads on this building are too much and my income from the school is no longer cutting it.

It's for this reason that I started building a new school about 40 minutes away from the city." *Was there anything this woman couldn't do?*

Muoy described how she had started building the school in the countryside, but news of the 'new school' had spread amongst the countryside villagers, and before Muoy was even finished and ready for business, the children began flocking to the new school.

"Before I knew it, I found myself running a school amongst a construction site, as well as the school in the city!" Muoy shook her head in disbelief.

Unfortunately, regardless of how engrossed I was by Muoy's fascinating life; it was obvious that a five-year-old Summer-Ruby was not as interested and quickly became irritable and progressively bored; climbing around the back of the sofa and playfully pulling at my hair. *Oh no! Not the affectionate mother-daughter plaiting routine.*

"Summer, stop climbing on the sofa…" I assertively darted her that motherly death stare whilst somehow maintaining a calm and collected tone.

"Sorry Muoy…" I pulled the 'I want the-ground-to-open-up-and shovel-me-in' face, feeling prematurely apologetic towards the immeasurably-honest lady that was standing before me; who had not only welcomed us into her home, but was also being incredibly honest about her personal journey by courageously pouring her heart out to a complete stranger. My gratitude was sky-high. Muoy owed me absolutely nothing and really didn't have to expose herself to me so vulnerably.

I could only hope that Summer's western ways had not offended this inspiring, multi-talented woman.

"Oh, she's fine." Muoy chuckled, sipping her graveyard tea.

"I would love for you to visit the school in the country and meet the wonderful children. Would you like that, Summer?"

"Yes please! Can we Mummy?" Summer turned her persuasive facial expressions on me. She was such a funny girl – I really didn't need persuading.

"If Muoy doesn't mind…"

"Of course not. Would you like to go tomorrow?"

I had planned to visit the Killing Fields the following morning, which was a memorial and education centre on the plot of land where the Khmer Rouge killed and buried thousands of innocent people. Now that Muoy had revealed her very 'personal link' to the Khmer Rouge, I suddenly felt apprehensive about telling her of our plans. The last thing I wanted to do was offend, and I would have been mortified if she had thought that we were visiting the site as an attraction in the city.

Nevertheless, I had to make a decision and quick. Taking a deep breath, I confessed.

"Who is taking you to the fields?" she asked after my confession, totally expressionless.

"We were just going to get a Tuk-tuk from the city."

"Nonsense! Take our Tuk-tuk driver, he won't rip you off! Ask one of my ladies downstairs to call him for you. He has been a family friend for many years, so you can trust him impeccably."

With that, I left Muoy's feeling rather overwhelmed by her astonishing and inspiring story.

***

I would like to thank Muoy for allowing me to print her personal story in this book.

Twenty-One:

Blinking away the tears

I would like to dedicate this chapter to Laureen, who sadly passed away from breast cancer within the year of our visit...

The next morning, we were fortunate enough to meet one of Muoy's best friends; a charming Canadian woman called Laureen.

Chatting to Laureen over our breakfast of melon, bread, butter and jam; she told us the tale of how she had met Muoy.

"Like you, I was staying as a guest here. Impressed by Muoy's exceptional achievements; I decided that I needed to support her in some way, so over the years that's exactly what I have done. On one occasion, I even stayed for an entire year!" she chuckled affectionately.

"A year!" shouted Summer in a very adult-astonished manner, making us all giggle.

With our laughter fizzling out, a man approached the table with a huge grin plastered across his face.

"Ahh, hello love!" Laureen greeted the man fondly.

"Guys - this is your driver, Rith. He will take you anywhere that you want to go – you can trust him!" Laureen put an affectionate arm around his shoulder.

Following our short but sweet introduction, we were soon speeding along one of the dustiest roads I'd ever experienced; heading to the dishonourable 'Killing Fields.'

I deeply regretted not thinking ahead and packing sunglasses for Summer, as the entourage of dust on the fast-moving road was painfully irritating. Mummy-hat firmly on, I decided to improvise by covering her face with a cardigan... *Well, what else was I supposed to do?* She actually quite liked it; turning it into a game of peek-a-boo!

With evil force, the wind and dust rapidly picked up pace.

The road was incredibly fast-paced, with lorries and motorbikes hurdling towards us; contributing heavily to the dry conditions of the road.

"I'll wait here for you," said Rith, Tuk-tuk wheels stopping to a holt outside the entrance.

"Oh, ok. Thank you. Feel free to grab a coffee or something..." I offered, feeling somewhat guilty that he had to wait around for us.

***

PLEASE NOTE - this section contains distressing content, which some readers may find upsetting.

Approaching the gates of the notorious 'Killing Fields,' Carl and I exchanged tangled glances towards each other. The sambre aura was so overwhelming. Death certainly immersed us in a way that I'd never felt before.

Joining the quietest queue I had ever experienced, we were given a head-set to guide us through each zone. My protective mother-mode prevented me from allowing Summer to have one. If I was honest, I still wasn't entirely sure how I was going to approach the subject of exactly where we were to her.

Carl and I had bickered extensively about visiting the fields just the day before. He was convinced that it was an irresponsible and outrageous place to take a child. But what was the alternative? I didn't have the luxury of a baby sitter. When would I ever have the chance to visit again?

"Summer, we have to be really quiet when we are in this area. Do you think that you can do that?" I gave her my 'serious mum' expression.

"Sure!" she shrugged her shoulders. *Honestly, sometimes it was like conversing with a teenager.*

Placing my headset firmly into position, I opened the map that detailed the route of each section.

The first walking-zone was the 'truck stop' that was responsible for bringing prisoners to the fields. A shiver travelled down my spine as I looked at the patch of land and contemplated the thoughts that must have been going through each prisoner's mind at that exact moment. *Did they instantly give up hope? Prey to die quickly?*

Listening intently, I stared emotionally towards a picture that showed a group of people being dragged from a truck.

Continuing forwards, it was difficult to visualise what happened on that very spot all those years ago. If I was to take a photo of the very land that I was standing on, you would be fooled to think that I was in a beautiful park. The fields were well-kept and peaceful...two words that certainly wouldn't have been used to describe them 40 years ago that's for sure!

Just as the wind picked up pace, the tape explained how sharp leaves and branches from the surrounding trees were used to slit people's throats.

Feeling as though I had been plunged into a deep, dark hole; a void opened in the pit of my stomach. Suddenly the picturesque trees didn't look so serene anymore.

I glanced at Summer as she skipped around one of those very trees. I had to portray a calm motherly façade so instead of reacting, I swallowed a deep gulp at the sight.

347

Never before in my life have I felt such raw pain at something that was a purposely direct cause from an individual...a member of society, nevertheless. Each stop on the tour felt like a fresh throb of pain.

With awkward timing, and acting as a complete paradox to my thoughts, Summer declared: "Wow! Look at that pretty tree, Mummy!"

I watched as she sprinted with glee towards a tree that was decorated with lots of colourful wrist bands.

"Mummy..."she called, reaching the tree and bursting with excitement.

"Why have people left their bracelets on the tree and fence?"

"Ummm, well..." I paused the tape, poorly stumbling for the correct words.

"It's because people died here Rube..." I said softly, bending down to child-height.

"So..." she screwed up her face in 'child-thinking' mode.

"In the way that we put flowers on Grandad Steve's stone. Over here people put their bracelets down?" She questioned, totally confused.

"Exactly!" I nodded my head encouragingly, smiling broadly towards my beautifully-smart daughter, whose life had not thankfully been tainted by tragedy or corruption.

"Why bracelets, though?" she suddenly asked as an after-thought, looking genuinely puzzled. *In truth, I had absolutely no idea!*

"Umm, well... there are no shops around here to buy flowers..." I stumbled for the best response that I could possibly come up with.

Playing the tape once again, the tree and its decoration of colourful bracelets were firmly on the agenda.

The narrator chillingly described how the trunk was once used to beat babies against.

With every further detail exposed, my mouth went Sahara dry and my stomach flipped sickly somersaults as though I was on a roller-coaster.

I paused the tape and stared at the tree before me, travelling back in time with fresh eyes. This colourful and pretty tree now seemed to have a black, torturous appearance and a disturbed soul. I felt physically sick.

Pressing 'play' once again, I listened intently whilst the narrator explained how some babies were thrown head-first into the trunk until their tiny, fragile and innocent bodies couldn't cope anymore. Others had their heads smashed in with rocks.

Feeling sick no longer cut it! I turned my lips up at the edges and shuffled past the disturbed tree faster than the speed of sound.

The next stop was a deep, square grave that was full with the skeletons of women that were buried next to their battered babies. Feeling as though I could cry at any moment, I bit my lip in distress and silently endured an entourage of pain as I stared motionless at the patch before me.

Moments later, I turned to glance towards Summer who was happily skipping along humming an innocent tune to herself. She had absolutely no idea of the brutal history surrounding her.

Despite being internally enveloped in grief, retaining my protective 'mum' stance, I had to fight back an onslaught of rage from sweeping across my face.

Continuing to play the tape, I learnt that Pol Pot became increasingly paranoid throughout his regime. It was for this reason that he killed anyone that threatened him or his mission.

Anybody believed to be wealthy, including those that were economically mobile through foreign contacts or with solid educational roots, were murdered; this left Cambodia almost wiped-clean of a skilled and white-collar workforce.

Love and sex were totally forbidden, and anybody caught displaying love or engaging in sex without official permission was instantly executed. Children were not allowed to go to school or play; sadly a child's future was a lifetime of prolonged and unjust labour or succumb to death itself.

I felt sick in the very pit of my stomach on learning that people were violently electrocuted; others had to bear having fingernails and toenails pulled off whilst conscious, and in extensive cases some were ruthlessly skinned alive. *I mean, really?*

Continuing past the mass graves and pits, Summer continued to silently walk alongside us.

Having gained the knowledge that extreme rainfall would often force bones, teeth and clothing to appear on the ground's surface because of the large number of bodies that are still buried in the pits, I felt physically on-edge with the knowledge that I was stood on those very pits.

Soaked in anguish, I examined the ground and for the first time actually noticed pieces of material peeping through the surface. It was a sight that certainly made me quiver.

Moving on, we came to a large glass-box that housed items of clothing and bones that had been found around the site, reminding me that each item recalled a harrowing tale of its owner.

Eventually, we reached our last stop. It was an odd-shaped building that was known as the 'stupa.' The building contained around 5,000 skulls and weapons, showcasing the grisly and honest truth from the genocide that took place less than 40 years previously.

Taking my turn to visit I approached the triangular building; alongside two strangers we squeezed our western bodies into the narrow viewing deck.

The stupa wad so savage that I found myself exchanging wrenched glances and gasps with complete strangers, as we observed some of the most disturbing items I'd ever seen in my entire life.

Alongside each skull sat a coloured sticker that indicated the weapon that was responsible for each murder. There were various axes, sharp bamboo – all kinds of armaments on display.

"Can you believe the state of some of these skulls?" A woman turned to me.

"It's just awful," I muttered as I absorbed an array of skulls that had huge cracks and holes, and others that simply resembled a jigsaw puzzle.

It was at this moment that a deep sadness filled my throat like a swelled lump, and I found myself blinking away the tears along with the stranger alongside me.

"Here..." the woman placed her arm around my shoulders in comfort.

Despite being complete strangers, the woman's arm remained slumped around my shoulder for the entire time I remained. The only sound was that of our sniffles.

***

Having experienced the full force of the field's appalling, heartless slavery; for the first time I was able to comprehend exactly what was meant by the term 'dark tourism.'

The word is associated with tourism that involves travelling to places infamous for widespread deaths and unfathomable suffering.

Excruciating as it was to be exposed to such needless inhumanity; it is not until you visit the killing fields that you truly understand the people of Cambodia; and I suddenly found myself examining the people very differently.

In all sincerity, it was incomprehensible to even imagine that any Cambodian over the age of 40 had lived and survived through the horrendous ordeal.

Pol Pot slaughtered an estimated 1.5 million people, wiping out between 1/4 and 1/5 of the country's entire population! The question remains: *what makes a man kill his own?*

Pol Pot was an ordinary child who was born into a comfortable middle-class lifestyle in the fishing village of Prek Sbav. His family were ethically-mixed (Chinese and Khmer) and even had connections with the Cambodian royal family!

Trying to psycho-analyse the mindset of this cold-hearted blood-thirsty leader, would have tormented my brain forever and a day; so I decided to place this thought into the deepest corner of my mind for exploration at a more appropriate time.

***

Lunch-time nearing, I asked Rith if he could stop at a café on route to Muoy's country school.

"Do you mind if I give the school a miss?" Carl asked, jumping on-board Rith's now familiar Tuk-tuk.

"Not-at-all! I think it's good for us to do our own thing on this trip. What are your plans?"

"I don't know yet. I might just relax at the guesthouse or catch-up on some reading."

"Sounds good!" I smiled, excited at the prospect of some much-needed mother-daughter time.

Minutes later and we had arrived at a café for lunch. The journalist in me wanted to discuss the turbulent history of the killing fields with Rith, an actual Cambodian resident. However, for a moment I lost my tongue completely. As eager as I was to press for more, it was awkward broaching such a sore and sensitive subject with a Cambodian whose family were obviously affected in some way or another.

As if reading my mind, Rith asked our opinion on the fields.

"That's a hard question to answer…" I stared at him with a plenthora of emotions hidden behind the surface of my eyes.

"I'm glad that I visited because it has provided me with the opportunity to better understand the history of Cambodian people. It probably wouldn't surprise you to know that I wouldn't want to visit again." I said honestly, before adding: "If I'm being totally honest, the fields have had a strange, eerie effect on me."

"Have you been to the Tuol Sleng Genocide Museum?"

"No," I said faintly.

"From what I have heard of the museum, I don't think it is a place that we could take the little-one to." I nodded my head towards Summer as I spoke.

I had actually researched the museum online whilst planning the trip. Otherwise known as the S-21 prison, the building was a former high school that was converted into a prison by Pol Pot during his regime.

Alongside the mass-murdering fields, thousands of Cambodians were imprisoned, tortured, interrogated and slaughtered in the prison.

The museum displayed paintings, photos and drawings that demonstrated the methods Pol Pot used to torture people into providing the names of their family members.

One image that stuck in my mind from researching was the water-torture technique. To my absolute horror, I had learnt how prisoners' bodies were suspended by their feet into barrels of water. Gruesomely handcuffed from behind, they were then dunked face-down into a dirty tank of water.

The only way to stop the torture would be to pass on the names of their family members who were then arrested, tortured and killed.

Despite wanting to expose Summer to the history of the world and open her eyes to cultural values and ethnics outside of her westernised experience; I did not want to scare her for life!

As much as I wanted Summer to learn about the world, it most definitely wasn't going to happen at the S-21 prison.

***

After lunch, we travelled back through the dust-clouds to Muoy's school in the countryside of Phnom Penh. This place was so out on a limb, I instantly felt isolated in remoteness.

Driving through the Phnom Penh countryside, I looked on from the comfort of our Tuk-tuk as I passed the skinniest cows I'd ever seen that were basking in the late afternoon sun. *I'd never seen ribs on a cow that was alive before!*

Speeding along, our Tuk-tuk was soon accompanied by a body of horses and carts, just as a Range Rover would cruise alongside my BMW at home.

Climbing from the Tuk-tuk as gracefully as possible, we were engulfed by a group of excitable children. I couldn't believe how many the school already occupied considering it was only half-built!

It was brilliant to see so many joyful pupils as they played on bikes, scooters and…wait – *is that skates?* Experiencing a total dreamlike moment, a young girl skated happily past me like an absolute pro! *Well she certainly knew what skates were!* I thought to myself as I recalled giving the girl in the Thai jungle Summer's skates; reflecting on that curious and slightly apprehensive expression, that told me she had no idea what they were.

Here we were with children in similar circumstances to those in the jungle school in Thailand, and clearly they very-much knew what skates were - and that was all thanks to Muoy.

Despite the school being a 'work in progress' the impressive facilities were certainly something to admire. The school looked absolutely incredible! *Imagine what it will look like when it's finished?* I nodded my head in disbelief, absorbing my incredible surroundings.

After waving goodbye to Carl and Rith, Summer and I found ourselves huddled alongside a group of excitable children and four westerners unsure of our next move.

"Hi, I'm Gabby - a volunteer!" said a young, plump Australian girl.

"This is Curtis, Alexandra and Megan."

"Hi!" I greeted them all.

Curtis, Alexandra and Megan continued to play with the children, whilst Gabby stayed with Summer and I.

"I'm Laura and this is Summer." I glanced down at my daughter as she clung to my leg, noticeably scared from the scores of eyes that were intently watching her every move. *The children were clearly fascinated by this curious-looking girl!*

We discovered that Gabby was a high school student from Melbourne who was travelling around the world on a national programme teaching children.

Summer's hand intertwined with mine, Gabby led us in the direction of Muoy. Noticing her in the distance, the 'incredible' Muoy was stood proudly amongst 10 or so children looking like 'mother hen' nestling her brood.

Spotting us from the corner of her eye, Muoy endearingly pulled us into the type of embrace that is usually reserved for long-lost relatives or air crash survivors. I admired this quality of hers. She seemed to have the power to magically eradicate your fears and instantly put you at ease.

"Welcome and thank you so much for visiting!" she beamed in front of the late-afternoon sun that still hovered in the background.

Touring the school grounds, we learnt that the land spanned over a couple of acres and housed a huge lake at the rear. With five bamboo huts, each had its own unique purpose.

"I fundraise for each part of the school," Muoy explained whilst we watched the construction workers (in t-shirts and flip-flops, but construction workers all the same) grafting away on the skate ramp.

354

Fascinatingly, as the work-force laid the concrete on one side of the ramp, the children nonchalantly climbed over the other side; playing what looked to be a game of tag. This all seemed to be completely amicable; the work-force and the children cohesively respecting each other's roles.

"The residency of the Australian volunteers has paid for the concrete that is today being laid." Muoy explained as I looked on.

"The lake will eventually act as a swimming pool. I'm hoping we can teach the children to swim and educate them about water safety during school hours.

"Outside of school hours, my vision is that we could open the lake to the public to bring in additional income for the school. Over on that patch of land..." Muoy pointed to another green field. "I would love tennis courts, and in another life - a high school.

"My dream is that the school will eventually cater for children and young people to the age of 18. We hope to offer a Montessori curriculum.

"I would ensure that psychology, life skills and subjects promoting human rights are given as much importance as the traditional academic subjects, because I truly believe that they're of vital importance to Cambodian children.

"Seametrey will offer excellent opportunities for children travelling from all over Cambodia, and not only those living in this neighbourhood!

"It will be a residential school with a distinctive difference!" Muoy placed one finger in the air animatedly whilst speaking (something I was now calling her 'signature' move.) You could clearly see the passion floating around her tiny body. In fact - her positive aura was slightly infectious.

"One parent or relative will be able to accompany the child and live at the school alongside them. The beauty of that arrangement is that it will enrich the adults experience, and slowly but surely they will absorb the environment and adapt their mind-sets too."

Muoy had clearly dedicated lots of time into creating her vision. I hoped for her sake that it all worked out. She certainly deserved for it to!

After the tour, I guided a still-terrified Summer over to a group of children that were playing nearby. Clutching to my leg like glue, I spotted a red, enticing ball in the distance.

"I have an idea!" I screeched enthusiastically, not entirely sure if the children around me even understood English.

"Everyone stand in a circle!" I eagerly shouted towards five-or-so children.

"Do you see this red ball?" I grabbed the ball from the ground.

"Everyone needs to throw it towards each other. Summer – you too!" I instructed, removing a reluctant-Summer from my leg and placing her alongside the children; forming a perfect circle.

Several minutes later and as I slowly backed away, Summer continued to laugh with the children whilst they tossed the ball to each other and giggled hysterically each time one of them dropped it.

I over-heard Summer tell a petite girl (who looked to be around three in age) to take her backpack off. Following the instruction perfectly, Summer then told the girl to sit on the ground.

I observed as my once-shy daughter excitedly ran towards her bag, took out her travel scrap book and excitedly flicked through the pages with the young girl; explaining every detail of each page.

In no time whatsoever, Summer had altered from the shyest child ever to the 'mother hen' role. Within minutes she had 12 children crowded around her, almost worshipping her leadership role. They looked in awe as she articulately explained the meaning behind all of her 'intricate' drawings documenting her travels so far.

It was fascinating watching Summer come out of her shell so confidentially, and I honestly felt like the children were genuinely intrigued by her.

It became apparent that some of them didn't actually understand all of the specific details that she was providing – unsurprisingly since they weren't English speaking. However, the children suddenly wanted to know who this little white girl was. I think they were enticed by her delicate features, creamy skin and rosebud shaped mouth.

Chakra was particularly fond of Summer. Only seven in age, Chakra was the perfect picture of cuteness with her delicately-placed navy Alice-band gripping her hearty-positioned black, bobbed hair.

Her English was impressive as she spoke in an accent that sounded almost American.

"What's your name?" I heard her ask Summer over the chatter of the children.

"Summer!" She not-so-confidently answered, immediately looking at me for the mother seal of approval. I grinned in response, to reassure.

"Well, come and play with us!"

Summer didn't need the slightest bit of convincing. With that, Chakra grabbed Summer's hand and dragged her towards the playground with another girl who seemed to be of a similar age.

Playing the role of over-protective mother, I wasn't entirely sure if I should stay within ear-shot of Summer. Within minutes, however, she had totally adapted to her surroundings and was dangling from the climbing frame alongside her new friends like an expert acrobat.

After 45 minutes of giving my arms a workout by spinning a skipping rope for two girls (and playing on a skate board with the cutest kid I'd ever seen) I decided to check in on Summer.

I laughed to myself when I watched her be totally engrossed in a game of chase with Chakra, another girl, and a few of the boys. *Some things never change!* I laughed as I watched Summer giggling as the boys' chased her.

Needing the toilet, one of the volunteers directed me towards a hut. Exiting the cubical, I spotted Muoy chopping vegetables in a nearby kitchen.

"Thanks for inviting us here Muoy. This place is truly remarkable." I let a pause fall before adding: "You should be incredibly proud of yourself!"

"Thank you Laura!" Muoy remained focused on the task in hand.

"The thing is, the education system in Cambodia faces many challenges. Firstly, there's a severe lack of qualified teaching staff. Then there is seriously low morale because of the terrible salary. Lastly, we are short of appropriate teaching materials.

With a heavy heart, I have to tell you that these unfortunate circumstances often lead to abusive and violent behaviour towards the children. What we have here is a million miles away from the largely competent education system in the UK, having worked in a children's nursey in London for many years."

"Yes, I can imagine there's a totally different approach to education here."

"In rural areas (such as here in Tonle Bati,) girls are expected to stay at home and help their families in the fields. You have to remember that in Cambodia; only 26 per cent of literate people aged over 25 have completed a Primary level of education!"

"Primary? What about high school?"

"Cambodia still has a poor intake - just one per cent of the population are enrolled!"

"One per cent?" I clarified in utter shock. *I'm not going to lie – I naively wasn't prepared for that! I mean – one per cent!*

"Is that typical of Asia?"

"No! That figure stands at around 20 per cent in most other Asian countries."

I was completely stunned into silence. Cambodia seemed to be significantly more deprived and 'third-world' than I'd even realised.

"Most of the children at this site are from disadvantaged families. They have no opportunities to travel so we have to bring the world to them! We offer that largely through the volunteers that pass through our doors." I nodded my head in awe, realising just how many years Muoy was dedicating to her vision.

I was mesmerised by Muoy's uplifting and thought-provoking words. Her outlook on life was stimulating. She was certainly somebody to admire and cherish with the upmost care.

Lost in appreciation, I began to convince myself that Muoy was the dictionary definition of 'giving' in the purest sense possible.

"My school has no option but to work Laura..."

I was hooked by Muoy's inspirational words and inspiring outlook on life.

***

A cloud of darkness hung over me when I realised that it was time to leave the school. Muoy had arranged for her friend to take us back to the city.

I couldn't believe my eyes when a super-sparkly, white, Lotus jeep arrived. Considering there was no public transport and we were in one of the poorest countries, I was certainly not expecting that mode of transport to arrive!

Travelling along in sophisticated style, the driver made a pit-stop at a drink-stall perched on the side of the road.

As I casually glanced out of my blacked-out window, I was stunned when I saw two teenage girls with their noses pressed up against the window glaring back at me. My eyes swivelled around to Summer as I paused for action.

Sharing the moment, we fell about laughing in unison.

"Open your window Mummy!" she screeched, totally energized by the sight.

The second our eyes met theirs, an excitement filled the air. In exasperation, the girls began squealing like animated piglets - pointing and laughing towards Summer.

"Oh-my-god! Oh-my-god! Oh-my-god!" they shouted in excited sync; whilst enthusiastically clapping their hands like a herd of performing seals at the 'Sealife Centre.'

Feeling unexpectedly overwhelmed, Summer buried her face behind a cushion.

Moving the cushion slowly away moments later, she revealed her porcelain-white features to her captivated audience once again.

After a quick glimpse at her pure white skin, beautiful and angelic face, the duo began shouting, "Wow! Wow! Wow!"

Immediately following the next high-pitched scream, an old lady appeared.

Removing the pillow from her face for the second time, the lady took one look at Summer and reacted in a copy-cat fashion to the young girls.

Moments later (and rather melodramatically) a whole Cambodian family were peering through the window staring at us as if we were suspects in a Police identity parade!

Summer and I were astonished beyond belief – I literally felt like we belonged to the Royal Family. It was all increasingly bizarre!

Out of nowhere, two huge coconuts full to the brim with coconut juice and enticing straws were passed through the window.

"Oh no – we can't take that." I politely declined the family's kind offer.

Disregarding me completely, the women continued to smile and generously pushed the coconuts back towards us. I didn't feel as though we could accept them from someone who was a great deal poorer than us.

I couldn't believe how much they were staring our way. I don't think anyone has ever looked at me in such depth before. It was almost as if they were examining every detail of our 'English rose' complexions, marking a map of our features to place forever in their scrap book of memories long after we had completed our journey through their home country.

Following that day, my mind remained focused on the family's generosity. Here was a family standing on the side of a deserted, country road armed with a few ice buckets selling drinks in one of the poorest countries in the world. And they were being hospitable enough to give free drinks to westerners travelling in a luxury vehicle. I found it totally dumbfounding! *How many people can say they would have given us those 'free' drinks if they were in that family's position?*

***

Twenty-Two:

Maybe it wouldn't work out, but seeing if it would turned out to be the best adventure of all...

Without a shadow of a doubt, one of the most special experiences on this trip was going to bed each evening fully consumed by the unique circumstances and newfound knowledge of that day; only to wake up contemplating the endless possibilities of our next adventurous day and what it would bring. We had learnt to adopt a 'new day, new adventure' policy, which always kept us firmly on our toes!

Today, Rith was driving us to the offices of the Cambodian Children's Foundation (CCF.)

I had stumbled across the charity (founded by Hollywood marketing executive: Scott Neeson) when I was researching Cambodia ahead-of the trip.

To summarise a long story, Neeson had embarked on a five-week trip to Cambodia back in 2003. Unbelievably, his travels altered his life in a huge but unforeseen way. Up until this point, he had a privileged existence with an incredible 26-year film-industry career under his belt. He had the unobtainable house that everyone dreams of; a fancy car, an entourage of celebrity friends, and even a yacht! Neeson spent 10 years at Fox and oversaw the release of iconic films such as Titanic, Star Wars, X-Men and Braveheart.

A drastic turning-point in his life, however, was the direct result of visiting a filthy rubbish tip on the outskirts of Phnom Penh.

Witnessing hundreds of needy, neglected and malnourished children scavenging through the rotting litter, ultimately led to Neeson resigning from his job, selling all his wealthy possessions and creating the 'Cambodian Children's Fund.'

Neeson's ambition was to transform the lives of underprivileged children into tomorrow's leaders; by providing them with shelter, education, healthcare opportunities and necessary support to their families.

CCF has grown tremendously over the years. Home to only 45 students in its first year, by early 2016 the charity had more than 2,400 students enrolled in its education programmes. Currently, 79 per cent of its high school graduates enter university. *What a magnificent achievement!*

Throughout 2015 alone, the charity provided over 300 homes to local families and approximately 4,900 loaves of bread.

Reading the CCF's uplifting website, I was absolutely hooked. Inevitably, I simply had to make contact and enthusiastically ask if I could visit during our trip to Cambodia.

Sitting in the western offices in Phnom Penh was surreal. I could easily have been in a western office in London, yet right outside the office walls we were surrounded by poverty. Sitting on the back of one of CCF's Tuk-tuk's with Summer and Carl whizzing through a part of Phnom Penh that I hadn't seen before, we ventured past one of the city's slums. *Perhaps it was the one that Scott had visited that inspired him to start the charity in the first place? I* pondered.

I was fully expecting to visit a school, healthcare centre and one of the residential homes, but I wasn't totally prepared to stomach the neighbourhood that we drove through to reach the primary school.

Prior to witnessing the sight of the slum with my own eyes; the most obvious indication that we were embarking on one was the distinctively overpowering smell of rotten sewage.

"Mummy it stinks!" Summer shouted over the roar of the engine, uncomfortably embarrassing me in front of our guide.

"Summer don't be so rude!" I hissed in motherly humiliation.

Leaning forward, I quietly said: "Just breath out of your nose - we will only be passing through for a few minutes."

Swiftly screeching around yet another sharp bend, it was hard not to miss the slum that occupied the entire right side of the road.

The housing conditions were like nothing I'd ever seen before, and were far worse than the Bangkok slum I'd experienced. *No wonder Scott felt compelled to do something drastic. If I had the money, influence and power that he has, I'd have done something similar myself!*

An endless array of scrap wood, plastic sheets, metal and corrugated iron had been formed into copious amounts of small battered huts, to resemble a line of houses. Unlike a typical row of terrace houses in the UK; these homes were residing next to excrement and toxic waste.

Feeling helplessly compassionate, I noticed filthy rain-water seeping through many of the roofs of the makeshift houses, and into puddles of yet more drenched rubbish that covered the floor underneath.

Scanning the area ahead, I took in the sight of the beautiful but extremely dirty children, who were dressed in filthy, torn clothes.

I felt overwhelmed with sadness as I stared at their hazardous and unstable play equipment - *If you can call dodgy ladders 'play equipment' that is...*

It didn't take a genius to work out that this deprived environment led to copious nasty diseases, which eventually led to a premature death.

"Many of the CCF children are from this village." Our guide explained as she manoeuvred her way through the gut-wrenching slum.

"Provided that children attend class every day, each family receives a bag of rice once a week. Unsurprisingly, since having this incentive the attendance record of the children is as high as 95 per cent as many families rely on that rice!"

"Mummy, why are the children so dirty and playing in the dump?" Summer vocally aired.

"It's not a dump darling - it's their home. Do you see how lucky you're that you don't have to live somewhere like this? It's so sad." I bowled my head, feeling sombre to my core.

My confused daughter looked at me glumly. At that moment, I felt as though we were both united in sorrow. Being so young, it was obviously difficult to determine exactly how much she understood; having said that - there was no denying that the expression on her face appeared to age her by years.

"I will be back shortly," said the guide as she arrived at a building that looked to be the school.

"Do you remember what we are doing here, Rube? We are going to visit a school and a doctor's surgery that has been specifically built for the people from that village that we just passed through; because if you are aware that someone needs help then you do your best to help them, don't you?" I rambled on to my largely bewildered daughter, not entirely sure if I was making any sense at all.

"I'm still not sure that bringing Summer here is a good idea!" Carl declared, shaking his head rigorously as if chastising me.

"Of course it is a good idea!" I hissed in irritation.

"I told you that you weren't obliged to come, Carl!" *Honestly, sometimes I just wished he would put a sock in it!*

The previous evening Carl had thought that it was appropriate to air his views about Summer seeing 'extreme areas of poverty' and how he'd never 'expose' his children to that side of Cambodia.

"To really understand the essence of Cambodia, you need to see the real country that is hidden beyond the depths of tourism, Carl! So here we are! This is it!" I flung my arms out wide like a mad woman.

"The glossy mall that we visited the other day covers up the truth behind Cambodia's forgotten people. I didn't scrimp and save for three years and fly half-way around the world to lie on a beach! I came to learn and open Summer's eyes to the real world, so that when we return home we can make small gestures to try and make a difference ourselves. I admit,

I'm not entirely sure how I will do this yet..." I rambled. "But I will. Whether that is simply by educating Summer and her class mates, holding some fundraising activities myself, or even sponsoring a child! But somehow I want to make a difference!"

"Hi guys. Are you ready?" the guide suddenly appeared by my side. *Phew! Little did she know that she had spared me from a complete and utter meltdown!*

Full of hope, we followed her into the school's courtyard, where we were immediately greeted by a row of classrooms. Distinctively, the rooms were small squares that were separated by a wall that stood merely the height of my waist.

In the first room were babies and toddlers, along with several volunteers.

"Hello!" Carl and I greeted the children enthusiastically, smiling warmly in their direction.

Summer on the other hand, clenched my leg like a koala and seemed completely unaware of what she should do.

Sitting on the floor with the young children, I placed Summer's tiny frame onto my lap, hoping it would calm her nerves.

Whilst I strived to build a tower with Lego blocks, a curious toddler waddled over and sat alongside us.

"Look Summer - he wants to play!" I giggled at the boy who had jet-black hair and bulging, brown eyes.

Cheekily, the toddler began removing the blocks from the tower I'd just built, meticulously placing each brick back onto the rug.

Considering where the children lived, they looked incredibly clean, smart and presentable, dressed in their CCF-branded navy-blue t-shirts.

We were soon led into another room where an abundance of tiny babies slept. It was hard to believe that the school even looked after such vulnerable infants.

Peering into one basket, I affectionately cooed at the miniscule baby who looked so tiny she replicated a plastic doll. Her perfectly formed micro-toes were peeping out cutely from her summer-blanket. Gazing at her delicate head, I couldn't help but notice her bed of luxurious, black hair.

Staring at her elfin frame, I had honestly forgotten how endearing babies were. Aged five now, it felt like a lifetime since Summer was that small.

Placing my hand on the baby's delicate skin, I gave her hand a maternal stroke. Barely seconds later and taking me totally by surprise, her tiny finger curled around mine. I instantly gushed like a grandmother meeting her grandchild for the first-time.

"She looks just like a doll…" Summer implored from behind, prompting me to spin on my heel and look at a small child who had entered the room behind her.

Clearly new to walking, I watched as the young boy wobbled precariously on his feet, before dramatically cascading onto his bottom. Undeterred by his padded landing; he hysterically clapped as though falling was all part of his hysterical plan.

Within moments, the room leader appeared by the doorway with a smile that illuminated the entire room. The boy giggled at the sight of her friendly face and frantically waved his arms for the pick-up that he knew was coming.

Smiling contently, my mind trailed off…It was scenes such as this that re-instated my faith in human kindness.

Swiftly moving into the next classroom, I observed as children of around five sat on long benches in front of a white board.

Upon entering the room, all eyes were on us. Once again, Summer suffered a bout of heightened shyness, nervously hiding behind my legs. *It was so funny how she dipped in and out of this nervousness!*

I bent down to her level.

"Why don't we hand out your stickers?" I passed her the backpack, gently egging her on.

"Good idea!" she instantly perked up.

Unlike the other schools we had visited, CCF didn't receive a box of gifts from us. I was previously told that the school had over 2,000 students and that it wouldn't be fair to provide presents to only a small proportion of children.

Knowing that I would feel awkward about turning up at the school empty-handed and with no fixed purpose, I chose to bring some personalised stickers that proudly declared: *'I met Summer from England.'*

On presenting the stickers, Summer had a totally mesmerised, captive audience.

My daughter really was a child of contradictions. One minute she was imitating the role of timid-mouse, and the next she was proudly playing the character of the much-loved leader.

Watching on like a spy, I inwardly smiled as I witnessed her confidently hand out stickers to rows of eager children.

It was crazy what newfound confidence the stickers actually gave her considering she was hiding behind me only minutes before.

With chubby cheeks that dimpled when she smiled, one child bounced in animation as a sticker was placed on her t.shirt.

"Would you like a sticker?" Summer cheerily asked the next child in the line as she clutched her 20 pages like a teacher with a clipboard.

I watched with amusement as one girl sneakily stole a page from Summer's grip without her even noticing.

Totally oblivious, my daughter continued in her mission of providing every child with that all-important piece of memorabilia.

Bending down to reach the mischievous girl's eye level, in my most-authentic cockney accent, I said: "Oy cheeky! I saw you take a whole page of stickers!" whilst chuckling to assure the young girl that I was only messing around.

The playful girl laughed in my face, which exposed a smile as endearing as a rainbow that almost spanned the entirety of her miniature face. She was truly adorable, that was for sure.

Against a volcano of giggles, the girl teased me by placing a sticker on each of her cheeks and one on the tip of her nose, making us both snort in unison. *See - friendships are not always built on knowing the same language!*

"Huh!" Summer huffed, clearly vexed as she marched towards us.

"Mummy – that girl stole a page of stickers from me!"

"It's ok; we have plenty so she can keep them."

"Cheeky!" Summer stated assertively, before carefully peeling a sticker from the girl's page and placing it playfully onto her chin, to match the rest of her now stickered-face. This mischievous act entertained the surrounding children and worked wonders for Summer's confidence – breaking through the shy undercurrent of her personality.

It was soon time to move on. Smiling broadly, I was ecstatic to witness the 'sunshine' in Summer emerge victoriously and confidently as she engaged alongside some of the most vulnerable children we had ever met.

Journeying further through the courtyard, the school seemed to become more unique and appealing with every step that we took.

Arguably, the most captivating aspect was its sense of enormous spaciousness because of its seemingly never-ending out-buildings that gave the appearance and feeling of a small village.

Advancing, it looked as though the older children were on a snack break as they bounced around the room in a hysteria of joy and freedom.

We worked at an incredibly fast-pace to try and provide each child with a sticker. Predictably, some returned despite already having several, others refused to budge - and some were even pushing to the front, frightening Summer and nearly knocking her clean off her feet at one point.

Before I even had the chance to say something, Carl protectively scooped my daughter up, and from the comfort of his arms she continued in her mission to pass each child a sticker.

Watching them both intently, I suddenly felt extremely grateful for Carl's presence. *Well there's a first!*

Noticing me staring in his direction, I mouthed the words 'thank you' over a sea of enthusiastic faces.

The small token of stickers for the children (and witnessing their smiling faces upon our visit) demonstrated that it was the simple things that filled you with happiness. It was these precious moments that truly signified the unity between human nature, regardless of ethnic makeup or social class.

Or next stop was the healthcare centre that resided inside another Phnom Penh neighbourhood.

Stepping into the medical centre, I was gobsmacked to discover that it resembled a western waiting room in the middle of a not-so western neighbourhood.

"Guys, this is Dr San...he's going to talk to you about the centre and how it helps this community. I'll wait for you outside," said our guide, ever-so attentively.

"Follow me!" Doctor San directed us into a side room.

"Everything in this medical centre is free and as you can imagine, we deal with a variety of medical-related problems therefore no day is ever the same."

"What's the most common problem that you see?" Carl asked with an air of curiosity; surprising me considering he hadn't muttered much since we had set off on the Tuk-tuk that morning - clearly objecting to the visit.

"Persistent infections - 80 per cent of which are water-related," the doctor explained insightfully.

"CCF provides purified drinking water to each school, and distributes 20-litre water bottles and a bottle cleaning facility to thousands of local families to try and break the constant cycle of infections. Sadly...offering the water to 3,000 plus families just isn't enough - which is why CCF relies heavily on donations."

"I noticed a wealth of tiny babies in the school we have just visited. Does the centre have a facility for supporting pregnant ladies?" I asked, intrigued and feeling hopeful.

"We offer a Maternal Care Programme, alongside a 'Welcome Home Baby Kit' to sustain the healthy development of newborns throughout their crucial first weeks. Since introducing the kits, infant mortality rates have reduced significantly! Whilst this is a giant leap in the correct direction, we are still lacking the full range of facilities that you have available in the UK." Dr San smiled, and at the same time glanced towards my clean, healthy daughter who was dressed head to toe in fresh clothes.

Summer innocently returned the smile by beaming back at him. I couldn't stop thinking about the irony of the situation. Here we were discussing the brutality of infant mortality that was no doubt happening around the corner at that very moment (many of which are caused by none-other than wealth circumstance) and here was my well-kept child without a care in the world.

Minutes later and as we left the medical centre, the guide explained how the charity also has a community centre.

"The centre provides free evening meals to anyone that arrives. It is important for you to understand that the CCF charity isn't about a hand-out. The charity is trying to break the cycle of poverty by educating the children who are the next generation capable of making change. We want them to leave their villages and move into appropriate employment and adequate homes. That way in 10 to 20 years' time, villages such as what you have seen today will no longer exist," she paused, stepping onto the Tuk-Tuk.

"In the meantime, we must help the families that are currently living with no running water and raw sewage," she continued to explain as she roared the Tuk-tuk into action.

"These people have no work, hope, and no respite. No one should have to live like that."

There were numerous bleak moments throughout the trip when I felt poignant to the very core of my heart. Seeing the slum and meeting its tiny occupants truly unlocked the key to my raw emotion. If I was honest, speeding along on that Tuk-tuk and thinking about what we had learnt and seen that day, along with the endless empathy that I felt, suddenly opened the flood gates to my feelings. I had to fix my thoughts far away to prevent the tears from cascading like a gushing waterfall down the contours of my cheeks.

My thoughts switched to the western world. Whereby we so often become pre-occupied with the silliest, most mundane things and do not appreciate the abundance of opportunities given to us daily. Not to mention the standard of living that we are persistently provided with. Heck! In Britain, if you have a child then you are given a home and regular money to get you by from week-to-week! And we still complain that it's not enough! *I mean, really?* How can one world be so different, depending on what country you are from?

***

"We also have a community outreach centre," the guide continued to educate, her voice impinging on my thoughts.

"Unfortunately, there are some children that are not able to attend one of our schools because their families need them to work. It is for this reason that we also offer a number of evening classes at the outreach centres to enable those children to get an education, too."

"You really are a life-line to this community, aren't you?" I said in ore as we sped through a dusty, dry road.

"Another thing that CCF offers..." the guide shouted over the roar of the engine, driving along at what was now a considerable speed.

"Is to provide teenagers lacking educational knowledge and achievements with 'life-trade skills' to enable them to become employable in the future; providing a pathway out of a lifetime of poverty. For example, it is common to train them to be a baker or pastry chef in the Star Bakery. That's the bread that is distributed to the Steung Meanchey families, who live on a garbage tip..."

"I am truly amazed! I had no idea that CCF offered so many life-changing things. Fantastic, isn't it Carl?" I spun to face my suddenly extremely quiet travel buddy.

"Yes, quite-so." he muttered in a small, distant voice.

Naturally, I couldn't work out whether he was deliberately being 'off' or whether he found it increasingly difficult to agree with me in fear of looking like a prized-fool because of his former objection to visit; pride well and truly broken!

"This is our last stop of the day - a residential home and school for some of our teenagers."

"This is Chea and he will be your guide at the house."

"Hi Chea..." we greeted the fresh-faced young boy that was waiting for us in the hallway of the building.

Waving goodbye to our former guide, we were left with Chea, our-new 13-year-old host.

Chea informed us that he had lived at the house for six years. Climbing the staircase to the first floor, he proudly pointed out his certificates which occupied a considerable amount of space on the wall. This made me feel empowered. Even though this was indeed a residential home and not a cosy, traditional 'family' environment, the walls housed the achievements of the students in much the same way that one would expect to find in family stairwells across much of the world.

Scanning one of the certificates, I read that Chea had been crowned 'Pupil of the Year' alongside another harmonious student.

"Wow - you are a master in karate?" I asked the young boy with a cheeky but reassuring smile dressed across my face.

"Yes my sponsor pays for it!"

I had read about sponsoring a child on CCF's website before arriving, however, throughout the day 'sponsoring' hadn't even been mentioned. This reassured me that we weren't invited purely as a marketing tool in the hope of the charity gaining a new sponsor. It was simply about educating us to the challenges that are faced in Phnom Penh. Undoubtedly, CCF was trying to make a lasting impression on us, but so they should – given the remarkable humanitarian efforts they were painstakingly executing every day.

Unsurprisingly, I now had a huge soft-spot for the charity; feeling somewhat inspired but not pressured.

"How does the sponsorship work?" Carl asked.

"A sponsor pays money each month for an individual child who is then able to use that money to participate in activities or experiences. So my sponsor paid for my karate lessons."

"Do you know who she is?" I asked, fascinated to know how it all worked.

"She writes to me often, and I write back – sometimes we skype! She's lovely and has given me many wonderful opportunities in life already."

I was curious to know whether he had ever met her in person.

"No never, but I would love to – just to say thank you properly, if anything."

Continuing down the hall, I peered into a room that was lined with computers.

"This is where we are able to skype our sponsors or write them letters." Chea continued down the hallway, stopping at a door with a sign that read: 'Councillors Office.'

"This is where we find our resident councillor and next door is the nurse's office."

"I have to say, I am absolutely stunned by your quality of English!" said Carl, suddenly intrigued and actually participating in the tour.

"When I arrived at my first CCF residence (aged six) I couldn't speak a word of English. CCF taught me from scratch! I owe everything to Scott!" Chea confessed, gratitude sparkling from his eyes.

"Oh, have you met Scott Neeson then?" *Call me naïve, but I just assumed that not every child would know Scott personally...*

"Oh yes, of course! He comes here all the time. Plus, I have been privileged enough to fly to the States and Hong Kong to fundraise for CCF."

"Really?" I was absolutely flabbergasted.

"Yes – I owe everything to Scott and my sponsor. I am very fortunate."

Chea explained that CCF is sponsored by 'Credit Swiss,' meaning that all the children are treated in exactly the same way. If one child has a sponsor and another doesn't, Credit Swiss pick up the bill until the second child has a sponsor that then takes over payments.

"That way the second child never misses out on opportunities..." Our teenage host continued to explain whilst we made our way down the staircase.

This made the situation at Muoy's school much clearer. It appears Muoy has steered clear of sponsors because it would not be feasible for her to make up the difference should a sponsor pull out.

"It's important to have a sponsor though," Chea continued.

"It allows you to build up a strong friendship with another person. Not all the children have parents or families, so it's nice to have someone to talk to, develop a relationship with and go to for guidance and advice."

Towards the end of the visit, Chea showed us a bedroom, and took us to a classroom where we watched a lesson take place. Before long, we were back on the busy city street, hollering a Tuk-tuk and heading back to Muoy's guesthouse.

The most important lesson I learnt from CCF was that a child will be unable to productively study if they are malnourished. Equally, a child cannot attend school if their family depends on them earning an income to put food on the table, or to look after their siblings. Families don't have the capacity to prioritise a child's education if they are homeless and lack access to healthcare or are struggling under the weight of crippling debt. CCF works on-the-ground to ensure that a family never has to choose between sending a child to school or putting food on the table.

Without a shadow of a doubt, I was impressed by the ground-breaking work of CCF.

When Hollywood marketing executive Scott Neeson took a five-week trip to Cambodia in 2003, I bet he never imagined it would change his life as much as it did. Maybe his vision wouldn't work out, but seeing if it would obviously turned out to be the best adventure of all... let's hope that Muoy would have the same success.

***

Twenty Three:

To travel is to take a journey into yourself

Whilst on our travels we had learnt that the vast majority of Cambodia's animals are under threat for a multitude of manmade reasons. The list includes land invasion, illegal logging and wildlife poaching. Despite the fact that I am openly not a member of the 'animal lover' club; the fact that humans were directly responsible for the mass destruction of a number of species did not sit well with me.

It was for this reason that I impulsively decided that we would work as 'bear keepers' at the conservation centre: 'Save the Bears.'

Standing outside Muoy's in the blistering heat, our transport to the centre finally arrived. My mascaraed eyes narrowed when a beaten-up Transit van stopped to a dramatic holt at our excited feet, sounding as though a tool-box was being shaken for added effect.

Peering out of the cloudy, dirty windows were none other than three rather-large Alsatian dogs that were panting and licking the grimy windows as they eagerly stared at the latest workers to join their gang. *Surely, they're not travelling to the countryside with us?* I gulped.

Hesitating for a moment, my hand hovered over my suddenly dry-mouth.

Breathing out of my nose to hold my breath minutes later, the odour of wet dog, combined with sticky, human sweat and the van's fumes, was enough to make me vomit at any second. *Where was air con when you needed it?*

Putting me further on edge, every so often I would see my young daughter glance towards me with increasing scepticism with every sharp turn and sickness jab that was felt. *Do not say anything about me hating dogs! Do not say anything about me hating dogs!* I mentally pleaded with my 'honest' daughter.

"Did you know that my Mummy is scared of dogs?" she embarrassingly declared to the entire fleet of dog lovers the van occupied.

Of course I am not 'scared' of dogs – I'm not really scared of anything. Of my life so far I have undertaken many dare-devil challenges, I'd hope you know. I've come face-to-face with a mammoth shark whilst snorkelling alone on the Great Barrier Reef, I voluntarily jumped out of a plane at 10,000ft, and I abseiled down a sky-scraper building. Not to mention getting into a pen with a 4ft shark in Mexico! When you consider this - it is hard to believe that I would be genuinely 'scared' of dogs.

I couldn't exactly tell a van full of workers (who were cuddling up to their dogs and chatting aimlessly about how adorable they were) that dogs really weren't 'my thing' and that the horrendous smell of them actually made me heave.

"I..errr…" *Oh bulls! I'll just go along with the tale – it's much easier to explain and less controversial.* I nodded to myself in internalised agreement.

"I cannot believe that you're scared of dogs? What is it about them that you find so terrifying?" One girl shrieked in confused horror at my 'confession.'

"I…ummm…" Quick Laura – think!

"I'm – well… to be honest... I just worry that they may attack me, you know?" *No - of course they won't know! Why did you say that, you dummy?* I mentally shouted at myself.

"Is this because of a bad, past experience?" the girl leaned forward in her chair inquisitively.

All eyes were on me as I was left to 'confess' my make-belief sad tale of being bitten by a 'scary' dog. *Jesus! How do I get myself into these situations?*

I glanced at Carl as he flashed me a brief smile. *Ahh that's nice! If I really did have something to confess, I would have appreciated his dodgy smile in that very moment.*

"Not all dogs are the same - just like people are not." The girl began speaking to me like a child.

"Just because one dog might have misbehaved, that does not mean that all dogs will. Dogs see the world differently to humans. Running away or screaming could be seen as an invitation to play. Why don't you stroke Alp? He is a friendly dog! Go on – just reach out and give him a gentle stroke…" she ordered.

"I – err… I'd sooner not. Thanks."

"It's super easy! And he won't hurt you. I promise!"

Oh god, the thought of touching the slobbering dog really did make me feel sick. And I had no hand sanitizer!

"There's nothing to be scared of Mummy!" Summer looked at me with those big beady eyes. She knew I wasn't scared of dogs! What was she playing at? If she's doing this to me at five, what will she be like as a teenager?

***

The final road to the centre was incredibly dusty. Worst of all, it was full of elderly people begging. Despite being so close to the end of our trip, I still hadn't witnessed begging on that scale before.

Literally every 20 seconds a severely frail, elderly person was perched at the edge of the road cupping their hands towards the bus in sheer desperation. It was painstakingly hard to watch and caused a knife-edge pain to hit the very pit of my stomach with every person that we sadly passed.

An eerie silence swept through the van ceasing all previous evidence of laughter and needless small talk amongst our group. To this very day, I don't think I will ever be able to remove that impoverished sight I witnessed from the grubby windows that morning.

"Mummy - why do the old people look like that? And…what are they doing?" Summer unsurprisingly asked into the soundless van with a five-year-old's air of innocence. The entire van remained silent as the occupants waited for my impending answer.

"Well…" I swiftly thought on my feet to ensure that I handled the situation delicately. *Unforeseen encounters like this always remind me of why motherhood is made unexpectantly challenging at times. Finding the right words and utilising them in a context fit for a five-year-old comes with its own difficulties. Not to mention the fact that children repeat everything to everyone so you need to ensure that what you tell them is audience worthy.*

"Well, these people don't have much money so as cars pass they put their hands out to see if anyone will offer them some…"

Needless to say, I was unhappy with my answer. Disappointed at myself for my half-hearted attempt, my internal thoughts raged.

"It is horrible to see but you do get used it eventually." One of the volunteers said in a small voice that was riddled with sadness. Remaining silent, I nodded my head in acknowledgment.

Arriving at Phnom Tamao Wildlife Rescue Centre, we were immediately taken into a bright and airy classroom that was adoringly decorated with children's drawings, stickers and paintings of various bears.

Emily introduced herself as our guide and educator for the day. She gave Summer an education pack that contained diagrams, leaflets, stickers and stories about the bears; and pictures for her to colour in – which of course she absolutely loved!

We watched a video that informed us about two of the centre's bears; the Sun and Moon bear. We were then educated in why the centre exists and the journey the bears took to get there. I learnt that Cambodia has 14 endangered species, and two of those include the Asian black bear and the Malaysian sun bear.

"The bears you will meet today have been rescued for a variety of reasons," Emily explained after the video finished.

"Believe it or not, there are restaurants in Cambodia that serve bear-paw soup to their diners."

"Bear-paw soup?" a stunned Summer shouted; clearly horrified and stealing the words right out of my mouth!

"Yes – it's awful!" Emily said with a glum expression.

"Others have been kept as exotic pets in bars and restaurants and caged simply for the amusement of guests. Some are seized from the black market; where their body parts are used for souvenirs; others have been saved from poachers that sell orphaned cubs for the illegal pet trade.

"We even have bears that have been rescued during attempts to illegally smuggle them into neighbouring countries for use in bear bile farms; and others who have been rescued from snare traps that were set in the forests to capture animals."

After a slight pause, she continued: "Some bears are donated by their owners who have neglected them as pets and no longer want them."

I was speechless beyond belief.

"Summer, would you like me to introduce you to Kong?" Emily crouched down to her level.

"Yes please!" Summer yelled with a look of wonderment glazing across her eyes.

"Kong was previously kept as an exotic pet so sadly, he's had a troubled life."

Within seconds Emily casually threw her tiny body over the almighty step of an off-white, mud-caked Defender truck.

"Guys, this is our truck for today so jump on board and we will head to Kong! It's hot today, huh?" Emily noticed our obvious discomfort in the face of the blazing heat and eye-squinting sun that was so bright; it was as if I was holding a golden medallion against a white sheet of paper.

In no time we had negotiated the rough drive along the sun-baked landscape, arriving at Kong's house.

"This is Kong," Emily introduced as she approached a large cage that housed a bulky brown bear that was busy chewing on a leaf.

I distinctly noted how often Emily lovingly bent down to Summer's eye level. Best of all, whilst speaking she would address Summer personally just as much as she would us grownups. Summer instantly warmed to her and was starting to view her as an approachable, trusting and warm adult. It reminded me of how Summer was with Mike, Laurie and Apple at the Elephant Sanctuary.

"Kong was from the Cambodian mountains when hunters caught him," Emily explained.

"The hunters tied him up and kept him in a tiny cage inside a noisy city bar. People would poke him and feed him strange food, which then made him sick.

"After a while Kong's vision started to fade and before he knew it he was partially blind."

"That's so sad…" Summer gulped.

Regrettably, the abuse and mistreatment of animals seemed to be a chillingly recurring theme across the parts of Asia that we had visited. First the elephants in Chiang Mai, then that poor Gibbon in the Phuket jungle who was being kept as an exotic pet in the most inhumane conditions; and now the tragic circumstances of the bears….

Kong's history was a reminder of the upsetting ability of mankind to be shamefacedly brutal.

"With the incessant noise, never-ending poking and the bizarre food," Emily continued. "It was a frightening time for Kong... well, until 'Free the Bears' came along that is!" Emily elevated her tone before smiling and squeezing Summer around the waist; prompting her to giggle in sync.

"How did you hear about Kong?" Carl quizzed.

"The centre was tipped-off so we rescued him and carried out surgery to amend his vision. With Kong's slightly intoxicating brown eyes widening, Emily informed us that miraculously he could now see.

"Can Kong see me, like - right now?" Summer screeched; her eyes glittering with enthusiasm.

"Yep! Come and watch this!" Emily offered Summer her hand before the duo walked on ahead.

Looking on, I couldn't help reflecting on the journey of 'transformation Summer.' I was so pleased that she was continually developing from a small quiet seed into a confident, flourishing flower... *'My Asian Summer'* had been born!

I prayed memories such as meeting Kong and hearing his story, stayed within her ever-developing mind and didn't vanish as quick as the trip seemed to be closing in on us.

"We have 21 forest enclosures and eight houses dedicated to the bears." Emily led-us across a patch of land, stopping at a clear fence.

"This is one of the houses. In each house you will see a pool, hammocks, climbing equipment and shady areas for respite from the hot sun."

"The bears look happy!" Summer beamed as we all stood and marvelled at a bear who was joyfully swinging on a climbing frame, and another who was sluggishly laying on a rock, eyes closed and head positioned towards the basking rays.

"Do you want to make the bears some lunch in the cook house?"

"Oh, Mummy, can I?" Summer tugged at my sleeve, forcing me to mischievously giggle.

"We have to make each house a food tray; so today we will make a tray for the house you have just seen." Emily grabbed a red plastic ball that was the size of a medium bowling ball and had a small hole on its side.

"You need to fill each hole with a cocktail of honey, dog biscuits, beans, bananas and other greens."

Making the balls was surprisingly satisfying and reminded me of the special time we had spent at the elephant sanctuary; mashing the bananas.

"Summer - can you help me push the wheelbarrow of balls to the house?" Emily placed the last ball into the dark-green wheelbarrow.

"Now I must tell you something important!" Emily warned with a stern shrillness to her voice.

"You must feed each bear at the same time - otherwise they fight over the balls. Got that Summer?"

"Yep! That's just like me, Sienna and Hope, isn't it Mummy?"

"Sienna and Hope are her cousins. Yes – just like you three!" I giggled uncontrollably.

"Oh Summer! You should never fight with your cousins. They're the first friends that you will have in life. You should cherish them dearly." Carl announced in an exceptionally serious tone; forcing me to dart him a strange and slightly irritated look.

"Well they're kids - that's what they do. Of course they're the best of friends five minutes later."

"You should still focus on the importance of not fighting from a young age, Laura!"

"Oh Carl: shut-up!" I declared overzealously but still managing to mask my inherent dislike of his elitist attitude with a hint of solitaire in my tone.

We came to a halt at the entrance of the bear house, and without a single bear in sight I wasn't entirely sure how we would get their attention.

"Summer!" Emily shouted.

"How does your mum tell you that it's tea time when you're at home?"

"She shouts, 'DINNER!'" Summer screamed, expending almost all of the air from her miniscule lungs.

"Wow! That was very loud." Emily giggled.

"Well, just as loud as that we shout the word 'more,' which in Khmer (the bears language) means 'come.'

"So, just as you did at the top of your lungs can you shout 'more, more, more!'"

Fast-forward a few minutes, and in sync the four of us were eagerly shouting 'more, more, more!' across the vacant enclosure.

"As soon as we see the bears heading our way, we need to throw the balls as high as we can over the fence - but not until I say so!" Emily declared.

"More, more, more…"

"More, more, more…"

"More, more - oh my god, there's one!" I screamed totally overjoyed, sounding more like a five-year-old than Summer herself.

"Keep shouting – you need to attract all three bears. More, More, More…" Emily bellowed at the top of her lungs.

In no time whatsoever, we had attracted the attention of all three bears.

"On the count of three - can you each throw your ball over the fence? We have to do this at exactly the same time. Ready: 1, 2, 3! Throwwwww…"

We watched on as each bear merrily found a ball, laid on its back, balanced the ball on its feet and skilfully used its long tongue to fish the food out of the hole.

"Mummy they look so funny!" Summer passionately laughed whilst we digested the fascinating sight of 'meal time' unfolding before our eyes.

"Right guys, our next stop is to meet one of our nine bear keepers." Emily led us inside an extremely dark bricked building and diverted into a side room.

"This is Bourney, one of our talented bear keepers. Bourney, this is Carl, Laura and little Summer."

Trust Carl to make us look totally stupid as he half-heartedly raised a limp hand in some sort of bizarre greeting to the keeper. Bourney must have been reading my mind, revealing a face that silently said: 'what the hell?' He looked at Carl oddly, darted his attention away from the weird greeting and smiled sweetly in my direction.

"Please…" Bourney placed his left-palm out wide, indicating for us to follow him into another room where we were met by several tiny enclosures.

"It's funny…" I giggled towards my travel buddies as I examined the contents of the room with my fascinated eyes.

"This room reminds me of a doctor's waiting room – only it's for bears and not humans." I continued chuckling at the uncanny resemblance.

"Well it's funny that you should say that as I am about to administer medicine to one of the bears."

Just as a human would stand patiently when a doctor approached, a black moon bear stood nice and tall for Dr Bourney.

A solid wooden door that was the height of my hip separated the bear and his doctor. My mind raced through all the possibilities of what we may witness.

"I'm excited!" Summer leaned in closely, flashing a wide cartoon smile that confirmed she was equally as exhilarated as I was.

"Should we be this close?" Carl hissed into my other ear. *Honestly, sometimes his words hit you like poison.*

"If something happens our travel insurance won't pay out because we chose to get so close..." he continued to ramble.

"You're a funny man Carl!" I laughed off his sombre comment in jest.

"It's not a joke, I'm serious!" his eyebrows stood to attention matching his words.

"I know – that's what I mean, 'you're a funny man!' anyway, shhh!" I silenced him with good humour as I instead focused my attention on Bourney.

I was so excited to see the doctor examining this magnificent creature, but king 'spoil sport' himself was droning on and on about bloody health and safety and ruining the moment completely.

"What's happening Mummy?"

"The bear is having his medicine. And he's not making a fuss, unlike when you have to take your Malaria tablets!" I giggled.

"So not funny!" she said in a grumpy, teenage-esque voice.

"That's not really a laughable matter is it Laura? You shouldn't encourage it." *Here we go again – Carl on the criticism!*

The bear was asked to complete a number of actions, such as opening its mouth, standing up straight, sitting down and turning around. As the bear turned, Bourney injected the medication into his backside without the bear even flinching.

After each command was complete the bear received a biscuit as a treat.

Bourney explained how he had worked at the centre for what seemed like a lifetime, and his favourite thing about the job was caring for the bears in the 'Bachelor House.'

"It's in the Bachelor House that most of the disagreements happen between the boisterous male bears." Bourney chuckled.

"It takes a long time to gain the trust of a new bear after the terrible experience they endured in their previous life."

"Bourney actually has an untouchable reputation for gaining the trust of the bears before the rest of the team." Emily entered the room, making Bourney blush scarlet-red at the compliment.

"Don't be modest Bourn…you have a beautiful, calm aura about you that shines through to the bears." She announced lovingly.

"Whilst the bears continue their health MOT," Emily turned to face us. "Why don't we go into their house and hide some treats. Would you like that Summer?"

"Like a treasure hunt?" Summer pondered, obviously not wanting to agree until she understood all the facts and exactly what she was signing up to.

"Just like a bear treasure-hunt!"

Entering the gigantic enclosure, I embraced my inner-child by climbing over the play equipment to hide the snacks.

"Mummy, put a biscuit in this tunnel!" Summer shouted cheerily, crawling out of a neighbouring tunnel.

"Don't put one in the tunnel if there's already one in there!" Carl reared his bossy head from a distance.

"What?" I shouted, confused by his interruption.

"Summer's asked you to hide a treat in a tunnel that she has already just hidden a treat in. Therefore, it isn't a good idea, is it? We are supposed to space the treats out; so that the bears use their skills to find them. I'm certain that we aren't supposed to make the task easy for them!"

I stared at him in utter disbelief.

"It's just a bit of fun Carl!"

"Who put this treat in here?" He angrily pointed to one of the hammocks.

"I did!" Summer yelled, totally unfazed.

"I think we need to re-group and strategize Laura. We only have 20 or so treats left, and so far they're being placed haphazardly. We have been asked to hide the treats to 'mentally challenge'" he finger quoted. "The bears, otherwise we would have been asked to simply throw the treats over the fence as we did with the balls."

Standing rigid and wracked with irritation, I stared directly at him for a good few seconds. Vexation spread through my body like the plague. Thankfully, the sudden grinding of a dustbin truck brought me immediately back to reality.

"Great job guys!" Emily approached the cage.

"The bears are ready to go back in now, so come out and we can watch them find their treats."

Watching the bears fiercely hunt to find their afternoon delights was extremely entertaining as they chased each other up and down the climbing frames.

Looking like they might rupture due to excessive food intake, the bears found all the treats in record timing.

"I think that's the quickest they have ever found them all!" Emily laughed.

"See! I told you!" Carl aggressively barked, shaking his head in troubled dismay.

"It wasn't a challenge for them at all - we should have re-grouped!"

"It is just a bit of fun Carl! More so for Summer than us..."

"Who's hungry?" Emily interrupted from outside the cage, clearly noticing the tension brewing.

"Me!" Summer shouted at the top of her lungs, a clear indication that she was comfortable in her surroundings.

Jumping back in the Defender, we soon arrived at a polished wooden platform that was suspended high into the trees. The entire team of keepers and volunteers were sat crossed legged on elegant wooden flooring; surrounded by plates and saucepans that were filled with traditional Cambodian cuisine.

"Guys!" Emily called out to get the attention of all the workers.

"This is Laura, little-Summer and Carl. They are our much-loved bear keepers for the day."

"Here!" shouted a blonde Australian man, tossing us each a can of full-fat coke.

"And plates for you…" a kind Cambodian man declared, making me feel comfortably at home.

"Dig in!" Emily shouted enthusiastically, unapologetically stacking her plate so sky-high the noodles were almost erupting over the confines of her plate like an uncontrollable volcano.

Feeling like the centre piece on a wedding cake; I shyly dished up a small helping of Khmer beef salad and sticky rice and pork for both Summer and myself. All eyes appeared to be fixed in our direction and as hungry as I was, I feared looking like the 'greedy volunteer.'

As I sat, it seemed Carl was already engrossed in conversation with someone, explaining about his 'lack of knowledge with animals because he is a Fraud Investigator by trade.' *I'd never have known…*

The best part of being on a volunteering project for the day was that we got to meet all sorts of intriguing people.

Jake, 22, told me that he was on a gap year from University.

"I am studying to be a vet in the UK. Incredibly, we were offered a gap year abroad to care for animals' native to other continents. I'm doing six months here with the bears, and six months in the wild bushes of Africa."

"That's incredible!" I smiled. "What do you think of this place? Were you shocked by people's attitude towards the bears, or were you aware of their bad treatment before coming?"

"I was aware of the cruelty that takes place: just not the sheer extent of it! When you think about it - every bear here has an inky-black past that has cast a mean shadow over their former lives." Jake paused thoughtfully.

He continued: "I have been at the Sanctuary for five months now and I've witnessed bears arriving a nervous wreck because they have spent so much time in a cramped, dingy cage. Some have had their paws chopped off, or have been endlessly tortured to create a food delicacy!" I raised my eyebrows and frowned.

387

Glancing towards Carl, I noticed that he had an uninviting mouth full of food and was visibly draining the life out of those surrounding him with his flat and dull tale about how he became the mighty, 'Fraud Investigator' winning numerous awards, don't you know...

"The most shocking thing I've learned since I've been here though," said Jake, thankfully breaking into my tiresome 'Carl' thoughts. "Are how bears are treated in the Chinese medicine industry - that outrageously, legally exists!"

"What happens?" I asked, totally clueless.

"Farmers milk a bear's gall bladder for its bile. It's then used for Chinese medicine!"

"What's bear bile?" I asked, genuinely confused.

"It's a digestive fluid that's formed in the liver and stored in the gall bladder. It's used in Chinese medicine because they believe it cures fevers, improves your vision and cleanses your liver."

Oh my...

"Unbelievably, farmers capture wild bears and lock them in tiny cages for several years at a time. They torture them by creating a permanent hole in their stomachs; allowing a tube to be fitted. This means that bile will drip out of the tube the entire time the bear is in the cage. I'm sure you can imagine the extensive psychological and physical damage that could do to a bear?"

"Gosh..." I squirmed, speechless for a second.

Instantly, darkness clouded over me. This level of man-made cruelty was impossible to comprehend.

"Umm..." I cleared my throat, put my fork down on my plate and reflected on the abuse endured by the bears I'd met that morning.

"So when the Police discover these farms, presumably they send the bears to you guys?"

"Unfortunately not! The farms are legal in China!"

"What? You're kidding?"

"Bear bile has been used in Chinese medicine for hundreds of years. As cruel as it is, it's hard to change old habits. Eventually, the bile is made into a powder and sold for just under £14 a gram. One major problem is that it is an extremely profitable business."

"Wow!" I quickly downed the last of my coke and glanced at Summer who was happily eating, silent in her own thoughts.

Emily was incredibly open throughout lunch, explaining who she was and how she had found herself working at the sanctuary.

Aged 26 and from Colchester, she had been working at the centre for a year and a half on a trip that originally started as a backpacking experience.

"I visited the centre and loved it so much that I couldn't leave," she chuckled through the last mouthfuls of her excessively-large lunch.

Chatting to her like this, I felt like I had known her for a seriously long time. Feeling totally at ease, I revealed that I was 29.

"Jeez! That really makes me feel like I need to grow up!" she laughed almost nervously.

"I'm 26 and my boyfriend is 31 and we're still messing around with animals in Asia!"

"But what a life you have!"

"What made you want to travel with Summer then? You're the first backpacker I've seen out here with a child."

I told Emily about my backpacking adventure at 18 and that I had always wanted to go again. However, life in general and becoming a mother halted my dreams for a while.

"So I thought, why not take Summer? she could learn so much from it. Just because I now have a child, my life hasn't ended. I can still backpack - I just have to adjust my trip slightly..."

"In what way?"

"I can't stay in a dormitory in a hostel because I can't guarantee the safety of Summer, so instead we stay in private rooms in hostels and guesthouses. It costs more and you of course meet less people but it's safer."

Glancing around, I became aware that I had several people's ears open around me. Upon discovering this fact, I cleared my throat self-consciously.

"Of course, I'm not going to make any plans to get excessively drunk at a 'Full Moon' party and wake up shame-faced next to a total stranger on the beach!" I laughed at the ridiculousness of this thought. "But other than the obvious, the trip is the same!"

"You must be really proud of your Mummy…" Emily turned to Summer, who responded most unimpressively by glumly shrugging her shoulders as if to say, 'none of this is a big deal!'

"Honestly, she's five going on 15!" I giggled, slightly embarrassed by her rudeness.

We were lucky enough to be introduced to even more adorable bears following lunch.

"This is Mokiyup, one of our sun bears." Emily clarified as we stared ahead at a handsome, miniscule, black-furred bear that had a yellow horseshoe shape of colour decorated on his chest.

"Mokiyup was a neglected exotic pet. He arrived in the most appalling state. Sadly he was kept locked in chains, stunting his growth considerably."

"I was going to say he looks incredibly small!" Carl interjected as he glared at the bear before him.

"Well sun bears are small, but Mokiyup is particularly small. When he was discovered he had a huge chain and padlock around his neck." Emily's voice plummeted.

"Despite the odds stacked against him, Mokiyup has grown in size, personality and confidence. He's our heroic, indestructible warrior – aren't you mate?" Emily peered her soft, calming face against the fence and smiled compassionately towards the bear.

Continuing across the land, Emily recalled stories of some of the other bears we passed.

"A few months ago, a cub called Anita arrived. She was rescued after being captured by hunters who used wire to tie her to a tree, hoping her cries would lure her mother within the gunshot range.

"My goodness!" Carl almost spat the words out of his mouth.

"It took ages for Anita to trust us after that. However, she's now a happy bear who is very playful and boisterous. She is forever making me laugh. She's such a joy to be around. A bit like your bear I expect, Summer?" Emily's eyes pointed towards Duffy who was of course firmly tucked under Summer's right arm.

Summer kissed Duffy on the head and weirdly wiped her snotty nose on him, making me frown at her.

Back in the Defender, Emily gave us some information about the Chief Executive of the sanctuary.

"Our CEO is an Australian man called Matt Hunt." Emily informed whilst accidentally driving over a sizeable pothole that made a remarkably thunderous crunching sound to suggest our enormous Defender wheels had somehow been swallowed by the vast earth below. Following the initial shock, everybody erupted into a bed of laughter.

"Women drivers eh?" remarked Carl to the van of women.

Hmmm, not content will earning the title of 'king kill-joy!' and the most peculiar man in the universe; Carl was unwittingly going for the full hat-trick of negative personality traits, now adding the title of 'male chauvinist' to his ever-growing list of awards! I shook my head in 'Carl' disbelief.

"Not the conventional route to becoming a CEO," Emily continued, ignoring Carl's rude remark. "Matt was originally on a working holiday at the Wildlife Rescue Centre…a placement that was only meant to last for a few months."

Although listening, my thoughts drifted to Lek, the owner at the Elephant Sanctuary in Thailand. She too had compelled her entire life to transform the fate of the mistreated elephants she came across. *What would happen if people like Lek and Matt didn't exist?*

Travelling certainly gives you the opportunity to take a journey into yourself and listen to your inner voice… a journey of thought-provoking, self discovery, some may say? *How many of us actually act upon the devastating things that we see, hear and learn about in our everyday lives?*

I'm not necessarily making reference to the type of influential people with the power and financial funds to set up a grand charity (like Scott Neeson with the Cambodian Children's Fund.) But the ordinary, everyday folk, who cry, get angry and do their upmost to make a change?

I urge everybody to listen to that inner voice if something they witness doesn't feel right…you never know what you

might find out – about the world, and yourself, and ultimately
go on to achieve...

***

Twenty Four:

Anger flowed fast through my veins just as a carp would through water...

Later that evening we ventured to a highly-recommended traditional Thai and Cambodian restaurant called 'Khmear Surin.'

Once inside, I couldn't peel my eyes away from the grand décor. With the walls draped in luxurious silk, the restaurant featured a perfectly polished wooden floor.

I found myself totally fixated on the alluring pot plants, sparkling fairy lights and attractive floor cushions. With all the guests sat around an arrangement of low tables, the top floor harboured spectacular balcony views of the street below.

"We don't have to sit on the floor, do we?" Carl triggered a dissatisfied look in my direction as we climbed the stairs to the floor we would dine on.

"Thank you..." I wai'd to the waitress as we approached the table, embarrassed by Carl's unforgiving rudeness.

"Mummy – look! Even Duffy gets his own floor cushion!"

With that Summer catapulted her tiny but robust body onto a cushion, closely followed by tough-old Duffy bear.

"Carl, lighten up! It will be fun!" I perched my ever-expanding bottom onto a floor cushion, excited about the array of culinary delights to come.

"Laura - we're both tall people! Our legs and back will ache after only a few minutes of sitting like a school child in a school assembly!"

"No they won't! Don't be so boring! Just sit down!" I tugged childishly on his arm.

Initially I embraced sitting on the floor, taking part in traditional Cambodian culture. As much as I hate to admit it, however, Carl was absolutely correct. Within 30 minutes my back and legs felt like they were about to break completely in half! I was desperately craving a chair. Of course, I couldn't tell Carl that! So, while he was tutting and shuffling around in an obvious way, I was a little more discreet with my ever-increasing aches and pains.

Stupidly rubbing my spine with my fingertips, "You're uncomfortable, aren't you?" a mocking smile edged across Carl's smug face. *So much for being discreet, Laura!*

"Not at all! I was actually thinking the total opposite!" I lied through my teeth, swallowing a huge dose of self-pity.

"I was actually thinking that I might ditch my dining room table and chairs at home and instead sit around the coffee table with a cushion in future. I think this style of sitting is actually very calming..." I shot a sly smile in Carl's immediate direction. *Ha! That got him!*

"Yes!" Summer punched the air in triumph.

"Mummy, can we do that? Pleaseeeee?"

I smiled through the agonising shooting pain that was at that very moment firing through the nerves in my knee to the bridge of my back. *I have to say...I was extremely proud of my first class acting skills in the heat of the moment. Carl would never have known!*

Even more insulting, however, was that we'd been in the restaurant for over 40 minutes and still hadn't been served our drinks. I only ordered a can of Sprite! Anyone would have thought that they freshly pressed the lemons, miraculously made the fizz and canned the lemonade themselves!

The novelty of my lie swiftly wore off when we still hadn't received our dinner an agonising hour-and-a-half later.

To our relief, Carl and Summer's food eventually arrived; my Thai green curry however, hit the table only 10 minutes before our driver was to collect us.

Finishing his meal, Carl ran to the driver and asked him to come back in an hour's time.

Unsurprisingly, my patience hit a brick-wall and I ended up arguing ferociously with the manager about the appalling service and ridiculously long wait for food and drink. Feeling increasingly uncomfortable in the restaurant, I put on a brave face for Summer and cheerfully suggested that we 'explore' the local area in search of a tasty dessert.

So consumed by an overwhelming desire to make a quick getaway; I gulped my curry down with forceful determination and barely enjoyed the flavours of the fragrant coconut milk and basil leaves touching my taste buds.

Exploring the road for a dessert quickly proved to be the wrong decision when we stepped out onto the leafy street and realised there was little on it. I hadn't paid much attention when I had walked from the Tuk-tuk to the restaurant a few hours previously.

"The danger of assuming!" Carl sighed under his breath when we literally had no where to go.

Walking to the furthest point on the street, we quickly found ourselves in an undesirable dark and dingy place. Attempting the opposite direction, we arrived at a rundown backstreet hotel that had cups and saucers, desserts and pancakes displayed in the window.

The cup and saucer instantly made me visualise home and crave a mug of sugary Tetley tea.

"I miss tea...the tea here is hardly Tetleys or PG tips, is it?" I pushed the door open with willingness.

"You're not seriously heading inside this dump are you?" Carl frowned, taking a step backwards.

"Well, yeah! As dodgy as it looks, it is safer than standing on this dark, back-street. We still have 40 minutes to kill... and they have tea and cake! What more do you want?" My face creased into a laughing position.

"I don't actually drink tea anymore," Carl confessed as we sat down with our drinks and doughnuts several minutes later.

"Why?"

"I don't like to be predictable. It is what British society expects and why should we behave in a way that they want us too? Haven't you noticed that whenever I come to your office I never drink hot drinks?"

"I've never really paid attention to be honest." I took a disappointing sip of herbal tea.

"Did you know that during their lifetime, the average person will drink 17,000 cups of tea?"

"Well that really depends on the tea. If it tastes like this interesting blend then I beg to differ!" Laughing, I gave up all hope of enjoying a homely blend of nostalgia. Instead, I placed my cup back on the table and took a greedy bite of my sugar ring doughnut.

"I love tea!" Summer blurted out in an extremely adult-chic fashion, as if she was having a stylish afternoon conversation with a group of well-to-do housewives in an upmarket neighbourhood. Seriously, she never ceased to amaze me on this trip. You never knew what you might discover next about my newfound 'Asian' Summer. It was certainly entertaining to watch.

"Really? You're only five! You shouldn't be drinking tea at your age! It's not good for your teeth. We never allowed our children to have tea..." He nodded his head towards me disapprovingly.

"Well, she used to have a non-caffeine children's tea but they stopped selling it for some reason. As a substitute, she now has a really milky tea in an espresso cup. I really don't think that small quantity will do much to her teeth." My anger at yet another 'parenting fail' comment from Carl elevated 150% and unfortunately the doughnut got the wrath of it. Purely out of irritation, I leant forward and took another rather-large bite.

I was becoming agitated beyond belief with his blatantly uninvited and less-than necessary opinions. This led to me taking another bite from the calorie-rich cake. *Comfort eating at its finest, ladies and gentlemen...*

"And whilst on the subject..." I rambled whilst chewing. "Can you stop giving me parenting advice? I have been a single mum for five years – not five minutes. It's insulting!"

"Oh! I didn't mean to offend you. It's just my opinion..." he shrugged.

"Exactly! Your opinion! Which means that you're not right and I'm not wrong. Just please..." I paused for maximum effect. "Enough of the advice! It's unwanted and unneeded!" I picked up the doughnut once again.

Realising my extravagant greed, I suddenly wrenched the doughnut from the firmly-fixed position in my mouth. Stealing a glance downwards, I caught a glimpse of an exotic ant desperately clutching to the side of the dough as if his life was about to dramatically terminate here and now.

"Oh-my-god!" I slammed what was left of the doughnut on the table.

"Summer - don't eat your cake!" I jumped up from my seat and went on a determined mission to find new ones.

Waiting patiently at the counter, I casually peeped into the display cabinet. *What the heck!* The entire display shelf was swarming in a parade of ants! There were literally hundreds of them! *How had I not noticed them before?*

***

Travelling back to Muoy's, we got chatting to our driver about his daily grind as a 'Tuk-tuk' driver.

"I have to earn an average of $20 a day to pay my overheads," he confessed.

"What's your average journey price?" I curiously asked.

"Around $2."

"Blimey! You have to make a fair few journeys before you make a profit then?" I said, completely stunned.

Whizzing through the almost noiseless back streets, my thoughts turned to how much we had been paying him every day. As soon as it dawned on me that he had barely been hitting his target, a wave of sadness swept through me. This man was busting his gut on a daily basis for an absolute pittance. Yet, despite that he was still asking us to choose how much we paid him after each journey.

"I'm so sorry that you have waited around for us and missed the opportunity to take on other fares."

"Not at all! In Cambodia we prefer to book clients for the duration of their trip. The alternative otherwise, is squabbling over fares with tens of other drivers in the street!"

Fully charged with a fierce electrical current, I felt overwhelmingly compelled to support this driver in some sort of way. *The question was: how?*

Some would argue that this driver's situation was no different to a UK taxi driver's difficulties. The difference, however, is that in the UK we are fortunate enough to have a government who supports us. This is certainly not the case in Cambodia! If the driver makes no profit that day, there is no child benefit to fall back on. The family will simply have to go without dinner that night.

Yet again, I felt incompetent. Entirely worthless to make instant-change and submerged head-to-toe in heart-wrenching grief. Regardless of the highlights, I often felt like I was progressively propelling myself into a tangled web of despair on this journey.

Vividly, I recalled the unspeakable torture inflicted on the majestically peaceful elephants at the Elephant Nature Park in Thailand; the harrowing living conditions of the young girl we repeatedly came into contact with at the train station in Bangkok; the vulnerable children we met in the countless schools we had visited; the dire situation facing Cambodia's ever-diminishing population of Sun and Moon bears. Not to mention the unthinkable barbaric mass murders carried out at the infamous 'Killing Fields.'

With my mind in overdrive, I knew I needed to find a way to help. Suddenly outraged with the widespread injustice I had experienced in Asia, my daily £3 flat-white Latte in Starbucks suddenly seemed significantly less appealing…

Darting through the bustling city streets, I was completely oblivious to what was happening outside. Glaring into a space of nothingness, I travelled into the deepest corners of my own thoughts.

***

Early the next morning and the three of us were standing on the side of a traffic-lined street, gazing at the gigantic 'Royal Palace' and its rather-striking gold-plated triangular roof.

With a French influence ozzing out of every detail and feature, the structure was truly breath-taking to say the least.

"Do the King and Queen really live here Mummy?"

"Yes of course! Why do you think it's laced in gold?"

Glancing over at the palace walls in anticipation, my mood fell into a pit of despair. Awkwardly propped up against the extravagant palace walls was a shoeless eight-year-old boy. Yet again, a total contrast in wealth as I stared at the lavish palace amongst a gloomy cloud of poverty.

"$1 please!" A tiny girl who was also perched on the pavement outside hollered towards us loudly.

"Can I give the girl one of Nanny June's bracelets?" Summer asked, displaying her compassion and kindness.

Placing my rucksack on the floor, I watched as my young daughter passionately rifled through the bag. A moment later and she produced a beautiful gemmed bracelet that glimmered gloriously under the morning ray's glow.

Smiling gratefully, the girl accepted the bracelet and walked off as she admired every detail of the crystal-like beads.

Under the shining sun, I looked at my young daughter passionately.

"That was a lovely thing to do Summer!" I gushed with pride.

Despite it being stupidly early in the morning, the entrance queue resembled a hectic Saturday at 'Chessington World of Adventures.'

Sonith (our guide) immediately pointed to the raised flag that smoothly danced through the cloudless, blue sky.

"The flag is raised when the King is home." He enthusiastically explained with a twinkle in his pupils as we walked into the grounds and passed several striking patches of greenery and pretty shrubs of flowers.

"Why is the palace white and yellow?" Summer asked; blissfully skipping in front.

"They should have painted it pink and lilac!" she elegantly spun in perfect circles.

"The colours represent the population of Cambodia. Yellow means Buddha and white stands for Hindu."

"My friend at school is a Hindu!" Summer proudly revealed.

Central within the palace's grounds, stood a magnificent cream building complete with white pillars and a gold-encrusted spiked roof.

"This is Throne Hall," Sonith clarified, leading us into the building that was literally crawling with tourists.

"This building is famous for royal ceremonies such as coronations and royal weddings."

"Coronations?" Summer squealed, causing Sontih to look at her in alarm.

"Like in the film, Frozen?"

Just like every other five-year-old girl chasing the princess dream; Summer was making reference to the iconic fictional character Elsa who has a coronation in the film to be crowned Queen. *Handy when a fairytale fantasy actually teaches your child about the ways of the world.*

"Yes Rummer! This is where the coronations take place."

I watched as her eyes widened with emotion...suddenly, she contemplated the King's throne in intricate detail; totally oblivious to the fact that Sonith had just referred to her as 'Rummer!'

Proceeding through the hall, Sonith informed us about Cambodia's traditional dancing; something we had witnessed many times since arriving into the country. We learnt that the different colour outfits worn by the dancers reflected the range of days in the week.

"This is not only showcased by women. Men also wear a certain colour shirt or belt depending on the day," he continued.

"Today's colour is red to reflect Monday," he touched the mannequin's blood-red shirt.

Intrigued by the knowledge we had absorbed, I could immediately see the benefit of having a guide. I didn't want to repeat the 'Angkor Wat' situation, when we were staring at impressive-looking artefacts clueless about the history behind them.

"This building houses the ashes of our former kings," Sonith revealed as we stared ahead at a tiny building that looked just like the Stupa, infamous for housing the skulls and weapons at the Killing Fields.

Next up was the history of 'Buddha.'

"This information would have been handy at the start of the trip Sonith!" I mischievously teased as he continued to explain the different hand movements in the traditional Cambodian dance.

Sonith even mentioned the monkey dance that the children had performed for us at the 'House of Peace' in Siem Reap.

"Anyone of any age can become a Monk..." he later explained as we ventured further through the remarkable grounds.

"Really? I honestly thought that your father had to be monk for you to become one? Or there would have to be a family-tie of some sort at least?" I asked with curiosity.

"Not at all! You could become a monk if you wanted to!"

"Mummy wouldn't shave her head - she loves her hair too much!" Summer giggled, making us all explode with laughter from her faultlessly timed wit and growing sense of humour.

Conversation thankfully moved on, I soon found myself informing Sonith about our chance meeting with the fortune teller in Thailand.

"In Cambodia, if a fortune teller says a couple are not compatible then they always separate!"

"My goodness!" blurted Carl, taking the words straight out of my mouth. *I couldn't have said it better myself!*

"So, how long have you been a guide?" I quizzed.

"I have worked at the palace for many years and during that time I've met the King several times. When he first came into post, he held a huge party for all of the staff and had an enormous cake!" A childlike expression of pure pleasure stretched across his face.

"Does your profession 'treat' you well?" Carl air quoted. *(Not again!)*

"Carl!" I interjected passionately. "That is so rude! You can't ask someone that!" *He really was embarrassing sometimes!*

"Of course you can! I work in the British public sector you see. It is a whole different 'kettle of fish' so to speak! We certainly don't get treats such as large parties with tasty cake... but to work for the King of Cambodia..."

Was he for real? Firstly, I doubt that Sonith really knew what the 'public sector' meant, and secondly, it was so damn obvious that he only showed an interest in Sonith's job because he wanted a forum to highlight his own job once again!

"Well...thank you Sonith. You have been very knowledgeable and attentive to our needs." I quickly changed the subject, offering a handshake.

"My mother named me well then..." he gracefully shook my hand.

I looked at him confused.

"Sonith means: good conduct and manners."

"Oh right!" I smiled peacefully.

"You're in the right job then - working for the King and all!"

***

Enduring a 30-minute wait for our driver, we headed to a children's park across the road.

Giddily skipping along the pavement hand-in-hand with my daughter, the fun moment was briefly sliced with a knife when I witnessed a lady perched on a picnic blanket; alongside a naked baby that was sleeping faced down on the side of the road.

Summer was clearly overwhelmed by the sight of the park to even notice the naked boy. She was so excited in fact, that it was as if it was the first time that she had ever experienced the delights of a climbing frame. It made me think about how much she was missing everyday things, and in particular how much she would appreciate them when we later returned home.

The park was stunning and surprisingly much better than any of the parks in our wealthy seaside fishing village back home.

Painted in a terracotta of colours; it featured pleasant looking flower beds and was meticulously sectioned into different areas according to age and ability. I found it hard to accept its extravagance given the destitute appearance of the children playing on the equipment.

Sadly, most of them looked as though they had stepped straight out of a rubbish tip. Shoeless, they had filthy skin and torn, mud-drenched clothes.

On leaving the park, we had to walk back along the road to meet our driver. Disappointedly, the naked baby was still fast asleep on the picnic blanket. Worse, the mother was nowhere in sight. Naturally, I stopped in my tracks and painstakingly looked around for her.

Where the hell is she? I blurted out in a blind panic.

"What are you doing? We have to go!"

"We can't just leave him here on his own Carl! He hasn't even got any clothes on!" I snapped at his sheer ignorance and blatant idiocy.

"Laura, half the children here are like this. All the parents seem to leave them for periods of time. It's just a different culture to ours..." he obnoxiously rolled his eyes whilst exhaling deeply.

"Why are you sighing at me like I am a massive pain in the backside? What if she never returns and the child is taken? He is so exposed, hugely vulnerable and totally defenceless."

In the corner of my eye, I spotted two women casually chatting in the distance.

"Wait here a minute!" I yelled, running at full-speed towards the women.

Approaching with haste, my memory was failing me - I actually couldn't remember what his mother looked like!

"Is that your baby?" I pointed up the street towards the child as I approached the women.

Both ladies gave me a look of confusion.

"Your baby?" I asked again (protective patience wearing thin) cradling my arms as if rocking a baby.

Total blank! *They clearly had no idea what I was saying!* I huffed as I stomped back towards the child.

"Mummy there's a little girl coming..." Summer pointed in the distance several minutes later.

"He has a mother..." the young girl declared.

"Where?" I threw my arms in the air out of sheer frustration.

"I don't know..." she innocently glanced around.

"Well we aren't going anywhere until she comes back!" I crossed my arms on the spot sternly.

Infuriatingly waiting with the baby, anger ripped through my entire body and was escalating at the speed of wild fire; hammering away at my moral conscience. Aggressively scanning my surroundings as a last-ditch attempt to seek out an appropriate adult, I spotted a police officer casually slumped against a nearby statue.

Running towards him in haste, I arrived slightly out of breath and found myself propelling the details about the 'discovered' boy at an almighty speed.

"And he's all alone..." I clutched the side of my rib cage from the stitch that had now formed.

After a moment's pause, he responded: "Ok," before returning to the game he was playing on his mobile phone. *How rude!*

"You obviously don't understand what I'm saying!" I began to repeat the story at an even faster pace.

"I understand!" he interjected mid-sentence devoid of all emotion, before immediately returning back to his game.

"Unbelievable!" I stormed back to the others.

"Seriously Laura! We're so late for the driver - he might leave us!"

"Well go and tell him to wait then Carl! I'm not leaving the boy!" I yelled, passion oozing from every morsel of my body.

"Why has his Mummy left him? And why isn't he wearing any clothes?" Summer continued to stare at the sleeping baby on the blanket in front of her.

"Honestly Rube, I don't know!" I grumbled under my breath, followed by a deep sigh.

Out of nowhere, the girl pointed to a lady who was slowly walking towards us in the distance.

With a face like thunder, my eyes swivelled around as I quickly gathered my thoughts.

Thankfully it was the mother - a very pregnant mother at that!

"Fantastic!" I muttered, absorbing her enormous bump and shaking my head from left to right in sheer frustration at the sight.

"Your baby?" I asked with a harsh tone to my voice as the lady waddled closer.

Not answering, she simply smiled and took a seat alongside her sleeping son totally oblivious to just how cross I was; this just irritated me even more.

"Why did you leave him on his own? Anything could have happened to him! You have been gone ages!" I viciously snapped at the woman. Carl, Summer and the girl glared towards me open-mouthed.

Silence filled the clammy air around us as I blinked rapidly, eyelids matching my heart rate.

Despite my angry tone, the woman seemed totally unfazed and unresponsive by my rant. I questioned whether she was plain stupid, ignorant or on a wind-up mission.

The woman's unresponsive reaction made anger flow fast through my veins just as a carp would through water.

I had a Laura-light bulb moment: "Can you translate into Khmear for me?" I turned to the young girl.

Nodding in agreement, the girl translated my rage; throughout which the woman continued to smile sweetly in my direction. *Was she hearing something different?*

"Oh, what's the point?" I shouted at the top of my lungs; becoming almost breathless.

Grabbing Summer's hand with meaningful purpose, I marched off like a storm trooper. Feeling like a fish in a net frantically jumping around in blind panic trying to establish its surroundings, the internal voice in my head was whispering to stay calm. I took a deep breath. *Exhale...*

"Why are you so furious?" Carl queried as I huffed towards the line of Tuk-tuks, hunting for our driver as we neared 45 minutes late.

"No wonder the country is in a state of disrepair with an entourage of children begging on every corner...they just irresponsibly pump children out willy-nilly with no real intention of actually looking after them properly!"

I shouldn't have taken my frustration out on Carl, but after the level of poverty that we had continuously witnessed throughout the trip (which mainly involved children) I was vexed that the women clearly couldn't clothe her child, yet there she was pregnant with another!

"That woman couldn't even clothe her child by the looks of it Carl, and there she is less than a year later ready to have another! It is pure insanity right? The whole system is twisted!"

"But that happens everywhere Laura, not just in the 'third-world'..." he air quoted robotically.

"I know you're right." I lowered my voice.

"That just really got to me - that's all..." I shrugged my shoulders depressingly, spotting our driver smiling sweetly towards us in the distance despite us being so late.

***

That afternoon I found myself sat in Muoy's guesthouse talking to Laureen about the lady at the park.

"It happens here all the time honey," said Laureen in her broad Canadian accent, sipping her 'herbal' tea.

"I know it's unjust and unfathomable, but you seriously need to let it go over your head and not let it consume you..." she advised.

"Honestly Laura, it is the way of life here...you will see similar situations countless times. If you let it anger you so fiercely, you will be red-raw with rage and on the verge of erupting throughout the rest of your time here!"

Swiftly changing the subject to lighten the mood, I explained Summer's delight when we visited the children's park, and how I guessed she was missing the little things in life.

"Have you been to the Aeon shopping mall up the road?" she asked.

"It is a western shopping centre that is brand new. It's full of western food outlets, a cinema, play centre and stores. To be truthful with you, I am not a fan. Morally, I can't justify the city having such a glamorous centre when the majority of those living here cannot afford to step foot in it!" she winced.

"In total it cost the Japanese around $200million to build! If that huge sum had been spent on much-needed facilities for the locals, Phnom Penh would no longer be in the dire state that it is in!" She shook her head in clear frustration.

Arching her head towards me: "Having said that - it does have a play centre which might be nice for little Summer..." she confessed.

"It features lots of luxuries that Summer would be used to."

Taking her advice on board, an hour later and with Laureen's directions to hand we soon arrived at the centre.

Aeon was enormous! Once inside I truly forgot what country I was in. It had an ice skating ring, cinema and humongous department stores. *How could such wealth sit in such a poverty-stricken country?* My mind rattled with every super-glossy step that I took.

Laureen was right - the play centre was just what Summer needed. She laughed and howled; diving from ball pit to ball pit, running around with her arms in the air like the crazy five-year-old that she was.

I later decided to treat Summer to a viewing of the latest Disney 3D blockbuster and a bucket of oversized popcorn. The cinema was the most glamorous cinema I had ever seen, with fluffy extravagant carpets and gigantic sparkling chandeliers.

As the adverts played out to the audience, 4D screenings were plugged, mentioning special lighting effects, moving seats, a wind and water machine! it was crazy what the cinema was offering, especially considering I couldn't name a single cinema at home that offered modern effects like that.

"Mummy, I've had the best afternoon!" Summer declared as we washed our hands in the toilets after the film.

"I thought you would like to do something that we do at home." I flashed a warm smile in her direction.

"This place is great for that isn't it?" interjected an American girl, washing her hands alongside us.

"I know! I actually can't believe it!" I spun to face her.

"Don't get me wrong, this centre fits my personality down to a tee...but somehow it feels wrong to be surrounded by all this wealth, when you step foot out of the front and there are countless people literally starving to death on the street." I confessed, feeling as though my moral compass was slightly imbalanced.

"I know exactly what you mean. I volunteer at a children's centre up the road and none of the families or the employees are able to visit the mall. If I'm totally honest, Aeon's existence has caused a storm in the local community. Many of the locals are disgusted. Controversially, I still visit - but that's just because it reminds me of home and I need a bit of normality every now and then, you know? Many of my American friends refuse though as they say it is too much of a culture shock."

"I can understand that!" I dried my hands on the super-intense Dyson-branded hand dryer.

"Personally, I think a lot of people use the building for its impressive air con!" The girl laughed over the roar of the dryer.

"The majority of the locals can't afford to use Aeon, and there clearly isn't enough tourists in the area to keep it full. Frankly, I find it more expensive than the malls back home!"

"Yes, I noticed that." I confessed.

Leaving the building shortly after was surreal. I felt as though we were quite literally walking from one planet and into another.

Inside the gold-lined confined walls of Aeon, you could see the rich throwing money away as though they were participants in the programme, 'Supermarket Sweep,' whilst a yard away there were swarms of people begging simply to stay alive.

Eventually reaching the pavement outside, I watched in horror as a man (so skinny he resembled a bag of bones) weaving precariously in-and-out of the traffic. The man was carrying a small girl who was drinking from a bottle of milk.

Witnessing him get as close as possible to the gridlocked traffic, the man held his hat as close as possible to the car's windows. I tried to contemplate how humiliated he must have felt living that desperate existence day-in, day-out.

***

Twenty-Five:

Life begins at the end of your comfort zone

An hour into the six-hour journey from Cambodia to Ho Chi Minh City in Vietnam; I watched fixatedly as our bus casually pulled onto the ramp of a ferry to cross the Mekong River from the town of Kandal to the countryside of the Prey Veng Province.

"Can I have your attention please?" the bus operator hollered down the aisle with authority.

"We will shortly be stopping for a toilet break. I request that you refrain from giving anything to the children that you see begging at the stop. Thank you."

It was a short yet slightly vague message. After witnessing the money and lunch-box fiasco at the toilet break on the last bus trip, however, I personally understood its necessity.

Whilst the bus painfully searched for a space to park, my eyes absorbed a group of street children that were desperately hanging around the passing cars with their palms firmly upturned, shouting for a dollar.

Gazing towards the emerging scene with curiosity, I watched as one car's passengers batted the children away like pesky flies. In total contrast, the driver of another vehicle threw a dollar bill out of the window. My heart sank to the floor. I felt like I was watching a mother feed the last slice of bread to a swarm of hungry swans; competing for what might be their last morsel of food for days on end. What unfolded was sadly much worse. Aimlessly falling through the air, the single note of cash started a full stampede as every child within eye-shot sprinted at full speed towards the scarce note.

Within seconds an almighty scuffle broke out between 10 or so children, making my stomach churn in displeasure. It was a scene that was hard to watch, that was for sure.

"Wow - did you see that?" An Australian man shouted in an excitable tone as if he was watching a prime-time boxing match.

"Yes mate! I'm filming it!" His counterpart gloated.

Stunned, my jaw descended to the floor as the guy pressed his Smartphone against the window to of course get the best possible 'YouTube' view.

"Really?" I announced across the aisle in a disgusted tone.

"You do realise that those children are no more than 10 years old, don't you?" I tried my best not to sound as rattled as I felt.

The man gave an apologetic shrug my way, before nonchalantly turning back to continue filming. *Unbelievable!*

With time seemingly standing still, my thoughts were consumed by those from war-torn Cambodia.

The country is still recovering from decades of war, massacre, confusion and loss. Regardless of this fact, the people we had met there were exceedingly poor but genuinely charming and some of the nicest people I had ever met in my entire life!

My mind drifted back to an image of us travelling in the Lotus from Muoy's country school. In spite of us appearing like the 'Rich kids from Beverly Hills' they handed us refreshing drinks completely free of charge.

The kindness that family demonstrated was exceptional. Generosity on that level clearly stemmed from humble beginnings.

What a remarkable quality to possess. *Wouldn't life be beautiful if everyone retained even an inch of that quality?* I stared with daggers towards the Australian guy (who had no-doubt already uploaded his video to social media and was racking up countless 'likes.')

Overcome with happiness to actually hit our first main town in Vietnam - boy did I notice the difference! There were traffic lights and a central reservation for a start! Motorbike drivers were wearing helmets (something I hadn't witnessed for some time) and there were even taxis!

Whizzing through the city streets, it was strange to see gigantic department stores and pleasantly presented buildings. After all, we had spent a considerable amount of time predominately staring at rundown units and street vendors.

Vietnam actually reminded me of Hong Kong, making me feel incredibly excited about the last leg of our adventure!

***

With her tiny nose pressed up against the taxi window, Summer admired the vast Vietnamese city of Ho Chi Minh City. It was fascinating watching her pupils dilate trying to digest every colour, object and landmark that we passed at speed. I had a flashback to being a child so excited by the prospect of Christmas, that I leafed through the Argos catalogue at lightning speed; pained with endless possibilities but too overcome with happiness to actually identify the one toy that I wanted.

Being totally honest, I also felt incredibly dazzled by the city's vibrant atmosphere. With hundreds of motorbikes speeding past us in all directions, against the racket of incessant horn-honking, and excessively noisy street vendors that were yelling from the top of their lungs at the passing trader, it was a lot to take in! You could say that the frantic-nature of the city hit us before we'd even stepped-out of our 'shiny' taxi. *Blimey! I was just grateful they even had taxis!*

"Arrghhh! This is so exciting!" Summer and I screeched in a mother-and-daughter fever pitch of happiness, scanning the streets as they rapidly darted past.

"Calm down you two!" Carl complained, clearly embarrassed by our over-the-top enthusiasm.

"Don't you find this exciting? I love nothing more than a fast-paced city!" I shrieked. I was met with the familiar sight of 'rolled' eyes…

Mid-flow of excitement, and my eyes nearly exploded out of my head when the taxi scarcely avoided a head-on collision with a car, moped and bicycle. Blinking several times to certify that this wasn't a bad dream, it appeared as though they were all determined to head straight for us! My stomach churned faster than a cement mixer.

"Phew!" I breathed, placing my head back out of the window like a dog travelling on the backseat for the first time.

***

Formally named Saigon, 'Hi Chi Minh City' is perched on the banks of the Saigon River. Having just five days left of the trip, I decided that we would end it in style by staying in the 5* Pullman hotel.

Previously having stayed in Pullman hotels in both Paris and Marrakech I knew what luxury awaited so I couldn't wait to finish the trip on an absolute high! Especially as the hotel was the latest establishment in its exclusive portfolio.

Our expedition so far had certainly offered us a mixture of accommodation that was for sure: with rundown guesthouses and hostels, quirky tree houses in the jungle, the occasional beautiful hotel; staying in Muoy's school, the 'con-artist' National Park hut; and to top off all of that sleeping on trains and buses! Therefore the plush hotel was a great way to end our voyage across Asia.

Coming to a halt outside the impressive skyscraper building, Summer's eyes glistened as she stared high into the sky at the diamond of a building that was the 'Pullman Spa Hotel.'

For a split-second, Summer's reaction reminded me of the film 'Annie,' when the orphan visits the rich man's house for the first time.

The Pullman had 306 signature rooms that each offered an individual style. Ours certainly didn't disappoint thanks to the bath tub that was sat directly in the middle of the room! The bath tub's odd positioning was something that both Summer and Carl found rather amusing! Personally, I'd just about had enough of Asian's bizarre bathroom and bedroom layouts.

When later exploring the hotel, we were left totally speechless as we peered over the top of the building's rooftop bar to admire the panoramic view. Our eyes glistened with intense pleasure. Stopping me completely in my tracks - my reflection in the pristine glass window suddenly caught my eye.

Oh – my – god! Look at the state of me! A part of me died inside as I shockingly absorbing the view.

I was clearly a stone heavier then when the trip had started, that much was for sure. Not only that but as I'd had no access to a hair dryer or products for some time, my hair had somehow morphed me into the cat-bothered maths teacher that no one liked at high school! My current surroundings were certainly no place for the baggy patchwork, quilt-like, backpacker pants and converse that I was also sporting!

Immediately feeling uncomortably self-conscious, I instantaneously felt out of place in the lush hotel with its beautiful guests who were sunning themselves in top-to-toe Givenchy whilst drinking vintage Veuve Cliquot like it was water.

Frantically tying my hair into a higher (hopefully more chic) pony tail, I checked my reflection once again. *Great! Now my pony tail resembled a dishevelleed fox's tail!*

I needed a drastic makeover and quick!

With the fantasy of sleek poolside Helmut Newton perfection, I was on a mission - *how hard could that be, exactly?*

***

With freshly blow-dried yet slightly humidified, frizzy hair, (*So much for Helmet Newton perfection, I looked more like a grizzled gorilla!*) I was finally ready to hit Saigon.

I have been to some tiring cities in my life, but Ho Chi Minh City is by far the most hectic place I've ever had the pleasure of visiting – and that includes the eccentric Bangkok!

With the toxic, fume-filled air, the ear-piercing sound of scooter horns, and the endless screeching of multiple bike brakes; the three of us resembled a trio of intensely-scared rabbits that were most certainly caught in the glow of the headlights.

Precariously standing on the pavement, we were attempting to cross what technically should have been a 'very normal' road!'

"This is madness!" Carl sighed, clearly running out of patience as we looked out to the wealth of scooters that were travelling in various directions as they weaved in-and-out of each other. Combine the mopeds with both cars and pedestrians, and attempting to cross seemed as eventful as climbing Mount Everest!

After waiting for far too long for a gap to cross, I came to the realisation that a break in the traffic may never happen. It was for this reason that all of the road safety I had taught Summer went straight out of the window.

"Run!" I screamed, expelling every last breath of air from my lungs as I clutched my daughter's hand for dear-life, sprinting between the streams of traffic.

Narrowly escaping with our lives during our first Saigon road-cross, we found the madness so encapsulating that we decided to sit in a coffee shop on the side of the street and watch the craziness unfold firsthand.

Experiencing the locals going about their everyday business was like prime-time TV viewing. Thousands of scooters whizzed around barely inches apart from one another; weaving through miniscule gaps that from the naked eye looked only big enough for 'Alice in Wonderland' to magically squeeze through; having consumed her suspicious potion. I found the irony somewhat amusing – a tedious everyday occurrence for the drivers, however; to the civilised British this spectacle was quiet unusual.

Like a multitude of other Asian cities, the mopeds carried many passengers, babies, even random objects - be that crates of vegetables or heavy, clunky furniture!

Perched at a table on the pavement, I sipped my Iced Coffee and admired Summer's picture of a 'typical Ho Chi Minh street.'

"Oh my…"

Out of nowhere, a scooter blasted past our feet at an immense speed as it manoeuvred in and out of the pedestrians and café tables.

"Why on earth is he driving on the pavement?" Carl barked, full of rage.

"Well look over there…" I pointed to the opposite side of the road where low and behold the same scene was unfolding.

"They must use the pavement when the road is too busy! How bonkers is that?" I laughed at the absurdity of the situation.

Walking through the city that afternoon, I was astounded by the mixture of architecture that the city offers. Modern high-rise buildings sat alongside traditional Vietnamese 'tube houses' (essentially skinny buildings.) Then there was the beautiful French Colonial architecture with its exquisite dazzling detail, plus the street-food and Pho stalls that sat right next to the 'high end' eateries. Not to mention the striking parks, crazy markets and exclusive shopping malls – it was an odd mix that somehow worked.

Our first scenic stop of the day was the 'Central Post Office,' which probably sounds like a peculiar place to visit ales you want to use its services, but all the guide books recommended it as a place to visit. As it was opposite the Notre Dame Cathedral (and close to the city's biggest shopping centre - the Vincom) it made sense to pop in and see what all the fuss was about.

Standing across the road from the bizzarely 'must-see' building, I'm not going to lie the structure did look impressive. With its rose and yellow façade, I read how the building was sculpted by Gustave Eiffel in 1886. (Who you have probably guessed was a French civil engineer and the architect behind the world-famous 'Eiffel Tower.') I even discovered that Gustave Eiffel had contributed to the architecture of the Statue of Liberty! *Who knew?*

The inside of the building was easily as impressive as the outside, with its polished dark, wooden counters and benches; aesthetically-pleasing tiled flooring; central clock and portrait of Ho Chi Minh himself that intently gazed across the post office floor.

"Summer..." I hollered, patting a bench that was placed in the middle of the shop floor.

"Come and sit..."

Aware of her growing interest in art, I tasked her with a challenge... she had to create a drawing of the Post Office adjacent to a sketch of the Eiffel Tower and Statue of Liberty.

"Have a good look around and take in every inch of detail!" I broke into a heart-warming smile.

We often spoke about the Statue of Liberty in New York; therefore she was able to easily draw it from memory. Pride oozed from every inch of me when 15 minutes later she presented her drawing with the addition of the two iconic landmarks that she etched completely from memory.

It didn't take long for the currency to become the bane of my life! Paying for things in Vietnam was certainly mind-boggling! Tiny amounts of pounds resembled thousands of dong! For example, £1 was 32,539 dong! Imagine how many notes you would carry on a typical day in the city! *We certainly were a robber's dream!*

Attempting to cross a zebra crossing was almost impossible. We found ourselves darting daringly through cars and mopeds that were driving in various directions over the crossing, despite the green man indicating that we could walk. *Confused? So was I?*

Within minutes of leaving any air conditioned building, we were sticky and drenched in sweat thanks to the high humidity.

Visiting in rainy season we were, but boy when it certainly rained. Within minutes of the rain starting the streets resembled rivers. As the rain drops started to fall a backup of bikes came to an almighty holt, with each driver stopping to don that all-important poncho! (Talk about prepared!)

Rain continuing to pour, I looked down from our sky scraper building and my eyes were decorated by the colourful sight of ponchos. It looked as though the drivers were heading through an epic river! It really was a unique spectacle that wouldn't escape my picture book of memories for some time that was for sure.

Scanning the sights from inside the taxi, my memory transported me back to Hong Kong. Not only because of the hecticness of the environment encapsulating me, but because of the over-confident and severely under-cautious attitude of the taxi drivers who openly scanned Facebook whilst ferrying you between destinations.

On one journey, I froze in sheer terror as I practically stared death in the face in what seemed like slow motion. Our driver was casually darting through the mayhem of traffic, missing passing mopeds as they weaved in-and-out of the interchange in a multitude of directions. Rather than give his fellow drivers his full attention, however, he was scanning the 'people you may know' section on Facebook! Worse - he 'friend requested' two people!

***

"Another market?" Carl complained like a broken record on repeat when I suggested a visit to the 'famous' Ben Thanh market.

"Laura, they will sell the same crap as they do in all the other markets we've visited so far!"

"How do you know? Have you been there before?" My eyes became dark and defensive. I envisioned being that girl from the golden-oldie classic television show 'bewitched,' mysteriously clicking my fingers to make Carl vanish into thin air. *How refreshing would that be…*

Blank response…

At 8pm, we made our way through a wide street that was laced with several stalls selling just about anything you could think of.

"Ooh peanuts!" Carl's eyes glistened.

"See, the market isn't so bad – is it?" I grinned like a cheeky baboon.

Busying ourselves bartering for an overpriced bag of peanuts, two young women approached and asked if they could take their photo with Summer.

"Sure!" I said, now used to the request.

What I wasn't expecting, however, was for one of the girl's to pick Summer up. This took us all (including Summer) totally by surprise!

"Err…I…" I muttered, suddenly taking in Summer's panicked face.

Before I had the chance to tell the girl to put her down, Summer's tiny feet had already touched the ground! On doing so she burst into terrified tears, burying her head deep into my legs.

"Ahhh!" the girls cooed at her hidden face, reacting as though it was cute seeing her so upset.

I bent down to Summer's height and hugged her close.

"I'm so sorry Summer!" I muttered into her ear.

"I honestly didn't know that the lady would do that."

"That scared me Mummy," she said in a barely-audible voice, struggling in-between a stream of sobs.

I felt like the worst parent in the world. *I shouldn't have let that happen!*

Cuddling her vulnerable body, the girl sneaked up from behind and tapped Summer forcibly on the shoulder.

"One more – blurry!" She frantically waved her phone in the air as if the task of capturing a prized picture of Summer was a life or death moment.

"No more!" Carl and I shouted passionately to the girls in unison. *Honestly, some people have no awareness of appropriate boundaries and when enough is clearly enough!*

"She's upset – can't you see that?" I barked protectively, still hugging Summer.

"I am sorry Rube!" I turned back to my daughter to face the blame.

"You don't have to have your photo taken with anyone you don't want to, ok darling?" I rose to my feet, kissed her forehead in an open display of affection and grabbed her hand tightly.

"Shall we have a look around and see what treasures we can find then?" I tried to salvage the situation even though I felt like a genuinely awful person.

"Yeah!" she sniffed away her last sob and wiped her nose on Duffy's ear.

"Here…" Carl kindly offered her his paper bag of treats to occupy her mind and dry the tears.

"How could I allow that to happen, Carl?" I whispered as we continued to walk on.

I was half-expecting him to say something that would make me feel like half-a-mother. However, humanity appeared to have landed at his doorstep for once, taking me completely by surprise.

"I feel awful too, but it just happened so quickly. From now on - no more photos!" *For once I actually agreed with him.*

I had heard on the grapevine that Vietnam is home to the most expensive coffee in the world, with one 'special' blend in particular selling for as much as $50 a mug across the world! Low and behold, I discovered the 'secret' behind the seemingly ludicrous price tag of this coffee; let's just say that the 'golden' price was affiliated to a rather 'unique' production process.

This may sound insanely peculiar but in order to achieve such expensive coffee, a civet cat is made to eat a batch of prepared coffee beans. While they're passing through the cat's digestive system, its stomach breaks down the protein that produces the coffee's distinctive flavour.

The beans are then defecated by the cat. (That's a posh way of saying that the cat poops them out!) After cleaning, the beans are roasted and - voila! You have your exclusive coffee beans!

Admiring a coffee stall, I noticed there were lots of 'weasel' coffee beans for sale.

Maybe I'd heard it wrong? Perhaps it wasn't a cat but a weasel?

"Excuse me..." I cleared my throat with assurance.

"Are these weasel beans like the civet cat beans?" Curiosity spilled from my tongue.

"They're from a weasel and not a cat. However, it's essentially the same thing - except that the animal is a weasel!" The stallholder smiled.

"The major difference is that they are much cheaper! "Her sidekick interjected, seemingly chuckling at her own comment.

"Has the weasel also pooped the coffee beans out?" I asked, being painfully inquisitive and not afraid to mince my words.

The lady emerged from behind the counter, pulling a chair towards me.

"Sit!" she instructed, with growing enthusiasm.

"The bean is within a berry, about the size of a grape," she explained as Summer took a seat on my lap and we both stared at the woman with inquisitive eyes.

"The berries are fed to the weasels that will choose which ones to eat and ignore. Being smart little cookies, they select the ripest and sweetest coffee beans available. As the weasel has acid and enzyme chemical's in its stomach," she continued. "It produces a less caffeinated brew with a deeper, slightly bitter taste as it is absorbed into the beans."

The three of us stared at the woman in fascinated silence. Not seeming to notice, she continued: "The beans are then washed and dried for three days under the rays of the sun and eventually they are roasted and sold. Stay here and I will make you a fresh cup!"

Before I had time to even blink, the lady had completely vanished; returning minutes later with a mug of piping-hot black, poo coffee.

"For you!" she proudly passed me the mug before busying herself serving another customer.

I was hesitant about tasting the 'poo' coffee I'm not going to lie... but I could feel the lady's eyes watching my every move. Not wanting to look rude, I slowly took a sip... *Oh yes I did!*

"Yuk!" Summer shouted, completely horrified.

"Mummy's drinking the 'poo' coffee!" She yelled to those around us, astonished by my 'revolting' actions.

Swishing the liquid around my mouth, I tried to mentally block out the fact that I was actually about to swallow a liquid that contained animal poo! I was also pretty certain I had turned an embarrassing tone of crimson-red. My cheeks were so poker-hot in fact that I could feel my body burning from the inside out! Having Summer repeatedly inform those around us that I was drinking 'poo' coffee was also making the situation worse as I couldn't escape the thought-process of what I was actually consuming.

Swishing the 'poo' liquid around in my mouth, the scorching drink travelled across the horizon of my tongue and coated every bit of enamel on my teeth. Desperately trying to erase all memory of the weasel-coffee ebbing across my teeth and sliding up and down the membrane lining of my internal mouth, I felt the tenseness of the woman's beady, chestnut eyes burning a hole right through me! I knew I would have to take one for the team and just swallow the dam stuff.

Just do it Laura! I mentally pleaded with myself.

Moments later and the weasel liquid pelted through my digestive system at 100 miles per hour. *How pleasant!*

A Vietnamese woman (who looked to be in her early 20s) approached with a baby in her arms, holding her hand out to ask for money. I nodded my head to indicate no, and instead stood to my feet to give the stall-holder her mug of 'poo-coffee' back.

Standing inches from my body; the woman with the child stared at me as if she was the Greek monster 'medusa' whose hair was made of venomous snakes.

The woman held her gaze towards me for so long it was as if she was about to turn my body into pure stone.

Suddenly, she pointed towards her baby as if she wanted to pull on my maternal heart strings and make me feel bad for ushering her away.

Ignoring the woman, I continued with my purchase of the coffee (*What? I couldn't 'not' buy it after the lady had made me a mug! That would have looked rude!*) My *Mum can have it or something…*

Walking away, the begging-woman blocked my path and again asked for money.

I felt incredibly ill-tempered. I couldn't believe the sheer audacity of the woman! She was clearly trying to make 'me' feel responsible that she was out at night with her baby begging. In fact, I felt the same stab of anger rise inside of me that I'd experienced in the park in Cambodia; with the abandoned, naked baby.

"He is cold!" The lady scuffled alongside me.

"You're the one that's choosing to sit out in the cold with him late at night! I'm more than sure you have somewhere else that you can go," I said, crossing the road.

I knew it was an insensitive, cruel thing to say but I couldn't help myself. I had seen so many disadvantaged children on the trip that it was now starting to make me furious.

They say life begins at the end of your comfort zone. I had most definitely reached that point! I suddenly felt uncomfortable beyond belief continuously witnessing local children being used as props to attract westerners and pull on our heart-strings to hand over our hard-earned money, only for the parents to have more children with no plan about how they were going to feed or support them. I really felt as though their core parenting tactic was to rely on westerners.

I knew it was a narrow-minded thought that didn't consider the complexity of their situation, and a part of me felt ashamed to have those thoughts. However, at that moment in time that was how my mind was working. I'd seen hundreds of deprived children across Asia begging on the streets and I was suddenly furious about it.

Following the tourists in their masses to the inside 'overpriced' market; we were continuously prodded and pulled by the vendors to buy their 'one-off' goods, that 'ironically' were identical to others sold in every market in Asia.

Combine that with the constant, "madam you buy..." gestures towards us (for items that were three-times the price of others I'd seen elsewhere) and I'd quickly had enough of 'Ben Thanh' and its pushy sales vendors.

"Oohhh McDonalds..." I called out, spotting the golden arches in the distance whilst we walked back to the hotel.

"Rube - do you fancy an ice cream?"

"Ooohh... yes please Mummy!"

"I wouldn't eat there if I was you." Carl immediately stopped in his tracks, adopting his spoil-sport tactics.

Giggling, I knew there was a conspiracy theory to follow...

"I once ordered an ice cream in 'said' restaurant and for some reason the guy made me two. Anyway, after I said I didn't want the second; he opened the top of the ice cream machine and actually – wait for it – tipped the cream from the cone back into the machine! Can you believe it? I mean, talk about cross contamination!"

"But it's frozen, so surely it would kill any bacteria anyway?" I questioned.

"Not only that - I tried to complain online and was repeatedly hit with the same 'error message.' Worse - there was a spelling mistake in the message! An actual spelling mistake! I refuse to shop anywhere that doesn't care if their online correspondence is correctly spelt!"

I couldn't help myself. I simply fell about laughing.

"Well feel free to wait outside whilst Summer and I get contaminated by our delicious but 'mis-spelt' desserts then." I chuckled, heading inside rebelliously.

After ordering, the server shouted to her colleagues in Vietnamese. Almost instantly three women ran to the till to sneak-a-peak at Summer.

"Oh she's so cute – just like a little dolly!" One of them cooed as they all suddenly fussed over her.

"For you, because you are beautiful!" another passed her a hot-red balloon.

"Here! Take this too..." a man passed her a 'Happy Meal' toy.

Out of nowhere, more staff appeared and were gazing over the counter at my rather-stunned daughter.

It was another one of those crazy moments in Asia where all you could do was laugh at the bizarreness of it all. Firstly, my travel companion was currently stood under the golden arches not even wanting to sit at a picnic table in fear of being 'contaminated' and siding with the 'illiterate' folk; and here was Summer and I in none-other than a fast-food joint, with pretty much every member of staff cooing over her giving us free bits and pieces! *Only in Asia...*

***

Twenty-Six:

Reaching the light at the end of the tunnel

My knees throbbed and my back pounded. Despite the obvious pain my body was experiencing, my mind was focused on maintaining a credible distance from the old man infront's bum. Inches away from the depths of his backside, it wasn't a comfortable experience that's for sure!

Desperately crawling on all fours, sweat-drenched, I came to an abrupt halt. The man in front was completely stationary. Stifled by the intense humidity in the claustrophobic tunnel, I felt the urge to hunch my shoulders to the right to see what was going on. We were in the midst of a full-on human traffic jam, 15 foot underground and crawling through the remainder of what was the Viet Cong's tunnels in the Cu Chi district, 40 miles northwest of Ho Chi Minh City.

In 1954, the country of Vietnam was divided with the decision that two years from that date there would be an election in both the North and South of the country to determine who would rule the entire nation. Unfortunately this election never transpired and by 1956 the split had become permanent.

North Vietnam was Communist (allowing the government to rule on everything) and South Vietnam (where we were in Ho Chi Minh City) was not.

The intention of North Vietnam was to unify both parts of the country under the banner of Communism. At the time, America was fighting the spread of Communism across the world. It was for this reason that the US president of that time promised to help any country that was vulnerable to the take-over of Communism.

US President, John F Kennedy, began deploying American military advisers to help the South Vietnamese army.

It was during this time that an American warship was attacked off the coast of North Vietnam, so Kennedy's successor (Lyndon Johnson) began sending American soldiers to Vietnam to fight the Vietcong and the North Vietnamese army. Astonishingly, by 1968 the US had half a million troops in the country!

Despite America being a modern country with up-to-date weapons, they seriously underestimated the North Vietnamese army who relied upon deceitful and vulgar tactics in order to retain power.

One major disadvantage for the American soldiers was the vast jungle terrain. Clearly, they were not best prepared for this 'alien' landscape.

Unbeknown to them, the Vietnamese meticulously dug covert-tunnels like a weave of spaghetti junctions that ran under the American troops' very feet and base camps.

In addition to housing thousands of people in the underground tunnels, passageways were successfully used as 'hideouts' for the Vietcong during live combat with the Americans. Worst still, they would often use their vantage point to trap American soldiers, catching them totally off guard.

Immaculately concealed beneath the American's weary bodies and demolished villages, the 'secret' tunnels soon became the hub of community life; offering underground schools and public spaces where couples married, babies were born and village life continued as normal.

One thing was for sure though: cozy it was not! Air, food and water were in sparse supply, resulting in the tunnels soon becoming infested with ants, poisonous centipedes, scorpions, spiders and mosquitoes. Naturally - when you're hiding, the residents were forced to remain underground for many days at a time. Sickness literally spread like wildfire; racing from body to body.

It didn't take long for Malaria to become the second largest cause of death by the end of the war.

When the US troops became wise to the tunnels, they tried everything in their power to combat them; even using toxic chemicals! However, with every attempt they were unsuccessful; for one reason or another…

In desperation, the US army began sending officers down into the tunnels with only a gun, knife and flashlight to their name. The often lone soldier travelled inch-by-inch down the narrow tunnel; attempting to identify booby traps which the Vietcong were by this point famously renowned for planting.

With the light from their battery powered lamps often not strong enough to withstand the enveloping darkness of the tunnel (and with no room to turn around) the soldier's fate would often result in underground fire fights, ensuing an unspeakable amount of deaths.

The 120-km complex of intertwining tunnels at 'Cu Chi' has since been renovated to create a war memorial park. Late November on a Tuesday afternoon we had found ourselves visiting the site.

"The tunnels were ploughed with bare hands during the 1940s war to gain independence from the French…" Dung (our tour guide) explained to our group of 20, as we stood in a circle staring at a miniscule circular drain in the ground. I can't tell you how odd it looked within the jungle landscape!

"During the Vietnam War (some 20 years later) the tunnels were lengthened to offer protection for the 'Cu Chi' people and become a hiding spot against the Americans.

"Now, who wants to climb into this tiny tunnel?" Dung inquisitively asked the group, resulting in us all glaring at each other in dead-pan silence.

The hole was almost pocket-sized, and looking around at the group the only person I thought that could realistically squeeze into the claustrophibic-looking space would be Summer.

"I'll do it!" a skinny American girl called out over-zealously, before scaling her slender size eight body into the ground. Her skeleton consumed the space so tightly that she resembled a fashion model squeezing every last morsel of skin into a figure-hugging, slim-line black dress.

"You should have done it Summer!" I daringly told my daughter as we later walked away.

"Absolutely no-way!" she widened her eyes like she had just seen a ghost.

"Scrabbling soundlessly beneath the feet of the American military, the tunnels linked secluded pockets of a 'Viet Cong' controlled zone; enabling them to carry out surprise attacks on the Americans." Dung continued to explain in a theatrical tone of voice that clearly indicated how much he loved his job. "

"As quickly as the Cong appeared, they would be gone like a fierce gust of wind!" he said.

"Who can tell me where the next hole is?" Dung quizzed the silent group as we continued to stare at him with straight-faces.

Gazing through the trees for a hidden tunnel, my eyes scanned the surrounding area, but I couldn't see a single thing!

"It's here!" Dung pointed enthusiastically at what looked like just another bush.

Cautiously lifting the lid, huge spikes appeared from both sides. Leaning a tiny amount of body weight onto the lid, Dung demonstrated how quickly it turned.

"A booby-trap!" he dramatically called out.

"If a soldier was running at a significant speed, they wouldn't be able to see the hole in the ground for it would be concealed by mud and leaves. When the soldier fell, bamboo punji sticks would painfully trap and pierce through his skin."

The group gasped.

Feeling considerably protective towards Summer, I instantly turned to face her. The expression on her face communicated that she was confused.

"If you fell into the pit you would find it impossible to remove your leg without causing severe damage," Dung ran the tip of his finger over the slant of the spike.

"The stakes would be sharpened into a spike, and on most occasions would have been rubbed with toxic plants to cause deadly infections."

"Blimey! The Vietnamese certainly used malicious tactics didn't they?" I leant towards Carl, who was clearly not impressed by my sudden conversation.

"Shhhh" he hissed offensively.

Although Summer's expression portrayed complete confusion, it seemed as though she was certainly following the story.

Continuing through the woods, we were met by an array of traps uninvitingly glaring at us. I was startled by the sheer variation and intensity of spikes we had seen; all in various shapes and sizes.

Just when I thought I had seen it all, my eyes loomed over gigantic balls camouflaged from head to toe in grass tainted with pulsating, threatening spikes that screamed torturous death.

It seemed as though the bamboo punji sticks (or spikes as I call them) were a common theme during the war, often placed randomly within the bushes to pierce through a soldier's foot as they walked.

Shockingly, we were shown a swing-door where planks of wood swayed violently thrusting spikes towards the so-called enemy.

"Trip wires were used to detonate a grenade - or release a box of scorpions onto their unsuspecting victims," Dung continued.

"Exasperated by an incompetence to overcome what actually was a poorly-equipped peasant army, the Americans (the most technologically- advanced fighting force in the world, remember) had no choice but to fight with their bare hands by sending their man power into the tiny, dark tunnels to engage in a deadly game of hide-and-seek..."

The term 'deadly game of hide and seek' instantly sent a shiver down my spine. *Imagine being that lone soldier thousands of miles from home and isolated by fear. That was someone's dad, son, brother, uncle…*

"Now…" Dung intruded on my thoughts.

"If you would like to experience a tunnel, this one in particular has been widened to accommodate Western tourists, but it's still incredibly small. Therefore, if you are claustrophobic I would advise you to not participate."

Half of the group opted to climb through - including me! Unfortunately Carl (rather predictably) chose not to embark on the challenge.

"There's no way you would catch me going down there!" Carl stared gloomily down the hole as if his existence would get lost down there for good. *If only…*

"I thought you were scared of heights? You didn't mention a fear of being underground too?" I asked, perplexed.

"Far too claustrophobic for me - god knows what is down there!"

"Just the two of us then!" I smiled sweetly towards my sidekick.

"There's no way Summer will go down there!" Carl warned as I attempted to grab her hand.

"Of course she will!" I smiled down at my adventurous daughter.

"Laura, it will be extremely dark and you have no idea how long it is going to go on for. There will be bugs and all sorts down there. It will give her nightmares!"

"Don't say that in front of her!"

"Carl's right - I don't want to go down anymore Mummy." Summer stared at me with her 'little girl lost' eyes.

"Are you sure? You were almost certain before and you won't get this opportunity again?"

"I'm sure!" she answered in a small voice, which told me that she genuinely no longer wanted to.

I felt like Carl had scared the living daylights out of her. Still, I didn't want to make her uncomfortable so I let her be. In my eyes, Carl had over-stepped the mark. Clearly, she was an impressionable five-year-old so would embody any fears he exposed. *He must have sensed the negative impact her was having on her, surely?*

I'd spent months showing Summer videos of the tunnels and telling her about how cool it would be to crawl through them. Mentally, I felt like I had prepared her for the job. Being that she was bubbling with excitement at the prospect of cramming her tiny body into one only hours before, I felt frustrated and personally stung by her refusal to now get involved.

Feeling incredibly vexed at Carl, completely alone, I made my way towards the tunnel.

***

My knees throbbed and my back pounded. Despite the obvious pain my body was experiencing, my mind was focused on maintaining a credible distance from the old man in front's bum. Inches away from the depths of his backside, it wasn't a comfortable experience that's for sure!

Desperately crawling on all fours, sweat-drenched, I came to an abrupt halt. The man in front of me was completely stationary. Stifled by the intense humidity in the claustrophobic tunnel, I felt the urge to hunch my shoulders to the right to see what was going on. We were in the midst of a full-on human traffic jam.

Climbing the steps to reach ground level, I saw Summer's face light up. She looked as though she was full of pride, staring down at her Mummy as I resurfaced from underground.

Enthusiastically tugging at my clothes, she questioned me before I'd even managed to reach the top of the staircase and absorb daylight.

"What was it like Mummy? Was it scary?"

"Not at all darling, you would have loved it!" I darted Carl an angry look.

"What about the creepy crawlies?"

"There wasn't any! I told you there wouldn't be!" I smugly glanced in Carl's direction as if to say, 'I told you so!'

431

"Oh…" she lowered her head.

Journeying through the grounds, we were shown how the residents of the tunnels cooked and later cleared the smoke without revealing their location.

"Chimneys were carved through the ground to diffuse the smoke, releasing it a considerable distance from where the kitchen actually was. The women would only cook in the morning - so the smoke resembled the early morning fog." Dung explained.

"Why was it only women who cooked?" Carl asked questioningly.

"I'm no feminist, but surely there must have been occasions when the men cooked? Personally, I pride myself on my cooking abilities…I mean, I do have a rather hectic job as a 'Fraud Investigator' but I think it's incredibly important to spare even just 30 minutes a day to cook a healthy, hearty, balanced meal!"

Along with the majority of the group, I stared at him blankly… *What was he doing?*

"Historically women cooked and looked after the children." Dung responded before thankfully moving the conversation on.

Sat under a gigantic net canopy that was tied to the posts of trees, we were fed a bowl of boiled tapioca strips, crushed peanut dip and mug of herbal tea. The mini-feast served as an introduction into the type of food eaten at that time.

"During the war Tapioca was the main (and sometimes only) source of food - not only that, but it was well-known for helping people to gain weight!" he raised his eyebrows suggestively.

"Oh god – I seriously don't want to gain any more weight!" I called across the table prematurely, before realising what I had said and how ungrateful I must have seemed.

Even so, I was being deadly serious! Unbeknown to everybody around me who seemed to think it was a joke; aimlessly chuckling at my comment whilst eagerly dipping the Tapioca into the delicious peanut dip.

"It increases blood circulation, prevents birth defects, improves bone health and even helps to prevent Alzheimer's.

Therefore, it is a healthy way to gain weight!" Dung laughed carelessly.

Whilst the group sipped their tea, Dung continued to educate us about the circumstances of the war.

"The war officially ended in April 1975 when South Vietnam surrendered. It was also the first televised war in America so many American reporters flocked to Vietnam in search of stories. The truth behind the war was candidly reported on the American television screens, with images of innocent Vietnamese civilians being killed, maimed and tortured.

"The coverage enraged the American citizens; many of whom quickly turned against the war. The South Vietnamese government (who the Americans were defending remember) were revealed as being extremely corrupt and anti–democratic as well! More and more images of Vietnamese civilians caught in the crossfire of fighting were released to the public, resulting in the US troops becoming progressively unpopular."

"That's right!" interrupted one of the American men sat around the table.

"The protests completely divided America, with many people furiously questioning the true intentions of the war."

"The death rate soared through the roof!" interrupted an English girl sat adjacent from me.

"People opposed the war because the death rate was so high, and the US government poured endless money into the war that could have been better spent elsewhere in the country." Dung continued.

"The music industry was even affected!" said another guy insightfully; sounding as though he was possibly German.

"John Lennon released that record - oh what was it?" he trailed off, captured in his own thoughts.

"Give Peace a Chance!" shouted another man, who was enthusiastically interrupted by a woman who cried out that Bob Dylan had released a record called 'Masters at War,' and both songs were used continuously during anti war protests.

I had learned more history that afternoon then I think I had ever digested throughout my entire time spent in high school. Once again, I reflected on the importance of travelling.

***

An hour later and the 'Cu Chi' tour had come to an end. Summer and I found ourselves stood (once again) outside a toilet block, but on this occasion we were actually waiting for Carl.

Scanning my immediate surroundings, I was totally lost in thought. It was hard not to be impressed by both the strength and determination of those who built the tunnels - not to mention the brave soldiers that later battled in them.

The tunnels, booby traps and stories from the war certainly demonstrated the will-power that the American's were up against and the sheer lengths that the 'Viet Cong' were prepared to go to.

Similar to the way that the Killing Fields made me feel, I found it all rather mindboggling.

Glancing through the crowds of people that the tunnels had attracted that sunny afternoon, I noticed Dung happily bouncing towards us through the horde.

"Hi guys! How did you find today?"

"Unbelievable! I've learned so much! It's crazy to think all that happened - and not even that long ago when you think about it!"

Dung nodded: "I was born a few months after!" he revealed.

"Oh really?"

"My parents were survivors. That's why they called me Dung."

I looked at him in confusion.

"What's Dung mean then?" I asked with a bemused look. *Another Asian person that knew the meaning of their name - they made us Brits look so boring!*

"Dung means strong, courage - bravery. My parents had me soon after. My mother survived despite carrying me, that's why I know so much about it as from an early age they wanted me to truly understand where I came from and that no matter what happens in life, I am to stay true to my name."

I was speechless, how utterly fascinating.

"Would you mind?" Dung held out his phone, pointing his eyes to Summer.

It wasn't that I wasn't used to the photo request, I just found it rather odd that our tour guide of all people would want his photo taken with a child who was on his tour. *Surely he saw them all the time?*

"It's up to Summer… Please don't be offended but we had a bit of a scary experience the other day when someone wanted their photo with her." I replied as honestly as I could.

"Summer - do you want your picture taken with Dung? Remember you don't have to…" I bent down to her level.

If Dung had been a person on the street then I would have said no outright, but as we had got to know him throughout the day I felt bad saying an outright no.

"Ok," Summer smiled as she peered into Dung's smart phone, displaying the cheesiest grin she could muster.

***

Twenty-seven:

Homecoming

That strange feeling had crept in…the last day of our travelling adventure had arrived. With a mixture of readiness to experience British home comforts and celebrate the looming Christmas holidays, a dark solemn feeling approached like a cloud above us. It reminded me that we would never capture these unique 'Asian' moments again.

In reality, it had only been six or so weeks that we had been away. However, days had felt like weeks and weeks like months.

Contemplating what was about to happen, I came to the realisation that we had seen and experienced so much that it naturally felt right that it was soon time to head home. However, after three excruciating years of saving and planning I struggled to believe that the trip was very nearly over.

After 10 years of using my backpack, the constant overloading had finally forced the zip to split. With two flights the following morning, I had no choice but to walk the streets of Ho Chi Minh in search of someone that could fix it.

At 10am the heat was already reaching a sweltering 30 Celsius! The city's sweaty odour (mixed with the uninviting stench of pollution) made me heave as we trudged along in the sticky heat.

Frustrating us further, every single tailor shop that we visited fobbed us off and simply directed us to another! I wanted to scream. I was hot, tired, and this was our last day!

"Oh Laura! Why don't you just throw the bag away and buy another to get you home?" Groaned Carl, whilst I pulled my camera out to take a photo of Summer skipping along the bustling, city street.

"This bag means a lot to me Carl, so I want to keep it! Now Summer, if you could just stand there and look out across the street...I want the picture to look as though you're on your own." I hollered.

Peering through my camera lens, I noticed an odd-looking plump man in his 50s walk towards us with a handheld bubble machine clenched to his palm.

Not wanting the man in the picture, I put the camera down and waited for him to pass. However, on his approach he began telling Summer to smile into the camera.

"I teach kindergarten, so I bought the bubble gun for the kids!" The man called out to me in an American accent.

Wearing thick black sunglasses, the man hadn't had the opportunity to see me look at the gun; so I thought it was rather peculiar that he was even justifying why he had such a gadget on display.

Continuing further down the street without a care, the man left the three of us to marvel oddly at his fading shadow.

"Laura, look at that guy - tell me what you notice!"

Alarmed, a chill swept down my spinal cord.

"That's weird, isn't it? Why would he do that?"

I watched as the man carried the gun in the palm of his hand but hidden from view inside a plastic carrier bag.

"Now, watch what he does when that child gets near…"

Frozen in suspense, my hand catapulted to my mouth in sheer horror! Each time a child was within reach, the man immediately yanked the gun out of the bag.

"I don't like that!" muttered Carl cautiously. And neither did I. *What was the man's intentions? It was as though he was trying to lure the children towards him with his 'special' gun.*

With the man's odd behaviour dictating our conversation, we headed into a nearby children's park

Just over 20 minutes later and swiftly heading out of the park's gates, a Vietnamese man and his two children entered.

"Ahh man! You're not leaving are you? My kids were actually excited when they saw you, they thought they finally had someone to play with!" said the friendly stranger.

Anxious about the need to find someone to fix my backpack, I just wanted to get the mundane task over and done with as quickly as possible. Time was zooming by and we didn't have long left. But, my moral compass had kicked in so I decided to complete a good deed of the day by staying in the park for a further 15 minutes.

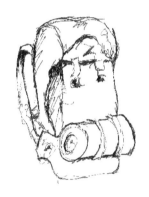

As you do, 15 minutes quickly turned into 60 where we discovered quite a lot about the man.

Born in Vietnam, he relocated to Canada during his early adulthood and was in Ho Chi Minh City visiting family.

"I'm really sorry," I explained.

"We are going to have to head-off. We leave tomorrow and I need to get the zip fixed on my backpack. So far it has been a nightmare trying to find someone to fix it."

Maintaining a calm silence, he simply smiled.

"Do you have the bag with you?"

Minutes later and with absolutely no tools in sight he miraculously fixed the zip!

"How on earth did you do that?" I stared at him impeccably.

"I'm Vietnamese – of course I can fix a zip!" Our 'friendly stranger' laughed pleasantly.

"Why have we had so much trouble trying to get it fixed this morning then?" I giggled.

Leaving the park like a weight had been lifted from my shoulders, I giggled at the craziness of what had just happened. We had no intention of staying in that park, but did so out of kindness alone. In return, we were repaid for our goodwill. Surely there's something that has to be said for that?

***

For our last 'special' evening in the city we headed to a restaurant called 'Saigon Grill' that was on a rooftop of one of the city's impressive skyscrapers.

Walking towards the building, a young girl was stood by a wooden podium displaying a menu. Informing her that we wanted to go to the restaurant, she enthusiastically asked if she could have her photo taken with Summer.

Waiting patiently at the lift, I watched as the girl uploaded the photo of the two of them to Facebook. *I'd love to have known what the caption was!*

Arriving onto the rooftop, the surroundings were absolutely stunning. BBQ grills laced each wooden table and the city lights gleamed from the high-rise skyscrapers; illuminating the neighbouring buildings and the constant flow of traffic below.

The menu presented us with choices such as: crocodile, ostrich and wild boar. However, it is safe to say that our earlier appreciation of this 'unique' dining experience was premature, when we waited for what seemed like an age for our raw meat to arrive…

Staring at the uncooked meat in ravenous hunger, Summer was the first to break the 'famished' silence.

"Mummy, I'm starving…"

"I am too Rubes. I'm sure it won't take much longer…" I nudged a piece of uncooked chicken in the hope that in the minute since I'd last nudged it, the meat would somehow of miraculously cooked.

"You can't deny that this is a pretty-good way to say goodbye to Saigon?" I quietly admired the view to distract my eyes from Carl, who was 'busy' moving all the condiments around the table in an agitated fashion.

"And I won't miss you doing that!" I raised my eyebrows sarcastically, smiling as I did so.

"Mummy, it's also a lovely way to say goodbye to Asia as we are going home tomorrow!" Summer beamed from ear to ear.

"Yes that's right!" I grabbed her by the waist and pulled her onto my lap, kissing her cheek lovingly. Cuddled in a warm embrace, we both gazed at the building to the right that was lit up like a Christmas tree.

"And to think it will be Christmas next week!" I oozed, drowning Summer in a shower of kisses.

Exhausted, my legs could barely carry me back to the hotel that night.

It had certainly been a jam-packed six weeks and in reality, it seemed as though we had been away for months.

Lost in silent memories, I guessed that Carl and Summer were reflecting too. Like every mother would be, I was desperate to know what Summer was thinking. She understood that we were going home the following day on an evening flight, and was excited about Nanny Jayne and Grandad Lewis collecting us from the airport. *If I felt as though I had been away for months, I could only imagine how she felt.*

***

Our flight from Ho Chi Minh City to Abu Dhabi was going to take just over seven hours. Exactly six hours and 20 minutes into the flight and I had one of the most dreadful experiences of my life...

We were sat in the middle aisle on a row of four. To my left was a woman who spoke little English, and to her left with an aisle separating them sat her husband and their three-year-old son.

The family appeared rather odd. Their son was clearly a brat who spent most of the flight throwing tantrums, resulting in a huge argument (in another language) between the parents.

Around five hours into the flight and as the majority of the passengers slept, my mind drifted through a carousel of thoughts. Every event from the trip vividly replayed, demanding analysis before I was allowed to sleep. Finally, when the carousel thankfully came to an end, I felt the blackness before sleep drift over me. My eyes dropped like an elevator whooshing through five levels.

With Summer's head soundly resting on my lap, I woke as though I had been electrocuted with a razor-sharp volt. The lady to my left was jamming her index finger violently and repeatedly into my shoulder, screaming at me in her language.

I blinked rapidly, taking in her 'yapping' frame for several seconds. Blurriness quickly fading, I was frozen in silence.

Her shouting was so intense that she not only woke me, but others too.

"I have no idea what you're saying!" I yelled in pure confusion.

The lady began aggressively pulling at the pillow resting behind my head.

"This is my pillow!" I shouted, which only prompted her vocal chords to rapidly rise too. *What on earth?*

Continuing to scream, the woman pointed to Summer's pillow.

"That's her pillow!" I scratched my head. *Was she accusing me of stealing her pillow?*

I searched the floor to see if she had dropped hers, but there was no sign of it.

"I've no idea what you have done with your pillow, but this is mine and that is my daughter's. We were each given one!" I shouted, outrage boiling by the second.

"What's going on Mummy?" A dazed Summer awoke.

In an Australian accent, a young man sitting in front awoke.

"Here: give her this and shut her up!" he purposefully tossed me his pillow.

"Thank you - that's really nice of you." I immediately passed it to the woman, without receiving as much as a smile or thank you from her in response.

Drama over, exhaustion dragged me back vividly towards another dream.

***

The next thing I knew, the cabin's overhead mood lighting had switched from a relaxing lilac to a vibrant yellow colour.

"We are sorry to wake you," a calming voice announced through the speakers. "We are just-under 40  minutes from Abu Dhabi so will shortly be preparing the cabin for landing."

Stretching my arms out wide, I didn't feel too good. A sharp pain darted through a tooth on the right side of my mouth. Within only a matter of minutes the pain had worked its way up my right jaw and into my right ear. I quickly held onto my face with the palms of my hands. Panic began to take over. *What was happening?*

Minutes seemed to morph into hours as the pain shot further up the right side of my face and across my forehead.

Clenching my head in terror, the throbbing become so intense that unannounced tears flooded my face, forcing me to sob like a child struggling to breath.

Feeling my cheeks stained with salt-drenched tears as my golden tanned-skin sunk in tone, I felt exhausted and helpless as I almost choked for breath. Before I knew it, the throbbing was so powerful that it travelled in circular movements around my head like a Ferris wheel at a funfair. It is amazing how alone you feel when you are terrified.

Reaching a new level of pain, I found myself screaming in agony. Unsurprisingly, the cabin fell silent around me. Feeling illuminated by spectators' eyes, I was absolutely mortified. The pain suddenly owned me - it dominated every thought and controlled every action.

"What's going on?" Carl and Summer yelled in fright, dragging me momentarily back into the world.

"I don't know. I'm in so much pain – my entire face is locked!" I screamed in a tone that I hadn't heard since I gave birth to Summer with no pain relief five years previously.

"Mummy, I don't like it!" Summer began to cry anxiously in concern. There was nothing I could do to console her. My

443

fingertips were rigid stiff as they stuck to the bones of my scalp like glue.

"Carl, can you please see to Summer?" I shrieked through inconsolable tears.

Several crew members stood in limbo around me unsure of what to do. Even the weird lady to my left glared towards my hysterical state as if I was a real-life gremlin being torched with sunlight and dying before her very eyes.

I had never experienced any form of discomfort whilst flying before and was petrified by what was happening. *Was I having some kind of brain aneurysm?*

By the time the flight touched down in Abu Dhabi airport, the pain had slowed to a pulsating thump. Understandably, I was too scared to remove my iced up hands from my rigid face.

"There are no other passengers left onboard if you would like to have a go at standing? Otherwise we can phone the on-call doctor to come and check you over?" a bewildered crew member leaned over me.

"It's ok..." I sobbed, still clutching my forehead with my frozen finger tips.

"I'll get off."

I felt completely humiliated and couldn't believe what had happened.

Slowly removing my fingertips from my face, my fingers felt numb and rigid where they had been locked against my swollen, puffy face for such a long time.

Glancing around through panda eyes, I took a glug from my bottle of water and with a final determined sniff; I stood defiantly to my feet, quickly gathering my thoughts.

Exiting the plane, tears flooded the surface of my face. I felt like a human penny slot machine. One tear after another precariously balanced on my soaked lashes for only a milli-second, before being violently plummeted off by another and landing dramatically on my burning, water-logged face.

Just over 40 minutes later and the pain thankfully vanished. Anticipating the long, three-hour wait before we boarded our next flight to Heathrow, I suddenly felt scared about what was to come.

Boarding the flight to Heathrow, my former tear-stained cheeks had returned to their usual colour and shape as I tried to push the memory of what had happened on the last flight aside.

Watching the runway from the small oval window, I prayed that the pain wouldn't return.

Even now (several years later) the memory of that flight still has the power to make me squirm.

Unfortunately, the pain experienced that day was not a freak isolated incident. Having travelled on ten flights since that trip, I have experienced that pain, albeit on a much lower scale, three times.

The doctor says it was caused by a build up of congestion, but if that was the case wouldn't it have happened on the Heathrow-bound flight too?

I am now so paranoid when flying that I take decongestion tablets a week before the flight, wear ear plugs continuously whilst in the air, and use a nasal inhaler throughout.

I've no idea why after flying frequently all my life this problem has suddenly developed in my late 20's. I cannot explain how scary it is. You feel as though your head is going to explode and I wouldn't wish that on anyone.

***

Arriving into Heathrow on a cold and grey December morning exactly five days before Christmas, Summer was glowing like a candle and was gushing at the thought of seeing her grandparents waiting at the arrival hall.

Emerging through the huge swing doors of terminal five, I watched as my mum and dad broke into wide-cheek-boned smiles as they took in the sight of Summer.

"Look at you!" They yelled as Summer sprinted towards them at full speed, arms-wide. She was dressed in royal-blue, loose tapered elephant trousers, along with a white long-sleeved t.shirt that was accompanied by a straw triangular hat; engraved in red stitching with the word, 'Vietnam' plastered across it.

"Summer! You little backpacker! You look amazing!" My mum embraced her tightly.

"And it seems as though Duffy survived to tell the tale too!" My dad screeched at the rather-dirty bear that was, as always, firmly tucked under her arm.

On the other-hand, I couldn't have felt further from amazing if I tried! I was a stone heavier then when I'd left, I had dishevelled plane hair, was in desperate need for a good wash, and was exhausted from the two back-to-back flights I had just encountered; not to mention the epic pain-fuelled break down I had experienced just seven hours before!

"Hi guys." I greeted them both with a kiss on their cheeks.

"Did you have a good time?" My dad bent down to Summer's height, patting her straw hat.

"The best! I made lots of new friends! And I was an elephant and a bear keeper..." she rambled on, before tucking a stray lock of hair behind her ear and yawning sleepily.

It was clear that we were all exhausted - and I wasn't surprised. We had certainly pounded some pavement over the weeks; I was surprised that ours legs didn't resemble bean-poles!

"Laura – are you not going to introduce us?" My mother looked towards Carl with curiosity twinkling from her eyes.

"Oh yes, sorry!" I apologised.

"Guys, this is Carl - my friend from work who accompanied us around Asia!"

I watched as Carl raised a limp hand in some sort of weird greeting towards my mother's curious face.

"I'm Carl...the Fraud Investigator from Laura's work."

"Oh yes that's right!" My mother's eyes twinkled at the 'job-drop.' *Mum – please don't sound impressed and set him off!* I mentally pleaded with her.

"How lovely to finally meet you, Carl. Thank you so much for keeping my girls safe. We were so worried about them travelling alone! I can't tell you how relieved I felt when Laura said that someone was going with them after all!"

I looked at my mother with cross-eyes. *I wasn't a child! And I certainly didn't need Carl to 'keep me safe!'*

"Well, I kept them out of harm's way don't you worry!"

I looked at Carl with extremely exaggerated eyebrows. *Really?*

"She didn't mention that you were an investigator though, how fascinating!"

Oh god – head in hands!

"Shall we go for a coffee before we head home? It's absolutely freezing outside! I brought you both a coat to keep you warm!" My mother proudly pulled two coats out of her bag.

"Again?" I laughed lovingly as a memory of when I had returned from Australia came to mind. It was a frosty February morning back then - snowing if my memory serves correct. Just like now mum brought me a coat to the airport, ensuring that I wouldn't freeze to death on the journey back home. You have to admire how a mother constantly displays their unconditional love in thoughtful and practical ways.

"The house looks very Christmassy!" Mum later squealed, sipping her hot chocolate cautiously.

"You wait until you see it... you will love it!"

"It's so colourful and cheerful the local paper even asked to photograph it!" Dad mocked.

"That doesn't surprise me!" I chuckled, taking a large gulp of hot chocolate, instantly warming my cold body up.

"What are your plans for Christmas, Carl?" My mum asked, instantly making me wonder where the question was heading.

"Oh. Nothing much. My children live up north so I won't be seeing them on the day itself. I'll most likely have a TV dinner and catch up on some reading."

My mum stared at his gangly face open-mouthed in disbelief.

I felt genuinely bad for him, and obviously so did she as before I knew it she was inviting him to spend Christmas day with us! What my family would make of his constant condiment arranging, foot tapping, incessant interrupting and extraordinary conspiracy theories, I didn't know. However, it seemed Summer and I hadn't escaped his 'strange' behaviour just yet...

"You won't feel out of place at our house Carl! Every year we seem to have a new waif-and-stray!" My mum giggled without a pause to thought, to which my eyes widened in disbelief at her chosen terminology.

"Mum!" I shouted across the table, embarrassed by her obvious faux-pas.

"What? I didn't mean it like that, but it's true! Remember Alf?"

"The chicken that Nan and Grandad tried to nurse back to health on their medication? The poor thing was high-as-a-kite for an entire month before they realised that he wasn't getting any better and that it was cruel to keep him alive, leaving them with no choice but to eventually kill him!"

"No, not him! God-rest-his-soul! Although, we did find him... so I guess he was a waif-and-stray in some sorts! But no! You know who I am talking about? Our Scandinavian friend who dad felt sorry for so gave him a caravan to stay in on the land?"

"Oh yeah!" I laughed at the absurdity of our so-called family Christmases!

"Isn't he in prison now?"

"Well yes, but that was very unfortunate...he was a lovely man, Carl, lived with us and everything!"

"Until he was done for murder, that is!" *If that didn't put Carl off the 'Pauley Christmas' offer, I didn't know what would!* I precariously placed my hot chocolate on the table. *Let's see what health and safety conspiracy theory he makes of that!*

"Anyway... enough stories Laura! Anyone would think you were trying to put Carl off coming!" My mother raised her eyebrows towards me in a manner that reminded me of being a mischievous ten-year-old being reprimanded. *Next she will be calling me Laura-Jayne!*

Oh, if only she knew what she'd let herself in for! We will see what she thinks when he starts frantically rearranging her condiments! She's very specific my mum...has an exact place for everything on the Christmas table.

"Well guys, this is sadly where I leave you!" Carl declared in a slightly over-zealous tone; indicating that he didn't really want to leave us at all.

"Laura, we're just going to head into the shop to get some snacks for the journey home..." My mum grabbed Summer's hand, heading towards WH Smiths.

"Snacks? We're at Heathrow not Timbuktu!" snorted dad, shuffling like a school boy behind.

Carl and I watched slightly baffled as the three of them wandered towards the shop, dad spouting about how heavy Summer's backpack was.

"There's no way you carried this around with you Rubes…"

"I did! I did! That's why I have huge muscles!" she giggled in good humour.

"They're nice people!" Carl laughed in a friendly and pleasant tone, making me turn away from my family to face him.

"I can see your mother in you too! Personality and looks…she seems very 'scatty!'" he air quoted.

"Oh right!" *Just when I thought he was being kind, he manages to offend me once again…and this time on my home turf!*

"Laura, look - I'm glad that we have got a moment alone because there are some things that I wanted to say to you before we return to only seeing each other once a month at the 'security risk' meeting." He air quoted.

I glanced at his gangly face suspiciously, dreading what was about to come next.

"I'm not going to lie - you have driven me insane over the past six weeks!"

"Erm…" I attempted to defend myself but low and behold, I didn't manage to get a single word out of my mouth before he filled the air again!

"No! Please…sorry - I know you hate me interrupting you when you are trying to speak but on this occasion, please - just let me speak!"

My eyes widened to prevent my mouth from erupting with frustration. Seemingly, it was easier to just nod in approval.

"There is absolutely no denying that you have brought out a whole new Carl on this trip!" His eyes twinkled with excitement and the pitch of his voice grew higher by a few decimals.

"I feel like a different person to who I was when we were last here at Heathrow! I have achieved things on that trip that I never would have imagined I could have done before! I think I have conquered my fear of heights completely; I've completed tasks entirely out of my comfort zone! For example, travelling on that notorious 'Tuk-tuk.' Not to mention that weird red truck thing in Chiang Mai that turned out to be a taxi. You have forced me to open my eyes to the endless possibilities offered by the world, Laura, and to actually take a more laid-back approach to life...I don't think that you actually noticed, but I have just completed two back-to-back flights without even being fearful!" he announced proudly.

My mind raced back to our flight to Chiang Mai when Carl was fully hyperventilating into the sick bag. I looked at him with impressiveness gleaming from my eyes.

"Oh my god! You're right - well done! I'm so sorry Carl! The whole weird head-episode on the Abu Dhabi flight completely distracted me...You were amazing on both flights and genuinely should be proud of yourself for that." I looked him directly in the eye so that he would be able to witness the genuineness in my pupils.

"When we were in Thailand, I told you that I had feelings for you."

I watched embarrassingly as his cheeks flushed a light shade of pink, quickly turning a deep shade of crimson; seemingly he was becoming extremely hot-under-the-collar.

"I am sorry for that...I can now see that we will never be 'romantically-entwined' and that we are instead destined to be life-long friends! And so our journey continues..." He coyly darted me a cheeky grin.

I looked at him a little dazed and confused. An awkward silence captured the space between us until Carl realised that I didn't have a Scooby-doo about what he was inferring.

"With me joining your family for Christmas I mean..."

"Oh right! Yes of course." I smiled, feeling like a prized idiot.

"You are very different from anyone I have ever met before Laura! You're clumsy and completely irrational in your decision making. However, above all else, you are witty, engaging and have a heart that is jam-packed with kindness. Also, I want you to know that you are an excellent mother."

I looked at him wide-eyed and stunned by the content of the conversation.

"After all the unwanted parenting advice you have given me, surely not?" I giggled like a naughty school girl.

"Thank you Carl..." I stretched onto the very tip of my toes and kissed him on the cheek.

"You're lovely too! And you know, you will find someone… you just need to stop talking about work! Oh, and tapping your foot!" I chuckled into the noisy terminal…

"I do not do that!"

"How can you say that? You know you do!" I snorted, playfully punching him in the arm.

Realising that our time together was definitely coming to an end, I decisively picked up my backpack and slowly wandered towards the shop that I knew my mother would no-doubt be maxing her credit card out in, buying unnecessary supplies for her tired campers.

One second of silence later and I just couldn't help myself – I gave him one last piece of relationship advice – come criticism…

"Oh… and the table thing! When you go on a date - do not insist on swapping seats if you're unfortunately left 'with your back to the room!'" I air quoted to mock him one last time, entirely in jest, of course.

"And DO NOT…" My pitch elevated passionately as I looked at him. "Re-organise the condiments on the table!" I fell about laughing.

"It's so weird – not to mention annoying…" I rambled on as the two of us giggled uncontrollably through the terminal.

"You know there's a theory behind why I do that don't you? You see, I believe that…"

As annoying as Carl was, he was undeniably unique. *Maybe he was right, perhaps we would end up as life-long friends?* I contemplated as he continued to ramble on about shootings in restaurants and how placing the condiments a certain way could save your life. (Or something like that.) If I'm honest, I wasn't completely listening…

***

451

Epilogue:

Four years on - where is my life now?

Love is unpredictable, so putting your faith in it can feel like stepping into a fragile boat on a choppy sea. After four-years in a cohabiting relationship that began in the local pub of all places, I finally have the life that I always wanted.

Exactly four months after returning from Asia and on a rainy bank holiday Friday, I found myself in my local pub. After several drinks, I left with my family and headed to my mum's for a coffee with my sister who was visiting from Manchester. My phone pinged.

"I have seen your profile online and I'd like to take you out."

"Mum – have you told someone that I joined that online dating website last week?" I vented, sipping my coffee cautiously.

"I know this text isn't real as my mobile number isn't on my profile."

"Well…" she swallowed a noticeable gulp. *I knew it!*

"I may have told Dad, but that's it." She sipped her coffee nonchalantly.

"Dad…who is currently at the pub with his friends - so this message is a wind up?" I huffed. *I was onto them within seconds. Funny joke, lads! Real funny!*

After a string of table tennis messages, I finally received a photo of my mystery messenger. It was a cheeky-looking guy that I'd never seen before, stood with his arm proudly draped around the shoulders of my brother in law, Paul.

"Oh that's Chris from the pub!" My mum exclaimed excitedly, glaring at the screen.

"He's such a lovely guy. His parents live next door. We've known him years! Your brother plays football with him and his sister Louise used to teach Ellie in Primary school. Kylie's the same age as him so even she knows him! He's been to many family parties; I'm surprised that you have never met him before!"

"Even I know him…" Summer suddenly glared over my shoulder at the screen.

"What? How?" I spun to face her alarmed, staring in wonderment at my shrewd daughter.

"Because he was with Grandad at the bar of the pub earlier, so I was giving him all my horrible jelly babies."

The next day and I received a Facebook request from 'Chris.'

This brave acceptance resulted in six days of non-stop messaging, which continued until 10pm on the following Friday when I impulsively found myself inviting this cheeky-chap to my flat.

With a soft cockney rhythm to his voice and standing at just 5ft 4inches, Chris instantly reminded me of my teenage crush, John Alford (Billy from London's Burning.)

Once in a great while, you meet someone with whom you forge a genuine connection with; when out of nowhere you both become submerged in a make-believe world of abrupt closeness. Feeling his gaze on my skin like sunshine, that night in my flat, Chris and I laughed like teenagers and shared stories until the sun came up at 6am.

Fast-forward to a year later and Summer and I were living with him on the agricultural farm that he manages, and I was pregnant with my second child, Cooper.

We are now several years down the line and with two boys together we are a strong family of five.

Within the last year of writing this book and pregnant with my third child, Casey, I was diagnosed with a blood clot on my brain which resulted in some rather inconvenient temporary memory issues. If that wasn't enough, the pregnancy was challenging to say the least - with multiple hospital stays which resulted in an unexpected inducement at 37 weeks following yet another E-Coli infection. At a time when everything should have looked scary, love seemed to cushion me against the hard knocks my body was taking... the emotional equivalent of bubble wrap if you will. Chris was my absolute rock throughout... I don't know anyone else that would sleep on a chair next to me in hospital for ten days. I now couldn't imagine my life to be anywhere but with Chris, Summer, Cooper and Casey. In my family of five, I finally have my happy ending. Well, I will when Chris finally pops the 'big' question, but that's another story... here's to the next chapter...

LX

Did you enjoy this book? What about 'My Summer Bump?'

If so, head over to Amazon and leave a review for both books…after you have done that share the books on your social media, pass them to a friend and tell them how much you loved them. (You did didn't you?)

- Don't forget that you can follow this book's journey by visiting the instagram account @laurapauley #myasiansummer #myasiansummeredits #myasiansummerillustrations
- You can also visit: www.laurapauley.com for more information about past and present projects.

Could you sponsor a child?

There are many ways to help the 'third world' and sponsoring a child is such a rewarding way to do it. After returning from Asia I looked at various charities and decided to sponsor through SOS Children's Villages. I regularly receive photos, letters and drawings from my sponsored child in Cambodia, and Summer loves nothing more than writing letters and sending little parcels to our child. It is such a fun way to educate your children about helping children in need.

For more information, please visit:
https://www.soschildrensvillages.org.uk/
You can also sponsor a child in Cambodia through 'Cambodian Children's Fund' (Scott Neeson charity…information below.)

Information on the places that we visited:

- **Elephant Nature Park, Chiang Mai, Thailand:** Where we worked as elephant keepers:
  https://www.elephantnaturepark.org/
- **Ban Ma Maeh School, Chiang Mai, Thailand:** This is the orphanage/school in the jungle that we visited. Unfortunately they do not have an official website but there is information about the school on various sites online.

- **'The House of Peace' Siem Reap, Cambodia:** This is the school that we visited in Siem Reap that hosted the community show: *http://www.santepheap.org/*
- **Seametrey Children's Village, Phnom Penh, Cambodia:** Muoy's school: *https://seametreycambodiadotorg.wordpress.com/*
- **Cambodian Children's Fund:** (Scott Neeson's charity.) Where we visited the school, doctor's surgery, slum and teenage house: *https://www.cambodianchildrensfund.org/*
- **'Free the bears' Phnom Penh, Cambodia:** Where we worked as bear keepers: *http://www.freethebears.org/*

Where will your next
adventure take you?

Lightning Source UK Ltd.
Milton Keynes UK
UKHW04f0638130918
328823UK00002B/451/P